# The Concept of Faith

*Cornell Studies in the Philosophy of Religion*

EDITED BY WILLIAM P. ALSTON

A full list of titles in the series appears
at the end of the book.

William Lad Sessions

# The Concept of Faith

## A Philosophical Investigation

Cornell University Press, Ithaca and London

Copyright © 1994 by Cornell University

All rights reserved. Except for brief quotations in a review, this book, or parts thereof, must not be reproduced in any form without permission in writing from the publisher. For information, address Cornell University Press, Sage House, 512 East State Street, Ithaca, New York 14850.

First published 1994 by Cornell University Press.

Library of Congress Cataloging-in-Publication Data
Sessions, William Lad.
The concept of faith: a philosophical investigation / William Lad Sessions.
  p.   cm.—(Cornell studies in the philosophy of religion)
Includes bibliographical references and index.
ISBN 0-8014-2873-4 (alk. paper)
  1. Faith—Comparative studies.   I. Title.   II. Series.
BL626.3.S47   1994
234'.2—dc20                                          93-30546

Printed in the United States of America

⊗ The paper in this book meets the minimum requirements
of the American National Standard for Information Sciences—
Permanence of Paper for Printed Library Materials, ANSI Z39.48–1984.

# Contents

# Preface

There are many different conceptions of faith; is there one concept of faith that somehow unites them all? This book sets forth six models of faith as helps to gaining a synoptic understanding of the concept of faith. The models clarify both the fine-grained differences among divergent conceptions of faith and their overarching unity as well.

I came upon these models after years of studying a great many conceptions of faith in both Western and Eastern traditions. Increasingly, it became apparent to me that certain basic conceptual features not only tended to recur but also to cluster. I tried various hypotheses to account for both the recurrence and the clustering, but finally during a single day's reflection exactly six groupings sprang into prominence. It was as if they had called attention to themselves, not as if I had sought them out or imagined them into being, much less created them according to my own designs. When I then reflected more fully and carefully on each grouping, I found that each possessed structure and content that could be articulated. It seemed to me that I was not making up such structure and content—arbitrarily devising and combining possible sets of features—but rather that I was being constrained by something independent of me, something that transcended my thought about it and occasionally surprised me, something already "there," something objective.

I am aware that merely subjective or cultural projections can also seem to have such objectivity, so I do not place too much stock in my apparently "Platonic" experiences. Nevertheless, the models analyzed in this book do seem to possess a structure somewhat independent of my devising. The more questions I have asked of them, the more detailed and coherent the answers have become, and I think there is a great deal more still to be learned. I do not present this piece of autobiography as evidence for the soundness of my results. The models are, after all, only heuristic hypotheses whose "proof" must lie not only in their theoretical perspicacity but also, and especially, in their empirical adequacy to actual conceptions of faith. Still, I continue to believe and hope that others will also find a certain welcome objectivity in the models as they explore with me this newfound land.

Two limitations of models are especially important to keep in mind. First, models are only abstract, sketchy, and limited intellectual instruments, not concrete, detailed, and versatile realities. One can of course do things with abstract instruments that one cannot do with concrete realities, but one should always bear in mind that instruments are no substitutes for realities. The value of understanding faith, therefore, should not be confused with the value of faith. Second, a conceptual model is only a limited fragment of a full concept, possessing but a few features to any degree of definiteness. Such limitation is the key to a model's success. It is precisely in virtue of its constricted compass that a model achieves whatever degree of intellectual illumination it may possess. But there is a darker side to this constriction: By strongly highlighting some aspects of faith, a model may therefore cast other aspects into greater or lesser shadow. Such conceptual chiaroscuro affects not only every model of faith but also every particular conception insofar as it exemplifies a model. One should therefore always beware of taxing any concept, model, or conception for what it does not make explicit.

Two hopes, somewhat grandiose, have helped to sustain this inquiry over the years. They concern the possible utility of this work and arise out of my own faith that true faith—faith that is genuinely faith according to some conception or other—need not exclude whatever truth or other value is to be found in the faith of others, even if it should be that what is valuable in one kind of faith cannot be obtained through another kind of faith.

One hope is for two kinds of "outsiders" to faith—those who

lack any particular faith at all (or so they believe) and those who have little sympathy for those who do have faith. I hope that a broader understanding of the concept of faith, of its rich and subtle variegation, may heighten their sensitivity to the ubiquity of faith and may deepen their appreciation of faith's deep mysteries and powers for good as well as for ill. To learn of faith is to learn of the human condition, and conversely.

Another hope is for "insiders" to various kinds of faith—especially those who think that remaining fast in their particular brand of faith entails rejecting, abjuring, or at least ignoring all others. I hope that a new way of viewing one's own conception of faith in concert with the conceptions of others may lead to grateful acceptance of other faiths even as one is strengthened and confirmed in one's own faith. To learn of faith is to become part of the wider human community, and also conversely.

Though personal pronouns are infrequent in this book, thanks to the use of symbolic shorthand, I have adopted the following convention at the inspired suggestion of Lesley Beneke: All personal pronouns in the text are feminine, while all those in the notes are masculine. This convention is arbitrary, to be sure, and it may occasionally startle readers accustomed to other ways of dealing with the issue, but it is no more arbitrary than any other convention, and it seems more elegant than most.

Many have helped, in many ways, and to these I am deeply grateful: To Washington and Lee University, for providing Glenn Grants over five summers (1987–1991) and a sabbatical leave during the fall term, 1990, and for furnishing ideal working conditions throughout. To Ed Craun, John Elrod, Peg Falls-Corbitt, Jim Keller, Mark Packer, and Minor Rogers, for graciously taking the time to carefully read and helpfully criticize various rough drafts. To two (anonymous) readers for Cornell University Press, for their useful critiques, and to William Alston, John Ackerman, Kay Scheuer, and Lesley Beneke, for their patient, painstaking, and invariably helpful editing. To Jacob Adler, Robert Audi, Harlan Beckley, Dan Bettendorf, Adrienne Hall Bodie, Alex Brown, Randy Harrison, Rick Heatley, Frank Hoffman, Harry Pemberton, Ann Rogers, Michael Smitka, and Tom Williams, for their cheerful queries, comments, and suggestions. To Betsy Brittigan, Sara Clausen, and Dick Grefe for friendly assistance in the Washington and Lee University Library. To Carrie D. Buckley, M.D., sine qua non, and to Karen Lyle, secrétaire extraordinaire. To my parents, Bill and Alice, who planted the seeds and nourished the shoots, and to my children, Alex and Laura, who helped them to grow—all of whom may be a little surprised by the flowers. And most of all to my wife, Vicki, who over the years has shown me the worth of that which transcends even faithful friendship: a life of love. With all this help, I have no excuse, but all the responsibility, for any errors or inadequacies that remain.

WILLIAM LAD SESSIONS

*Lexington, Virginia*

# The Concept of Faith

# Introduction

Countless words have been written about faith, and doubtless there will be more. "If it were all to be recorded in detail, I suppose the whole world could not hold the books that would be written" (John 21:25; NEB).

This particular book about faith ventures a novel approach by offering a new answer to an ancient problem of great interest, a problem which daily gains urgency in a global village filling up with tribes of different faiths. The problem may be expressed quite simply, if somewhat misleadingly: What is faith? A better way to ask the question is this: What is the concept of faith? But why should faith or the concept of faith be a problem, what kind of problem is it, and why is it important to consider this problem?

## A. The Problem

Clearly faith is very diverse. Different people differ in the faith they have or follow or live. The faith of a Polish Catholic priest is not the same as the faith of a Hindu *bhakta*, and neither is the same as the faith of a Zen monk, a Sikh guru, a Shiite imam, a Sufi dervish, an Anglican divine, a Yoruba *oba*, a Jain *acarya*, a Sioux holy man, or a pentecostal televangelist—not to mention the (un)faith of a "secular humanist." In addition, faiths differ in different ways. People have faith in different things (different "objects"); they have different degrees or amounts of faith (different levels of intensity and ranges of involvement); they have very different ways of expressing their faith (different credos, symbols, and theologies as well as different rites, practices, and institutions); and they hold differing attitudes toward their own and others' faith (different evaluations and judgments). Moreover, not all faith is religious. People have faith in themselves and in one another, in institutions amd in ideals, in the practice of science and in the performance of art, in the business of business and in the business of life.

But there is another, mostly unrecognized, kind of diversity in faith. Different people think of faith so differently as to be using different *conceptions* of faith; they have different views as to what it is to have faith, what the essential features of faith are, what faith consists in, what faith is. In Chapter 4 we consider in detail seven distinct conceptions of faith, and we glance at many others; but a moment's reflection will serve to confirm the point: Different people have and use quite different conceptions of faith, both within and across traditions of faith.

All these varieties of diversity of faith, but especially the diversity in conceptions, contribute to the overarching problem of this book, the problem of understanding the concept of faith, when faith as a global human phenomenon is so diverse. Our central concern may now be stated as follows: How is the concept of faith to be understood, such that it can apply to all of the diverse varieties of faith? (Can it? Can a single univocal concept—what one might call a universal *category of faith*—handle all the various cases? Could any of the manifold conceptions of faith be adopted, amended, or revised to serve as such a category?) This is a conceptual problem that demands for its resolution the careful clarification of the concept (or concepts) of faith. Here the methods and tools of philosophical analysis are likely to be most useful, and this is why we pursue a "philosophical investigation" into "the concept of faith."[1]

---

1. By no means do I wish to imply that this problem is only of philosophical interest; it may also intensely concern the faithful, especially those who are religiously concerned. As H. Richard Niebuhr notes, "Faith [Christian faith] seeks understanding in a double way. It seeks to understand what it believes but also how it believes" (Niebuhr, 1989, 23).

## B. The Importance of the Problem

It may not be immediately obvious why gaining philosophical clarification of the concept of faith is important. Some might suggest that we just muddle through, using whatever insights we have accumulated over these past millennia of use and reflection on faith. In my view, however, our current resources are insufficient to solve the problem, and we should seek still greater clarity in our view of faith.

First, there can be little doubt that faith—whether religious or ordinary, past or present, Western or Eastern—is not well understood, even though it is of vital and continuing importance in human life. To be sure, faith's importance is ambiguous, for faith is both a many-splendored and a much-besotted thing. Faith has inspired much of the highest and deepest in human history, from works of art to acts of love; but it has also conspired with much of the worst, from holy wars to witch-hunts. Still, even a self-consciously "secular" age cannot deny faith's importance. But something so important cries out for understanding, and clarity of concept forms at least part of such an understanding. However, current explications of the concept of faith are inadequate, for they tend either to promote one conception against the others or else to distill a vague and vapid "essence" of faith. Either case fails to account for faith's full conceptual diversity. We need a clarification of the concept that respects diversity.

Second, misunderstanding of the faith of others is as frequent as it is consequential. Perhaps the misunderstanding that leads to intellectual rejection ("your faith is nothing more than irrational belief") is merely opportunity lost; but the misunderstanding that leads to personal, social, cultural, or ethnic rejection ("their faith is heresy, perversity, untruth") is often the prelude to and pretext for violence and bloodshed. Wars have been fought for and by people of faith against (what they took to be) people of different faith, and much of this antagonism has been rooted in misunderstanding of faith. But it is not just the faith of others that has been misapprehended; there has also been widespread failure to understand others' conceptions of faith as well. Insofar as greater conceptual understanding can eliminate or mitigate the ravages of antipathy, it is worth pursuing.

Third, technological advances in transportation, communication, and medicine, among many others, have produced two important explosions within the confines of our interdependent globe: an exponentially increasing human population and an informational supernova. Despite vigorous reactionary efforts, different human communities or individuals are increasingly unable to maintain their distinctiveness by mere isolationism or imperialism. At the very least, they must take account of those who differ from themselves, and this includes others' concepts as well as cultures. In particular, it is becoming harder for divergent views of faith to hide their differences. More outsiders are looking in, more insiders are looking out, and both are noticing things that can make profound differences in their lives. It is unwise to presume the adequacy of one's own conception of faith for understanding the faith of others. Even worse is to shield one's ears and eyes. In the end, ideas as well as material products compete in global markets. Increasingly, therefore, people of faith must confront others whose faith is different from their own—and this means different in conception as well as in other respects. If this confrontation is to go well, all sides must gain a clearer grasp of the concept of faith.

## C. Obstacles to the Inquiry

Although the problem of understanding the conceptual diversity of faith is an increasingly urgent one, there are many obstacles to inquiry in this area, of which three are most prominent: One is the great variety of conceptions of faith, the details of which are often accessible only to specialists. There are in the world today very many views—both primary and reflective—as to what faith is. It is not always clear how such views differ from and resemble one another, in part because they are often only minimally explicit, and are often clearest in their polemical rejection of deviations ("heresies"). A more adequate account of the concept of faith should help to clarify these differences and agreements; the multitude of conceptions need not be reduced to unity in order to be seen more synoptically.

Another obstacle is the deep fervency of faith—especially the great intensity of belief, devotion, commitment, and passion displayed by persons of faith about their own particular conceptions of faith. Such fervor may be praised or condemned, but its presence makes calm and level-headed discussion difficult in two contrasting ways. In one, emotion clouds conception, making it difficult to discern the distinctive features of particular conceptions; in another, so much is felt to be riding not only on faith but also on the correct conception of faith—as if one were saved, not *sola fides* but *sola conceptio fidei*— that one is not free to explore alternatives. An adequate account of faith should at least not inflame these passions; and, if it can help to clarify the *conceptual* divergences, it may provide some balm.

A third obstacle is the modern attenuation (or degeneration) of the concept of faith into the concept of irrational propositional belief, a reduction that is found in many popular and intellectually so-phisticated circles (see Chap. 5, sec. A). For many people today, having faith comes merely or centrally to mean stubbornly believing certain unfounded, often bizarre propositions. Such a conception of faith no doubt has its uses—chiefly polemical ones, to indict the holders of confused, unsupported, or indefensible views—but it pro-motes at best a shallow misunderstanding of faith. A more adequate account should show why the account of faith as irrational propo-sitional belief is superficial and misguided and also why it is so seductive. Investigating the concept of faith in all its rich diversity cannot be easy, but the obstacles only add to the urgency of our inquiry.

## D. The Proposed Solution

It would be a great exaggeration to claim that this book fully solves the problem as presented; the problem is much too vast. What I present is a proposal for clarifying the concept of faith that, in concert with other approaches, may yield some of the understanding we so urgently seek.

The proposal, in brief, is this: There is no category or categorical concept of faith. That is, there is no single substantive concept that applies univocally, in virtue of shared characteristics, to everything reasonably labeled "faith." But concepts can be more or less unified without being univocal, and they may gain their content in other ways than by containing or implying features common to all their instances. This is the case with the concept of faith. In exploring the writings of those who have reflected on faith, one does not find a single shared category. Rather, there are many different conceptions of faith, differing and resembling one another in many overlapping ways, that have been held by different persons and groups in every age and place. Such great conceptual diversity simply cannot be comprehended in the univocal embrace of a category.

Since many people think faith is universal, something generically human,[2] my denial that the concept of faith is a category may seem to deny that there is a concept of faith at all. This is not so, for concepts need not be categorical. They can be more or less unified without being univocal, gaining their semantical content in other ways than by containing or implying features common to all their instances. This is the case with analogical concepts whose various instances resemble one another in various ways, without there being a single feature or set of features common to them all. The concept of faith, I maintain, is just such an analogical concept or analogy. Before elaborating this contention, I need to make clearer just *which* conceptions of faith require uniting in one concept.

Particular conceptions of faith may be either primary ones, those actually used by particular individuals or groups in their religious or other experience and practice, or reflective ones, those more theoretical and abstract conceptions that emerge out of primary conceptions via reflection on them. Since primary conceptions tend to be vague and unarticulated; since even individuals belonging to the same community of faith need not share or articulate the very same conception of faith; and since the reflective conceptions of a few people often control a tradition, articulating primary conceptions of faith can be a long and arduous affair. That is why I have chosen reflective rather than primary conceptions as data for this inquiry. Reflective conceptions are more precise and better articulated than primary conceptions, and, since they have been made explicit in writing, they are also more accessible. Still, we must remember that reflective conceptions of faith ultimately depend on primary conceptions of faith.

2. Here I have in mind primarily Wilfred Cantwell Smith, 1964, 1977, 1979a; but he is by no means the only one who has ever sought this end. Others include Dewey, 1934; Ellul, 1983; Hegel, 1977; Marcel, 1951a, 1964; McTaggart, 1906; Schuon, 1975; Van Der Leeuw, 1963; and Yandell, 1990.

Actual reflective conceptions of faith are those that have been articulated by someone, sometime, and somewhere. These, like possible conceptions of faith, differ from one another in a wide variety of ways. The claim of this book is that there is no single feature or group of features (aside from a few very formal, abstract, and useless ones) shared by each and every actual reflective conception of faith. Hence there is no category of faith. Still, these conceptual differences are not the only, or the final, word. There are also many resemblances, likenesses, and similarities among these conceptions. Could there be enough resemblances in all the myriad conceptions of faith so as to constitute a single concept—unified now not by univocity but by analogy? I contend that faith is indeed just such an analogy or analogical concept, more varyingly complex, but also perhaps more intriguingly unified, than many have heretofore appreciated.

It might be helpful here to think of the concept of faith, à la Ludwig Wittgenstein, in "family resemblance" terms. Faith is like an extended family whose various members are all different, sharing no single feature or group of features, but who are more or less closely related by differing kinds of likeness and by some partially overlapping common features. In the case of faith, family and members are both concepts, and so I introduce the following stipulative usage: "concept" is reserved for the overarching (analogical) concept, and "conception" for the actual (mostly univocal) reflective concepts of individuals and groups.[3]

Two features of analogical concepts deserve special notice. First, analogical unity is a matter of degree, not of digital presence or absence. One analogical concept may be more or less unified than another, and neither need be very unified at all. The greater, more numerous, and more fundamental the resemblances among its instances, the greater the degree of unity the concept possesses; conversely, the greater, more numerous, and more fundamental the differences, the lesser degree of unity it has. Second, analogical concepts are fundamentally and irreducibly vague. Such concepts do not have intrinsically sharp and distinct boundaries; instead, a twilight region of indeterminate application surrounds more clear-

3. I sometimes use "concept" more broadly, to refer indifferently to categories, concepts, conceptions, and models, but I trust there will be no confusion between the broader and the narrower uses.

cut paradigm cases. Of course, someone may choose to draw a distinct boundary around the concept for some purpose, but since different people may draw such boundaries differently (more or less tightly or sharply), it follows that people may well disagree about whether a particular conception falls within the concept's range. However, differing boundary-drawing decisions need not be haphazard or arbitrary, even though they will undoubtedly be influenced by various kinds of commitments and biases. Just because no single line can be drawn, it does not follow that all lines are equally well drawn, with equal justification.

The overall concept of faith displays both features—it is loosely unified and inherently vague. Its instances—particular conceptions of faith—share no common features, but neither are they a mere jumble. There are enough resemblances and overlapping features to constitute, or to consider, them all as conceptions of the same concept. Our problem of clarifying the concept of faith may now be put as follows: How are we to comprehend in one analogical concept the vast diversity of actual reflective conceptions of faith? How can the analogy of faith be clarified, both in its unity and in its diversity?

A number of approaches might be adopted. One might, for example, conduct a detailed inquiry into a single historical conception of faith, or a comparative inquiry into several such conceptions, as recorded by particularly clear-minded and influential thinkers.[4] Or one might trace the historical development of a conception, or of several conceptions, within or through a tradition.[5] With sufficient breadth of scholarship, one might even compare conceptual histories across traditions.[6] Also, one might abandon history to seek some kind of ahistorical comparison, a typology of various conceptions across time and traditions.[7] Or, one might propose a more or less

---

4. See, e.g., Fey, 1976, or Ferreira, 1980, on J. H. Newman; Hatch, 1917, or Ljungman, 1964, on Saint Paul; Park, 1983, on Chinul; Pieper, 1963, or Persson, 1970, on Saint Thomas Aquinas; Shepherd, 1983, on Calvin; Ueda and Hirota, 1989, on Shinran.

5. See, e.g., Bultmann and Weiser, 1961, and Hals, 1980, on the Bible; Lührmann, 1976, and Kinneavy, 1987, on early Christianity; Gilson, 1938, on the Christian Middle Ages; John Baillie, 1956, on twentieth-century Protestantism; K. L. S. Rao, 1971, on early Hinduism; Murty, 1959, on Advaita Vedanta; and Dobbins, 1989a, on Jōdo Shinshū.

6. See, e.g., W. C. Smith, 1964, 1977, 1979a.

7. See, e.g., Chirban, 1981; Connolly, 1980; Fowler, 1981; Schuon, 1975; Sullivan, 1979.

*Table 1.* Outline of the six models

---

1. The Personal Relationship Model:
   S has faith$_P$ in A only if S is in a personal relationship with A, S trusts A, S believes certain propositions about A, and S's coming to be in that relationship with A is (at least partially) caused by A.
2. The Belief Model:
   S has faith$_B$ that p only if S believes that p, S is (firmly) convinced that p, S has inadequate evidence for p, and S's belief that p is nonevidentially based.
3. The Attitude Model:
   S has faith$_A$ toward X only if S's attitude toward X partially but radically constitutes a self-world horizon that is prepropositional, fundamental, totalizing, and significant (bestowing as well as embracing significance).
4. The Confidence Model:
   S has faith$_C$ (or S faiths$_C$) only if S is in a nonrelational conscious state that realizes S's deeper self, that is characterized by a profound feeling of (self-)confidence (serenity, tranquility, calm, peace), and that is conditionally imperturbable.
5. The Devotion Model:
   S has faith$_D$ in W only if W is a way of life open to S, which S voluntarily chooses, to which S is committed wholeheartedly and lastingly, and in which S perseveres.
6. The Hope Model:
   S has faith$_H$ in G only if G is a supreme, future, apparent good that S greatly desires and confidently awaits, anticipates, and expects, despite G's improbability.

---

new (at any rate reconstructed) reflective conception based on one's own individual or community experience with some primary conception.[8] I pursue none of these paths, however useful they may be.

Instead, I propose and investigate six models of faith. A model is an idealized, reflective, moderately abstract, explicit but open-ended concept. Its role is partially like that of a Platonic Idea. While never found in its pure form (or Form) in actual practice, it has a kind of objective and publicly ascertainable structure that enables it to measure the messy actual world and thereby to serve the cause of understanding. Hence, we should not expect to find models of faith actually being used by individuals or groups in their daily or religious lives. A model's utility is not a function of its use in ordinary, concrete contexts, but rather flows from its theoretical perspicuity: Does it help to clarify, amplify, or deepen our under-

8. See, e.g., Hick, 1957; Muyskens, 1979; Pojman, 1986b.

standing? The goal in constructing models of faith is to provide fairly well structured sets of reasonably well-delineated conceptual features that may be used as patterns to place alongside the somewhat amorphous and opaque, but also tangled and complicated, reflective conceptions of faith. Models help to clarify particular conceptions of faith and help us to understand the overarching analogical concept of faith. We may think of models as analogical probes.[9]

In effect, I substitute these six models for the single category of faith sought by many scholars. Each model is a univocal and (nearly) universal concept, but it is their ensemble, not any single model, that clarifies the concept of faith; the unity of the concept of faith is the (limited) unity of these models taken together, not separately. Instead of a single category of faith, we must be prepared to think on three different levels.

1. The (one) generic *concept of faith* is not a category (that is, a universal, univocal concept) but rather an analogy or analogical concept that serves as a way of gathering together a "family" of variously resembling and differing conceptions of faith.
2. The (many) particular *conceptions of faith*, whether primary or reflective, are the various concepts of faith actually used and articulated by different persons at different times and places. These conceptions resemble and differ from each other in many complicated ways.
3. The (six) theoretic *models of faith* highlight distinct, coherent sets of fundamental features prominently exemplified in some group of conceptions of faith. Each model is something like a category, or a Platonic Form, but with a more limited range and ambition than an overall category of faith. Taken singly, each has an objective (though nonactual) structure; taken together, the models shed new light on the generic concept of faith both by the ways in which the models are interrelated and by the ways in which different groups of conceptions of faith exemplify and diverge from the models.[10]

9. Two cautions are necessary. First, models do not constitute or portray a higher realm of being; their ideality is not separate from or more real than actual things but merely provides one way of (partially) understanding actuality. Second, there is no implication of causal or other dependence. Particular conceptions are not made up out of models or their elements, nor do they "participate" (in some formally causal sense) in the models they more or less exemplify. To repeat, models are heuristics in the service of understanding.

10. A fuller account of the nature of models, and their roles in relation to the

## E. The Method

Books on faith tend to divide into the sectarian and the scholarly. Sectarian literature is practical-minded, written from and primarily to a particular tradition of faith, aiming to stimulate faith in the unfaithful, sustain it in the faithful, and defend it against the infidel. Scholarly writing is more theoretical and cosmopolitan, aiming to clarify and comprehend various aspects of faith in every time and place. This book is a piece of scholarship, but it differs from the usual type. Most scholarly works on faith focus on four areas: the "objects" of faith (what faith is "in" or oriented towards), the degrees and amounts of faith (how much faith there is, and how effective and influential it is), the causes and effects of faith (what produces faith, what faith produces, and how), and, perhaps most prominently in Western philosophical circles, the rational warrants for and against faith (why faith should or should not be held). Moreover, most of these are fragmented and partial in their purview, delighting in the minutiae of various segments of various particular traditions of faith.

These are all legitimate paths of inquiry, but this book takes a different road. It aims at a synoptic and global understanding of the myriad conceptions of faith by viewing them in terms of the six proposed models. The goal is not to find a way of choosing for or against faith, or between different conceptions of faith; instead, it is to shed some light on all of the various conceptions of faith held in all ages by countless faithful people around the globe. In short, I seek a philosophical portrait of faith.[11] This seems a daunting and immodest task, but it is modestly undertaken. No claim is made to finality, completeness, or basicality, either in approach or in particular results. This book is a conceptual, ahistorical, nonsectarian, synoptic inquiry at a moderate level of reflection, abstraction, and explicitness, focusing on individuals.

---

concept and conceptions of faith, is given in Chaps. 2 and 3, but one further point needs to be emphasized here. The relation between model and conception is not one-to-one; some conceptions may exemplify only one model, but most exemplify several models (though no consistent conception can fully and nonparadoxically exemplify all the models since, as we shall see, they are mutually incompatible). Conversely, a given model may be exemplified, to varying degrees, by many (though again not by all) otherwise differing conceptions.

11. See Nozick, 1989, 12–14, on how a portrait differs from a photograph.

1. It is a conceptual account, or inquiry, seeking a better understanding of faith by tracing some of its complex conceptual contours—or the different contours of illuminatingly similar concepts. I seek to chart some major ways in which the English term "faith" has been used in an effort to discern some philosophically interesting aspects of the term's "grammar." Such an account is distinct from what I term causal, theological, psychological, and sociological accounts of faith. A causal account locates the causes or antecedent conditions—whether temporal or transcendent—of someone or some community having, coming to have, or developing faith of a particular kind, according to a particular conception of faith. A theological account elaborates and defends the content or "object" of faith as particularly conceived—what faith, on that conception, is in or about—and thereby establishes the metaphysical or ontological status of faith. A psychological account portrays the mental, mostly conscious, state of one who has faith: what it feels or seems or is like to be a person who has faith. A sociological account treats the social structures and behaviors shared by—and perhaps created by, or at any rate expressing the views on faith of—those who have the same, or similar, conceptions of faith. All of these kinds of accounts of faith are helpful, sometimes, to some people. But they are not conceptual accounts, for they do not focus on the very conceptions of faith—their structure, implications, and meaning—whose antecedents, contents, phenomena, and communities they describe.

There are, of course, many ways to explore and describe conceptions, and there are degrees of comprehension. One way—appropriate when inventing and clarifying technical concepts—is to state the necessary and sufficient truth-conditions of its attribution ("something is *this* if and only if these conditions hold"). Another way—necessitated by the irregular twists and turns of natural languages—is to catalog usages and contexts ("we informed native speakers would, or would not, say *this* in *that* context"). My procedure lies somewhere between these paths. Conceptual conditions are proposed, somewhat constrained by usage, experience, and reflection. Each of the six models of faith can be viewed as a partially idealized or rationally reconstructed concept that takes as central certain features and ignores or downplays others. The hope, of course, is that all or nearly all actual conceptions of faith can be illuminated—if not by one or another model, then at least by some combination or the ensemble of six.

2. It is ahistorical. Although many accounts of faith have influenced this work, and although it was written at a particular time and place by one not unaffected by historical currents, this book is not primarily a description or analysis of the conceptions of faith actually used by some individual or group of individuals at some time or over some period of time; nor does it trace the growth, development, or alteration of such conceptions.

To some historicists such a procedure will seem absurd, irrelevant, or self-defeating, for, they will surely note, the concept of faith itself is not a timeless Platonic Form but a human contrivance. Of course such a historicist must be burdened by the very weight of history that renders extraordinarily difficult, not to say surpassingly tedious, any attempt at completeness. It would far transcend anyone's competence, life span, or interest to trace and record the extraordinary twists and nuances of various conceptions of faith over all of recorded history, throughout the world, in all of the various traditions and communities of faith, and in the hearts and minds of every faithful individual. But although completeness is a will-o'-the-wisp, it nonetheless marks the ideal limit of what a historicist would consider the only authentic way to approach the full concept of faith; the gate is strait and narrow, passing solely through particular, historically conditioned conceptions of faith. So, on the historicist view, either one presents the historically conditioned conception of faith held by someone or some group or else one does not deal with the concept of faith at all.

While I grant that all conceptions of faith (and perhaps even all concepts *simpliciter*) originate and develop at particular times and places, and perhaps also have idiosyncrasies marking them as belonging to some particular person(s), I deny that there is no room for any other account of concepts. In my view, it remains open for someone—a philosopher, say—to discover or rationally reconstruct concepts that not only bear some stronger or weaker analogies to the actual conceptions held by others in human history but that also, in virtue of possessing features such as explicitness, precision, and clarity, may help to illuminate those actual conceptions. Of course if the goal is to devise a single concept that applies univocally to what anyone at any time has called "faith" or thinks of as faith (or, even more stringently, to find a conception that anyone at any time would accept as coinciding with what they consider faith to be[12]), then one is hopelessly condemned to irrelevancy or vagueness. A general concept applicable to all conceptions or recognizable by all persons would be so thin and tenuous as to be worthless. Our ahistorical goal must be more modest, but also, I hope, more attractive and attainable: To articulate some rationally interesting models of faith that variously resemble, and illuminate, the historical conceptions.[13]

3. It is a nonsectarian account. By this I mean far more than that it goes beyond being an account of some particular traditional conception of faith. It does, of course, range more widely than this—in fact perhaps too widely, for it seeks to take into account any self-nominated conception of faith; its scope is global and encompasses all traditions of faith. But in addition, the account is nonsectarian in not attempting to inculcate or insinuate some particular variety of faith, and in not claiming that one kind, form, or instance of faith is superior to all the rest. There is no hidden agenda of promoting one conception of faith over another.[14] Finally, the account is nonsectarian in that while its primary interest is in religious as opposed to secular forms of faith, it neither defends nor promotes one kind against the other. It makes sense to compare and contrast religious with secular conceptions of faith, but this does not entail assuming either that they are the very same conceptions or that one kind is preferable to the other. In short, the goal of this work is a better understanding of faith in all its bewildering variety throughout human history.

The obvious problem arises: Is it possible to understand faith without actually experiencing or having faith, and can someone have

---

12. This seems to be the goal of W. C. Smith, 1981, in proposing "corporate critical self-consciousness" as the criterion of religious (self-)knowledge.

13. Ideally, historical and philosophical accounts are mutually supportive: History supplies a diversity of conceptions nourishing and guiding a philosophical search for understanding, while philosophy supplies a unity of concept guiding a historical quest for understanding. Methods and materials may differ, but the two kinds of understanding should not be separated.

14. This is easier said than done, of course. Quite naturally I have my own origins and biases (basically Protestant), but I have endeavored to deal fairly with all varieties of faith.

faith without having some particular kind of faith, that is, living with and according to some particular conception of faith? If not, then how can understanding avoid sectarian bias? Even if a person cannot understand faith without having some particular kind of faith, and even if this entails having some particular conception of faith, I do not think one need be blinded to the meaning and merits of alternative conceptions of faith. The kind of conceptual understanding I seek does not require having a given kind or level of faith—as opposed to having some faith or other—nor does it require looking favorably upon any particular version of faith, or all of them. It asks only that the inquirer be willing to pay careful attention to those who speak and think in different ways about faith.

If I take a stand at all on this matter, it is to lean toward the views that faith is a generic, or at least a very widespread and important, phenomenon in human life over the millennia and that the concept of faith (if not particular conceptions of faith) is not a private possession of any sect or tradition. To be sure, one cannot discount or ignore the maelstrom of questions as to which conceptions are superior to the others; which ones represent "true," "authentic," "genuine," or "real" faith; and which ones desperately need to be instanced and enacted—or, alternatively, to be excised and exorcised. Such normative questions are vital, but it is imperative to seek greater understanding of the alternatives before plunging into the maelstrom.

Seeking a nonsectarian understanding of alternative conceptions of faith is rare in any age, but never has it been more needed. Far too often writers on faith are advocates or despisers of some particular version of faith, especially of its propositional affiliations and psychological and social consequences. This kind of conceptual sectarianism rarely conduces toward understanding the varieties of faith, particularly in today's conceptually and fideistically pluralistic world.

4. It is a synoptic account. Synopsis is seeing together, and I propose a way of seeing the world's myriad conceptions of faith all together, as varying exemplifications of the six conceptual models. No doubt there are other routes toward a synoptic vision: One might gain historical synopsis via mastery of the details of various traditions; or sectarian synopsis via extrapolation of some particular tradition's conception of faith to other traditions; or revisionist synopsis

via stubborn viewing of other conceptions of faith as versions of or deviations from one's own (carefully tailored) conception. However, since on reflection it seems to me that no single actual conception of faith both says something rich and significant about faith and also characterizes all or nearly all conceptions of faith,[15] I embark on the path of exploring a number of ideal concepts or models. Such six-fold philosophical synopsis faces two kinds of difficulty: Are the six models internally and mutually coherent, and do they all present recognizable portraits of faith? Are all or nearly all actual conceptions of faith indeed illuminated by one or another of the models? I treat the former question in Chapter 3 and the latter question in Chapter 5, section A.

5. This account operates at a moderate level of reflection, in both materials and results. Its ultimate materials are of course primary conceptions of faith actually used by people—especially but not only by religious people—as they live their daily lives, in activities ranging from more or less formalized practices such as public prayer, Bible reading, and credal affirmation, to more or less individually modulated episodes of conversation, confession, and dark nights of the soul. But its more proximate materials are reflective conceptions of faith—resulting primarily from efforts by those within communities of faith to think about their primary conceptions of faith and the lives they inform—which have been recorded by those with sufficient talent, leisure, interest, and opportunity to write them down.

The results of this study, the six models, are also reflective concepts; however, since they are used to survey other reflective conceptions (of faith), they can be considered second-order reflective concepts.

The uses of reflective concepts, of course, may diverge from, or even clash with, the uses of primary concepts, as the pious occasionally remind the more speculative in their midst. The ways I use reflective models are not necessarily the same as those uses made by theologians of their own reflective conceptions of faith. Without minimizing these possible divergences, I wish to stress a contrary truth: The three kinds of notions (primary conceptions, reflective conceptions, and models) need not be so disparate that no one con-

---

15. At this point the reader need not accept my claim; support for it is assembled in the rest of this work, especially in Chap. 4 and Chap. 5, sec. A.

cept could ever span their distance. More particularly, it is possible that a reflective conception or model that is used to think about a primary conception might be the same concept, or something very similar.

We should never forget, however, that reflective concepts are dependent on primary ones. The models of faith proposed here exist only for the sake of illuminating primary conceptions of faith that exemplify them. Ultimately, the meaning of a reflective concept must be tested against the meaning of primary conceptions.[16]

6. It is a moderately abstract account. I give examples of conceptions of faith that have been used, or described, by actual persons, but these tend to be the somewhat abstract conceptions of theologians, philosophers, or scholars and not the concrete usages of primary conceptions by particular individuals or communities. Moreover, the language I use involves a heavy dollop of abstracting abbreviations—"S believes that p," "S has faith in A," and the like—and this makes for convoluted and inelegant English prose. I would encourage the reader unaccustomed to symbolic notation and abstraction to persevere with the following account. As many have discovered, both have their uses.

The major benefits of symbolic abbreviation are precision, concision, and clarity; as in mathematics, complicated structural ideas may be expressed briefly but perspicuously. The complicated ideas resulting from abstract philosophical thinking also lend themselves particularly well to symbolic abbreviation.[17] Further, abstract thinking is necessary for comparative understanding at a reflective level. Two concepts are not reflectively compared simply by explicating each one separately; the two must be put together in order to be seen together, and this means involving, if not invoking, some "third term" more abstract than either of the two being compared. The two resemble each other in some ways and differ in others, but

16. Of course, this does not mean that someone using a reflective concept of faith to clarify and understand a primary conception must share the faith expressed by the primary conception.

17. Coincidentally, one obtains an unexpected bonus in abbreviated reference to persons as well as to propositions and other kinds of entities. By using capital-letter abbreviations for persons—such as "S" and "A"—one may avoid the briar patch of gendered English personal pronouns: "S believes that p" does duty for "He or she believes that such-and-such is the case." Such avoidance may be welcomed in an age that has yet to find an elegant and universally acceptable stylistic solution.

insofar as the resembling and dissembling features can be concep-
tualized at all, it will be by means of some concept(s) more abstract
still.

The level of abstraction in this essay, while essential, is moderate;
it falls somewhere between the actual thinking of individuals in-
habiting the valleys of faith and the idealized thinking of angels on
the pure categorical clouds above, looking out on the conceptual
landscape from a central hill.

7. The account is a moderately explicit one. An implicit concept
is one whose meaning is disclosed, if at all, only in concrete use; an
explicit concept has at least part of its structure and content set forth
either at a primary or a reflective level, in definitional, truth-
conditional, or some other form.[18] Explicitness is a matter of degree,
and perhaps no informative reflective concepts can be made completely explicit. Still, it seems desirable to be as explicit as possible.
Once again I seek moderation—a moderate degree of explicitness—
by proposing a number of partial definitions and truth-conditions
that should conduce toward understanding the largely implicit primary conceptions of faith.

8. Our account focuses on individual faith, the faith of individual
persons. This point needs careful qualification, however, for no one
could reasonably deny that faith is tied to community. Communities
of faith engender faith and inform faith; they nurture faith and guide
its expression; the very articulation of a conception of faith bears
implicit witness to a linguistic community, and the appeal of such
a conception is embodied in a communal tradition of faith. Indeed,
though it is people who have faith, community penetrates their faith
to the core: Individual selves can live and move and have their being
only in a society of selves.[19]

Nevertheless, despite the inescapable communal context and con-
notation of faith, the present account takes individuals as the proper
subjects of faith. Faith is modeled and conceived as the faith of some

18. Note that primary conceptions may be explicit and reflective ones implicit,
though the tendency is in the other direction.

19. "Selves are social knowers who live in covenant relations" (Niebuhr, 1989,
42). Niebuhr's emphasis on the social dimensions of faith— what he calls the "organic
or social order" (45)—is not at odds with the present account. As Niebuhr notes,
faith is a complex whole that can be variously analyzed, and his own analysis
considers only a few aspects of this whole.

individual. While communities may be necessary for faith, individuals have what communities make possible. This claim is partly an ordinary linguistic claim, partly a commonsense ontological one. When we speak of a community's faith, what we most often mean is the faith that individuals in that community share; a community embodies faith only insofar as its members have the same faith. In short, faith is thought to be a property primarily of individuals and only secondarily of communities; individuals are the primary subjects of faith, communities and traditions the secondary subjects.

Second, a focus on individual subjects of faith does not preclude openness to social implication, even when the latter is not explicitly affirmed. All six models (as described in Chap. 2) share this openness. The devotion model, for example, treats faith as an individual's commitment to a way of life, while leaving open how this commitment might be socially formed, shared, expressed, modulated, and the like. Saying nothing of the communal dimension of faith does not entail that nothing can be said. Third, when various particular conceptions of faith are considered in light of the models (see Chap. 4), the examples selected are not a haphazard collection but represent diverse traditions (communities) of faith.[20] While faith's vitally important communal or social dimensions receive little explicit attention in the present study, they are not underestimated, forgotten, or denied outright.

## F. Outline of the Work

This book contains three major parts.

1. Models. Six thematic models of faith are elaborated in Chap. 2. No claim is made to exhaustiveness or completeness, such as could be established by a Transcendental Deduction. There may be other models. But these six seem relatively prominent, and they are revealingly independent of one another; that is, they highlight fundamental and distinct facets of faith or groups of conceptual features of faith. They are indispensable and sufficient for our purposes here, even if they should yield to a deeper account.[21]

---

20. In addition, of course, they have an intrinsic richness, articulateness, and appeal; see Chap. 4 for additional criteria.

21. See Chap. 3 for further suggestions on these issues.

Each model is an idealized, abstract, explicit, reflective concept that takes some one element found in a group of primary conceptions of faith and makes it central, though also incorporating many of the other elements (in different ways). Each model highlights something vital in faith; each fails to capture the whole of faith. Each makes certain questions and issues prominent while relegating to obscurity or unimportance other matters of concern. The six models are some-what arbitrarily titled; in each an account of essential conceptual features is conjoined with a brief treatment of conceptual opposites where such features are absent or altered.

The personal relationship model accents a distinctively personal kind of ongoing relationship between two people. This relationship varies greatly depending on the people involved as well as the con-texts and limits of their relationship, but it is centered on one person's trust of (or in) another. Such trust involves acceptance, loyalty, and love, and it grounds certain propositional beliefs on the other's au-thority. One such belief is that the object of faith is the agent-cause of the faith relationship. The major opposites[22] of faith, on this model, are lack of trust and distrust in another (either of which may derive from trusting or distrusting a third party). I use "S has faith$_p$ in A" (where 'S' and 'A' name distinct putative persons) as the standard locution for this model of faith.[23]

The belief model brings the epistemic side of faith to the forefront. Faith is most saliently a matter of firmly or confidently believing—believing with conviction, or being convinced—that certain prop-ositions are true without adequate evidence for one's beliefs; indeed, one does not believe on the basis of evidence at all. Still, such beliefs

22. In each model, the focus is on two kinds of opposites—absence and contrary—although in one case (the confidence model) these kinds coalesce into one, and in other cases more than two kinds of opposites can be discerned. For example, in-difference and malevolence are both opposites of benevolence, but perturbability is the sole opposite of imperturbability in the confidence model, and there are several opposites of hope (despair, certainty, hesitancy, and dread).

23. In putting forth a locution as "standard" for each of the models, I do not mean to imply either that this is the only ordinary form of words appropriate to a given model or that this form of words in ordinary usage always or often conforms exactly to the model's conditions. The "standard" locutions are somewhat quixotic and idiosyncratic, but they call attention to the characteristically different stresses of the six models. Simply to use one locution for all models—such as "S has faith in X"—would mask these differences. The different subscripts on "faith" reinforce the differences in locutions.

need not be evidentially irrational—contrary to the person's own available or obtainable evidence—and may even be rationally justified on some nonevidential basis. Such faith aims at removing doubt, at making certain unavoidable important decisions, or at gaining some great good, but not at achieving knowledge. Opposites of faith, on this model, are suspension (or withholding) of belief, disbelief, evidential belief, and tepid belief. The standard locution here is "S has faith$_B$ that p" (where 'p' names a proposition).

The attitude model emphasizes the totalizing or all-encompassing quality of faith. Faith is a basic prepropositional attitude (or set of such attitudes), an existential holistic orientation that connects with, and indeed creates, a fundamental "horizon of significance" for a person in relation to a world. It is a person's deepest way of "being-there"—how one most basically takes, interprets, or relates to one's environing whole—just as it is the world's most fundamental way of "being-here"—how the environing whole impinges on oneself. Specific propositional beliefs about self or world are therefore relatively superficial manifestations, though they are not entirely dispensable. Opposites are the lack of an appropriate attitude (the absence or attenuation of a certain horizon) and the presence of an opposing (or mutually exclusive) attitude/horizon. The standard locution will be "S has faith$_A$ toward X" (where 'X' names S's environing context as "seen" or "taken" by S in the attitude of faith).

The confidence model highlights the psychological or even ontological condition of the faithful person. Faith is a "personal quality" (W. C. Smith, 1971), a fundamental, totalizing, and enduring quality of a concrete living person. Faith is a state of being conscious characterized by an underlying sense of tranquility, serenity, peace, or assurance in the face of such perturbations as doubt, despair, and anxiety. Faith is a kind of feeling, but much more than an ordinary transient affect; it is something much more fundamental and enduring. The sole opposite is the lack of serenity, which turns out to be the same as the presence of perturbability. I use "S has faith$_C$" (with no "object" expressed), though it is tempting to introduce "faith" as an active intransitive verb into the English language: "S faiths$_C$."

The devotion model focuses on decision and agency. Faith is a person's willing engagement in a way of life, constantly reaffirmed, in the face of alternative paths and obstacles. Faith is a matter of willpower and the powers of will: choice among alternatives, resolution in the face of danger and hardship, resistance to temptation, perseverance against long odds, reliance on others, adherence to a goal or plan. Opposites are impotence, ignorance, and irresolution. The locution is "S has faith$_D$ in W" (where 'W' names some path or way of life).[24]

The hope model places desire and longing for a supreme (and future) good on center stage. Faith is confident expectation of and fervent yearning for an improbable but anticipated good that includes but transcends the highest imaginable good for oneself. It involves living "as if" the articles of faith are true, but not necessarily believing that they are. Opposites include despair, evidential assurance, hesitancy, and dread. The standard locution is "S has faith$_H$ in G" (where 'G' names the good desired), though at times it will be convenient to use "S has faith$_H$ that G" or even (somewhat artificially) " S has faith$_H$ for G."

2. Comparisons. The six models are examined together in Chapter 3. Such examination displays comparatively and perspicuously some central strands of resemblance and difference in the concept of faith. I consider first some relations of models of faith to other models, then some relations of models to conceptions of faith, and finally some relations of models and conceptions to the concept of faith.

3. Conceptions. In Chapter 4, the six models of faith are applied to seven reflective conceptions of faith.[25] My goal here is to show how the six models of faith can shed new light on some important conceptions of faith that have actually been used and thought about throughout world history. Since the same six models may be combined in an inexhaustible number of ways, one should not expect to discover pure instances of each idealized model; some models are realized more fully than others. But all are instanced, more or less, in various combinations with other models, and all help to illuminate

---

24. Alternatively, one might say "S has faith$_D$ to $\phi_w$" (where '$\phi_w$' names the living of the way of life W).

25. Although I choose to view particular conceptions from the standpoint of reflective models, the illumination could just as easily shine in the other direction. But that is a job for some participant in a tradition of faith—or perhaps a task for a custodian or historian of a particular conception—and not the work of a philosopher.

hitherto unnoticed differences and resemblances among the myriad primary conceptions of faith.

Further, although the major focus of Chapter 4 is on how different actual reflective conceptions of faith exemplify different models, I also take note of how there are different exemplifications of the same model—variations on the same theme. The variations I consider are only samples—at best paradigms—of an enormous (potential) endeavor. Extending this endeavor is left as a decidedly nontrivial exercise for the reader.

Most of the seven conceptions are offered by people attempting to make explicit what the founders and seminal thinkers in a tradition of faith have somehow seen, invented, or instituted but also kept implicit, unreflective, and even somewhat vague, ambiguous, and unclear. Since the conceptions of faith that have received the greatest articulation tend to be elements of religious traditions, it is not surprising that six of the seven are religious conceptions of faith (or perhaps one should say they are conceptions primarily of religious faith); but we should remember that a conception of faith, or even a tradition of faith, need not be a religious one.[26]

All seven conceptions are selected according to the following criteria: they are reasonably definite (fairly complex, precise, articulated, unified, and explicit); they exemplify different models in different ways; they represent different major traditions of faith; and they are relatively accessible to a nonspecialist audience. In addition, they are all presented by authors who advocate the conceptions they depict, authors who sometimes overstate but rarely overlook important features of their own conception.

The seven conceptions of faith are:

A Thomistic Christian conception (Josef Pieper) that clearly exemplifies the personal relationship model.

A Calvinist Christian conception (Victor A. Shepherd) that also, though differently, exemplifies the personal relationship model, combined with elements of the belief model.

A Lutheran Christian conception (Gustaf Aulén) that primarily exemplifies the personal relationship model (again distinctively), but also the attitude and devotion models.

A contemporary reconstructive conception (James Muyskens and

26. See Hardwig, 1991; Moravcsik, 1988.

Louis Pojman) that clearly exemplifies the hope model, along with
features from other models.

A tripartite Hindu conception (Satchidananda K. Murty), two parts
of which reflect the personal relationship model but one of which
combines, somewhat precariously, the belief and confidence
models.

A Shin Buddhist conception (Yoshifumi Ueda and Dennis Hirota)
that paradoxically juxtaposes the personal relationship model with
several other models.

A Sŏn Buddhist conception (Sung Bae Park) that chiefly exemplifies
the confidence model but allows for (and encourages) auxiliary conceptions of faith exemplifying other models.

Finally, in Chapter 5, I discuss the diversity of conceptions of
faith (particularly those that may be viewed as deviations from the
personal relationship and belief models) over against the analogical
unity of the concept of faith. The book concludes with a brief look
at a dense cluster of remaining problems.

# Six Models of Faith

We begin with models, not conceptions, of faith; this is a useful order of exposition, not an order of actual discovery or recommended inquiry. The six models I describe are the result of my reflection on a great number of conceptions of faith, but clarity of philosophical understanding flows in the opposite direction.

By a "model" I mean an idealized, reflective, moderately abstract, explicit, open-ended, univocal concept that can be used to gain greater theoretical clarity concerning a multitude of particular conceptions.[1] Ideally, a model should have the clear-cut structure and edges of a Platonic Form: Its features should fit together more tightly and neatly than anything messily empirical; its relations with other

---

1. My understanding of models has considerable affinity with Avery Dulles's characterization: "a relatively simple, artificially constructed case which is found to be useful and illuminating for dealing with realities that are more complex and differentiated" (Dulles, 1985, 30). In contrast, however, a model for Dulles has or is based on a unifying metaphor or image and serves purposes of explanation as well as of understanding. Moreover, his five models of revelation do not closely correspond to my six models of faith, even though revelation is intimately associated with faith, in part because Dulles considers only twentieth-century Christian conceptions of revelation, whereas I cast my net of faith more widely across time and traditions. Dulles focuses on "how and where revelation occurs" in order to locate "the crucial moment of revelation," whereas I consider more pervasive logical structures: what kind of property or relation faith is. I should also note that I arrived at my six models, and the conception of model they exemplify, some time before reading Dulles's useful book.

Forms should be crystalline (clear, rigid, and regular); and there should be a certain independence of human authorship in its constitution. Exploring a model, therefore, should seem like discovering (perhaps even "recollecting") antecedent reality; it should not feel as if one were inventing or creating something new. Models should have an objectivity like that of mathematical structures. The following six models are not quite perfect Forms, but they do have different structures.

## A. The Personal Relationship Model

This model will seem most familiar to Western readers, but its familiarity should not breed complacency, much less contempt. Since it is a model, one should beware of identifying it too closely with any actual primary conception or family of conceptions. The essential features of this model may be summarized as follows:

> S has faith$_p$ in A only if S is in a personal relationship with A, S trusts A, S believes certain propositions about A, and S's coming to be in that relationship with A is (at least partially) caused by A.

1. In faith, two persons are in a personal relationship.[2] A personal relationship is a real, ongoing relation between actual persons qua persons. A personal relationship is, necessarily, a relation between persons—both S (the "subject" of faith) and A (the "object"[3] of faith) must be persons. Moreover, the two must be related to one

---

2. Of course, the converse does not hold; not every personal relationship between two persons is a matter of faith. Also, for simplicity's sake I speak as if faith were a relationship between exactly two persons, but clearly more may be involved: S may not just have faith in A and faith in B separately but also faith in A-and-B (perhaps relying on their voluntary cooperation with each other), and S may gratefully share faith in A with another person (it is not just S's faith in A and T's faith in A but S-and-T's faith in A). But the complications raised by introducing more players cost more than the accuracy they add, since the following points remain unaffected.

3. This sense of "object" is not the one opposed to "person" or "human being," but is rather a convenient name for one of the roles in a personal relationship, regarded from the standpoint of one person, a role that can only be played by another person.

another in a distinctively personal way, that is, in a way in which persons, and persons alone, can be related. Spatial relations are not distinctively personal, but love, trust, and (possibly) belief are.[4] Further, a personal relationship requires time. It endures through time; it grows, develops, and thrives over time; and it withstands the vicissitude of time (that is, the uncontrollable and usually adverse changes in time). One may have a day-old personal relationship, a relationship that has barely begun, but not a relationship that lasts for only a day. Considerably more time is needed to initiate, establish, cultivate, and maintain a relationship with another person. Finally, personal relationships are reciprocal, involving active give and take on both sides; they are constituted and conserved by a series of actions—transactions, exchanges, cooperations—finely attuned to the other person, to the history and present status of the relationship, and to the wider context as well.

Several problems arise in thinking of faith as a personal relationship. Quite often we speak of faith in something other than a person, for example, faith in democracy (a political system), the Communist party (a particular organization), the American Way (a way of life), the church (a religious institution or tradition), love (a fact, or perhaps an ideal), or even, in an advertisement, faith in Michelin tires (a consumer product). On the personal relationship model of faith, such talk is strained or inappropriate save as a misleading way of indicating that the object of faith is or depends on persons. "Faith" in Michelin tires—if it can be called "faith" at all—is really, or finally depends on, faith in their manufacturers, purveyors, and advertisers; faith in democracy is faith in the citizens who instantiate its principles; and so forth. On the personal relationship model, then, talk of nonpersonal objects of faith is merely a manner of speaking and not central or standard.

"S has faith in A" implies that A exists and that there is a real relation between S and A. Can there be faith in nonactual things (such as ideals and imaginary entities) or in actual but mistakenly apprehended things (such as idols and false prophets)? There are

---

4. Hence "complete or absolute (existential) dependence" could not count as faith on this model, since mere existential dependence is not distinctive of persons; but this prohibition would not apply to "consciousness of complete or absolute (existential) dependence," since consciousness is a distinctive characteristic of persons—at least it is distinctive of human persons!

three cases here. In one, S quite correctly does not believe that A exists—S may even correctly believe that A does not exist—yet S nonetheless has faith in something that A personifies (ideals). In another, S mistakenly believes that A exists and S has faith in A in part only because of this mistaken belief (imaginary objects). Finally, S correctly believes that A exists but S also has certain mistaken beliefs about fundamental or essential properties of A—beliefs which if corrected would block or remove S's faith in A (false prophets).

For those who have faith in ideals personified by (nonactual) persons, surely there is the belief, or the presumption, that the ideal can be realized, that is, made actual or at least approximated. But this belief, in turn, cannot stand on its own. Ideals such as principles, norms, or values are not self-actualizing; they are abstract entities that can be actualized only by antecedently actual beings with the twin capacities to apprehend and to actualize ideals. Actual persons have such capacities. Apparent faith in a (nonactual) ideal may be the guise of a real faith in some (actual) person or persons believed to be capable of actualizing that ideal. In this way, faith in an ideal may exemplify the personal relationship model of faith.[5]

Concerning imaginary objects, either of two lines might be followed. One could say that faith on the personal relationship model requires only an intentional relation between an actual person and her intentional object (and not a real relation between two actual persons); or else one could say that where the supposed object of faith does not exist there is no faith at all, but only delusion, superstition, or mere credulity. I incline toward the latter, more natural alternative: S has faith$_p$ in A only if A exists; if A does not exist, but S thinks A exists, then S does not really have faith (on this model) but is deluded, mistaken, or under the spell of an illusion.[6]

Concerning actual objects mistakenly conceived, the situation is somewhat different. Here no doubt faith in some sense exists, insofar as a person is the actual object of faith, but if the object is misconceived or misapprehended in some fundamental way, the faith is

5. I do not mean that all ostensive faith in ideals fits this analysis; but if it does not, then it is not faith according to the personal relationship model.

6. Though lack of an actual object precludes faith on the personal relationship model, it does not necessarily preclude (genuine) faith *simpliciter*. S's faith in an imaginary A may exemplify some other model such as the attitude model.

more or less deficient or defective;[7] presumably it would be abandoned if the defective apprehension were corrected. For example, if S trusts a false prophet, the prophet is a real person who is unworthy of S's trust or incapable of satisfying or sustaining it. S does have faith, but it is a defective faith.[8]

Since affirming "S has faith in A" on the personal relationship model commits one to the existence of A, how can nonbelievers or disbelievers in A even talk about S's condition? In a religious context, how can agnostics or atheists talk about a person's "faith in God"? Is faith on the personal relationship model a concept only faithful insiders can use? No. According to this conception of faith, atheists, for example, can certainly affirm that theists think they have faith in God, even though they will not be able to say that theists do have faith in God. Indeed, on the atheist view no one has faith in God, since there is no such person as God in whom one could have such faith.[9] Further, atheists could credit theists with faith in other human beings such as priests, prophets, and popes, on whom their (allegedly delusive) faith in God is based. But to affirm that S does have faith, on the personal relationship model, is to acknowledge some actual object of that faith, however defective, misguided, or destructive

7. Defective in what senses? Defective perhaps in rational justification (since an essential belief or presupposition is false, and S may be rationally unjustified in believing it) or defective in worth (since there is an air of illusion or delusion about the "relationship," though such relationships need not be totally lacking in worth), but not necessarily defective in effect on both the faithful one and others—grand illusions may lead to great good as well as to great evil.

8. There are some difficult borderline cases, however. What if S trusts some object O that is not a person, while (and because) S believes O to be a person? Here I am still tempted to count this fundamentally skewed relationship as faith, albeit defective faith. Perhaps the dispute between impersonal monists and personalistic theists could be cast in these terms: The monist thinks that the theist mistakenly considers and treats as a person something that is not a person—the universe as a whole. Both monist and theist may therefore agree that the theist has faith, and indeed faith in God, but the theist thinks this faith is sound while the nontheist considers it defective.

9. For an atheist, then, all putative faith in God is mere delusion or superstition—not, as for an impersonal monist, defective faith. To clarify the distinction between defective faith and delusion, consider an analogy with love: Does S love B (the beloved, the object of S's putative love) if B does not exist or if B is fundamentally misapprehended by S? If B does not exist, then S is deluded, not loving; S thinks he is in love with B but he is not in love at all. If B exists but S fundamentally misconceives of B, then S's love is defective; S still may be in love, but his love is not a love of B (i.e., S does not love B as B truly is).

one may consider such faith to be. It is conceptually incoherent, on this model, to think that someone has faith in a merely intentional object.

How can anyone—faithful and nonfaithful alike—tell whether someone has faith? Is the person in question the best judge of whether she has faith? Not necessarily. First-person experience may be inconclusive as to whether its object exists or has the fundamental character it seems to the subject to have. At the very least, it seems that genuine faith in an actual person could well be phenomenologically indistinguishable to S from delusive "faith" in a nonexistent object or from defective faith in an existent object fundamentally misapprehended. But all this means is that S, simply by introspection or by considering her own experience, need not be in a privileged or the best possible position to tell whether S has faith. Faith is not incorrigible; one could think one had faith and be radically mistaken.[10]

2. In faith, one person trusts the other. The concept and conditions of trust are fairly complicated. According to Diego Gambetta, "Trust . . . is a particular level of the subjective probability with which an agent assesses that another agent or group of agents will perform a particular action, both *before* he can monitor such action (or independently of his capacity ever to be able to monitor it) *and* in a context in which it affects *his own* action."[11] This notion of trust is excessively narrow; it is confined to subjective probabilities, beliefs, particular actions, capacity to monitor, and effects on self. My use of "trust" here is considerably broader and involves three inseparable features: acceptance, loyalty, and love. These features are specified from the subject's standpoint; though important for both, trust is central for the subject in a different way than for the object.[12]

10. It is quite another question whether one could have faith and not think that one had it. In other words, must S believe that S has faith in order for S to have faith? The personal relationship model leaves this issue open.

11. Gambetta, 1988, 217. The view that faith essentially involves trust is very widespread, though variously construed. See, e.g., Barber, 1983, for three social-scientific senses of trust as expectation, as well as for some social functions of trust; Droege, 1983, for a developmental psychological interpretation; and Moravcsik, 1988, for trust as essential to community and irreducible to self-interest or duty.

12. To be a trusted object involves being or being considered trustworthy as a reliable authority and an adequate object of loyalty and love. I do not explore these object-centered features of faith.

Faith involves the subject's *acceptance* or acknowledgment of the object. S does not necessarily accept every aspect of A, nor does S accept A in every respect, but S must at least accept A as an authority.[13] More concisely, A is an authority for S. An authority is someone on whom a person relies for truth, guidance, or value;[14] hence one may distinguish among epistemic (or cognitive), practical, and axiological authority.[15]

S acknowledges A as an epistemic authority when S believes, or is prepared or willing to believe,[16] whatever A proposes for S's belief; when A proposes something to S, S believes it on A's authority. A need not be an unqualified or unlimited epistemic authority for S. A's authority may be (regarded by S as) restricted to a certain subject matter, and A's word regarding any part of that subject matter might be an occasion for S merely to consider that item (and not to believe it, much less to know, or to be certain about it). But if S trusts A then S somehow relies on A for obtaining and/or certifying truth, whatever the scope or degree of A's authority for S.

S acknowledges A as a practical authority when S obeys or follows, or is prepared or willing to obey or follow, whatever A commands S to do; when A commands S to do something, S does it on A's authority. Practical authority may combine with epistemic authority, so that A may command S to believe that p—that is, for S to perform whatever actions are sufficient to bring it about that

13. Peg Falls-Corbitt asks: Does this condition apply to a parent's faith in and trust of a child? It may, if the parent accepts the child's (limited) authority for its own words and deeds—that the child will keep its promises, speak truthfully, act responsibly, and so on. But it may not, if the parent's trust is more a matter of Gambetta's subjective probability—the parent trusts (believes, predicts) that the child will behave in a certain way. Only the former could be a (somewhat marginal) case of faith on the personal relationship mode; the latter case, if it is indeed faith at all, instances the belief model but not the personal relationship model.

14. Could this reliance be merely hypothetical? That is, could it be that S would believe, obey, or value A if S thought A had spoken or commanded something, or if A were in a certain condition or had certain properties? Insofar as the trust is merely hypothetical, so too is the faith. In order to have actual faith there must be some actual reliance.

15. Such acceptance of the trusted one's authority is present even where one trusts another to do something for you. Part of what distinguishes trusting someone from depending on his predictable behavior is relying on his word: He is taken to be an authority not simply on what he has done or promised to do but on what he will do (because he wills to do it).

16. Or perhaps, more weakly still, if S is only prepared to try to believe? But this is scarcely acknowledgment at all.

S believes that p. Also, once again A's authority may be limited: A's command may range over only a certain kind of action (for example, prescribing certain duties within the confines of A's epistemic authority), and A's command may establish only a prima facie or weak duty. But if S trusts A then S relies on A for obtaining guidance for acting, however far or fully S is prepared or willing to follow A's commands.

S acknowledges A as an axiological authority when S values, or is prepared or willing to value, whatever value A exemplifies; whatever values in A shine forth to S, S is prepared to value them on A's authority. Axiological authority may combine with epistemic and/or practical authority. S may be inspired to obey A's command to believe because of A's radiant value. Once again, A's axiological authority may be limited. A may exemplify only a restricted range of values, or may exemplify them only to a certain degree, or both. A may be a "pretty good" leader or philosopher but a "lousy" carpenter or wife. But if S trusts A then S relies on A for illumination regarding value, to whatever extent or degree S is prepared to value A's exemplified value.

Faith involves S's *loyalty* to A (and to their personal relationship), a loyalty that is free, lasting, and tends toward ultimacy and totality. Faith's freedom implies that S is responsible (and can be held responsible) for S's loyalty to A, and this implies that S intends to be loyal to A (S "knows what she's doing" and "means it") and does so voluntarily (S is neither ignorant nor coerced in her loyalty). But this aspect of S's personal relationship to A should not be overemphasized; it is not as central here as it is in the devotion model (Chapter 2, sec. E). In particular, loyalty should not be viewed as the instantaneous creation of a radically free (but ultimately arbitrary or "gratuitous") choice or decision, or primarily a matter of willpower. Rather, the loyalty essential to a personal relationship is only gradually achieved, being founded on an ongoing series of interactions and transactions; both parties play roles in initiating and sustaining it.[17] Also, faith's loyalty is not necessarily (nor usually) deliberate, planned, or calculated; it seems more like a gift gratefully accepted, or behavior spontaneously and unreflectively emitted, or

17. See Gambetta, 1988.

a "passion" that comes to one unsolicited and sweeps over one unbidden, than like an "action" under one's command and control.

Faith is ongoing, sustained, lasting; loyalty is not momentary, occasional, episodic. Faith cannot be confined to some particular time or encompassed in some brief interval, but necessarily endures through larger periods of time.[18] Moreover, the extent of faith's duration cannot be specified in advance, as one might lay down the temporal conditions of a contract. Instead, just as faith seems to come to one as a gift, so faith's continuing loyalty appears temporally open-ended—or even, in a sense, unending.

Faith's loyalty is a matter of degree, *tending* toward ultimacy (a person's final, deepest, most important or overriding loyalty) and totality (a loyalty that involves all of one's capacities and includes or subsumes all of one's loyalties). Someone's loyalty to another is more clearly a case of faith in the personal relationship sense, other things being equal, precisely to the extent to which the whole person is more ultimately and totally involved. If S's loyalty to A is minimal, claiming S only to a very limited degree, or claiming only a limited part of S, then it may no longer be faith but some lesser loyalty. But if S is finally and fully involved—with all S's "heart and soul and strength" (Deut. 6:5; NEB) then we are clearly dealing with faith.[19]

Faith involves the kind of conation that may fairly be called "*love*": a firm, deep, and lasting desire for personal relationship with the other person. It is not merely that S believes that personal relationship with A is valuable (for S and otherwise), but also, and more important, that S tenaciously recognizes the value of the relationship, deeply desires it, and feels strongly about it. As a result, faith is a motive for action, often a powerful or even a dominant motive. Once again, recognition, desire, and feeling are not momentary, episodic, or delimited, but persist in an open-ended way, shaping

18. One could distinguish between commitment at a time and loyalty over time; faith as personal relationship requires both, of course, but especially the latter.

19. While ultimacy and totality are not necessary for faith as such—there may still be genuine faith that is less than Tillich's "ultimate concern" or Aquinas's all-inclusive "charity"—these seem to be characteristics of specifically religious (or at least of religiously desirable) faith. See Penelhum, 1983, chap. 8, for a similar distinction between "ideal" and "actual" faith.

not only vivid passing experiences but also solid enduring characters and hence establishing whole persons. Because of its powerful motivational force, faith if wrongly aimed can easily become an angry, hateful, destructive fanaticism. But this devolution is not inevitable. Though faith may lead to hatred (especially hatred of those who do not share one's faith), it is founded not on hatred but on love.[20]

In sum, then, S has faith in A, on the personal relationship model, only if S trusts A, and S trusts A only if S accepts A as an authority, is loyal to A, and loves A.

3. In faith, one person believes certain propositions about the other, on the other's authority.[21] This condition has often been so prominent as to eclipse the others; propositional belief is, in fact, the central feature of the next model of faith, the belief model. But by listing it as only the third aspect of the personal relationship model of faith, I mean to signal that propositional belief is not the sole, primary, or deepest aspect of faith in the personal relationship model even though such belief is nonetheless essential to such faith. Those who would reduce such faith to propositional belief are mistaken; they confuse the skeletal beliefs held on faith with the entire living organism of faith. But equally in error are those who would dispense with propositional belief; they forget that living organisms need skeletons to support their many vital functions.[22]

The personal relationship model of faith claims that S has faith in A only if S believes that p on A's authority (where "p" stands for a special set of propositions). But why should personal relationship require propositional belief at all—as opposed to some other propositional or nonpropositional attitude—and which propositional beliefs (which kind or set of such beliefs) are required? Moreover, how convinced must the faithful one be, and how is the object of faith an authority in faith?[23]

20. How excessive or improper love of one person who is an object of faith can become or join with hatred of another (or the same?) person who is not an object of faith deserves detailed psychological study.

21. This bald contention will be qualified shortly, when we distinguish between secondhand (v. firsthand) authority and implicit (v. explicit) belief.

22. For further discussion of conceptions that reduce faith to propositional belief, see Chap. 5, sec. A below.

23. Further questions about belief, particularly those concerning knowledge, are considered in sec. B, on the belief model.

For S to have faith in A, S must *believe* some propositions. It is not enough for S to suppose, presuppose, assume, or presume these propositions true, or to think that they are merely possible or probable, or simply to act as if they were true.[24] S must actually hold these propositions to be true, and in this sense to believe that they are true.[25] Such beliefs are called propositional because what is believed is a proposition, something capable of having a truth–value, of being true or false.

Some will reject this requirement of propositional belief, maintaining that the truth (or falsity) of faith lies elsewhere, and that anyway the notion of propositional truth is opaque.[26] We may agree with much of this critique. Surely there are various nonpropositional senses of the word "true"—for example, those that mean "genuine," "original," "authentic," "real," "superlative," or "an exemplary instance"—and often these other senses are ascribable to some aspects of faith. For example, S's loyalty to A may be "true" in the sense of being genuine, or S's faith may be "truer" than T's because it is more lasting or wholehearted. Many faithful persons, with reason, regard such features of faith as more important than propositional truth. Finally, we must concede the notorious difficulty of characterizing "true" in the distinctively propositional sense. But none of these points obviates the need for propositional belief.

Of course, the requirement of propositional belief is double-edged. It is how faith on the personal relationship model acquires a cognitive foothold, but it is also how the rational justifiability of faith can be called into question; the latter is the price of the former (a price, incidentally, that is not always actually paid). Accounts of faith as lacking propositional belief must either devise some nonpropositional account of cognition or else give up cognitivity for faith altogether. Neither alternative seems very attractive—at any rate neither is attractive on the personal relationship model. Concerning the former, nonpropositional knowledge or cognition may be (essentially) involved in personal relationship, but this cannot be all

24. Contrast sec. F, the hope model.
25. It is a further question as to whether these beliefs must be professed, confessed, or otherwise publicly affirmed. See Fries, 1969a, chap. 3. Also, articles of faith need not form a creed, a set of public beliefs authoritative for some group. See C. Plantinga, 1979, and Schaff, 1983, vol. 1, preface.
26. See, e.g., W. C. Smith, 1971.

that is involved. Even the best of friends or lovers needs to hold
some view as to the truth of certain important propositions about
the other's character, beliefs, intentions, and desires ("he is trustworthy," "she loves me"). Concerning the latter, without the cognitivity entrained by propositional belief, we could not talk about
good or bad personal relationships in ways that seem essential, as,
for example, delusive or defective, in the senses proposed earlier.
No doubt it is vital that personal relationships can be good or bad
in ways that do not involve (believing) propositions, but this is no
reason to extirpate propositional cognitivity from faith altogether.

It is not easy to specify the range of propositions that must be
believed in order for there to be faith on the personal relationship
model, in part because these propositions vary from person to person.[27] But let us begin by calling the subject matter of S's faith in
A all those propositions, true and false alike, that are about A and
A's relationship to S.[28] Now S need not believe all or even most of
the true items in the subject matter of S's faith; much here is optional.
Still, there are minimal elements of S's subject matter that are necessary, though not sufficient, for S to have faith in A at all. Let us,
following Aquinas, call these necessary beliefs "*articles of faith*."[29]

Though articles of faith may differ from person to person and
may be structured differently even for the same person, it may be
useful to arrange articles of faith under aspects of the personal relationship model of faith we are now considering.[30] S must believe

27. Does faith require that any propositions be disbelieved? E.g., where S's faith
in A requires S's belief that p, must S also disbelieve not-p? Or is it enough that S
not believe not-p? But why cannot S both believe p and believe not-p if, as some
would hold (Aulén, 1948), paradox is the essential preservative of mystery, and
faith is a mysterious relation to that which is essentially mysterious? Also, what
about disbelieving propositions the negations of which need not be believed? Further,
must any propositions be suspended or withheld (neither believed nor disbelieved)
in order for there to be faith? My account of the personal relationship model leaves
these questions unanswered; different conceptions of faith each exemplifying this
model might specify different answers.

28. Some of this subject matter is directly about A (and A's relationship to S),
while the rest is indirect (what helps, hinders, leads to, bears on, or results from
S's relationship to A). See Aquinas's implicit distinction between truths about God
and truths in reference to God, in *Summa theologiae* 2a2ae 1.1 Responsio.

29. Penelhum, 1983, calls these "core beliefs." Henceforth we use "q" to stand
for any article of faith for S, while "p" continues to name any proposition whatsoever, whether or not it is an article of faith.

30. The argument for this is as follows: Let us abbreviate the concept of faith

that A exists; that A is a person (of a certain kind, with certain capacities); that A is really related to S in faith; that S trusts A (accepts, loves, and is loyal to A); that S's trust in A is not misplaced (A must be worthy of acceptance, love, and loyalty); that these very beliefs are required for having faith in A; and so forth.

Of course, S need not, and rarely will, believe only articles of faith about A; S's beliefs within the subject matter of faith typically range much more widely, albeit optionally. Moreover, to say that S must believe that q does not mean that S must dwell on q—be constantly aware of q, scrutinize its meaning, worry about its truth—but only that S holds q to be true. In short, propositional belief need not be a prominent part of S's faith; perhaps it comes to the fore only when S's faith is under some kind of intellectual or practical challenge. Still, such belief is never absent.

S's embrace of articles of faith must be firm and tenacious; S must be *convinced* that q. However, S need not be certain that q (an epistemic judgment) in order for S to feel certain or be convinced that q (psychological judgments), and conversely. Certainty implies that one is rationally justified (to a very high degree) in believing that p, whereas conviction only implies that one is personally involved (to a fairly high degree). In faith, S's firm conviction of q exists somewhat independently of the evidence, arguments, and experiences that necessarily bear on certainty. This does not mean that S cannot be certain as well as feel certain that q, only that the former is strictly irrelevant to S's faith$_p$ in A (faith according to the personal relationship model). One must be careful here. Though somewhat independent, faith's beliefs are not necessarily contrary to evidence,

---

as personal relationship as ⌐F₁¬ [read "⌐F₁¬" as "the concept of F₁", where "F₁" abbreviates "faith of the personal relationship kind"]. Two claims are then plausible: (a) S can have F₁ only if S has or understands ⌐F₁¬. (b) S can have ⌐φ¬ [where "φ" is a variable for anything of which S might have a concept] only if S believes the necessary conceptual conditions of ⌐φ¬. If both (a) and (b) are true, then S can have F₁ only if S (minimally) believes the necessary conceptual conditions of ⌐F₁¬. Listing those conditions of the concept of faith is therefore a useful way of organizing the beliefs implied by S's faith in A. Of course this arrangement differs from that of Aquinas, for whom articles of faith are those propositions revealed by God which are directly or indirectly about God and to believe which is essential to human salvation, and who accepts the authoritative structure of the traditional Apostles' (Constantinopolitan) Creed. The two arrangements do not necessarily yield the same set of propositions, though there is some overlap in the Catholic Christian case of faith as a personal relationship.

experience, and argument. To be sure, people sometimes do believe things on faith that go against or beyond evidence, argument, or experience, but not always or even usually. Often articles of faith are entirely consistent with rational grounds and criteria, even if they are not based on them.

As already noted, S accepts A as an authority in various ways, not least as an authority on belief. Not only does S accept A's authority with regard to believing in general, but S's believing some articles of faith about A also essentially *depends only on this acceptance*.[31] However, some articles of faith cannot be accepted on A's authority, for they are presupposed in accepting A as an authority: especially the beliefs that A exists and that A has the requisite authority-making features.[32] But the remaining (nonpresupposed) articles of faith in A—since this remainder is a proper subset of q, let us call it q*—must be accepted on the basis of A's authority, such that:

a. If S did not believe that q*, then S's acceptance of A's authority and S's belief that A authorizes q* would suffice to generate S's belief that q*;
b. If S were to believe that q* solely on some basis other than on acceptance of A's authority, then S would cease to have faith in A; and
c. S does believe q* on the basis of A's authority and on no other basis (in particular, S's belief that q* is not based on evidence).[33]

We must be careful on this last point. The claim is that, according to the personal relationship model of faith, there is no other basis for S's belief that q* (some nonpresupposed article of faith) in so far as q* is a matter of faith for S. This does not mean that such articles of faith are the only beliefs S has about A. Moreover, another

31. This is one sense of saying that S holds or believes something "on faith" or "on the basis of faith" (and not on some other basis).

32. It is difficult to specify these features more precisely; indeed in the case of religious authorities, S may not have any clear idea as to what they are, or even what "exists" means in this context.

33. Is such a belief on faith properly basic? Is it even basic? Alvin Plantinga's widely influential account of belief in God as properly basic (1979, 1981, 1983) seems irrelevant to faith on the personal relationship conception; at the minimum he has omitted a treatment of believing on another's authority, and how it is or is not basic, much less properly basic. See Grigg, 1983, 1990.

person (or S at another time) could well believe q* on some other basis—on evidence, perhaps—or "in the (properly) basic way." Furthermore, if S were to hold one and the same proposition to be true both on faith and on evidence, this would require S to have two different beliefs about the same proposition: "S's belief that q* on faith" and "S's belief that q* on evidence" would have to be different beliefs, not the same belief with different bases. Finally, S could believe q* on faith according to some model of faith other than the personal relationship model.[34]

S's belief that q* may be on *firsthand* or *secondhand* authority. The former is a belief that directly depends on accepting the authority of the object of faith, where S believes something about A on A's authority, by accepting A's authority. The latter is a belief that directly depends on accepting the authority of some other person (perhaps as a necessary condition of accepting A's authority, or as a means to learning about A) where S believes the proposition about A on B's authority.

Could S have faith in A if all of S's beliefs about A were on secondhand authority? No; this would not be faith in A but faith in someone else. S has faith in A only if S believes at least some proposition(s) about A on the firsthand authority of A. Which beliefs may be held on secondhand authority? In addition to some (but not all) nonpresupposed articles of faith, S may also believe many other propositions about A on another's authority. Further, S may believe p about A on the authority of both A and B (firsthand and secondhand authority for the same belief), though in this case firsthand authority takes precedence qua authority.

Multiple authorities may be necessary for faith's belief. Sometimes, and quite often, these cases are vital to an ongoing community of faith, a tradition. Consider the simplest case, where there

34. Two additional questions not answered by the personal relationship model of faith warrant further inquiry. First, are there any propositions that, if believed at all, could only be believed on faith? These would be propositions for which no one—in this life, at least—could obtain adequate supporting evidence or experience yet which would still be requisite for faith of some kind. And second, are there any propositions that could not be believed on faith? These would be ones that either cannot be believed at all (e.g., because they are too complex or employ concepts incomprehensible to humans), or else if believed must always be believed on evidence or grounds (e.g., because their truth is self-evident or obvious to everyone who is capable of believing at all).

are two authorities, A and B. Suppose that S accepts A's authority with regard to p but cannot find out A's precise position on p from A directly. Suppose further that S accepts B's authority with regard to whether A in fact says (asserts, holds, teaches) that p. If S should learn from B, on B's authority, that A does say that p, then S would believe that p. Here A is S's firsthand authority with regard to p, B is S's firsthand authority with regard to A's position on p, and in this way B is S's secondhand authority with regard to p.

S's belief that q may be either *explicit* or *implicit*.[35] S's belief that q is explicit for S just if S (actually) believes that q; it is implicit just if S does not in fact (actually) believe q but would believe q if q were proposed to S for belief (and S understood it). In particular, since S accepts A as an authority with regard to q*, S would believe that q* if S should authoritatively learn that A says (asserts, teaches, communicates) that q*, or perhaps even that A holds (believes, knows, is certain) that q*.

S may have faith in A if some, indeed most, of S's obligatory beliefs (articles of faith) about A are implicit. Could S still have faith in A if all of S's beliefs about A were implicit? Here one must make another distinction: S's belief that q may be implicit qua belief about A or it may be implicit qua belief based on the authority of A. S could not have faith in A with beliefs all of which were implicit in the former sense, but in the latter sense S could. Concerning the former, S has faith in A only if S explicitly believes that q (at least some of the articles of faith); completely implicit belief here yields only implicit (potential) faith, not explicit (actual) faith. But concerning the latter, none of S's explicit beliefs about A need be held explicitly on the authority of A—indeed, the articles of faith presupposed by acceptance of A's authority cannot be held explicitly *or* implicitly on A's authority. Still, all of S's beliefs—both explicit and implicit—about q* (that is, all nonpresupposed articles of faith about A) must be held at least implicitly on the authority of A. S has faith in A only if S at least implicitly believes every q* (nonpresupposed article of faith) on the authority of A. But S might very

---

35. As defined here, explicit belief is actual belief and implicit belief is potential belief (in one sense of "potential"). Other ways of construing the explicit/implicit distinction describe it as conscious versus unconscious belief, conscious versus nonconscious belief, occurrent versus dispositional belief, or expressed versus unexpressed belief. See D. Evans, 1980, chap. 6.

well trust A without explicitly believing q* on A's authority—either because A has never spoken to S about q* or because S does not believe that A has so spoken—so long as S would believe q* if (S came to believe that) A proposes q* to S for belief.[36]

Finally, we come to the question about whether faith on the personal relationship model can yield or constitute *knowledge*. Propositional knowledge on faith is a distinct possibility on this model. If there are constraints here, they are due to the nature of some special object of faith and not to the nature of faith as such. The central idea is as follows: If S has faith in A, A knows that p, A is an authority for S with regard to p, and A proposes p to S for S's belief, then if S believes p on A's authority S also knows that p.

Suppose that S has faith in A, and therefore that A is a (firsthand) authority for S with regard to q (where q is an article of faith for S about A). Suppose further that A is a legitimate or reliable authority in this area, and S so believes. Now A may be merely a doxastic authority for S about q, that is, A's authority may warrant S only in believing q; S's say-so yields (at best) justified belief. But A may be more than this; A may be a cognitive authority for S about q, that is, A's authority may warrant S in knowing q. So under the latter circumstances, if A proposes q to S and S believes q on A's authority, then S knows that q.

Of course, some will resist allowing that there can be knowledge (as opposed to some less weighty category) on authority; and these resisters are not entirely wrong. Knowing on authority is somewhat defective when compared with other kinds of knowledge—in par-

---

36. The points on firsthand and secondhand authority and explicit and implicit belief may be combined. Clearly beliefs can be held explicitly or implicitly on firsthand authority: If S accepts A as an authority with regard to r (some proposition about A), then S does (explicitly) or would (implicitly) believe that r on the basis of A's authority if S learns or were to learn that A asserts (holds, knows) that r. But beliefs may also be held explicitly or implicitly on secondhand authority: If S accepts another person B as an authority with respect to some proposition r about A, then S does or would believe that r on the basis of B's authority if S learns or were to learn that B asserts that r. Further complications arise in cases of mixed authority: S might believe r implicitly on the firsthand authority of A and explicitly on the secondhand authority of B; or S might believe r (implicitly or explicitly) on the firsthand authority of A only because S believes (implicitly or explicitly) on the firsthand authority of B that A has said r. Such complications are often important in "real-life" cases of faith, even though they are not specifically addressed by the personal relationship model.

ticular, it does not allow the knower's direct personal (firsthand) verification of her knowledge (while remaining knowledge on faith); it is essentially secondhand, dependent upon another. Still, the question should be whether such defects prevent believing on authority from becoming or being knowledge at all.

The first point to note is that these defects do not entail a lack of evidence. After all, if evidence is roughly whatever bears on the truth of a proposition, then a legitimate authority's word is a kind of evidence ("if A says that p, then probably p"), and the more perfect the authority the better the evidence. Rather, the essential defect lies in the kind of evidence and hence the kind of knowledge the knower has: S may know that p on A's authority, but S does not thereby know why p. If all goes well and the authority tells the believer what is true but not why it is true, then S has knowledge on authority, but this knowledge is reason-defective.[37] This defect does not necessarily prevent believing on authority from being knowledge; lack of knowledge why p is true does not prevent one from having knowledge that p is true.

There are, however, some further complications. Note first that S's knowledge, gained essentially through reliance on A's authority, need not be the same as, or as epistemically excellent as, A's knowledge. S's knowledge is based on A's knowledge and authority; A's knowledge need not be based on anyone else's authority. Second, knowledge on authority need not imply certainty or absence of doubt; at least S may have doubts (for example, about possible evidence) where A is certain.[38] Third, knowledge and (epistemic)

37. Why cannot A tell S not only that p but also why p, that is, why cannot A give S some correct reasons (evidence, grounds)—or even S's own reasons—for believing or knowing p? This would not make knowledge on authority any less reason-defective. There are two cases. Once given reasons for p by A, S would or would not continue to believe them on A's authority: (a) If S continues to believe the reasons for p, or that they are reasons for p, only on A's authority, then S continues to lack insight into why p is true. S might now know not only that p but also that these are the (A's or S's) reasons why p is true, but S still would not know why these are the reasons, and hence would not know why p. Such knowledge on authority is still reason-defective. (b) If S comes to believe the reasons for p (and that they are reasons for p) not on A's authority but because of S's own insight into their truth and bearing on p, then S may indeed acquire knowledge why p and not merely knowledge that p, but now S does not know p on A's authority. Such knowledge that is no longer reason-defective is no longer knowledge on authority.

38. Contrast the view of B. Mitchell, 1973, chap. 6, for whom knowledge precludes all doubts.

authority need not coincide. A could know that p but not be a reliable reporter or communicator to S of this knowledge (or perhaps A is wary or chary of so communicating), so that S might not come to know p on A's authority; conversely, however, A could not serve as a knowledge-authority for S without authoritatively knowing the subject-matter herself. Fourth, the trail of transmission of knowledge by authority must start with someone's knowledge; if S knows something on A's authority, and A on B's authority, and so forth, then there must be a first knower, or else there is no knower at all (via authority). Conversely, knowledge may be lost, or reduced in quality, through authoritative transmission from someone who knows. Not only may the informational content of the message become degraded (as anyone realizes who has ever played the parlor game of "Gossip" or its real-life counterparts!), but also the broader context (reasons, point of view, attitude and aim of speaker, behavioral implications) may be lost; tone of voice and purpose are not always easy, or desirable, to communicate. The odds of losing information will increase in direct proportion to the number of stages in the trail of transmission.

What does "A proposes p to S for S's belief" mean? The simplest case would be where A directly says something to S that S understands and that clearly indicates A's own cognitive state: "I know that p." But there are other ways. A might say "You should believe" or "Believe p (trust me)." But A might possess sufficient skill to propose p for S's belief in other ways. A might get B, who is also authoritative for S, to say to S: "A knows p" or "A knows p, because A told me so." Or A might bring it about that S comes to believe that a certain book was authored by A in an authoritative way, or that certain experiences occur to S that S likely will or at any rate could interpret as communications or "signs" from A.

I conclude, therefore, that in principle nothing precludes believing on (legitimate) authority from becoming or being knowledge.[39]

4. In faith, the object plays a causal role. Whereas the two previous conditions focused on S's role and standpoint in the personal relationship between S and A, this condition treats the causal role played

39. See the belief model (sec. B) for further discussion of whether believing on authority yields knowledge or only justified belief. This is an important difference between the personal relationship model and the belief model.

by A, the object of faith: S has faith in A only if A (in a certain sense and respect) causes S's faith in A.[40]

The causality in question is not that of being a necessary (background) condition, or a precipitating event, or a coincidental occurrence; rather, it is agent-causality, where A as a person acts to bring about or cause or even create S's faith (at least in part). Since faith is a distinctively personal relationship, and persons are necessarily agents, agent-causality, not event-causality, must be involved.[41] Faith is not (just?) something that occurs or happens to persons; it is something persons do or bring about. Conceivably S could trust A or even believe a number of propositions about A on A's authority, without A acting so as to create this trust or belief (for example, S is credulous or gullible), but this would not be faith according to the personal relationship model, which requires that the object of faith be a creative source of the subject's belief. Still, attributing such causality to A is not saying a lot, for the concept of agent-causality is obscure; in addition, there are three further problems.

The first problem centers on to what *extent*, and in what respects, A is the agent-cause of S's faith in A. Is A's agency a cause or the cause of S's faith—part of the cause or the whole cause? Here we must note a tendency toward totalization, as well as some troubles this tendency entrains. Note first that the possible range of A's causal activity is very wide. A could produce: S's awareness of the propositions to be believed; the believing of them; S's acceptance of A's authority; the basing of S's believing on S's acceptance of A's authority; S's trust (acceptance, commitment, love) of A on which S's acceptance of A's authority somehow rests; S's very capacities for acceptance, trust, and belief; the accompanying emotions or passions; the personal relationship itself between S and A, which includes all of these; and so forth. Within this range, A's agency may produce stronger or weaker degrees of each aspect, may work with or against other causes or agencies, and may create tendencies and inclinations as well as capacities and actualities. In all of these respects, the personal relationship model of faith leaves considerable

40. This causal criterion serves as one basis for the Christian distinction between human and divine faith. See J. F. Ross, 1969, 77–78.

41. It is another question whether agent-causality can somehow be analyzed as or reduced to event-causality.

room for variation in particular cases. A might produce acceptance of A's authority more extensively, or to a greater degree, in one person than in another, or B might produce a greater variety of propositions, or greater tendency to believe them, than A does.

Given this wide variation, there nonetheless seems to be a tendency among those who have faith to assert a very wide, and ever-widening, sphere of influence by the object of faith: ultimately all areas of the subject's life are encompassed. In part this is due to the tendency of the acceptance of authority to spread or strengthen as one invests proportionately more of one's life in the relationship. In part it is due to the apparent conflict between restricting the object's causality and having faith. If, for example, A is not the cause of S's acceptance of A's authority, then it seems that either the subject or alien causes must determine it. But neither source is satisfactory to faith. Alien causes are indifferent or inimical to faith's concern, while self-determination appears to faith as self-reliance—the very opposite of trust in another. So there is a tendency in faith toward totalization.

However, reaching totality (ascribing an unsurpassable maximum of causal efficacy to the object of faith) is not required by the personal relationship model of faith. In particular, the object of such faith need not be a supernatural agent or deity with maximal power. All that is required is that the object of faith play some causal role, however limited, in producing faith in it. Even so, the tendency toward totalization is frequently pushed to the limit—where S thinks of A's causal activity as extending to and sufficient for the whole of S's faith in A. It is here that we run into an age-old but still quite formidable thicket of perplexities: How could S's faith be free if it is completely determined by its object? How then could S be, and be held, responsible for any aspect of S's faith? How could a faith that is completely determined by its object even be considered someone's (that is, some human subject's) faith at all? These perplexities are part of the old conundrum variously labeled "human free will versus divine omnipotence" or "freedom versus grace." I do not pursue these questions here except to address a distinction frequently employed in this connection (see Chap. 5, sec. C).

Could A's activity be a supernatural cause of S's faith even while there are (other) natural cause(s) of that faith? It is scarcely clear what natural causality involves; supernatural causality deepens the obscurity. But the supernatural/natural distinction does not seem to relieve the problems created by faith's drive toward totalization. To the extent to which both kinds of causality can be expressed in terms of (essential) part and whole, or necessary and/or sufficient conditionality, totalization seems to require that A's supernatural causality be the whole cause of—both necessary and sufficient for—S's faith. But this is incompatible with some natural cause being either necessary or sufficient for S's faith, and so S's own agency or ownership of faith is in jeopardy. Conversely, if natural causes are both necessary and sufficient for S's faith, then supernatural causality is impossible or redundant. Of course, both kinds of cause may be jointly necessary, or they may be separately or conjointly sufficient, but in neither case is the supernatural/natural distinction helpful in checking the tendency toward totalization.

The second problem for the concept of agent-causality is the notion of faith as a *gift*. To say that something is a gift is to say more than that it is due to another's activity. To call what A gives to S a gift also implies that: the gift is something good for S overall (a plague is not a gift, unless perhaps it is the necessary means to a greater good); it is intentionally brought about by A (an accidental effect, however good, is not a gift); and it is brought about for the end or purpose of giving an overall good to S (a good for S produced by an action designed to serve some other purpose is not a gift for S in the strict sense, even if it is a good given to S, but rather a "lucky break" or "good fortune").

Perhaps some cases of faith have all three additional features of a gift, but clearly not all of them do. For example, not all instances of faith seem good for the faithful, much less for others (fanaticism); some faith is at best a foreseen consequence of what the object of that faith does or intends (someone may acquire authority and convey truths about herself that are believed on her authority without intending that others rely on the former and benefit by believing the latter); and sometimes faith is intentionally produced to benefit others and not the subject of faith (political manipulation, religious cults). So faith is not always a gift, however much it might appear to be a gift to those who greatly treasure faith.

The third problem can be formulated as a question: If A (partially) causes S's faith in A, must S (correctly) *believe* that A does so? An answer to this question is suggested by a brief look at the concept of revelation.[42] Revelation—at any rate propositional revelation—involves both causality and belief: A reveals p to S only if A causes S to believe that p. But, it seems, A's causing S's belief must be coupled with S's awareness of that very causality, or else S has merely a belief produced, not a proposition revealed. Is this claim too strong? Is there not a kind of (partial) "revelation" where A gets or leads S to believe that p without S knowing, believing, or being aware of A's role in producing this belief? This is revelation without a revealed revealer, and is therefore incomplete. In the full or realized sense of revelation, A successfully reveals p to S only if A at least in part causes or brings it about that S believes that p, and only if S believes that A has (at least in part) caused or brought it about that S believes that p.[43]

If the parallel with revelation is apt, it would seem that some (correct?) belief by S concerning A's role in causing S's faith in A is necessary to S's having faith in A, or at any rate to having full or realized faith. We may therefore add a condition such as the following to the personal relationship model of faith: S has faith in A only if S believes that A causes S's faith in A.

5. The opposites of faith are lack of trust and distrust. One way to understand the meaning of a concept is to see what it excludes;

---

42. For further discussion of the concept of revelation, see J. Baillie, 1956; Bavinck, 1953; Brunner, 1946; Downing, 1964; Dulles, 1985; Latourelle, 1966; McDonald, 1959; Mavrodes, 1988; Moran, 1966, 1972; Söderblom, 1966; Swinburne, 1992; Thielicke, 1977, vol. 2; and Trembath, 1991. A further list of mostly Roman Catholic sources is found in O'Collins, 1981, 368, n.1.

43. Further questions arise. What if the aspects of S's faith in A that are in fact caused by A differ from the aspects that S believes are caused by A? Or what if S believes that A somehow causes some part or aspect of S's faith without any clear idea as to which part or aspect? (For instance, S's belief that p could be produced by A without S realizing or believing that it was, even though S believes that A has produced some other aspect of the personal relationship between S and A.) Are any of these cases still faith, however defective or deficient, or must S's beliefs about A's causal role in faith be at least approximately correct? What about a possible regress of causes and beliefs? If, in order for S to have faith in A, S must believe that A causes S's faith in A (A has revealed p to S), must this belief also be caused by A in order for there to be revelation? If so, must S additionally believe this (that A has caused S's belief that A reveals p to S)? And then must A cause this further belief, and must S believe that A has done so? Where, if ever, should this regress be terminated, and why?

if something is affirmed, what is denied? I call a concept's denials its "opposites." There are, of course, many kinds of opposites for any concept. In this and subsequent treatments I focus on two major types of opposites, which I call "absence" and "opposition," though some treatments go beyond this distinction or even call it into question.[44] The absence of a central conceptual feature F is its mere lack: non-F. The opposition of F is the presence of another feature, G, which either prevents or somehow conflicts with the occurrence of F: anti-F. (Hence absence and opposition are distinct properties, although opposition may imply absence.)

Now faith, on the personal relationship model, has as its major opposites the lack of trust (absence: S's not trusting A) and the exclusion of trust (opposition: S's distrusting A). For the former, S's lack of trust need not take the form of actively doubting, suspecting, or even opposing A; it is enough that S simply does not trust A. Further, this lack of trust by no means implies that S lacks all personal relationship with A, though the range of their personal interaction will necessarily be severely constricted. For example, S might play poker with A but would be sure to cut the cards and keep a keen eye on A throughout; S might sign a treaty with A but would make sure that there are safe and reliable means of verification; and so on. In short, S might have very little, if any, trust in A and still be able to maintain some kind of (minimal) personal relationship with A. Still, total lack of trust does tend toward impersonality—the kind of relationship one can have with even inanimate objects, and they with one another—for without trust one cannot have very many or very extensive dealings with a person as a person.

For the latter, S's lack of trust is due to some feature or condition of S that opposes by positively excluding S's trusting A. Distrust here is the product of some attitude incompatible with trust, whether or not that attitude is rational for S to have. For example, S might have been betrayed once, long ago, by A and ever since has refused to extend to A the credit of goodwill; or S might be quite irrationally prejudiced against A's racial or religious group and hence be unable

44. Two points can be made about focusing on these two kinds of opposites. First, there are other kinds of opposites insofar as each of the partial necessary conditions of a model can be independently absent or excluded by another property. And second, even where opposites are distinguished in principle, it may be very difficult in practice actually to notice and name their instances.

to trust A; or S might falsely believe that A is S's enemy. Such exclusionary attitudes are the opposite of impersonal. Not only can one not distrust a nonpersonal entity, but distrust may come to form the core of some quite enduring, even all-consuming, relationship that is all-too-personal ("my enemy A"). Even though personal, however, the relationships formed by distrust are antithetical to those required by faith on the personal relationship model.

Further, either lack of trust or distrust may stem from trust; trust may, but need not, breed further trust. Sometimes, of course, S's trust of one party, A, has no effect upon S's trust (or lack of trust or distrust) of another party, B: A may have nothing to say about B to S, or if something is said, S may just ignore it. But quite often trusting A tends to increase or decrease S's level of trust in B: trusting one apostolic successor tends to reinforce or increase one's trust in the others and gossip tends to undermine confidence in its victims. Sometimes trusting A even blocks trusting B (and conversely): sometimes S cannot be the slave of two different masters (Matt. 6:24; NEB), nor trustfully follow the lead of two antagonists.

To recapitulate: According to the personal relationship model of faith, one person has faith in another only if the first is in a distinctively personal relationship with the second, a relationship centrally characterized by trust (acceptance, commitment, love), on the basis of which the first person believes (on the other's authority and with conviction if not with certainty) certain crucial propositions about the second and their relationship (articles of faith), and where the second person plays (and is believed to play) an agent-causal role in the relationship. Faith is absent when trust is lacking, even if distrust is not present. There are undoubtedly many loose and indefinite ends to this model (some of which have been mentioned), but it should now be clear enough to be useful in shedding light on some actual reflective conceptions of faith (see Chap. 4).

## B. The Belief Model

Whereas propositional belief is a secondary, albeit vital, ingredient in the personal relationship model, here it appears to constitute the whole of faith. But appearances are deceiving; there is more to the belief model of faith than belief. The essential features of this model may be summarized as follows:

> S has faith$_B$ that p only if S believes that p, S is (firmly) convinced that p, S has inadequate evidence for p, and S's belief that p is nonevidentially based.

1. Faith is propositional belief. On this model of faith, two features predominate: belief and propositions. Belief here is not "belief in," belief in another person, but "belief that," belief that such-and-such is the case, or belief that a certain proposition is true. Believing and propositions therefore dovetail. Believing is a certain attitude that human persons can take toward propositions and only toward propositions; and propositions, not persons, are the requisite objects of this attitude. In fact, the two are so closely linked that in ordinary usage the same word, "belief," is sometimes used for both: "belief" is what a person believes (the proposition) and it is also the person's attitude toward it (the believing).[45] It is better to keep the two distinct.

Many will object that the belief model either provides no concept of faith at all, since it omits a number of vital features of faith, for example, trust and commitment, or else is only an "outsider's" conception of faith, not one that would, or could, or at any rate should, be used by someone who actually has faith.

Concerning the former point, this model seems to be a model of one kind of faith, even if it does not include all features found in many prominent conceptions of faith. Any appearance to the contrary is due to focusing on features of faith not expressed by the model yet permitted by it, that is, by wrongly treating what is not explicitly included in the model as implicitly excluded by it. Faith

45. Some (e.g., Kellenberger, 1989, 76) are tempted to treat "S has faith in A" as equivalent to "S believes in A" and "S has faith that p" as equivalent to "S believes that p," but the temptation should be resisted, for despite considerable resemblance there are important differences. For one, "S has faith that p" is not equivalent to "S believes that p"; other conditions (e.g., firmness of conviction) must be met by belief to convert it into faith. For another, one may believe in things other than persons (ideals, institutions, or principles) while one can have faith ultimately only in persons. For a third, believing in A entails believing that certain propositions about A are true, whereas having faith in A does not entail that one has faith that certain propositions about A are true (although it does entail believing that these propositions are true).

on the belief model does not say that S must have a trusting personal relationship with A, but neither does it preclude such a relationship; noninclusion is not exclusion. In fact, as we shall see, accepting authority is an important way in which nonevidential grounding for the requisite beliefs might be obtained. No doubt the belief model is only a partial concept of faith, but so is every other model; partiality does not prevent the belief model from being a concept of faith. It highlights a coherent set of features (belief, propositions, conviction, evidence, basis) that are prominently exemplified by some actual conceptions of faith, and that are therefore useful for analyzing and understanding those conceptions.

The latter point contains a large element of truth. The belief model of faith largely is an outsider's conception. In part this is understandable, even innocuous. It is easier to understand a relatively limited set of propositions than to comprehend an entire living faith; easier to abstract, discuss, and criticize propositions believed than to enter into the unendingly subtle nuances of a personal relationship; easier to think about carefully circumscribed propositions than a whole life's fundamental orientation. But there is a more ominous side to such propositional simplification. Exclusive focus on propositional belief may seek to reduce faith to a paltry set of inadequately evidenced but fervently held propositions, and this can easily become an important part of a policy that seeks to reject all faith as irrational, unworthy, trivial, or untrue.

Still, one should not concede too much to this critique of an outsider's viewpoint. First, it is simply false that no insider ever would or could think of her faith in terms of what she believes. It is, in fact, perfectly natural for her at least to begin to answer a question about her faith by affirming some of her important beliefs, even though she may not characterize them as beliefs and will quickly go on to say that such affirmation is inadequate and incomplete in various ways: Simple expression fails to capture the richness and profundity of her beliefs; mere statement fails to convey the full importance of these beliefs for the whole of her life; profession of belief, however fervent, cannot convey the vitality or totality of her devotion; it is hard to make it clear on what (nonevidential) bases her beliefs rest; the importance of other persons in gaining and maintaining her faith cannot be ignored; and so forth. Despite all these inadequacies, however, it still seems plausible to think that beliefs are (sometimes) a tolerable first approximation to a person's faith, and it is this approximation that the belief model highlights.

As I use the terms, a "proposition" is whatever can have a truth-value of true or false; a "statement" is the linguistic expression of a proposition, inscribed (or uttered, or whatever) in some particular "sentence." Persons may take various "propositional" attitudes toward propositions; they may entertain, doubt, affirm, or assume them.[46] Belief is one such propositional attitude.[47] Minimally, if S believes that p, then S holds p to be true. This holding-to-be-true must be sharply distinguished from allied propositional attitudes such as supposition, presupposition, assumption, or presumption. Belief is not simply thinking that p is possible or probable,[48] nor acting or being disposed to act as if p were true, nor claiming that p is true or likely to be true, or that it is rational for S to hold that p is true. S must actually hold p to be true for S to believe that p sincerely and explicitly. There are, of course, many complications, of which I note the following.

Could S believe that p without expressing p in a statement? Is belief independent of linguistic performance? Could S believe that p without even being able to express p in a statement? Is belief independent of linguistic competence? I tend to think that it is not possible for S to believe that p without S being able, in some way and to some degree, to give linguistic expression to p. After all, how could someone hold some proposition to be true but have no way of expressing which proposition she is holding? Would she properly be said to be holding anything at all to be true? I think not, and hence I assert that the belief model requires the propositional

46. Not all propositions need be expressed, or even expressible, in human statements; not all sentences instance statements (there are also questions, exclamations, and so forth); and there are grave difficulties in characterizing more precisely such notions as "proposition," "truth," "statement," "sentence," "language," or "attitude." Fortunately, our characterization of the belief model does not depend on resolving such issues.

47. For alternative views of belief, see Bogdan, 1986.

48. Nor, contrary to Swinburne, 1981, 3–8, is belief just a matter of thinking or holding that p is more probable than not-p (where $P(p) > .5$). Actually, Swinburne's claim is only that "normally to *believe* that $p$ is to believe that $p$ is probable" (4; emphasis added). This may or may not be acceptable as an explication of what is believed, the content of belief (not that p or that p is true but that p is probable), but it sheds no light on what it is to believe, the propositional attitude involved, for there it is patently circular ("to believe this is to believe that").

beliefs constituting S's faith to be at least statable or expressible by S.

Could S believe that p without understanding p? Yes, in part. Most typically, of course, the propositions that S believes on faith are taken to be but tiny points of light surrounded by a vast cloud of important obscurity or mystery; very little of the great web of a proposition's entailers and entailments need be understood by S. Even the very propositions believed are often felt and affirmed to be understood or even intelligible only in part and unclearly, "in a mirror dimly" (1 Cor. 13:12; RSV). It is quite possible, then, for S's faith to pass beyond S's understanding in various ways; p may be vague, ambiguous, or otherwise unclear to S, and perhaps some aspects of p may transcend S's powers of comprehension altogether. Lacking such understanding, therefore, S may believe that p is true solely on the authority of another. In fact, S need not even understand exactly which proposition is actually expressed by the statement that S accepts on the authority of A, or how this statement expresses that proposition. Nevertheless, the belief model of faith cannot dispense with all understanding on S's part or else there would be no beliefs of S remaining. Very minimally, in order to believe that p, S must understand (and also believe) that the statement expressing p that S accepts on another's authority does express some genuine proposition and that there are some propositions, which S can articulate to some extent, that the statement does not express— or else there would be nothing for S to believe in the propositional way. A person cannot say, "I believe whatever A tells me to believe—though I have absolutely no idea what A tells me to believe." S must have some understanding, however dim, of what it is that A tells S that S is supposed to believe.

Could S believe that p without being aware of believing it? Yes and no. For every time t at which S believes that p, S might not be aware of believing p at t; S might not occurrently believe p at t. Instead, S might believe p at t dispositionally, such that S would occurrently believe that p at t if certain conditions were satisfied. The category of dispositional belief is very expansive. Certainly it accommodates beliefs of S that are (currently) subconscious—all could be brought to S's occurrent awareness under the right conditions, though some conditions are more easily satisfied than others (a moment's image may jog a particular memory-belief, but years of analysis may be required to bring deeply repressed and profoundly threatening beliefs to light). Similarly with implicit beliefs: even if S does not actually (explicitly) believe that p, nonetheless S does so potentially, and so there are conditions—if p were proposed to S for belief by an authority for S, for instance—under which S would actually believe in such a way as to be or become aware of so believing.

However, the danger here is that "dispositional belief" is too expansive a category. Since there are conditions, however fantastic, under which S would believe that p, for any p, it might seem that S must believe everything (dispositionally, of course). The solution is twofold. One part is to rule out conditions—grounds—that do or would causally produce the belief that p. The other is to see that normally when one asks whether S dispositionally believes p one has in mind a certain range of consciousness-raising conditions (undergoing psychoanalysis, trying to remember, thinking through the logical implications of an occurrent belief), and given those conditions it will not be true that S believes everything, even though it is likely that S believes (dispositionally) more, often far more, than S is aware of believing (occasionally).

Must someone—in particular, must S herself—always be able to tell or determine the facts about S's believing-state, (a) given that S believes something or other, to tell which proposition S believes? and (b) given any particular proposition, to tell whether S believes it? Not necessarily, in either case. There are of course many obstacles in the way of either determination: S's belief that p may be repressed, or masked from S by unconscious desires and motives; S may be in error, or even self-deceived, about S's capacities for telling whether S believes that p; the belief may be implicit and the conditions for making it explicit may never arise or may be difficult or impossible for S to realize; and S's belief that p may conflict with, or even contradict, important beliefs of S, making it hard for S to be honest with herself. Moreover, the criteria for verifying or determining the presence of beliefs—whether these are internal, phenomenological criteria or external, behavioral ones—may themselves be open-ended and indeterminate, so that their application may sometimes be inconclusive. In short, no one may be able to tell whether S believes that p, and it may even be indeterminate whether S does so believe. Nevertheless, these indeterminate cases have minimal impact on the belief model of faith, which is concerned not with telling when or whether belief is present but with describing how faith is constituted by belief when it is present.

Do the logical principles of excluded middle and noncontradiction hold with regard to belief? No doubt believing p while disbelieving not-p is the standard case, but it is not the only alternative open to S. S may suspend or withhold belief that p or not-p (entertaining but neither believing nor disbelieving), or S may just not believe that p or not-p (not considering or even never being in a position to be able to consider them). But could S both believe and disbelieve (or at any rate both believe and not believe) that p? Perhaps so. Believing a logically contradictory proposition (believing that p-and-not-p) is not itself a logical contradiction, though it is usually irrational. Moreover, believing each of mutually contradictory propositions (believing that p and believing that not-p) is also not logically contradictory, and holding both beliefs at once may even (just barely?) not be irrational, if one could have equally strong and good reasons for both.[49] Finally, it seems possible for S both to believe that p and not to disbelieve that not-p.[50]

None of the above complications need be denied; the expression "S believes that p" clearly covers a multitude of senses, or at least a great many complications. But none of them destroys the belief model of faith; these complications merely complicate.

2. Faith involves firm conviction. According to the belief model, for S to have faith that p, S must believe that p in more than a tepid, halfhearted way. S must be thoroughly convinced that p; S's belief that p must be a matter of firm conviction. Two questions naturally arise: What is conviction, and how firm must it be?

On the first question, conviction is a matter of actual psychological resistance to change of belief-status; it is the tenacity with which S holds that p under varying conditions, the difficulty of changing or

49. It is a further problem whether S could have (rationally or not) faith$_B$ that p together with faith$_B$ that not-p, since faith according to the belief model involves more than belief.

50. In all the cases of this paragraph, it would be difficult, if not impossible, to determine exactly what S does believe, since one could not infer what S believes from what S disbelieves or does not believe, and conversely, so long as S believes even one contradiction, is inclined to believe a contradiction, thinks it rationally proper to do so, or would tolerate so believing.

removing S's hold on p. Such tenacity comes in degrees, ranging from very low to very high; the degree of tenacity cannot be zero, since that would amount to no belief at all, nor can it be infinitely high, since that would fly in the face of the alterability of any belief, given suitable conditions. Conviction need not be proportional to evidence; one may believe with greater or lesser conviction than one's available evidence allows, and nonevidential conditions may alter one's convictional status. Moreover, the conditions that affect conviction need not be consciously entertained; conscious entertainment of information and evidence certainly affects people's level of conviction, but so may unconscious psychodynamics or subconscious physiology, in ways and to degrees quite unknown to one.

Conviction should not be confused with two other notions, certainty and subjective probability. Both of these are fundamentally epistemic notions tied to evidence, whereas conviction is a psychological notion independent of evidence. One may, of course, feel certain independently of evidence, and in this sense "feeling certain" may mark a very high degree of conviction. But being certain is essentially tied to evidence; one could not be certain without having adequate evidence. Nor is conviction measured by subjective probability. Subjective probability estimates depend on what S takes the evidence to be (p has probability P on evidence e, as S views e and measures P), whereas conviction need not be tied to evidence even in this slender way: S may be convinced that p even though S thinks p is a long shot (that is, p's subjective probability is low).

Although conviction is not essentially tied to evidence, this does not mean that evidence is necessarily irrelevant to conviction. S may in fact base much (though probably not all) of S's conviction about p on the evidence, or on what evidence is available to S. But people differ in this regard, and another person not only might have a different level of conviction on the same evidence (or the same level of conviction on different evidence) but also her conviction might be more or less constrained by the evidence, perceived or actual. Conviction as a psychological condition may diverge more or less widely from the epistemic ideal of certainty.

As to the question of how firm conviction must be for belief to constitute faith, when conviction is lacking or too low, then clearly there is no belief and hence no faith. Perhaps S merely considers p, or assumes p (for the moment or in this context), or acts as if p, or hypothesizes that p. On the other hand, when conviction is quite high, then clearly belief is present. One must cross over a threshold level of conviction in order to enter the halls of belief, yet that threshold is incurably indeterminate, and it varies from person to person. This is not just a matter of being unable to tell whether a certain level of conviction is sufficient for someone to believe; it is a matter of real indeterminacy. It is simply not the case that, for every proposition of which S is (to some degree) convinced, S either believes it or does not believe it. Such indeterminacy is theoretically messy, and it may also be existentially anguishing for someone desperately searching her soul for signs of the presence of saving belief. Nevertheless, indeterminacy is unavoidable on this model.[51]

3. Faith's belief lacks adequate evidence. This point is crucial for the belief model. S's faith that p is not at all a matter of proportioning one's belief or degree of conviction to the evidence, and any conception of belief that essentially ties belief or level of conviction to evidence must forge a different conception of faith.[52] This does not mean that S, in believing that p, necessarily lacks evidence for p, but that whatever evidence S has is less, perhaps much less, than what is needed to rationally justify belief or firm conviction that p, and much less than what is needed to constitute knowledge or certainty that p. In short, what evidence S has is inadequate for the degree of conviction with which S believes—or perhaps even for S to believe at all. Unlike rational conviction or knowledge, faith's believing involves going beyond, perhaps far beyond, the evidence—it requires an evidential risk or "leap."

Before proceeding further, some terminological conventions will be helpful. I use "evidence" in a broad sense to mean anything that bears on (makes more or less probable) the truth or falsity of a proposition.[53] Absolute evidence for p is God's evidence for p, what-

---

51. Of course, conceptions of faith exemplifying the belief model may specify some more or less precise and determinate level of conviction as a requirement for belief, and may even stipulate tests (behavioral or introspective) for telling when this level is reached. But these conceptual restrictions are not part of the belief model as such.

52. As Swinburne, 1981, 19, does: "S believes that *p* if and only if S believes that the total evidence available to him makes *p* more probable than any alternative."

53. In this sense of "evidence," not only propositions can be evidence, even though I focus mainly on propositions. Other kinds of items that at least sometimes

ever in principle bears on p's truth. Objective evidence for p is humanly obtainable evidence, whatever a human being could obtain that would bear on the truth of p. Subjective evidence is a particular person S's evidence. I also distinguish among obtainable, available, and actual evidence. S's obtainable evidence is whatever evidence S could get, using such methods and capacities as S possesses (without gaining or creating new methods or capacities), in a given situation. S's available evidence is whatever S has gained through S's methods and capacities in a given situation, evidence that S could use, but need not, by being aware of it. S's actual evidence is what S actually makes use of in judging, knowing, or believing in a particular situation; clearly it is a proper subset of S's available, or S's obtainable, or God's own evidence.

As noted in the previous section, belief (in human persons at any rate) is somewhat independent of evidence. S may believe that p not only contrary to absolute and objective evidence but also contrary to S's subjective (or even S's actual) evidence. I say that S's evidence is adequate for S's believing when it suffices for belief in a fully rational person. More fully: S's subjective evidence $e_s$ is adequate for S's belief that p with degree of conviction c just when S would believe that p with c on $e_s$ if S's belief that p with c were solely determined by S's fully rational appraisal of $e_s$, that is, if S were a fully rational person and S's apprehension of S's subjective evidence would suffice to generate belief with the requisite conviction.[54] Further, $e_s$ is inadequate for S to believe that p just when it is not adequate for S to believe that p; on the assumption that S's evidence can never be adequate both for p and for not- p, it follows that S's subjective evidence for believing p is inadequate just when S's evidence is adequate either for disbelieving p or for not believing p.[55]

---

constitute evidence include experiences, facts, beliefs, hopes, desires, and, in general, completed propositional attitudes (the attitude together with its associated proposition).

54. It does not follow, of course, that when $e_s$ is inadequate for believing p that it is therefore rational for S to disbelieve that p, since $e_s$ may also be inadequate for disbelieving p. In this latter case, one is tempted to say that the evidence is adequate for not believing that p. This is acceptable, so long as one does not equate evidence-rationality with the full rationality of believing. Proportioning conviction (and belief) to evidence need not be the only way of being rational in one's doxastic economy, for there may well be nonevidential considerations bearing on rational believing.

55. In this and other formulations I ignore complications arising from the dif-

On the belief model of faith, S's belief that p necessarily lacks adequate evidence: S's subjective (actual, available, or obtainable) evidence for p is inadequate to support S's belief that p.[56] S's believing on faith therefore, is simply not a rational function of S's evidence.

However, one must be careful not to overdramatize such evidential inadequacy. In particular, one must not equate belief lacking adequate evidence with irrational belief, much less with irresponsible fanaticism. Sometimes, no doubt, faith on this model is indeed irrational, for example, when not only adequate evidence is lacking for the belief but also the evidence positively and conclusively counts against believing or the evidence is adequate neither for believing nor for disbelieving, and there are no other rational considerations for believing. But inadequately evidenced belief is not always irrational belief. It is at least possible that a belief that lacks adequate evidence nonetheless is rationally quite in order—if the corresponding disbelief also lacks adequate evidence, so that there is a kind of evidential standoff or balance, and there are nonevidential considerations that make the belief rationally appropriate.


4. Faith's belief is nonevidentially based. Not only does S lack adequate evidence for believing that p (evidence that would rationally produce and justify S's belief and/or S's high level of conviction) but S's belief is not based on evidence at all. This does not mean that the belief has no basis; it simply means that its basis is not an evidential one.

It is hard to give a precise characterization of "basis," and my usage is somewhat broader than most, since I allow any completed propositional attitude[57] to be based on any attitude, whether prop-

ferent kinds of evidence: S's actual evidence could be inadequate but S's available or obtainable evidence could be adequate, and so forth.

56. In fact, if S has faith that p then S's belief that p is not based on evidence at all, so that even if S did have adequate evidence for p, nonetheless S's belief (on faith) that p would not be based on that evidence. Nevertheless, S does lack adequate evidence for p; this is a necessary feature of the belief model of faith.

57. By a "completed propositional attitude," I mean someone's particular propositional attitude together with its corresponding proposition, that is, S's belief (want, desire, hope, wish, fear, confession, affirmation, acknowledgment) that p.

ositional or not.[58] Basis is a considerably wider notion than evidence but somewhat narrower than necessary condition; nor is it quite equivalent to "cause." The basing relation is asymmetrical (if a is based on b, then b cannot be based on a), irreflexive (a cannot be based on itself), and transitive (if a is based on b and b on c, then a is based on c). Although I construe basis as a one-one relation, it can also be expanded to one-many, many-one, and many-many situations. The intuitive idea is that basing expresses both existential and justificatory dependence, so that removing the basis would remove the based,[59] and whatever justification, if any, possessed by the based rests, at least in part, on the justification, if any, possessed by the basis. More elaborately: A completed propositional attitude $\Phi$ is singly based on another completed (but not necessarily propositional) attitude $\Psi$ just when S holds $\Phi$ and $\Psi$, S would not hold $\Phi$ if S did not hold $\Psi$, S's $\Phi$-ing is rationally justified only if S's $\Psi$-ing is rationally justified, and the justification for S's $\Phi$-ing flows through the justification for S's $\Psi$-ing.

Some bases provide evidence for propositions believed on their basis. Suppose that S's belief that p is based on S's belief that q and that q has some bearing on p's truth; then S's believing q to be true provides at least some evidence that p is true. But other bases are nonevidential. Suppose that S's belief that p is based on S's wish for some good. Now since wishes are notoriously nonevidential—wishing for something does not make it so nor even more probably so—it follows that the basis for S's belief that p is nonevidential.

There are many different kinds of evidential and nonevidential bases,[60] but here we may return to the notion of authority in order to show some of the subtleties of the distinction. If S believes p on A's authority, S's belief that p is based on S's acceptance of A's

---

58. Plantinga is typical in restricting the basing notion to beliefs. For him, a belief can be based only on other beliefs. Since a belief is only one kind of completed propositional attitude, Plantinga is forced to distinguish "basis" from "ground" in order to distinguish "proper" (rationally justified) from "improper" (unjustified) basic beliefs. Properly basic beliefs are appropriately grounded (in experience). See A. Plantinga, 1981, 1983. My broad use of "basis" incorporates not only Plantinga's sense of "ground" but also much else.

59. This holds only insofar as there is just one basis; with multiple bases, matters are more complicated.

60. These include global attitudes, commitments, and hopes, which I consider under later models of faith.

authority (plus other attitudes, both propositional and nonpropositional, such as S's belief that A has proposed p for S's belief, S's trust in A, and so forth). Is the acceptance of authority an evidential basis for the belief held on authority? That depends.

Suppose on the one hand that S's belief that A is an authority (at least with regard to p) is correct; A is an authority here. Then it seems that A could supply evidence for what S believes: If A, the authority, says that p, then it is likely that p; A's say-so is evidence for what A says. (Still, S need not believe p on this evidence; S may continue to believe that p on faith because S accepts A's authority. A's word may be evidence even though S does not treat it as evidence.) But suppose, on the other hand, that A is not an authority about p, despite S's belief to the contrary. Then it seems that A's say-so is not evidence for S's beliefs; A's word is evidentially worthless, and S is mistaken in thinking otherwise. (Still, S may believe p on A's authority, and this belief may even be rationally justified, although A is not in fact an authority.)

But there are further complications. For one, what S takes to be evidence is a function of what S believes, and if S accepts A as an epistemic authority, whether A is in fact such an authority, then S will tend to count A's advice as evidential gospel, even if the "good news" is erroneous and does not in fact provide evidence for S's beliefs. On the other hand, of course, A may well be an epistemic authority, such that A's advice could provide evidence for S's believed propositions, even if S does not accept or even recognize A as an authority. We must sharply distinguish between A's being an authority for S and S's accepting A as an authority, and both of these from A appearing to S to be an authority. Only if A is an authority does S's acceptance of A as an authority actually open up an (optional) evidential basis for believing; otherwise one only has the appearance of evidence.

Another complication is of considerable importance especially in religious contexts. S may not have, nor be able to obtain, evidence for A's authoritativeness; S may not be in a position to determine whether or not A is indeed an authority (for S with regard to p). Conceivably A's advice to S could provide S with evidence for S's belief that p, S could (correctly) believe that A does so, and yet S have no evidence for this latter belief. Here one might say that whereas S's belief that p is evidentially based, S's second-order belief that this is so is only nonevidentially based (if indeed it is based at all)—it might simply be based on trust "all the way down." It is important to specify precisely which order of beliefs one has in mind in asking whether they are evidentially based.

A third complication is that the notion of subjective evidence is ambiguous. The subjectivity can be a matter of individual constriction of the items that can or do serve as evidence or a matter of individual construal of the evidential relation itself. On the former construal, whether S's belief that p is evidentially based depends on the scope of S's personal "data base"—the items bearing on the truth of p that are possessed by S, available to S, or obtainable by S. On the latter construal, whether the belief is evidentially based depends on S's view of the relevance of an item in S's data base: Does S believe that a (putative) piece of evidence e within S's data base bears on the truth of p?[61] On the former construal S could have evidence for p but not be aware of it, so that the belief is not in fact evidentially based (though it could be). On the latter construal S could believe that e is evidence for p yet be mistaken. As applied to believing on authority, on the former construal, S's acceptance of A's word and words could be an evidential basis of S's belief that p even though S does not believe that it is (for example, S does not remember what A said, or that S accepted [accepts] A's authority). On the latter, S's belief that A's authority provides evidence for S's belief that p may be mistaken (again, A may not have spoken regarding p, or A is an authority but not with regard to p).

The gist of the matter is that accepting someone as an authority may well provide, under some conditions, an evidential basis for believing what the authority says; under other conditions such acceptance will be a nonevidential basis; and under yet other conditions it will be no basis at all.

That a belief is nonevidentially based does not entail that it is not rationally justified, if rational justification for beliefs is not simply a matter of evidence. This is a controversial topic.[62] Everyone grants

61. This version of "subjective evidence" may be too subjective for some to count it as evidence at all. Yet from a certain ("Idealist") perspective, beliefs, including beliefs about what counts as evidence, are bedrock.

62. The controversy is more than a contemporary one. Pascal's "wager," Kierkegaard's "leap of faith," and William James's "will to believe" may all be read as attempts to provide nonevidential but nonetheless rational justification for religious

that the notion of rational justification per se is wider than evidence or proportioning belief or conviction to evidence. Actions, emotions, and attitudes may all be rationally justified, and not always, or even often, is this justification a matter of evidence. Sometimes evidence is simply the wrong sort of thing to worry about, as when a lover exactly proportions her love to evidence of her beloved's worthiness to be loved. Still, in the case of beliefs or conviction, many would want to restrict the notion of justification to what I call evidence-rationality: evidence and evidence alone rationally justifies belief or level of conviction.

The force of evidence-rationality derives from the obvious interest of reason in truth and hence in believing true rather than false propositions;[63] since evidence is what bears on the truth of propositions believed, reason takes note of evidence. All goes well so long as the evidence is adequate for belief or (less clearly) disbelief. But faith according to the belief model precisely lacks adequate evidence and in fact is not even based on evidence. What then? Should we adopt W. K. Clifford's view that "It is wrong [that is, at least rationally unjustified, and perhaps also morally prohibited] always, everywhere, and for anyone, to believe anything upon insufficient [that is, inadequate] evidence"?[64] Is it wrong to base one's belief on something other than evidence? Is truth the only interest of reason in believing?

These questions should all be answered in the negative, for some beliefs can be rationally justified on nonevidential bases, under such conditions as the following:[65] S's subjectively obtainable evidence is inadequate for belief that p as well as for belief that not-p; S's belief that p is nonevidentially based; and the nonevidential basis for S's belief that p is itself rationally justified.[66] For example, suppose that

---

belief—or at least to show what such justification would look like. See Pascal, 1966; Kierkegaard, 1941, 1970, 1985; James, 1979. For one way of reading these works see C. S. Evans, 1978; for another, Sessions, 1980b, 1982, 1985.

63. Is an interest in truth a necessary (but not a sufficient) condition of reason? Or does this interest rest on a deeper interest, such as that in consistency (since truths can never be mutually inconsistent)?

64. Quoted in James, 1979, 18.

65. This is obviously not a complete analysis of nonevidential rational justification; there are many more loose ends than can be tied up here.

66. Of course, it may be difficult to tell or show whether the nonevidential basis is justified, but it should not be impossible, at least in principle.

S believes that p on the basis of hoping thereby to obtain some great good for S; then, if there is no adequate evidence that S could obtain either for or against p—either S can obtain no evidence regarding p at all or else all such evidence is neutral or balanced with respect to p's truth—and if S is rationally justified in hoping for the good, then S's belief that p is rationally justified.

It seems, therefore, that we should reject evidence-rationality as a necessary condition for the rationality of beliefs. Hence it is possible for faith according to the belief model (nonevidentially based, confident, propositional belief) to be rationally justified.[67]

Whereas on both the personal relationship and the belief models, faith requires propositional believing, the former permits and the latter excludes propositional knowing. According to the personal relationship model, if S believes that p on A's (legitimate) cognitive authority, and if A knows that p, then A's say-so may constitute evidence for p, and it is possible in this way for S to acquire evidence that is adequate not merely for believing p with some high level of conviction but (also) for knowing that p.[68] According to the belief model, however, even if S believes that p on A's legitimate authority (and the other conditions are met), this does not constitute knowledge, although the believing may be fully rationally justified in some nonevidential way. But why do these two models differ with respect to faith and knowledge?

Mostly the disagreement is terminological. Both models agree that a belief held on authority may be justified and true, and that such a justified true belief differs from other kinds of justified true belief that do qualify as knowledge (for example, self-evident beliefs, experimentally highly confirmed beliefs, and so forth). Moreover, both note that in some cases of faith—particularly in religious contexts—there may be no way for the believer in this life to conclusively verify the authority's (putative) competence or (alleged) communications. Finally, both agree that believing on another's

67. Similar remarks apply to the personal relationship model, particularly with respect to the (nonevidential) rationality of accepting an (evidential) authority as an authority.

68. As the analysis of knowledge is notoriously unclear, I do not try to specify what, if anything, beyond (or perhaps instead of) adequate evidence is needed to convert highly convinced belief into knowledge.

authority (or "hearing") is second best to finding out for oneself (or "seeing").

There is one key disagreement. Could the authority's word constitute adequate evidence for the believer's belief? The personal relationship model answers "yes," holding that if the authority is indeed reliable, a stable condition may be induced in the believer with respect to truth—like a human apprentice who has learned well from a worthy master. What the legitimate authority proposes are true beliefs that the authority knows to be true; the authority's word therefore can provide evidence—indeed, very good evidence—for the truth of the beliefs induced. The belief model answers "no," noting the evidential risk (from the standpoint of the believer) inherent in the acceptance of anyone's authority without being able to obtain evidence (at any rate conclusive evidence) for that authority's legitimacy, like a traveler who has no way, in this life, to conclusively ascertain whether she is on the right or best path, or perhaps no way even to understand the true nature and final destination of the path she is presently traveling. The propositions proposed for belief may well be true and known to be true by the authority (the authority may be legitimate), and the believer may accept these propositions on the other's authority. But the believer has no way of conclusively determining this authority to be legitimate, objective, or correct. S takes A's proposals to be evidence, but does not know that they are. Evidential risk is therefore ineradicable for the belief model, and it prevents faith from pretending it is knowledge. On the personal relationship model, however, S can obtain experiential evidence for A's authoritativeness in and through the personal relationship itself—enough evidence to certify A as a knower and knowledge-donor.

Where the personal relationship model speaks of the compatibility of faith and knowledge—indeed, it insists that faith yields knowledge, of a kind—the belief model holds that faith and knowledge are incompatible and that faith yields only justified belief at best. The former stresses the reliable hold on truth produced by justified acceptance of a legitimate authority's word; the latter emphasizes the evidential insecurity of accepting another's authority and the nonevidential basis of faith's belief.

Nonevidential believing-that is ubiquitous. We believe with conviction, but not on evidential bases, in situations where evidence cannot remove the possibility of grave doubts but where to have such doubts is demoralizing or crippling—where doubt passes into despair and prevents one from living an even ordinarily happy life, much less one of great and noble purpose. We believe in this way when we greatly desire to do so, when (we believe that) believing on faith is requisite for some great good we seek. And we have such belief when we simply cannot help it, when we are faced with unavoidable and important life-choices—decisions that make all the difference for self and others—that are undetermined or underdetermined by the evidence available. Most if not all of our most important life-choices are of this nature. But even if we were purely cognitive beings, possessed only by a burning desire to know the truth, we should still occasionally need to believe on faith. Cognitive humans cannot live by evidence alone.

This point deserves further emphasis. Suppose S wants only to know the truth, and suppose knowing the truth is a matter of knowing which propositions are true, and why. Now if S knew everything there is to know, then S would have no need for faith. But suppose, reasonably enough, that S falls somewhat short of perfect cognition. Then even if S could come to know all truth—or at least this were possible for S's species—and unless all truth were simply given, S would nonetheless need to strive to gain such truth. In short, a finite, would–be knower needs to inquire if the desire to know is not to be frustrated.

Certain forms of inquiry, let us suppose, have tended to succeed, though the upward path often has been rocky, winding, and steep (and the inquirer knows all this). Since inquiry has required such effort in the past, why should S continue inquiring? S cannot be in a position to know that future inquiry will always succeed, even by successful induction from past successes; the only way that S could actually know that further inquiry would succeed in knowing all truth is, contrary to our assumption (and to fact), by actually knowing all truth. So S does not and cannot know that further inquiry will always prove successful, and if it does not S will be deeply disappointed. But then, it seems, S is faced with a choice: either to surrender S's (supposed) only desire, or else to continue to inquire on the basis of this desire (and not on the basis of evidence).

Of course, in the real (human) world we are not purely (much less perfect) cognitive beings. Instead, we are filled with a myriad of desires in competition with the desire for truth. Further, we want the truth, but not only the truth, and not truth at any cost. In such a world a fairly profound confidence in the continued, indeed complete, alethic efficacy of inquiry may be necessary for one to pursue inquiry with lifelong intensity, persistence, and creativity. Is this not a place for faith along the lines of the belief model—the dogged but inspiriting belief that continued inquiry will indeed succeed? S certainly lacks fully adequate evidence for this belief, leaving it open for S's belief to find a nonevidential basis—perhaps S relies on the encouraging word or example of an impressive mentor, or a profound trust in the reasonableness of things, or a deep hope for future results, or an abiding confidence in the competence of S's own powers of comprehension.

In short, even for the cognitive purposes of a finite (cognitively incomplete) being, faith according to the belief model seems indispensable. How much more is such faith essential in light of our many noncognitive aims and ends?

5. Faith's opposites are nonbelief, disbelief, evidential belief, and tepid belief. Each opposes the central conditions of faith according to the belief model, but in different ways.

*Non-belief* that p is the lack of belief that p; it is simply not believing. Not believing p is not the same as disbelieving p; to disbelieve p is to believe not-p, whereas not to believe p is compatible both with believing not-p (disbelieving p) and with not believing not-p (not disbelieving p and therefore suspending belief that p). Nonbelief opposes faith as its simple absence or lack.

To *disbelieve* p is to believe not-p. The propositions involved, p and not-p, are (at least) contraries— they cannot both be true. But belief that p and disbelief that p are not contraries, for it is possible for S both to believe p and to believe not-p; a person may have inconsistent beliefs.[69] Of course, it may be thoroughly irrational to hold inconsistent beliefs (in nearly all cases?[70]), but it is certainly

69. See Da Costa and French, 1990.
70. Some have urged that, in some cases, inconsistent beliefs are not only possible but desirable and even rationally required: They may be necessary in order to characterize truly paradoxical mystical experiences in a literal and straightforward way. See Henle, 1949; Katz, 1978; Pletcher, 1973; Stace, 1961.

possible to do so. Disbelief is an opposite of belief not because it necessarily excludes belief, though it may, but because it is in powerful tension with belief. When recognized, it requires to be dealt with either by removal (eliminating one or the other or both of the inconsistent beliefs), rehabilitation (showing how the beliefs do not really conflict), or by reconciliation (explaining and justifying how inconsistent beliefs may or need to be held).

*Evidential belief* that p is believing p on the basis of, and only because of, adequate evidence; if S lacked evidence for p, S would not believe that p.[71] Further, in evidential belief, S's degree of confidence or conviction about p is proportioned to S's evidence for p, so that if S had only a slight balance of evidence favoring p, S might believe that p but would not have a great deal of confidence that p. But in faith according to the belief model, S believes that p not only despite inadequate evidence for p, but also not on the basis of any evidence at all; moreover, S's degree of confidence that p is not tied to S's evidence for p. Evidential belief opposes faith (on the belief model) by excluding it. If S evidentially believes that p, or does so with a degree of confidence determined by the evidence, then S does not have faith that p, and conversely.

S has a *tepid belief* that p where S believes that p but with little or no conviction. Faith on the belief model requires firm conviction; hence, faith excludes tepid belief. Note that the tepidity of belief may or may not be evidentially based; if S's lack of firm conviction is based on evidence, then of course either the evidence or the basing must be inadequate; but even if S's conviction is not based on evidence, its tepidity nonetheless disqualifies it from being faith.[72]

To recapitulate: According to the belief model, a person has faith only when she firmly believes a proposition—tenaciously holds that proposition to be true—while resting that belief not on adequate evidence but on some other basis. The belief is a matter of conviction, not certainty. Nonevidential firm belief is central to faith on

---

71. This may be due to S's subscription to a Cliffordian principle of evidence-rationality.

72. Tepid belief may be nonevidentially based but still opposed to faith in either or both of two ways. It may inadequately or improperly rest on an adequate nonevidential base (i.e., a base that could but does not serve S for faith's firm conviction). Or, it may properly rest on an inadequate base (i.e., a base that could not yield firm conviction even if properly used).

this model, as is shown by faith's opposites: Not believing, as well as believing contrarily, on evidence, or tepidly, all center on how (or whether) a person holds some proposition to be true.

## C. The Attitude Model

The first model of faith focuses on a kind of personal relationship, a relation between two persons, while the second highlights a kind of propositional belief, a relation between a person and a proposition. The third model makes central a more fundamental and global kind of attitude: a person's basic orientation, interpretation, perspective, or "onlook"[73] toward the world; how the person "takes" or "sees" or "experiences" the world. This attitude essentially generates a "horizon of significance," a kind of prepropositional boundary both between a person and her world and also around them both. A horizon at once divides, unifies, structures, and limits both self and world. Because a horizon-forming attitude is fundamental, totalizing, and significance-engendering, it has all the earmarks of distinctively religious faith; indeed, on this model, there may be no such thing as nonreligious faith, no merely mundane, limited, or ordinary faith. Let us begin, as before, with a summary depiction.[74]

> S has faith$_A$ toward X only if S's attitude toward X partially but radically constitutes a self-world horizon that is prepropositional, fundamental, totalizing, and significant (bestowing as well as embracing significance).

1. Faith is a partially, radically constitutive attitude toward the world. I use the term "attitude" in a very broad sense: a distinctively personal relation toward something. The subject of this relation

73. For a comprehensive treatment of onlooks, see D. D. Evans, 1963, chap. 3.
74. Portions of this model resemble features of other accounts of religious faith from which I have learned much. In particular, I am indebted to John Whittaker's discussion of profound and guiding "principles" (1981); to John Hick's various treatments of "total interpretation," "experiencing as," and "the interpretive element in experience" (1957, 1969, 1973a, 1978, 1989; see also Helm, 1973a, chap. 8); to Karl Rahner's notion of "transcendental experience" (1967, 1978b; Rahner and Vorgrimler, 1981; Rahner and Weger, 1981; see also McCool, ed., 1975; O'Collins, 1981); and to William Lynch's talk of "image" and "imagination" (1973).

must be a person, and the relation must relate the subject qua person; but the object (or objects) may be anything at all—persons, things, events, states of consciousness, relations among things, abstract entities, propositions.[75] Persons may even have attitudes toward the world, the person's widest environing context regarded as a limited whole. A world may be limited in some or all ways without thereby being in all aspects finite; it may include only a few kinds of actual and possible objects, but infinitely many of them. Moreover, these limits need not be spatiotemporal ones; limits of significance will especially concern us later.

A basic division among objects of attitudes is that between propositions and all else; hence the distinction between propositional and nonpropositional attitudes. In addition to subject and object(s), attitudes also necessarily involve a relation between them, a relation that possesses at least two distinctive features: S has some kind of intentional or directed awareness of the object(s); S has a reflexive awareness of S as the very person who has this awareness of that object (those objects). Attitudes are therefore essentially "subjective," not necessarily in the senses of being unique or idiosyncratic, much less private or erroneous, but in the sense of thoroughly involving an individual person as the self-aware subject of the attitude.

An attitude is constitutive of something when it contributes essentially to that thing—completely constitutive when it contributes

75. There may be one or many objects of one attitude; but can there be more than one subject of the same attitude? Two or more subjects may share the same attitude ("same" in the senses that it is directed toward the same object(s) or that it is the same kind of attitude, or both) without there being multiple subjects of a numerically single attitude. For groups of persons to count as subjects of attitudes in a strict sense, they must have attitudes irreducible to (though not necessarily independent of) the various attitudes of their members. In a steadily loosening way, we often ascribe attitudes to human collectivities ("Iraq wants Kuwait's oil"), to collectivities not comprised of persons ("the migrating flock is seeking a proper nesting site for the night"), perhaps even occasionally to inanimate objects or events ("the stone wants to fall to the earth," "that is an accident just waiting to happen"). But these are derivative, or degenerative, cases. In the full sense attitudes presuppose personality and agency, and we may well doubt that groups of human persons are themselves personal agents. (This is not to deny, of course, that there are many group features that have important effects on individual members of the group.) At any rate, to avoid such complications, I restrict subjects of attitudes to individual persons; henceforth, an attitude is a one-to-one or one-to-many personal relation, never a many-to-one or many-to-many personal or impersonal relation.

all that is essential, partially constitutive when it contributes an essential part. Every attitude is, trivially, partially constitutive of itself as a particular relation. But not every attitude constitutes either its ongoing subject or object, much less both of them at once, or in the same respect. Instances of the attitude of contemplation, for example, may constitute part or all of some particular objects, but the particular subject of contemplation qua contemplator, much less qua enduring consciousness, is not thereby constituted. The purely imaginary "object" that I am now contemplating is completely a figment of my contemplation, and does not constitute me as an enduring self, for I could well contemplate something else and still remain the same contemplator; this particular flight of fancy is not essential to the story of my conscious life. Still, a subject is partially constituted as a contemplator in virtue of taking up, and being able to take up, an attitude of contemplation, no matter what objects are contemplated; therefore an account of my mind that failed to take note of my powers and episodes of contemplation would be seriously defective, and any detailed autobiography would need to note the time I spend on contemplation—at least what kinds of objects I tend to contemplate and which particular ones I have actually contemplated at crucial moments of my life.

An attitude may be radically constitutive in either of two senses: extensively, if it constitutes both subject and object (in relation to each other); or intensively, if it qualifies or conditions other constitutive features of subject or object. Faith, on the attitude model, is a partially radically constitutive attitude in both senses combined. If S has the attitude of faith toward X, this partially constitutes S as the kind of being, a self, that is appropriately related toward X via that attitude, thereby also coloring other fundamental capacities and attitudes of S; S's attitude of faith also partially constitutes X as an appropriate widest environing context or world for S's way of being in this attitude. In brief, faith on this model is (partially) internal both to self and to world, and interpenetratingly so.

Faith on this model should not be seen as the specification or instantiation of a prior and ongoing attitude, as, for example, believing propositions about God may be thought a specification of the attitude of believing propositions, whether the propositions be about this or that, things or features, gestalts or goods, gods or

God. Instead, faith is more radical; it partially[76] constitutes S as a certain kind of being-in-the-world,[77] such that S with faith-toward-X is a fundamentally different—though not a completely different—kind of being from S without faith-toward-X. A person who engages the world in faith is a profoundly different person from one who does not—a "new person," to use primary religious language, a different kind of "self" in the language of this essay—and a person with one manner of faith differs profoundly from someone with a different faith. Such difference in self or selves, in fact, is a criterion for difference in faith or faiths, at least according to the attitude model.

Of course the "new" person is not completely new, for many particular beliefs, attitudes, and features remain, and there is continuity of general attitudinal capacities as well. But faith is more than new objects for old attitudes (new wine for old wineskins?); it is also a new kind of attitude, perhaps even a new capacity, a new way of relating to the world, and a new way of being a subject. As a result, a person who comes to have faith possesses a new character or even new identity as well as a myriad of new attitudes and dispositions not previously exhibited. New attitudes and dispositions, such as accepting certain kinds of authority, willingness to engage in worship or other activities, or tendency to value and disvalue certain things, arise only with and through faith, not conversely. Faith first makes a new kind of self and then conditions that self's

76. The constitution is partial, not complete, because there are many other kinds of attitudes, and other capacities and features, that are also essential in faith. In the attitude of faith, one does not discard but retains various attitudes involved in believing propositions, speaking and understanding a natural language, or intending and deciding. Though partial, however, faith's constitution is radical since most or all of the other essential attitudes and features become qualified or conditioned by, and through, the new attitude of faith. In faith, one believes new propositions, seeks and understands a new language (or understands a familiar language in new ways), and intends and decides new kinds of actions.

77. Jim Keller asks: How does one individuate kinds here? What does "kind" mean in this context? I do not have anything approaching a theory of kinds, and my usage is fairly broad, but I do take it that not all properties generate or underlie kinds; kind-properties are relatively general, quasi-essential, yet nonindividuating. For example, moral virtues are kind-properties: A courageous person differs in kind from a cowardly one, and yet may still be one and the same person (individual). On the other hand, physical attributes tend not to be kind-properties: A plump person does not differ in kind from a slender one.

attitudes and activities. This is what is meant by saying that faith is partially, radically constitutive of the subject's concrete personality.[78]

Faith on this model is not properly viewed as a way of relating to a previously constituted environment, as, for example, coming to disbelieve a proposition one had previously believed, or coming to know new facts about familiar objects, or seeing new or unusual instances of the usual kinds of objects. Faith is more radical; the object ( = X) it constitutes (though again only partially) is a world— or rather it is the world limited in a certain way, with a certain horizon—such that this world exists essentially in and for the faith (indeed, for this faith) that apprehends it. Faith's world arises with faith because it arises through faith, and not conversely. It follows that the world for one person's attitude of faith differs fundamentally (though not completely) from the world for another's different faith. One is even tempted to say that a person with a certain faith inhabits a "different world" from someone without faith or with a different faith, but this means no more than that the world is different for persons of different attitudes of faith. The different worlds of persons with different attitudes of faith partially overlap and interpenetrate; they are not totally incommensurable, differing in all respects. Hence miscommunication, misunderstanding, mistrust, and enmity across such "worlds" are not inevitable. But just as faith's constitution of a world is only partial, so the overlap of differently constituted worlds is only partial; partial incommensurability is the price one must pay for partial constitution.[79]

Note that the subject of faith, S, and the object of faith, X, are correlative to each other, in the sense that they are appropriate to one another because they are jointly (partially) constituted by and through the same attitude of faith. A person's faith exists only in a fitting context, and such a fitting context exists only for such a faith. This is another aspect of what it means to say that faith is radically constitutive of self and world.

But here we must guard against an excessive epistemological idealism. A world as a limited whole is always the object of its cor-

78. I put aside the questions as to how such a radically constitutive attitude could ever be brought about or terminated. See Chap. 5.

79. One may speculate that these partialities are inversely proportional: The more completely faith constitutes a world, the less completely that world overlaps with a different world (one with a different horizon).

relative limiting attitude, but it does not follow that a world as such is only an intentional object.[80] Environing contexts causally press in on selves in ways neither fixed nor anticipated by those selves. But what it is that presses in upon one is (at least partially) constituted by what one is prepared and able to countenance. What was it that Moses saw before him at Horeb? Was it "a flame of fire out of the midst of a bush" (Exod. 3:2; RSV), the appearance of an "angel of Yahweh" (ibid.), a rare case of vegetative spontaneous combustion, a mirage, a dream, a hallucination? Doubtless something happened to Moses, but what that something was need not be agreed upon. Moses saw something through the eyes of his faith that would be— has been and is—seen differently by those with different partially constitutive attitudes.

2. Faith's attitude constitutes a self-world horizon of significance. Since the appropriate conception of horizon is a bit arcane, it needs to be derived from more familiar notions.[81] Paradigmatically, the horizon is what divides sky from land and sea, where heaven and earth begin and end, the place where they meet—though occasionally, as on misty mornings, it is more an uncertain zone of transition than a sharp line of demarcation.

The main features of this ordinary notion of horizon are as follows: A horizon is a boundary between two fundamental regions; it divides without separating them. It also unites what it divides; a horizon is where the regions come together, somehow a mutual boundary. This boundary limits what it comes between; it is where each region ends and that by which each is circumscribed—an edge and a bound. But a horizon need not be a one-dimensional line; it may be a zone or indeterminate margin. A horizon also implies a structure in and of that which it bounds—whether spatial, material, conceptual, or otherwise. Finally, horizons are not given all at once or unalterably but may expand or contract, or at any rate may be widened or

80. I am grateful to Jim Keller for pressing this concern.
81. I thank various readers of earlier drafts of this section for demanding greater clarity on this topic, though I doubt my revised account fully meets their demands. The notion of horizon I develop spans both phenomenological and analytical philosophical camps. For the former see Husserl, 1931 ("*Horizont*"), §§27, 44, 47, 82–83; Heidegger, 1962, 4, 63, 416; and Rahner, 1978b ("transcendental experience"), 20–21, 32–35, 52, 57. For the latter, see Wittgenstein, 1953, §§68, 71; 1961 ("*Grenze*"), especially 5.6–5.641.

narrowed by us; we may push beyond or ahead or above our current position in order to gain access to a wider horizon, which is just our current horizon widened.

This initial notion is partially transformed in the concept of a *perceptual horizon*. Here a horizon is the limit of a perceptual field, a field that usually and to some extent can be narrowed or broadened, filled or emptied, clarified or made opaque, by the perceiver. A perceptual horizon bounds what is perceived from what is not perceived. But what is not perceived is not inherently unperceivable; the perceptual horizon lies between the actual and the potential, not between the possible and the impossible. Indeed, the currently unperceived is continuous with the currently perceived, capable of being perceived under suitably different conditons. A perceptual horizon divides seen from unseen, heard from unheard, or felt from unfelt—but this boundary is never fixed for all times, places, and persons, nor even for any of these. Shifting a perceptual horizon is at least partially under the control of the perceiver, though other factors may intervene as well (light, weather, accidents, other people). Finally, the perceptual field is no longer literally spatial but only spacelike: the geometry of the visual field is sometimes at odds with the geometry of physical space, and the fields of other senses— hearing, smell, taste, touch—are "spaces" only in extended or metaphorical senses.

It is a further step to think of a *horizon of perception* as not merely accounting for the divide between actual and potential perception within a field but as also circumscribing the field itself as a field of possible perception. Here the horizon of vision demarcates not only what is seen from what is unseen but also what counts as something that can be seen—the "visible" is understood in the sense of the possibly seen, as opposed to the not possibly seen. Such a horizonal limit—however closely it may be approached and however fully it may be described or understood—cannot be broadened or narrowed as such, though it may be exchanged for another. No matter how wide the horizon of vision, for example, one simply cannot see (visually, literally) a smell as such; smells belong within another horizon of perception altogether, outside vision's view.[82] Sights and smells occupy different perceptual "spaces," each with a distinct

82. But what about synaesthetic perceptions?

structure and limit—in short, they are perceived within different horizons of perception.

Now let us take the notion of "horizon" one metaphorical step further and speak of a horizon of significance.[83] Suppose something is (seen as) significant; then its horizon of significance encompasses anything that is structurally continuous or commensurable in significance with it, anything that can be sensibly linked to it (even by antagonism)—but not anything incommensurable with it. Some suppose all significance has a single horizon (the Good is one), others propose distinct and incomparable realms of significance (there are many goods). Some believe significance is totally or largely under the control of the perceiver, others think significance may be discovered or recognized but is never, or not centrally, in the eye of the beholder alone. However these and other disputed issues are resolved, a horizon of significance has these properties:

    a. It divides a region of significance from another region, whether from an incommensurable region of significance or from a region lacking significance altogether;
    b. It unites as it divides, fitting together what it demarcates, marking where (one kind of) significance ends and something else begins (perhaps another kind of significance);
    c. It structures the region it horizons, constituting it as a kind of significance-"space" wherein different actual and potential instances of significance can be located; and
    d. It limits what it horizons, though the limits it sets may go unrecognized or unappreciated.

We are now in a position to connect our extended notion of horizon with the previous discussion of faith as a partially, radically constitutive attitude toward the world. A world is (regarded as) a limited whole and hence has a horizon at its limit(s); the world has many such horizons, for it is—or may be seen as—limited in many ways. The attitude of faith (partially but radically) constitutes a self-world horizon, particularly a self-world horizon of significance, and the most fundamental way of differentiating faiths is in terms of the different horizons of significance they generate. The significance of neither self nor world is limited and structured independently of the

83. Under the umbrella of "significance" I include such things as value, meaning, importance, worth, and the like.

other; their horizon is a common one, uniting as well as dividing them. Faith's correlativity (the mutual appropriateness of subject and object) is a function of self and world sharing the same horizon of significance. This does not mean that the kind of value, meaning, importance, or worth (thought to be) possessed by the self must be continuous with those features (thought to be) possessed by the world, much less that the two must share the same kind, degree, or amount of significance. Rather, it means that the self-world horizon links as it distinguishes their respective kinds of significance, so that the significance of the self is essentially related to the significance of the world, and conversely.

3. Faith is prepropositional. As a radically constitutive attitude, faith is logically, and often temporally, prior to propositional attitudes and specifications. This priority needs to be carefully circumscribed. Though a transformed and "new being," S is also partially the same person before and after acquiring faith, and this means (in part) that S retains some of S's prior propositional beliefs and that, more broadly, S's attitudinal condition (including beliefs and other attitudes) remains partially the same, in ways that can be partially characterized in propositional terms. Moreover, the new aspects of S's faithful condition are also somewhat susceptible to propositional characterization. Likewise S's world before and after faith has many features that may be characterized in propositional terms.

Nevertheless, propositional belief and characterization are secondary in the new horizon of significance that faith brings. A horizon of significance itself is neither a set of propositions (not even a logician's maximal set of propositions or "possible world") nor a set of propositional beliefs (not even a metaphysician's complete system of beliefs or "worldview"), but that which gives meaning to all kinds of propositional attitudes, including propositional beliefs. Acquiring faith, therefore, is not centrally a matter of acquiring a new set of propositional beliefs; it is not even fundamentally acquiring any kind of propositional attitudes at all. Propositional beliefs and other attitudes are relatively superficial manifestations or aspects of faith, not its essential kernel. Beliefs are feeble and fallible attempts to express, describe, and inculcate faith—feeble not simply because they always fall short of completeness of characterization but more deeply because the significance of beliefs and other prop-

ositional attitudes to faith is part of the horizon of significance engendered by faith. The horizon is prior to the beliefs, not vice versa.

Some are tempted to go further and claim that the attitude of faith
is quite independent of propositional attitudes such as belief, that
such beliefs are completely dispensable for faith, or perhaps even
that they are inimical to faith.[84] These temptations should be resisted.
Beliefs and other propositional attitudes are not easily (or not at all)
expunged from beings like ourselves who have the capacity, and
the strong predilection, for taking such attitudes, even in and for
the faith that is a radically constitutive attitude. To see this point,
it is worth exploring two questions: Could the person who has faith$_A$
toward a world dispense with propositional attitudes altogether?
Could such a person dispense with propositional beliefs?

Having any attitudes at all (in the distinctively personal sense of
"attitude") seems to imply having at least the *capacity* for propositional attitudes. A being who lacked the latter capacity would
scarcely count as a person at all (or at any rate as a human self).
Even if S's attitude toward X is initially and primarily nonpropositional, therefore, it must be at least possible for S to have or take
some kind of propositional attitudes toward X, or else S would not
be a person (or human self). A being which could only take nonpropositional attitudes toward things in general seems barely conceivable, if that, and a being which could only take nonpropositional
attitudes toward a certain object or kind of object is scarcely more
intelligible. Certainly it is difficult to imagine a distinctively human
attitude toward anything that does not also permit some kind of
propositional attitudes toward that thing[85]—even if it is just contemplating relevant propositions; or acknowledging, confessing, or
witnessing to their truth; or being guided by their depiction of a
goal or practice connected with the object.

But, further, there are very good reasons for S actually to use S's
capacities for having propositional attitudes—good reasons for S
wanting or even needing to have or take propositional attitudes
about S, X, and S's relation to X.[86] Consider the following case.

---

84. See W. C. Smith, 1964, chap. 7; 1979a, chap. 1; see also Chap. 5, sec. A.

85. This is not just a matter of having propositional attitudes to some propositions
or other—the capacity in question is for attitudes to propositions that concern that
very nonpropositional attitude, as well as its particular subject and object(s).

86. Of course, none of this in the least implies that nonpropositional attitudes

Suppose that S loves B with a kind of love that is or essentially involves a prepropositional attitude. S could adore, admire, desire, and in general be aware of B in various nonpropositional ways. These ways might well be prior to any propositions that could be formulated or entertained, so that any test of any such proposition's meaning, scope, appropriateness, and veracity must lie in the non-propositional experience of love, and not conversely. The question then is whether this love could exist (and persist) without S enter-taining and believing some propositions about herself, her love, and her beloved. Clearly S could take up propositional attitudes toward any of these if S wanted to, for S as a person has the requisite capacities. But why would or should S want to adopt such prop-ositional attitudes? It seems unnecessary to do so, and S might de-stroy the love she propositions.

No doubt some kinds of propositional attitudes—a distancing "objectivity," a self-interested calculation, a passionless detached contemplation, for instance—are irrelevant or harmful to love and the lover(s). But none of this prevents someone else from taking such attitudes toward S's love, nor does it block S from taking other kinds of propositional attitudes toward S's love, such as thinking that B is lovely, remembering that their anniversary is next week, recognizing that B likes this and not that, knowing what B wants from S, and the like. Indeed, there are very good reasons for S to want to take such propositional attitudes, for doing so is an im-portant part of what it means to love another. Someone who ignored or refused to traffic in such propositions would be an irresponsible lover, unconcerned with the facts of the matter about the loving attitude and the beloved other. If this case may be generalized, it seems that propositional attitudes need not be at odds with prepro-positional attitudes; indeed, there may be very good reasons for wanting to have certain kinds of propositional attitudes even where the prepropositional attitude is (partially) radically constitutive.

If some propositional attitudes or other are practically unavoid-able, or at least often desirable, what about propositional *beliefs*?[87]

_____

are reducible to propositional ones, nor that they could be replaced (without loss) by the latter.

87. I mean, of course, belief in the minimal sense of holding a proposition to be true, not in the fuller sense of being strongly convinced of that proposition's truth independently of the evidence.

Belief seems to be involved or implied, innocuously enough, in most every kind of propositional attitude: acknowledging p, for example, involves at least holding p to be true; contemplating p involves a whole host of hypothetical or conditional beliefs (for example, that if p were true then q would also be true); and so on. So even if belief is not the central or determinative propositional attitude, it seems nearly omnipresent. But we may go further than this.

Faith as a constitutive attitude requires certain attitudes—ultimately beliefs—toward certain propositions describing crucial features of self and world. These features are at the forefront of faith's awareness, those which to S are the most prominent features of S, X, or their relation. Faith's propositions describing these features certainly do not amount to a theory of the object or attitude of faith, much less to a theory of faith itself. They need not be very clear or precise, nor believed very passionately, explicitly, or consciously; the features must be prominent, not propositions describing those features. Moreover, the same fundamental attitude is consistent with somewhat different sets of propositional beliefs, or with a changing or developing set of such beliefs; no specific creed or set of explicit articles of faith will adequately convey the fullness or even the foreground of faith. The important point is this: Propositional beliefs, however inadequate and distorting they may be, nonetheless cannot be totally absent from faith on the attitude model. In having faith-toward-X, S must have certain beliefs about how X is or appears in relation to S, and about how S is or appears in relation to X, precisely in order to remain in that relation as a being possessing the developed capacity to have any propositional attitudes at all.

The upshot is that even though faith, on this model, is a non-propositional attitude prior to any propositional specification, this fact neither excludes nor renders undesirable continuing efforts at having, and improving, one's propositional attitudes as well. Though propositional belief may not be prior or central to faith as attitude, it is not therefore dispensable or undesirable.

4. Faith is fundamental. Here is one of the several ways in which faith, according to the attitude model, is ultimate or absolute. The attitude of faith is fundamental in that it is basic, not based on anything else, though much else may be based on it. In particular, faith is not based on any other attitude, while other attitudes are

based on it. Earlier a rough and ready characterization of the basing notion was given. Where A and B are completed propositional attitudes (not necessarily beliefs), A is based on B when A at least partially depends on B for its existence and justification. This notion can be expanded to permit talk about A and B as nonpropositional attitudes, experiences, and the like. Since faith on the attitude model is prepropositional, it follows that such faith is not based on any propositional attitude. But could it be based on other nonpropositional attitudes or experiences?

Nonpropositional attitudes may be based on nonpropositional experiences, as when meeting someone "in the flesh" entirely alters one's previously distrustful attitude toward that person. Similarly, one nonpropositional attitude may be based on another nonpropositional attitude, as when hatred of a certain group seizes upon this particular member of the group, or when envy seeps from one acquaintance to another.

Faith, as a fundamental attitude, is not based on any other attitude or experience, whether propositional or not. But though faith is not so based, it may still presuppose such attitudes or experiences. John Hick has presented an account of religious faith as a kind of total interpretation.[88] According to Hick, just as a moral total interpretation of the world presupposes (and supervenes on) a physical total interpretation, so does a religious total interpretation presuppose (and supervene on) a moral total interpretation. Here there is existential dependence (faith could not exist without morality) but not justificatory dependence (faith might not be justified by, or only by, morality), whereas both conditions are required for the basing relation. Faith, on Hick's view, though fundamental, is not necessarily justified, and it may even be fundamentally mistaken. This is part of the riskiness of faith. One risks being wrong—not trivially but profoundly wrong—in the fundamental way or ways one's self and horizon are constituted.

It is worth emphasizing that although faith is not based on any other attitude, other attitudes (and much else) may be based on faith. For example, one may entertain, consider, and hold, with varying degrees of conviction, some propositions to be true—one may more or less strongly believe them—on the basis of faith. But the attitude

88. See Hick 1957, 1969.

based on faith need not be a propositional one: loving someone, feeling confident, or hoping for some good may all be based on faith as well. Being based on faith, these attitudes would neither exist nor be justified if faith were absent or unjustified.

5. *Faith is totalizing.* Here we encounter two more ways in which faith may be said to be ultimate or absolute. Faith involves the whole person and that person's whole environing context.[89] Because faith according to the attitude model is totalizing in both ways, it has a distinctively religious cast.

On the one hand, faith is an attitude of the *whole person*, an attitude that encompasses all important aspects of a person—not just the intellectual, the emotional, or the volitional, but all of these and everything else. Certainly such faith is not mere notional assent, no matter how profound the propositions affirmed, but neither is it real assent if such assent only involves believing propositions. Likewise, such faith is no mere momentary impulse of feeling, no matter how overpowering its intensity, nor is it a lifelong, all-consuming passion that involves nothing but feeling or emotion. Faith is not merely behavior or action, no matter how momentous the consequences, nor is it some profound choice of one's fundamental character ("existential choice") involving only volition. Each of these is the expression or realization of some distinctive part (or capacity) of a person, and however inescapable and important that part may be, it is nonetheless only a part. All these parts are involved in faith, but none by itself is faith. Two questions bear on this issue.

Must everyone always have at least one such totalizing attitude, and therefore some faith or other, at all times? Some have answered yes,[90] thereby cheaply purchasing a kind of universal apology for faith, if not quite a universal baptism into one kind of religious faith. But this answer seems very doubtful. Why must everyone always

89. This point is not at odds with my earlier claim that faith is only a partially constitutive attitude. There the claim was that whatever faith constitutes, whether a particular thing or a whole environment, it contributes only a part of that thing. Here the claim is that faith contributes to the whole self-world horizon of significance. Combining the points, faith contributes (an essential) part of the whole self-world horizon. Moses did more than meet a stubbornly persistent fire; the significance of his life and of his whole world were altered; his horizon of significance was transformed. But not everything in Moses or in his world altered.

90. See Tillich, 1958.

have some totalizing attitude or other? Could S simply have various kinds of attitudes encompassing more or less, but never all, of S's whole self? One might argue that a person without a totalizing attitude has a self that is less unified (and perhaps less valuable or fulfilled) than a person with a totalizing attitude—but that is another matter, since what is desirable is distinct from what is possible.[91]

Must everyone have at most one such totalizing attitude, and therefore no more than one faith, at any moment? Some have answered yes, often in a missionary effort to move people from (what is taken to be) one form of faith to another. This is a dubious undertaking. A person with more than one totalizing attitude might well live a disorganized life, with divided allegiance and dichotomous understanding, but it does not follow that it cannot be done. It does not even follow that such a fragmented life is dishonest or self-deceived. Someone may adopt two or more different totalizing attitudes, may honestly see no way of reconciling them, and yet may muddle through in a fully authentic way. Once again the evaluative question (Would a person with more than one faith live a worse or better life than a person with one or none?) is distinct from the modal question (Would such a life be possible?).[92]

On the other hand, faith is an orienting attitude toward one's context as an *environing whole*—treating it not as something itself contextualized by a wider whole, but as the widest whole itself—not a region of attitudinal "space," as it were, but such space itself. This is what being a "world" entails. Still, such totalization is not easy to thematize. The attitudes on which we ordinarily focus are limited and particular ones, oriented toward a delimited part, region, or aspect of some wider whole. We are conscious of this object, worry about that group, believe this proposition is true, hope for that state of affairs to occur—and all of the objects of such attitudes are particular and delimited. Faith as a totalizing attitude involves something else; it reaches out toward the whole of which these are but delimited parts, subregions, or aspects. It means grasping things whole, if not necessarily in concepts or very clearly, and glimpsing

91. I do not mean to suggest that the unity of personality secured via some totalizing attitude is always preferable to all kinds of disunity. On the contrary, some kinds of self-totalization are the very essence of blind and hateful fanaticism.
92. Once again, I mean to pass no evaluative judgments.

the horizon of significance that extends beyond and around the foreground of one's life.

Once again we may ask whether exactly one (at least one and at most one) environing whole is required. On the one hand there is no need for S to have an attitude toward experience that constitutes it as a limited whole; for every context there may be a wider context, with no ultimate horizon(s). Granted that everyone will in fact stop somewhere, and that most will not go far, there still is no logical requirement that someone stop here, or indeed stop at all. In addition, some absurdists or nihilists will refuse to ascribe significance to the world at all; their horizons of significance lie well within the world, or do not exist at all. And still others (agnostics, sceptics) believe they can suspend commitment to any horizon-fixing attitudes at all. On the other hand, there is no need to have only one environing whole, only one horizon of significance over one's entire life.[93] Granted that there is pressure to connect up one's fundamental attitudes, there is still no necessity of doing so; one may simply be unable to bring together the various horizons presented in differing constitutive attitudes.

Faith therefore involves the whole self and the whole world, but does not constitute these wholes in every respect, and it is not an obligatory attitude possessed by everybody who has any attitudes at all.

6. Faith is significant, bestowing as well as embracing significance. Faith engenders a horizon of significance of the kind I call "meaning-and-value." At its richest and deepest, faith does not merely provide instances of preexisting structures of meaning-and-value but rather brings into being a certain whole new kind of meaning-and-value, a new meaning-and-value for the whole as well as for new aspects of the parts in relation to each other. For example, theistic faith does not merely restructure ontology, add new imperatives, or provide new instances of antecedent values and virtues; it casts everything in a new light—where human destiny, vocation and agency, life itself, even matter-energy and space-time all acquire new and special meaning-and-value. Everything in life, and life itself

93. See Hick's hierarchy of total interpretations (natural, human, divine); one can have a higher-level supervening interpretation only if one first has the lower-level one (1957, chap. 6).

(at least potentially), acquires a novel significance, whether *sub specie æternitatis* or *sub specie dei*. Two aspects of the new kind of significance that arises with faith need to be stressed.

I call this kind of significance *"meaning-and-value"* to signal that it is not restricted to any single area of human concern. To be sure, faith does impinge on intellectual significance—the intelligibility or comprehensibility of the whole and therefore of the parts of the whole. But faith also aids in making sense out of one's life, in finding life meaningful and worthwhile, or in gaining direction in one's lifework. Faith also gives guidance in ascribing value, and kinds of value, to the various kinds of things in the world, indicating what counts, and why, and how much—therefore revealing (in part) what should and should not be done, desired, and given devotion.

Faith both *bestows* and *embraces* significance. Faith creates meaning-and-value—brings into existence novel significance—and also recognizes meaning-and-value—discovers prior significance. Faith as a radically constitutive attitude is both the act of bestowing a significance on things that they would not otherwise have and also the response of embracing a significance in things that would not otherwise be noticed.

But an apparent contradiction looms. How can significance be both created and discovered? Are these mutually exclusive? Does one need to decide between a subjective and an objective account of significance? Not necessarily. Recall that faith as a radically constitutive attitude partially constitutes (the whole of) both subject and object of faith, self and world, in relation to each other; neither subject nor object has the significance it does apart from this relation to the other. This implies, on the one hand, that the significance in and of the world (faith's object) depends on the self (faith's subject); this world would not have the significance it does were it not this self's world. In the sense of depending on a self, therefore, significance is a "subjective" creation. A world's significance is bestowed on it in and through faith. But the attitude of faith also implies, on the other hand, that the significance of object and subject is a correlative significance, and that neither is the mere by-product of the other. A world's significance is found in faith—not made up, invented, or willfully projected from something prior to faith. It is as if the world's significance were already "there" for the self to embrace, even though it makes its appearance only in the relation of faith. In sum, faith both makes and finds significance in self and world—perhaps one could even say that faith's own significance as a fundamental attitude is this engendering discovery of a horizon of significance.

7. Faith's opposites are lack of faith and having a contrary faith. Lack of faith here does not mean lacking some constitutive attitude or other; if S has any attitudes at all, S cannot avoid having some at least partially constitutive attitudes, since every attitude (trivially) partially constitutes itself. Instead, S may lack a totalizing significant constitutive attitude or S may lack a radically, partially constitutive attitude. Having a contrary faith does not necessarily mean lacking all faith, but it does mean having another partially, radically constitutive attitude that is at odds with one's initial faith. Let us consider these three cases.

First, a person may lack a constitutive attitude that is both totalizing and significant. Either S's constitutive attitudes are not totalizing (producing a fragmented self and a chaotic world), or else they are not significant (yielding a meaningless and valueless self and world), or both (chaos is pointless). Such lacks help us to see better what faith according to the attitude model involves.

Second, a person may lack a constitutive attitude that is both partial and radical. Here there are two possibilities: S's constitutive attitudes are completely radical (not partially radical), or S's constitutive attitudes are partial but not radical. Both possibilities are worth exploring in greater detail. What would it mean for S to have no partially constitutive attitudes, but only ones that are completely constitutive? A completely constitutive attitude contributes all that is essential to self and world, a totalizing horizon of significance that envelops the individual and exhausts the environment, constituting the entirety of S and S's environing context. Someone in the grip of a completely constituting attitude might be able to conceive the bare possibility that there could be other alternatives to seeing self and world in this way, but she would be unable to imagine or appreciate this as a real possibility.

Why cannot such an all-consuming attitude (or set of attitudes) be faith? Here the kind of risk proper to faith on the attitude model is significant. On the attitude model, though faith tends to be totalizing, it is inevitably pluralistic: There are many such totalizing attitudes, even though there may seem to be only one for a person locked in the grip of one. Such a person may grow so comfortable, confident, or confined in this attitude that she fails to see that there are indeed alternative attitudes with equal powers of constitution. When this happens, one may say one of three things: S has faith but does not recognize that she does (because she mistakes a partially constitutive attitude for a completely constitutive one); S's faith is irrational or fanatical (S unwarrantedly discredits or discounts other possible horizons); or, S has passed beyond fanaticism into what I call blindness, an inability even to recognize that there are alternatives to her current constitutive attitude. Ignorant faith and irrational faith are still faith, but blindness excludes faith, is an opposite of faith.

What would it mean for S to have partially constitutive attitudes that are not radically constitutive? Recall that an attitude is radically constitutive in either of two senses: extensively, if it constitutes both subject and object (in relation to each other); or intensively, if it conditions other constitutive features of subject or object. Faith, on the attitude model, is a radically constitutive attitude in both senses. Failure of a constitutive attitude to be either (or both) is a lack of faith. In the former case, the attitude could fail to constitute self or world, making it less than fundamental; in the latter case, it could fail to touch all the aspects of self and world constituted by other attitudes, making it less than totalizing or significance-bestowing/ embracing. In both, the partially constitutive attitude does not cut deeply enough into the person's mode of existence to qualify as faith according to the attitude model.

Third, S may have a contrary faith, a contrary constitutive attitude that is also partial, radical, totalizing, and significant. It is not that S lacks faith altogether but that S has more than one faith; the risk faith involves—there are many possible constitutive attitudes that might be taken—is internalized, not just recognized as an abstract possibility. S's initial faith is put in jeopardy by another, different faith, in either of two ways. The contrary faith may come to displace the initial faith. Since radically constitutive attitudes tend toward exclusivity, such displacement is a live possibility. It is also possible for S to have two (or more?) contrary faiths at once, where their essential opposition is expressed in conflict and disharmony. The two faiths coexist, but unstably, in ways that threaten to undermine the fundamental and total nature of both: The self and the world of one constitutive attitude are at war with the self and world of another. While retaining both attitudes, S has the unenviable options of oscillating from one to the other or else being torn asunder in a vain attempt to cling to both.

To recapitulate: According to the attitude model, faith is a partially, radically constitutive attitude, one that extensively and intensively contributes an essential part of both the subject's and the object's identity and character—with faith, a self in relation to a world via a horizon of significance (partially) comes into being. Such an attitude precedes but does not preclude—nor even avoid—propositional expression; it is fundamental (basic), totalizing (of self and world), and significant (both giving and finding meaning-and-value). Its opposites are lacking a constitutive attitude that is totalizing and significant, lacking one that is both partial and radical, or having another, contrary faith.

## D. The Confidence Model

This model of faith differs quite radically from all of the others in one crucial and consequential respect: the other models are all *relational* ones, conceiving of faith as a relation between a person and some object (another person, a proposition, a world, and so forth). The confidence model is a nonrelational view, conceiving of faith as a quality that characterizes a person (or a self, or a state of mind of a person or self) without essential reference to anything else—without there being any intentional or real object of that person's state of mind.[94] For some readers a nonrelational model seems like no portrait of faith at all—there cannot be faith without an object, they insist—but I would ask that judgment be postponed until after the confidence model has been described and (in Chap.

---

94. This description calls to mind W. C. Smith's characterization of faith as a "human quality" (1979a). But since Smith does not distinguish between quality and relation, the resemblance is only superficial. Its deeper affinities (and actual antecedents in inquiry) are to mystical and extraordinary experiences reported in all times and places. See, e.g., Forman, 1990; Katz, 1978, 1983; Oakes, 1990; Stace, 1961; and Woods, 1980.

4) applied to some actual conceptions of faith. The main features of the confidence model may be summarized as follows:

> S has faith$_C$ (or S faiths$_C$) if S is in a nonrelational conscious state that realizes S's deeper self, that is characterized by a profound feeling of (self-)confidence (serenity, tranquility, calm, peace), and that is conditionally imperturbable.

1. S is in a nonrelational conscious state. By "conscious state" I mean a state or condition of a person in which that person is conscious or aware, whether the person is conscious or aware of anything.[95] A conscious state is relational if it contains both a distinction and a relation between a subject and one or more objects of awareness; the subject and object are two (distinct) yet together (related). There are various kinds of objects, and various ways of classifying them. One scheme divides them into real objects, those that exist independently of someone's awareness of them, and intentional objects, those that exist only in and through someone's awareness of them, either as kinds (ideas, unicorns, fictional characters) or as particulars (this imaginary friend, this object of my present attention) or as something in between (fictional characters). A conscious state is nonrelational when neither the distinction nor the relation between subject and object is present in the awareness, either because the state lacks any object or (if this is even possible) because it lacks both subject and object. In a nonrelational state there is no object of awareness, only a state of awareness; there is no awareness of anything, whether or not there is some subject that is aware. I call such a state "pure awareness."[96]

It is important to distinguish between two kinds of *pure awareness*, or rather two versions of the character of pure awareness. The first holds that pure awareness is not a separable or independent kind of

95. The restriction to persons is for convenience only; I do not believe only persons are conscious, but only conscious states of persons are of concern here. Further, no definitions of the notoriously elusive terms "consciousness" and "awareness" (here treated as rough synonyms) will be given. I can only assume that we all have some understanding of awareness insofar as we are aware.

96. Other terms might serve as well, e.g., "introvertive mysticism" (Stace, 1961) or "Pure Consciousness" (Forman, 1990). The authors in Katz, 1978, in effect argue that there are no such "pure" states; their arguments are effectively rebutted in Forman, 1990.

consciousness but only a distinguishable modality of awareness that, while taking no object itself, necessarily accompanies states of mind that do have intentional or real objects (though it need not accompany all such states). I call this the "accoutrement" version. According to it, pure awareness is an accoutrement of separable or independent states of consciousness, not a separable or independent state in itself—a kind of underlying tone, mood, quality, or feature of an experience, not an experience capable of occurring all on its own. Such an accoutrement may be a more or less prominent feature of experience, and one may of course consider it on its own, taking it as an independent topic of attention or inquiry, but the feature itself cannot exist independently of the conscious states it accompanies. The second version is more radical, and therefore more problematic. I call it the "independence" version. On this view, pure awareness is a state of consciousness that, while it may accompany some or all other states of mind, is also capable of existing by itself, at least in principle. Pure awareness is not only a distinguishable accoutrement of independent states of awareness but also an independent and separable state of awareness on its own.[97]

The following discussion favors neither account of pure awareness; its points should apply equally well either to the accoutrement version or to the independence version. Some might be tempted to deny that there is, or could be, such a thing as pure awareness, but they would be swimming upstream against a torrent of empirical evidence, or at any rate of testimony, to the contrary. A great many persons of indisputable integrity have attested to the existence, and

97. The independence version allows for two gaps between the potential universality of pure awareness and its apparent actual rarity. (1) The detection gap. When pure awareness does accompany ordinary states of experience it may be hard to detect. Skill, training, special techniques, or extraordinary experiences may be required in order to discern what is there to be discerned. Further, without such special helps, it may be impossible to distinguish between the independence and the accoutrement versions by means of practice or ordinary experience. (2) The achievement gap. Achieving such independent states of consciousness will typically be regarded as open to everyone, since pure awareness is supposed to accompany everyone's experience. But not everyone actually achieves such states, due to the many and great difficulties of isolating and separating pure awareness from ordinary subject–object consciousness. Special effort and insight are required, and special techniques such as meditation may be all but indispensable. (At least there seem to many to be great difficulties in achieving pure awareness, though there is some contrary testimony in schools of "sudden enlightenment" that this state can be gained simply and easily, or at any rate quite abruptly.)

therefore the possibility, of a kind or quality of experience that differs markedly in its phenomenal properties from ordinary, intentional, subject-object consciousness.[98] But even though the existence of (something like) pure awareness is undeniable, its nature and value are obscure. Most would agree that it is at least a *psychological* condition, a state of mind, or at any rate a state of (some) human minds. But is it more than this? Is it an ontological condition transcending ordinary empirical waking or dreaming experience in reality, insightfulness, and value? Is pure awareness the highest form of consciousness, the key to truth, the highest bliss, identical with the ground of being, one with ultimate reality, not other than Brahman? Such questions, however fascinating, are not addressed here. My concern is only to describe features of faith as highlighted by the confidence model, and these features do not presuppose or imply controversial ontologies or soteriologies. Just as in the personal relationship model one may understand what S's faith$_p$ in A means without thereby endorsing the existence and a certain description of A, so also here in the confidence model one may understand what S's faith$_C$ means without thereby endorsing some sweeping theory of ultimate reality and human salvation.

Since faith on the confidence model is a state of pure awareness without any (intentional or real) object, it cannot be a *constitutive* attitude, for such attitudes constitute both subject and object of awareness and therefore presuppose a relational awareness. Indeed, such faith cannot be an attitude at all, or any other kind of relation of one thing (a self or subject) to something else (an object or objects). Such faith is therefore "nondual," without an "other," and this is why, in order to avoid ordinary assumptions about faith having an object, it might be worth trying to use "faith" as an active intransitive verb: "S faiths." But nondual faith as confidence need not amount to a profound experience of mystical union, a state of complete nonduality (the independence version of pure awareness). Faith as nonrelational may only be a distinguishable, more or less prominent aspect of an experience that contains various relations between a subject and one or many objects of awareness (the accoutrement version).

98. For some of the evidence, see especially Forman, 1990, pt. 1; and Stace, 1960, 1961; also Katz, 1978, 1983; Otto, 1932; Underhill, 1955; and Zaehner, 1957.

Since faith on this model is not an attitude (toward some object) it cannot be a *propositional* attitude. Faith is not a matter of believing propositions, or of holding them in any way to be true, or of acting as if they were true. Moreover, faith as pure awareness is not even a prepropositional state of mind, in any of three different ways:

a. Prior expression of propositions about pure awareness (by S or anyone else) is neither conducive nor necessary to having it;
b. Pure awareness does not naturally give rise in S (at some later time) to propositions descriptive of it or its contents; and even
c. For S at t to have attitudes toward propositions descriptive of pure awareness is not compatible with S at t having pure awareness.

In other words, there are no logical or ordinary causal links between pure awareness and propositional attitudes, except of a mutually exclusive kind.

From none of these points, however, does it follow that there are or can be no true propositions about pure awareness, or that S could not make, assert, or understand those propositions, if S wanted to do so. But it does follow that S does not and cannot have any attitudes toward these propositions in having (or while being in) such a state of awareness. Thinking propositional thoughts about a nonrelational conscious state is possible, but such thoughts cannot occur in such a state, even when the propositions one thinks truly describe that very state.

Since faith as confidence is not a propositional attitude, it is also neither a *doxastic* nor a *cognitive* propositional attitude. That is, faith is not a matter of believing or feeling certain about propositions, nor is it a matter of knowing or being certain about propositions; there is no question of beliefs, knowledge, truth, or evidence. In fact, this model goes even farther; it does not think of faith in doxastic or epistemic terms at all (whether propositional or not), but rather in psychological or ontological ones. Faith is a state of awareness or being, not a state of believing or knowing. If faith on the confidence model is thought to provide access to another or higher reality, it is not that it yields insight into, or information about, such reality but that it constitutes a foretaste or imperfect realization of that reality.[99]

99. No judgment is made here as to the relative cognitive, epistemic, or soter-

Since faith precludes propositional beliefs (for the person who is in a state of pure awareness), it precludes *causal* propositional beliefs about the state of pure awareness for that person. Precluded are not just propositional beliefs about the (phenomenological or ontological) state of pure awareness itself but also propositional beliefs about the causes and effects of such a state. All are incompatible with having pure awareness. Of course, such beliefs are precluded for S only while S is in the state of pure awareness; for someone who is not in such a state—or for S at some other time—causal beliefs (and indeed propositional attitudes of all kinds) are both possible and possibly useful. In short, faith as confidence is explanatorily as well as propositionally opaque to itself. It necessarily takes no thought about today or tomorrow; it has no propositional attitudes concerning its own causes and effects.

While faith as a nonrelational conscious state necessarily is *not identical* with relational kinds of faith (faith according to the other models), nevertheless there may be causal or other kinds of connection between them. For example, it may be that faith as personal relationship is a useful means to the goal of faith as confidence: trusting in the right guru may enable one to learn and do that which is necessary to gain nonrelational faith. On the contrary, achieving nonrelational faith may block relational faith. Achieving states of pure awareness may lead to complete self-reliance, trusting no authority beyond oneself. The particular sorts of causal connections that do in fact hold is a matter for empirical investigation, not a priori legislation.

2. *S's state of mind realizes S's deeper self.* All models of faith involve self-realization of some kind, in the sense that some important capacity, potential, or "dimension" of the self is actualized. For example, trust not only opens up an entire world of personal relationships but also develops the kind of self who can enjoy and thrive in such a world. But self-realization is an especially prominent feature on the confidence model of faith. This is because the pure

iological merits of nonpropositional versus propositional conscious states. Moreover, there is no presumption that propositional knowledge is the highest possible cognitive condition. Whether God's omniscience is propositional or nonpropositional (see Taliaferro, 1985; Alston, 1989, chap. 9), it is precisely not (human) faith but something higher.

awareness required by such faith does not reach out to another, to some object of awareness; all it can do is to alter the antecedent quality or condition of the subject of awareness, and this subject is (taken to be) the self—or the Self. This alteration of the subject is no trivial matter; it is all-important. Confidence becomes the fundamental quality of the whole person, and any account of S must include, first and foremost, a depiction of this nonrelational conscious state that S was (is, will be) in.[100]

This conscious state may be said to realize S's deeper self in several distinct senses of the word "realize:"

a. It may mean that S recognizes or becomes aware of this deeper self—though not necessarily as an explicit object of thematic recognition. In fact, the locution "aware of" is misleading here; perhaps it would be better to say that in achieving pure awareness S (necessarily) becomes self-aware or an aware self.

b. It may mean that S makes real or actualizes S's deeper self—not as creation but as fulfillment or achievement. In pure awareness S makes actual a potential self, the deeper self that S potentially is.

c. It may mean that S becomes identified with S's deeper self. Not only is S no longer unaware or ignorant of this deeper self, but also S is no longer distanced from this self; S moves from self-estrangement or self-alienation to self-fulfillment or self-actualization.

d. Most controversially, it may mean that S becomes identical with this deeper self, so that all traces of duality between self-conscious self and true self disappear.

These senses, though distinct, are compatible; self-realization can involve them all. But it need not do so. Since each sense takes one

100. Two questions arise. First, does the state of pure awareness abolish or replace the self instead of realizing it? (Is pure awareness as self-less as it is content-less?) Perhaps, but the overwhelming majority of testimony about pure awareness also speaks of a pure self or at any rate a "pure subject" of that awareness. Of course this pure self is said to be no ordinary kind of self, and it is possible that it is nothing more than the state of pure awareness itself (or a series of such states). Still, it is hard to talk of a state of awareness without also talking of something (a subject or self) that is aware, even if this is only a figure of speech. And second, why does the confidence model require self-realization if pure awareness is possible without a self? Here this model simply follows majority testimony and common usage in regarding pure awareness as realizing a deeper self. If (some form of) pure awareness does not require or is not equivalent to a (nonordinary) subject or self, then it will not count as faith on the confidence model. Indeed, some kind of self-realization seems common to all (models of) faith.

a step closer to an "independence" view of pure awareness (so long as it is held that the true self can exist independently of the ordinary phenomenal self), it may be that one would wish to stop before arriving at full-fledged identity.

3. S's state of mind is a profound feeling of (self-)confidence. The nonrelational state of consciousness, pure awareness, possesses a fundamental phenomenological quality as unmistakable as it is difficult to characterize. I call this quality "confidence," in a special sense of the term, but there are other terms that might serve equally well: "serenity," "calm," "peace," "tranquility," and "assurance." It is a quality of awareness that might be expressed, though very feebly and misleadingly, by such phrases as: "nothing can harm me," "nothing (fundamentally) is wrong," "all is well," "all is as it should be."[101] Moreover, some light is shed on the quality of confidence by noting S's state of awareness when S lacks confidence (when "S does not faith"): confusion, trouble, doubt, hesitation, distraction, awkwardness, disturbance. To borrow an old Asian metaphor, an ordinary troubled consciousness is like the moon's dancing image in a rippling pond—distorted, shifting, broken, dull—whereas confidence is like the moon's steady reflection when the waters are stilled—clear, unwavering, whole, brilliant.

Although confidence cannot be characterized completely or exactly, it does possess the following conceptual features:

a. Confidence tends to *persist* through time. It is not some momentary, intermittent, or sporadic feature—if, indeed, it is an occurrent feature at all, something that happens. Though it may begin in and with some extraordinary experience, confidence continues throughout subsequent experience, at least to some extent; it is an ongoing trait.

101. This sentiment finds wide and various expression. "In the woods, we return to reason and faith. There I feel that nothing can befall me in life,—no disgrace, no calamity (leaving me my eyes), which nature cannot repair" (Emerson, 1957, 24). "Nature never did betray/ The heart that loved her", such that nothing shall "disturb/ Our cheerful faith, that all which we behold/ Is full of blessings" (Wordsworth, "Tintern Abbey," lines 122–23, 133–34). "I will mention another experience straight away which I also know and which others of you might be acquainted with: it is, what one might call, the experience of feeling *absolutely* safe. I mean the state of mind in which one is inclined to say 'I am safe, nothing can injure me whatever happens' " (Wittgenstein, 1965, 8).

b. Confidence tends to *endure* over time. It has considerable power to withstand—and indeed to overcome—the manifold "perturbations" of life. Doubts may trouble the soul, inclinations tempt it, dilemmas vex it; but a confident self has the strength to resist and conquer these vicissitudes of existence. Confidence perseveres and prevails; it is a triumphal trait.

c. Confidence is *deep*. It is no superficial veneer for a behaviorally manifest personality, much less a self-deceived or hypocritical facade, but is rather a fundamental feature of an entire person. Like a constitutive attitude, confidence is fundamental and totalizing for the self (although unlike a constitutive attitude there is no correlative horizon). Confidence plumbs the self's depth; it is a profound trait.

d. Confidence appears as a *feeling-tone*. It is therefore a "passion" of sorts, but it is not a flickering affect or a violent eruption from animal depths, something that disrupts other mental functioning and subverts rational thought. Instead, this passion is more like a powerful yet tranquil mood, a frame of mind, a feeling-tone that infuses and strengthens all awareness, thought, and action. Confidence is felt awareness; it is a pervasive trait.

e. Confidence is a *positive* quality. Any state of mind that it characterizes is experienced as immensely desirable, attractive, or valuable. When lacking, it will be sought out and sought after with considerable energy. Confidence is a positive feeling; it is an attracting trait.

f. Confidence is basically *self*-confidence. It is not fundamentally trust in or reliance on another, or conviction that something good will happen, although these may be more easily achieved when one is confident. Nor is it the mere absence of self-doubt—that ultimate weapon of the salesman—although all such doubts do cease. It is not even trust in oneself, insofar as that implies duality and relationship of trusting self to trusted self. Instead, it is the sense of deep-seated security in a world of woes, a condition of well-being not based on future weal but on present worth (or the worth of the present)—a quality or indeed the essence of the self, though not a relation of the self to itself. Confidence is self-confidence; it is a self-affirming trait.[102]

4. Faith's opposite is conditional perturbability. Since confidence is a positive quality, it may be lacking; but what then might stand

102. "Trust thyself: every heart vibrates to that iron string. . . . Great men have always done so, and confided themselves childlike to the genius of their age, be-

in its place? Initially, one might think to distinguish two noncon-
fident conditions: the presence of some quality antagonistic to confidence (I call these qualities "perturbations"); and the absence of
both confidence and perturbation, a neutral condition either without
feeling-tone altogether or with only a nonperturbing (but also non-
confident) quality. But this distinction is not truly fundamental.
According to the confidence model, confidence is the absence not
merely of (actual) perturbation but also of (potential) perturbability.
The quality of confidence is not just an actual positive feeling-tone
that displaces other feeling-tones because its presence is incompatible
with theirs. Rather, confidence is also an incapacity to be perturbed,
a positive disposition of imperturbability.

This may sound strange. How can a state of mind be imperturbable, not liable to disturbance by doubts, fears, distractions, and the
like? To see how confidence might be imperturbable, two senses of
imperturbability need to be distinguished. S (or S's state of being
or feeling) may be imperturbable in that S possesses a fundamental
quality Q such that, so long as S has Q, S cannot have any of the
various kinds of particular perturbations.[103] However, since Q itself
may be lost—though we need not suppose that it can be lost quickly
or easily—S's imperturbability is at least in principle vulnerable. We
may call this sense conditional imperturbability. S may be imperturbable in a stronger sense when S possesses a fundamental quality
Q* such that so long as S has Q* S cannot be perturbed and such
that S cannot lose Q*. Such imperturbability is not vulnerable; it is
a quality that can be gained but not lost. We may call this sense
absolute imperturbability.

Faith on the confidence model requires only the weaker sense of
imperturbability, conditional imperturbability. Faith when achieved

---

traying their perception that the absolutely trustworthy was seated at their heart,
working through their hands, predominating in all their being. And we are now
men, and must accept in the highest mind the same transcendent destiny" (Emerson,
1957, 148).

103. What might Q be, according to the confidence model? One kind of possibility is internal: S might be able to maintain S in such a state, or perhaps the very
state of awareness itself is somehow resistant to change—or even outside the causal
nexus altogether (although this possibility would more naturally be associated with
absolute than with conditional imperturbability). Another is external: A very powerful being—God, perhaps, or a super-scientist—might maintain S in the condition
of self-confidence. A third is both internal and external: Confidence might lie in the
very (nonpersonal) nature of things.

(or granted) excludes all perturbations and also the capacity to be perturbed. But this imperturbability may be lost (or removed), and then even if actual perturbations do not appear there still exists the capacity, and perhaps the tendency, to be perturbed. Still, the model does not exclude absolute imperturbability; there is nothing in this model to prevent a particular conception of faith from requiring absolute imperturbability.[104]

Since, therefore, confidence is imperturbable, at least conditionally, its opposites are not two (perturbation and lack of both perturbation and confidence) but only one (perturbability). If S is perturbable in any way—if the fundamental quality of S's state of mind is such that S can be perturbed—then it matters little, according to this model, whether S is presently perturbed, or how much or in what ways. Someone who is merely susceptible to perturbation lacks faith as much, and in much the same way, as one who is filled with doubt, suspicion, despair, and other perturbations.[105] Here faith on the confidence model differs importantly from the other models, all of which have at least two distinct kinds of opposites.

To recapitulate: According to the confidence model, faith is a nonrelational conscious state of a person, a state that lacks all objects or contents of awareness though not, in all likelihood, any subject of awareness. This state of awareness realizes the person's deeper self in various senses, and is characterized by (self-)confidence, a profound and positive feeling-tone that persists, endures, and excludes both perturbations and conditional perturbability.

## E. The Devotion Model

Each model brings a distinctive feature to the forefront and views faith from its perspective: trust, propositional belief, fundamental

104. Indeed we later meet with some actual conceptions that do just this. See Chap. 4, secs. F and G.

105. To recur to the image of the moon reflected in the lake, we must imagine the lake to be calm not just accidentally, due to a lull in the customary storm, but calm of necessity, due to a long-term or even permanent alteration of climate. Perhaps we could imagine that something, or someone, will ever after keep the winds from roiling the waters—perhaps even that, somehow, the stillness perpetuates itself, a (self-) conscious soliton.

attitude, feeling-quality. The devotion model highlights a different kind of feature—volition and commitment, the powers of will and willpower—and sees all other aspects of faith in its light. One could perhaps call this model "commitment," "loyalty," "fidelity," or "adherence," but "devotion" (though not "worship") resonates better with some of the particular conceptions of faith I consider in Chapter 3. A summary depiction of the devotion model is as follows:

> S has faith$_D$ in W only if W is a way of life open to S, which S voluntarily chooses, to which S is committed wholeheartedly and lastingly, and in which S perseveres.

1. Faith's object is a way of life. Unlike the confidence model, the devotion model permits and requires faith to have an object—something in which a person has faith. But the object of faith on the devotion model is unique. With the personal relationship model the object is some other person (S has faith$_P$ in A); with the belief model it is some proposition (S has faith$_B$ that p); and with the attitude model it is some horizoned "world" (S has faith$_A$ toward X). Here the object of faith is a way of life.[106]

By "way of life" I mean a pattern or kind of living, not some actual particular life that exemplifies that pattern. A way of life is therefore an abstract entity, not a concrete particular. But it is a very complicated abstract entity. Its complexity includes specification of the full panoply of personal capacities and resources necessary to live in a certain way—including individual dispositions of thought and feeling, as well as institutional arrangements and ceremonies—and especially specification of the (kinds of) actions that persons may deliberately choose to perform. A way of life is instantiated only when someone intentionally lives his or her life in that way and does not merely think or feel what it would be like to live in that way, or pretend to so live, or do so unwittingly, unintentionally, or involuntarily. Instances of ways of life are not centrally personal relationships, moods, or dispositions, nor are they personal states or conditions (though of course all these are involved). Instead, they are temporal processes consisting of a number of personal actions. As a pattern of living, therefore, a way of life may be instanced in

---

106. See Luijpen, "Faith is primarily a way of living" (1973, 87).

many different ways—by any life consisting centrally of a series (perhaps a sequence) of appropriately intentional actions.[107]

A way of life is a pattern for a whole life and for a complete life, though not necessarily for a total life. A way of life encompasses (at least potentially) the entire temporal span of a person's life; it cannot be confined to just a single time or period of life, nor can it be "merely a stage" one goes through. It is a pattern for a whole life. It provides for a life that lacks nothing essential for being a life one could voluntarily choose for its own sake. Since it will specify all the particular details and general aspects of a way of life that are essential to living that way of life and to rendering it eligible for election, it is a pattern for a complete life. But it does not (could not?) specify every particular detail or general aspect of a whole and complete life. A way of life is more like a blueprint than a scale model. It is not a pattern for a total life.

What constitutes a "pattern"? In one sense any finite sequence of actions or events illustrates some pattern or other, just as any finite sequence of numbers instances some finite formula (indeed, an infinite number of such formulas). In this sense every life, no matter how bizarre and disjointed, would necessarily instance some way of life. Muddling through, taking no thought for the morrow, accepting whatever comes one's way, going with the flow—all would constitute ways of life. But this is too broad. There are four further restrictions on the concept as I employ it here.

First, since a way of life must be capable of being chosen by some (finite) agent, it cannot be infinitely or excessively complex, or completely or excessively obscure, in its main features. Of course S could choose something that is in fact infinitely complex or completely obscure, but S could not choose it as such, for there would

---

107. A slight complication arises. Is faith according to this model primarily devotion to a way of life (an abstract entity) or rather devotion to the *living of a way of life* (a concrete particular entity or process exemplifying that abstract entity)? The two are inseparable. One cannot be devoted only to an abstract entity as such (though one may admire, inquire into, or defend such entities); the devotion always extends to its exemplification in some concrete life. But conversely, one cannot be devoted only to a concrete particular entity as such (though one may have other kinds of relation to it); the devotion is always to a particular life as exemplifying some abstract way of life. So perhaps one could speak of the object of faith on the devotion model as an abstraction *in concreto*—an exemplified way of life. Hence the standard locution for this model of faith could be either "S has faith$_D$ in W" (where 'W' names some path or way of life) or "S has faith$_D$ to $\Phi_w$" (where '$\Phi_w$' names the concrete living of W).

be no way for a subject with finite capacities to know how to follow such a pattern as an alternative.[108] A way of life must be simple and clear enough to be discernible by any agent who could choose to live her life in accordance with it.

Second, ways of life vary on an active-passive scale.[109] At one end of this scale there are a great number of particular activities that constantly need to be examined, planned, prepared for, worked at, remembered, evaluated, and the like—an exacting affair of active management. In addition, "taking control of one's life" often means wresting control from others and from the environment, and so struggle, effort, and competition are required. At the other end of the scale there is acquiescence or even quiescence, not management or manipulation; one quietly waits, observes, accepts, does not contend, and lets pass all that transpires.

But whether a way of life is more or less active, less or more passive, there still will be some overarching pattern of behavior, of self-initiated as well as environmentally responsive action/inaction. There is a certain consistent and connected way in which S acts and reacts; S's life is not sheer randomness.[110] Even drifting through an apparently passive course of inaction may satisfy (though just barely) the criteria for a way of life. Insofar as this life is not simply a matter of being buffeted by environmental forces, the self exercises its powers of intentional action largely by refusing to initiate or guide (some kinds of) controllable events.[111] It takes to the extreme such maxims as "going with the flow" and "taking (or accepting) life as it comes."[112]

108. There are many possible complications. W might have a finitely complex main pattern with infinitely complicated details; W's finite pattern might be loose enough to permit an infinite number of quite distinct instantiations; W might have various levels of pattern; the pattern that S grasps and follows may only approximate the pattern that W truly is; and so forth.

109. There are of course many kinds of action and inaction, and so a single scale is an oversimplification, but it will do for the present.

110. To be sure, one might want a certain amount of randomness in a life: S might want occasionally to decide what to do by flipping a coin. But this does not avoid pattern since S must determine how and when to randomize, and what use to make of the results of such procedures. Randomness is always constrained by pattern. While there may be more or less randomness in a life, an overall random life—much less a random way of life—turns out to be inconceivable.

111. Also, of course, the entire pattern of relative inaction must be capable of being voluntarily chosen.

112. Such an apparently "passive" way of life resembles the Taoist notion of *wu-wei*, usually translated as "nonaction" or "inaction." The Chinese term is re-

Third, a way of life is correlative to character. In living a certain way of life, S both forms and expresses a certain kind of character; conversely, a certain kind of character is needed to follow and live a certain way of life. Following a pattern produces dispositions or habits to recognize, follow, and extend that pattern. As Aristotle stressed, performing actions of a certain kind develops settled dispositions to perform such actions; doing courageous acts is how persons become courageous. But conversely, in order to perform the actions proper to a certain way of life, S must perform them in the right way, in the way that a skilled, adept, or "virtuous" person would perform them, and this requires having the settled disposition. Hence, a way of life can often be recognized in and through the characters of the people who follow them.

Finally, ways of life need not be exemplary. An immoral way of life is as much a way of life as a moral one; similarly with ways of life displaying such other characterological qualities as laziness, laxity, irresponsibility, indecisiveness, hypocrisy, and self-deception. S's life can display a pattern of refusing to take responsibility as much as a pattern of responsible obedience.

It is of course always possible to characterize or describe any way of life to some extent, but one cannot capture all of it, for the full complexity of a way of life defies complete characterization. Any depiction of a way of life must fail to represent fully the extraordinarily intricate, subtle, rich, and interpenetrating details of that way. Because of this complexity, learning how to live or follow a way of life cannot proceed by first understanding explicit descriptions of that way, by reading an operating manual. Even if there could be an operating manual for a way of life, one could not learn how to follow that way just by reading and understanding the manual; other kinds of instruction would be required. Typically, to learn how to follow a way of life, one becomes a follower of a follower, following in the footsteps (that is, the examples, not the precepts) of someone who already knows how to follow that way. Occasional

---

markably ambiguous, however; *wu-wei* may mean any one or more of the following: doing nothing at all, doing nothing artificial, not contending, doing nothing willfully, doing nothing rigidly or forcibly, doing nothing against one's (and others') nature, and (perhaps) acting without attachment for the results of one's actions. All of these meanings are compatible with the point that *wu-wei* is, or can be, a way of life.

advice, precept, and admonition—given in the right way at the right moment[113]—will be useful, but words are secondary aids to exemplary deeds.

At this point it might seem that faith as devotion to a way of life essentially depends on, or even collapses into, faith as personal relationship to another person. However, this is not the case. Learning how to live a way of life—coming to have devotion—may depend on trusting another person's authority, insofar as examples are essential, although some ways of life seem to be discovered or created by extraordinary individuals on their own. But living or following a way of life is not so dependent on others. Once one has learned how to follow a way of life, one is "on one's own," (necessarily) able to make one's own decisions, not only about whether to persevere in that way but also about how to pursue it—indeed, about how that way goes or should go. Faith as personal relationship (trust) is at best an essential, or at any rate a typically useful, means to the end of faith as devotion; it does not constitute that end, the following of a way of life.

Still, someone might object, devotion seems to be primarily commitment or loyalty to a person, not to a way of life.[114] In particular, theistic devotion is passionate commitment to a personal deity. From this standpoint, then, the devotion model of faith could only seem a variant of the personal relationship model—with trust in another's practical, pragmatic, or deontic authority assuming the upper hand. Undoubtedly there are instances and conceptions of faith that construe devotion most fundamentally as commitment to a person and therefore primarily exemplify the personal relationship model of faith. But there are also other instances and conceptions of faith in which a way of life, and not a person (institution, ideal, principle, cause), is the primary or basic object of devotion. These fit another pattern: the devotion model. The models are distinct, even if they are occasionally combined, or blended, in particular instances or conceptions.

113. Even an operating manual for a way of life that includes a chapter on "How to teach someone how to follow this way of life" would not be able fully to specify what constitutes a "right moment" for saying the proper words, even if it could specify the proper words (which it cannot).

114. I am grateful to Peg Falls-Corbitt for helping clarify the remainder of this section.

According to the devotion model, then, devotion to a person is basically devotion to a person as exemplifying certain characteristics—as having a certain character or as living a certain way of life. If the person did not have that character or live that way of life (in a particularly vivid, supple, expert way), one would not be devoted to her; and conversely, if someone else equally excelled in having that character and living that way of life, one would also be (as?) devoted to her. The devotion is primarily to the way of life, not to the person; even though for some learner the two may seem inseparable or even indistinguishable, the distinction will be more apparent on separation from one's guru.

Further (again according to the devotion model), a devotee treats the way of life to which she is committed not as a mere means to something better, but as an end in itself, something worth pursuing for its own sake even if it does not lead on to something else. A way of life requires no goal or end or result beyond itself; it is self-sufficient. S does not follow W in order to achieve or realize some good G that lies beyond W (whether or not G includes W as part of itself). Rather, W is the supreme good that S seeks. It is the final end, the end-in-itself.

Finally, if a devotee seeks a personal relationship with someone who exemplifies the desired way of life, typically this relationship is sought not as an end in itself but rather as a means to achieving the devotee's own exemplification of that way of life. A serious devotee does not desire to be a slavish follower of another (seeking relationship for its own sake) nor to be another's "groupie" (basking in the other's reflected glow). Instead, a devotee desperately wants to live the other's way of life, that is, to live the very same way of life as the other lives, and to live it on her own, by herself (though, of course, not necessarily for herself alone).

In these ways, therefore, the primary object of faith on the devotion model is a way of life, not a person. Those completely wedded to a personal relationship model of faith may seek to reduce or subsume such devotion to personal relationship. Nonetheless, it is apparent that the devotion model is distinct from the personal relationship model, however fused the models may be in particular conceptions of faith. Living a way of life is the primary object, goal, or end of faith according to the devotion model, even if instances of this model of faith are also instances of some other model.

2. Faith's way of life is voluntarily chosen. To be devoted to (living) a way of life is not merely to so live intentionally; it is also to choose or decide, voluntarily and freely, to live in that way and not any other. A way of life lived out of habit or ignorance, or under duress or coercion, would not be devotion, for such a life would lack the feature of voluntary choice. Without attempting to define "voluntary choice," we may note seven of its elements:

The chosen way of life must be *open* to the agent.[115] An open way for S is at least a way of life that it is possible for S to choose to live. In addition, S must be aware of this way as an option for S, the way must be sufficiently attractive to S (though not necessarily the most attractive way open to S), S must be able to choose to live this way, and S is neither constrained nor coerced into choosing it (alone).

The chosen way of life must be an open *alternative* selected from among other open alternatives (that is, when S chooses a way of life there must be at least one other way of life open to S that S does not choose). To choose is to decide, and to decide is to select one from a number of mutually exclusive alternatives, and thereby to "cut off" those not selected. These other alternatives must be attractive to S, but they do not have to be exactly as attractive as the way actually chosen (in fact, they may even be more attractive).[116] Further, S need not spend much if any time contemplating the road(s) not taken, or grieving about not being able to take any one or all of them. The important point is that there must be such open alternatives. For S to choose a way of life (in the relevant sense) there must be other ways of life open to S that S does not choose to follow (or that S chooses not to follow).

This point may be disputed. Might the "alternative" to a way of life that S might choose simply be no way of life at all? Might S choose not to live any way of life, to follow no way of life? And might S simply not choose any way of life at all? No. No one can avoid living some way of life or other; the only question is whether that way is a matter of choice or of default.

---

115. What I am calling an "open" option resembles William James's notion of a "living option" (1979, 14).

116. There may even be good reasons for choosing a less attractive way open to one, for example, if it is more likely to be achieved or to pay off, or if it is more difficult or easy to achieve or sustain, and so forth.

S could choose not to live this or that way of life, but in doing so S would be choosing to live some other way of life. This is because S cannot choose not to live some way of life or other, nor can S not choose to live some way of life. The former is ruled out because it would mean trying to completely randomize one's life—a self-defeating choice. The latter does not prevent S from living a way of life; it just means that the way of life that S ends up living will be a way of life S has not chosen to live.

So S must live some way of life or other, and the only question is whether S chooses the way of life S lives. There are, however, two further complications. What if S is unable to choose any way of life? This is a more extreme case than might initially appear. Recall that the ways of life among which S can choose must all be open to S: S cannot be ignorant of nor unattracted to them, nor can S be unable to choose them (for example, due to coercion or impotence). The question therefore is: Could there be no open ways for S? Perhaps, but at great cost. To the extent that the number of ways of life open to S are constricted, so is S's range and indeed power of choice. In the extreme I suppose all options could be stripped away, but then one would be left either with a self whose volitional powers could not be exercised or with no volitional powers at all. The former is a self without the occasion to exercise its fundamental volitional capacities—a very weak and ineffectual self—and the latter is a being without such capacities—no self at all.

The second complication may be phrased as, Could S choose more than one way? There are two cases: multiple ways over time and multiple ways at a time. Clearly S could choose different ways at different times—perhaps alternating between two or three, perhaps progressing through some limited range, or perhaps just jumping from one to another indefinitely. In some of these cases there is a metapattern (a sequence of development, or stages), in others not. If there is a metapattern, this again can be chosen—for example, to proceed through this as opposed to that sequence of stages—although I suspect further iterations (of meta-metapatterns) will not typically lie within a person's powers of choice due to the complexity involved. But if there is no metapattern, then there is no choice. (It cannot be that S consistently chooses out of immediate inclination, or randomly, for this is a pattern.) Choosing different ways of life for different times of life is certainly possible and perhaps even, on certain views of human development, quite desirable, with or without a metapattern.

What about choosing more than one way at a time? There seems to be no problem with choosing mutually compatible ways of life. But what about choosing ways that are mutually incompatible? Newton Da Costa and Steven French have developed a nonclassical "paraconsistent" doxastic logic in which the holding of inconsistent beliefs is quite possible,[117] so I assume that a paraconsistent logic of choice or decision could also be developed. If so, it is at least logically possible for S to choose (to follow, to live) two or more mutually incompatible ways of life at one time.[118] The question I wish to raise, however, concerns not possibility but rationality: Would it be rational (if possible) for S to choose both W and W* (which are mutually incompatible)? I believe not. It is irrational to (try to) serve two masters at once, even if it is possible; and it is also irrational to (try to) live two incompatible ways of life at once; a rational person would try one or the other, or one after the other, or neither one nor the other—but not both. Still, since irrational choices are possible, we must allow room for them in the devotion model of faith: S may be devoutly committed to an undesirable because irrational way (or combination of ways) of life.

Since a way of life must specify a whole and complete life (though not all of a life), it must be chosen as a *whole and complete* life. This does not mean, of course, that S must have a clear and distinct view of the entire way of life in each—or indeed in any—moment of decision; any glimpse of a way of life, particularly one in the making, is partial. Rather, it means that every essential or important part of the whole must be chosen, for to balk at an essential or important part is to balk at the whole. Moreover, S's choice of a way's essential parts should aim at connecting them into a completed whole, at least one that would be recognized as completed in hindsight; and the life lived in accordance with this whole pattern should be valued in and for itself, as a completed or final whole.

S's choice requires *self-control*. Choosing a way of life obviously involves self-discipline, doing one's best to ignore, restrain, or over-

117. See Da Costa and French, 1990, which provides a good bibliography on the subject, especially of Da Costa's earlier work.

118. Surely there is some [indefinite] upper bound on how many ways of life S could choose to live at once, but this limit will vary from person to person.

come any contrary inclinations that would prevent one from living that way of life.[119] But it also involves self-control, bending one's self toward following that way—not just making an effort but devoting one's heart and soul and mind and strength to the task.[120]

S's choice must be *constantly reaffirmed*. It is not that S must spend every waking moment consciously and explicitly reaffirming a way of life; that would allow little time for anything else. Rather, the reaffirmation, for the most part, will be implicit in the various actual explicit choices S makes, as well as in the tendencies developed and dispositions cultivated by S. Perhaps we can best capture the notion of constant reaffirmation subjunctively: each of S's actions (and series of actions) is such that S would explicitly reaffirm it as part of S's chosen way of life were it to be brought to S's conscious attention.

S's choice is *free from external constraint or coercion*. Clearly a prisoner is not free to walk away from her cell, and so cannot meaningfully be devoted to a way of life that requires such movement. But what counts as a constraint may not always be so clear. Is a wall outside of one's normal or actual lifetime range a constraint? Is gravity a constraint for travelers? What about lack of ability or opportunity? We shall have to leave the notion of "external constraint" rather vague and open-ended.

A consequence of the previous conditions is that S is *responsible* for choosing the way of life S attempts to follow. S's choice of a way of life will rarely if ever be the sole cause or condition of the life S actually lives; there will normally be many other contributing factors. But S's voluntary choice is the crucial element for assigning praise or blame to S; it is what makes S responsible for living that way of life. S's devotion to a way of life is praised or blamed not (primarily) on account of the consequences of the devotion, nor (primarily) for the sake of altering future commitments by S, for S may be praised or blamed for having chosen a way of life even if nothing has or will come of it. What matters is that S chooses devotion to W, since responsibility for that choice belongs to S.

119. But what if S's will is too weak, and though S tries as hard as S can, S still cannot control such wayward impulses? Does it still count as faith?

120. As Peg Falls-Corbitt points out, self-control—as well as the kind of wholehearted and lasting commitment treated in the next section—are in considerable tension with choice of mutually incompatible ways of life: It is not easy to pursue an irrational way of life, even if it is possible.

A final aspect of a devotee's voluntary choice—S is committed to a way of life in a wholehearted and lasting way—is so important that it deserves a section of its own.

3. Faith requires wholehearted and lasting commitment. Here is another, volitional sense in which faith can be considered a passion: whereas in the confidence model faith's passion is construed as a fundamental and all-embracing quality of feeling, here faith's passion is construed as a fundamental and all-consuming "choice" or "decision" to follow a way of life—a commitment that is wholehearted and lasting.[121]

The commitment is wholehearted because it involves the whole of the self, or at least the major and essential sides of the devotee's soul. All (important) aspects of S's personality are energized by this commitment, all are bent by S's will to the end of following this way of life, and all achieve some measure of fulfillment in living this way of life.[122] All faculties, dispositions, capacities, and abilities of S are oriented and hence subordinated to S's living this way of life, but they are also enrolled in such a life. No faculty should tug in a contrary direction, but neither should any faculty remain completely dormant or unused.[123]

The commitment is lasting because it encompasses the entire (remaining) temporal span of the devotee's life—it cannot be a fitfully sporadic attempt, much less a single episode. Such a commitment

121. The use of "choice" or "decision" signals faith's volitional roots, but these terms can be misleading. Choice and decision are episodic, occurrent, seriatim, whereas faith requires an "act" of will that is also enduring, dispositional, and continuous. I therefore use "commitment" as the more encompassing term. See C. S. Evans, 1985, chap. 8.

122. It is not a necessary part of this model that in such wholehearted commitment to a way of life all (major, important) sides of the soul receive complete fulfillment, or even greater fulfillment than they could possibly receive in following any other way of life. Such claims have been made on behalf of some conceptions of faith, but it is hard to see how they could be substantiated. No way of life can fulfill all of one's potentialities, for they are not compossibly actual. Devotion to a way of life therefore involves loss, or at any rate the lack of opportunity to develop some other talents to their fullest—opportunity which may be available in another way of life.

123. Of course, this is the ideal, rarely if ever fully achieved in practice, where one usually finds only varying degrees of approximation to wholeheartedness. Some devotees are more committed than others, and possibly none is committed in a completely wholehearted way.

need not be made at or by any particular age in life, and some may spend all or most of their lives without making such a commitment. Still, faith's commitment is lifelong in the sense that once undertaken it lasts for the remainder of the devotee's life qua devotee.[124] This does not mean that the level of commitment is unvarying, for there will be volitional ups and downs; nor does it mean that the commitment cannot be lost altogether, for devotion may die; it simply means that the commitment remains while there is any devotion at all. A life-lasting commitment is the only appropriate response to the demands of a way of life: Just as a way of life patterns a whole and complete life, so a devotee must endeavor to make complete the whole of her life lived in conformity or approximation to that pattern.

4. Faith requires perseverance. Faith not only lasts, it perseveres. To persevere is to live resolutely, resisting the inertia of inaction, as well as to prevail against obstacles, overcoming forces in opposition to one's will.

Faith on the devotion model requires resolute action. Instead of merely drifting—which is less than just waiting, or even continuing to continue[125]—devotion involves creative response to the forces and events that impinge on one. Even acquiescing in attractive influences is a matter of choice, since accepting these influences entails not accepting and even not seeking competing attractions or demands. Faith as devotion, then, is a resolute effort of will, often a strenuous effort, to shape not just some but all actions and reactions into accordance with a way of life, so as to live that way of life. To exercise such resolution throughout one's life is to live what some have called an "intentional life." An intentional life is more than a life each of whose constituent actions are lived intentionally; it is a life wherein the shape, significance, and tendency of all that one does are expressions of one's intentional choice.

But faith on the devotion model requires more than resolution; it requires perseverance against obstacles. It is not just that one must resolve to follow this as opposed to that path, but that one must

124. This is the devotion model's analogue to the (conditional) imperturbability of the confidence model.

125. Waiting "for Godot" is no mere waiting. Indeed, perhaps there is no such thing as "mere waiting," if waiting is always waiting for something or someone.

resist and overcome forces that oppose one's will while one is following this path. There are many kinds of obstacles: the attractiveness of incompatible alternatives, the difficulty and danger of the way, the inadequacies of one's resources, the opposition by others, the riskiness of a course of action, or even a whole way of life. But there is no faith, on the devotion model, without such obstacles to be overcome through persevering voluntary action. Without obstacles there may be persistence (or inertial movement) but there will not be perseverance.

5. The major opposites of faith are impotence, ignorance, and irresolution. There are of course many ways of construing opposites of faith on the devotion model; each of the conditions mentioned above, and their subconditions, might be removed or replaced in turn. Moreover, there is a sense in which devotion to any way of life is the opposite of devotion to any other, insofar as following one precludes following the other (in a rational way). Nevertheless the three features of impotence, ignorance, and irresolution capture, I think, the major contraries of devotion: S may fail to choose W voluntarily (as a result of impotence or ignorance) or S may fail to be sufficiently committed to W (irresolution, encompassing several distinct kinds of failure).[126]

S may fail to choose W voluntarily because S is *impotent*, that is, because S is unable to choose W. It is not that S is unaware of W or unattracted to W, but that S lacks the ability to choose W. Such impotence does not entail that S does not follow W; other persons (or accident) may see to it that S does live according to W—but still, S does not choose W because S cannot, even though S would choose W if S could. S's impotence may be generic (inability to choose any way of life) or specific (inability to choose this or that way of life), and may last for a shorter or longer period of time. Further, S may possess the power to choose but lack the opportunity to exercise it (on this occasion or even for a life), or S may lack

126. Note that these opposites have to do with some lack, failure, or deficiency on the part of S, not on the part of W. This is because deficiencies in W (so long as W is a way of life and not some more limited project) do not prevent S from being devoted to that way of life; they simply render S's devotion irrational or otherwise unsatisfactory. But such kind of irrational devotion is still faith. Further, recall that rejecting all ways of life and not choosing any way of life are ruled out, so long as a person is able to choose among open ways of life.

both ability and hence opportunity for exercise (in which case S is hardly a self at all). The important point is that simply following or even living a way of life does not guarantee that one has faith, for S may not be able not to follow that way. If S is unable to choose a way of life, following that way of life in however accurate a manner cannot be faith on the devotion model.

S may fail to choose W voluntarily because S is *ignorant,* that is, because S does not know to choose W. It is not that S finds W unattractive or that S is unable to choose W, but rather that S is not aware of W as a possibility (indeed, an open alternative) for S. Perhaps S would choose W if S knew about it, but S is crucially ignorant. Such ignorance may be wholesale (S knows nothing of W) or retail (S lacks knowledge of certain aspects of W); it may be momentary or more lasting. Although wholesale ignorance of W cripples voluntary choice of W, not all retail ignorance does so; for example, S might not know some inessential details of W, or might know only the first essential steps one must take in order to acquire more essential knowledge later, or might know later but not earlier steps. Moreover, S's crippling ignorance may be either of W or of S. S might be unaware of certain features of W that would (if known by S) make W attractive to S, or S might be aware of these features but still not realize that these features are indeed attractive to herself.

S may be *irresolute,* that is, S may fail to be committed to W. Such irresolution takes many forms. S's devotion may be partial and tentative (less than wholehearted), fitful and fleeting (less than lasting), timid and tepid (less than resolute), or faltering and diffident (less than persevering). It may lack full or effective self-control, and may seldom if ever be reaffirmed. A wavering, halfhearted, weak commitment is not devotion but dalliance or hedging one's bets.

Most of these points seem obvious, but something should be added about lack of perseverance. Surely someone who quickly tires of following a way of life lacks faith in it, but what about someone who finds it easy to follow a way of life, who does not have to struggle against obstacles: Does such a person also lack devotion? Such a question may seem impertinent, for whether there are obstacles appears to lie beyond the person's control, whereas devotion seems a voluntary choice within a person's control. But the matter is more complicated. Not all obstacles as such are beyond S's control, and control is not all there is to devotion.

On the first point, many obstacles, insofar as they are obstacles, lie somewhat within a person's control. Temptations, for instance, seem to come from outside the self, but they require a temptee as well as (even more than?) a tempter: S is given or finds temptations along the way, but it is up to S to allow them to tempt, to find them tempting, to be tempted by them, and all this is (relatively) within S's control. Absence of obstacles such as temptations, therefore, is at least partially under S's control, and may indeed (partially) flow from S's perseverance instead of occurring independently of it. Sometimes absence of obstacles is a sign of faith.

On the second point, faith also sometimes lies beyond S's control, to a greater or lesser extent. Traditional theistic doctrines of grace have always recognized this point (although they have tended to lean too far in the other direction, ascribing all control to the object of faith), but it may be made independently of theism.[127] Just as the ability and knowledge necessary for S to choose W may be lacking or compromised, so may S's commitment—through no fault of S's own. We often think of our commitments as entirely within our own control, but this need not be the case. We may find ourselves committed more or less fully than we have chosen. One way in which this may occur, surprisingly enough, is also where obstacles to commitment have never presented themselves due to factors beyond one's control. (Perhaps S, living in a homogenous community in an isolated region, has never seen or vividly imagined anyone pursuing another way of life.) If following W has in this way always been easy for S, then S's powers of perseverance may never have had the opportunity to develop fully. In such a case, S might follow W fairly closely, but would not continue to do so if (externally presented) obstacles were to arise; hence S would lack perseverance and therefore not have faith on the devotion model.

Someone who does not have to persevere against obstacles in following a way of life may be said to be devoted to (or to have faith in) that way only if the person would persevere if there were

---

127. Indeed, the point extends beyond the devotion model of faith. All models allow for at least the possibility that acquiring and retaining faith is not simply the responsibility of the subject of faith. This is clearest, perhaps, on the personal relationship model (where the authority, A, plays a vital causal role in bringing about the relationship), but it is just as true of the other models.

externally presented obstacles and the fact that there are no internally generated obstacles is under S's control.

To recapitulate: According to the devotion model, faith is living a whole and complete way of life which one has chosen voluntarily (freely, knowingly, without coercion, and responsibly) and to which one is wholeheartedly and lastingly committed, living resolutely and persevering against obstacles, thereby avoiding the pitfalls of impotence, ignorance, and irresolution.


## F. The Hope Model

Once again a new feature is central, giving a distinctive cast to our final model of faith. Faith on the hope model is not personal relationship, propositional or prepropositional attitude, feeling-quality, or volition; it is the deeply rooted, heartfelt desire for some important future good.[128] As a standard locution for this model I use "S has faith in G" (where 'G' names the good desired), though at times it will be more convenient to use "S has faith that G" or even, rather artificially, "S has faith for G." An outline account of this model is as follows:[129]

> S has faith$_H$ in G only if G is a supreme, future, apparent good that S greatly desires and confidently awaits, anticipates, and expects, despite G's improbability.

1. The object of faith is a supreme, future, apparent good. Each of these features is treated separately, and there are several loose ends in our account, but ultimately all features must be combined.

The object of faith is an *apparent good*. Apparent goods are person-relative[130] and primarily correlative to desire:[131] G is an apparent

128. Here is a third sense in which faith may be thought a "passion." Desiring is not the same as feeling or willing, however intimately they may be related.

129. This model partially resembles but significantly differs from accounts of faith offered by Muyskens, 1979, and Pojman, 1986b; see Chap. 4, sec. D below for a fuller treatment of their particular conceptions.

130. Although the present account is restricted to persons, arguably it could be extended further: to all sentient or conscious beings, or perhaps even to all life-forms. Doing so, however, would add unnecessary complications.

131. Apparent goods as the proper objects of faith on the hope model are not

good if and only if G seems good to S (that is, to some particular person or other); and G seems good to S if and only if S desires G. Hence, every apparent good contains an implicit reference to the person who desires it: G is good to S. By "desire" I mean minimally a person's attraction to some actual or potential object: S desires G just when S is attracted to G or when S finds G attractive.

Apparent good is contrasted with real good. The hope model is not committed to any particular account of real good; it does not even require that there be real goods. All that is needed is a contrast with the notion of apparent good.[132] This contrast may be elaborated in either of two ways: Real goods are not person-relative, at least not relative to particular persons: G is good whether any particular person (or even all persons, save a divine person) desires G.[133] Or, real goods are good overall, whereas apparent goods are good only prima facie or in a limited respect.[134]

Apparent goods cannot exist independently of particular persons; an apparent good is always good to someone, the person who desires it. However, an apparent good need not be, nor be thought to be, good for the one(s) to whom it is good. The beneficiary and the subject of an apparent good may differ; what S desires to have or obtain (even for the sake of S) need not be something that in fact benefits S. Further, present desire for a future apparent good is not the same as future desire for a (then) present apparent good. The G that S desires now may when obtained turn out not to satisfy S's desires then, that is, S may no longer want G, or may then want something else more than G.

What sorts of things are apparent goods? Since an apparent good is an object of desire, the question becomes: What sorts of things

only desired but also awaited, anticipated, and expected. What is said in this section concerns only such goods qua desired; not all of these features need carry over to them qua awaited, etc.

132. Even so, our treatment of apparent good is compatible with an account of (and commitment to the existence of) real good such as that of Rawls, 1971, chap. 7. Rawls notes (400, n. 2) that he is following a rich tradition stemming back at least to Aristotle's *Nicomachean Ethics*.

133. Real goods in this sense need not be totally independent of desires. Rawls, 1971, for example, defines real good in terms of what it is rational to want or desire, but rationality itself is not a function of desire.

134. In this sense real goods may also (but need not) be person-relative: G may be a real good for S precisely because S does (or would) desire G, all things considered, whether S is aware of this fact.

are objects of desire? Here we encounter a peculiarity of ordinary English usage that is unexpectedly consequential. Contrary to the way many philosophers talk,[135] it would be odd in ordinary English to say something like "S desires that p"—as if desires were ordinary propositional attitudes and apparent goods were propositions or the extensions of propositions. In ordinary usage, persons do not desire *propositions*, nor do they desire the truth of propositions, that propositions are true, that it is the case that a proposition is true, or anything of the kind. If Jane wants the cat on the mat, she does not desire the proposition that the cat is or will be or should be on the mat, nor that it is true that the cat is (etcetera) on the mat, nor that it is the case that the cat is (etcetera) on the mat. Rather, what persons desire are actual or possible entities: things, persons, events, states of affairs. If a "that-" clause should go with "desire" at all, it must be conveyed subjunctively: the desire that a proposition be true, that a state of affairs obtain, that an event occur, that something exist, and so forth.

Now let us suppose that it is possible to translate all uses of "desire for" entities into some kind of "desire that + (subjunctive clause)" expression. Could all of these latter subjunctive usages be collated into a single idiom containing a nonsubjunctive proposition—"S desires that p be true"—where "p" describes a state of affairs concerning S's desired object, the obtaining of which S desires? For example, could "one desires the cat on the mat" become "one desires that the cat be on the mat" and this become "one desires that it be true that the cat is on the mat," which has the form "S desires that p be true"? No. The subjunctive "p be true" is not equivalent to the indicatives "p is true" or "p will be true" or even "p should be true." In fact, "p be true" is really not a proposition at all, unlike "p is true" and "p will be true." Hence, desire is unlike propositional attitudes such as believe, know, think, and contemplate. S may believe that p or that p is true, though not that p be true; but S can only desire that p be true, and not that p or that p is true.

This may seem heavy laboring over a triviality. Why should it

135. James Muyskens holds that "S desires that p" is a necessary condition of "S hopes that p" (1979, 18). Louis Pojman is more ambiguous, claiming that "hope entails desire for the state of affairs in question to obtain or the proposition to be true" (1986b, 162); but apparently he takes "desire for a proposition to be true" to mean "desire that the proposition is true."

matter that desire takes a propositional object only subjunctively? The primary consequence, I believe, is this. Desire, which affirms that p be true, implies a different kind of attitude toward p than standard propositional attitudes, such as belief, which affirm that p is true. To believe that p is to (attempt to) grasp hold of the truth of p, however firmly or weakly, with or without adequate evidence, and so forth. But to desire something is, in part, to miss or yearn for the truth of p in the absence of the truth of p; it is to do without the truth of p. So whereas belief is a (partial) fulfillment with respect to truth, desire is a (partial) lack. This lack is essentially tied, in desire, to futurity. A future entity is present only as a potential entity, and hence as an actual lack; a future good is presently lacking.

The object of faith is a *future* good. As we have just seen, the object of desire contains a present lack that is fulfilled, if at all, only in the future. There may be various present foretastes of the good—encouragements, assurances, partial glimpses, premonitions, and the like—but as desired this good is not (yet) fully realized.[136] Such futurity is central to faith as hope, but it is either missing or not as pronounced in other models of faith: Trust points to the past as the ground of authority, belief need have no future relevance, confidence takes no thought of the morrow, and so on. Of course, all six models do tend to think of faith as a deeply settled disposition that persists through time—lasting, enduring, even persevering—but there is not the hope model's insistence on the future as the essential domain of faith.

Faith's object is a *supreme* good. A supreme good is more than an ordinary object of desire. At the minimum it is a good that transcends the ordinary run of particular apparent goods, by being desired more intensely or in a different and incommensurable way. For example, a state of mystical unitive bliss is often held to be more attractive than any number or kinds of ordinary dualistic experiences, or at any rate to be incommensurably attractive in comparison with them. At a higher level, a supreme good not only transcends ordinary goods but also encompasses or includes them, by providing for their satisfaction in its satisfaction. For example, happiness, Aristotelian *eudaimonia*, and self-actualization are often

---

136. "Fully realized" here includes realizing all of G, realizing all aspects or dimensions of G, realizing a higher or more desirable form of G, and so on.

held to encompass and satisfy most of the major desires of a person. Transcendence and encompassing are independent of each other. A transcendent good may exclude instead of encompass other goods, and an encompassing good need not transcend the goods it encompasses. Any supreme apparent good for S must at least transcend, and preferably should also encompass, many or all of the ordinary apparent goods for S.

Further, G is supreme in the sense of being desired by S at the highest level on balance or overall; G is supreme to S in that, all things considered, S desires nothing more than G. We may say that G is, to S, an unsurpassed good. It does not follow, however, that G is therefore necessarily unsurpassable, in fact or in thought, or necessarily unique or existent. These points deserve further explication.

While there is a threshold of desire for apparent goods to count as supreme goods, there is no upper bound on how great a supreme good can or must be. Different goods will be considered supreme by different persons at the same or different times, or even by the same person at different times. A good such as the Kingdom of God, which transcends and encompasses most of the ordinary goods for S, may be desired more highly by S than S's own good alone. But this need not be the case. S may hold out hope only for herself, or only for a few friends. For such a private good, others need not apply—even though there may well be a higher good (apparent even to S) that includes this private good and much else (for example, others' goods as well). A good that is in fact supreme to S need not be unsurpassably good.

G need not be unsurpassable in thought, that is, the highest good that S can imagine or conceive. A good that is actually supreme to S may differ from a higher good that S can imagine but does not think is plausible or likely enough to merit strong desire. For example, S might admit that a good including sheep and goats is better than one including only sheep (herself and other right-thinking sorts), but may think only the latter is actual, or stands any chance of being actual, or at any rate is what S really wants.

There is no uniqueness clause. S may desire more than one (apparent) supreme good. Two goods—even two incompatible goods—might be ranked equally highly by S, and S might pursue either or both of them, perhaps at different times, with equal intensity and seriousness. That G is a supreme good to S does not imply that G is the only actual or possible good that is supreme to S.

Neither is there an existence clause. There need be no good that is supreme to S at all; it may be that all of the goods S desires are just particular, ordinary, and humdrum, with no transcendent or encompassing desires among them. This might be the case even if there is some deep-rooted and universal human desire for the transcendent,[137] for such a desire need not be expressed or effective in S's life.

Why must the object of faith be a supreme good? Why cannot nonsupreme goods serve as well? The answer is that supremacy of the object of desire is what distinguishes the hope that constitutes faith from the hope that does not. Ordinary hopes for ordinary goods typically do not generate the requisite strength of desire and expectation to constitute faith. An ordinary apparent good just is not good enough—neither transcending nor encompassing—to inspire the necessary fervor of faith; only a supreme good will do.

Quite often, but not always, the object of hope is a good *promised* by another, toward which hope is the appropriate or justified response. A good promised is another's assurance that a future good will be realized. While hope may originate or be energized as a desiring response to such a promise, it need not do so; it is possible that S first imagines G and only thereby becomes attracted to it. Similarly, a promise is often a (vital) clue to the likelihood or possibility of some good; were G not promised to S by another, S might not consider G to be possible, likely, or worth taking seriously. But, again, this is not necessarily the case, for S might also become convinced of G's possibility quite independently of another's promise; the object of hope need not be a promised good.

While most objects of desire are *possible*, not all are. Perhaps a completely rational person would not tolerate inconsistent (and therefore impossible) objects of desire, but few actual persons are so intolerant. As just one example among many, who among us has not quickened to the commercial jingle "Who says you can't have it all?" Impossible dreams are indeed possible—not in the sense

137. See Saint Augustine's famous claim: "Our hearts are restless until they rest in Thee," *Confessions*, 1.1.

that they can be realized but in the sense that they do occur and energize behavior, occasionally even consuming entire lives. Still, a skeptic might insist that at least S must believe or think that S's object of desire is possible, even if it is not: How could S go on desiring something S thinks is impossible (whether or not it really is impossible)? Once again, this condition seems more an ideal for completely rational persons than a description of how real persons actually live. Some people, at least, pursue dreams that they acknowledge to be impossible, even in the full glare of rational scrutiny. It may be irrational to do this, but it is not impossible. So, according to the hope model, the object of faith, insofar as it is an object of desire,[138] does not need to be, nor need it be thought to be, possible.

2. The faithful person greatly desires this good. Since goods are the objects of desire, and nothing is desired more than a supreme good, it may seem analytic to hold that a supreme good is greatly desired. But this is not the case, for the strength of S's desire for G may vary independently of G's supremacy as a good to G; even a transcendent or an encompassing good need not be greatly desired. To see this point, assume that S has a lukewarm (or even icy) temperament, such that there is nothing that S desires very much at all; S does not even strongly desire to satisfy all of (the rest of) S's desires. A supreme good to S is a nonordinary good than which S desires nothing more. Now if S desires anything at all strongly enough for it to count as an object of hope, and if S desires any supreme good, then S must desire a supreme good strongly enough to count as an object of hope, since nothing is desired more than a supreme good. But since, we are supposing, S desires nothing very strongly, S does not desire even a supreme good (if any) very strongly, and so none of S's tepid desires may be strong enough to qualify as faith according to the hope model.

What, then, counts as "greatly desires"? What is it to "desire strongly enough"? Clearly such desire is the opposite of idle wishing, and it is considerably more than lukewarm preference. More than this, the desire should equal or exceed in strength any other desire

138. The qualification is crucial; S must believe that G is possible insofar as G is an object of expectation.

of that person, for that is what it means for something to be (desired as) a supreme good. It is difficult to be more precise than this. There seem to be two ways of measuring strength of desire: first, via the intensity of feeling aroused by satisfaction and/or frustration of a desire; second, via behavioral tendencies of a desire, especially in energizing a wide range of persistent behaviors to overcome obstacles. There are problems with these measures. As we have seen, persons differ in general level and range of strength of desire. Would even the strongest desire of an icy-tempered person be strong enough to constitute faith? Here the feeling-intensity criterion may diverge from the behavioral-tendency criterion: The strongest desire may generate only tepid feelings but wide-ranging and persistent behaviors. Both criteria are intrapersonal at best. One would like to be able to find, or stipulate, some minimum interpersonal threshold, but this seems impossible, as there is no universal coinage of desire.[139] For these and other reasons, therefore, we must be content to leave the meaning of "greatly desires" somewhat vague and imprecise; this means that there will inevitably be borderline cases where we will not, and cannot, be sure that faith is present or absent.

3. The good is improbable. The probability in question is a "subjective" one: G (or G's obtaining) is not probable for S, with respect to S's knowledge, beliefs, or information, and the good that is not probable relative to one person may be probable or improbable for another person. Broadly, then: G is not probable so far as S's evidence goes (including S's self-evidence). It does not follow, nor is it precluded, that, on S's evidence, the negation of G (not-G, or G's not obtaining) is certain for S. On the evidence S has, G's obtaining may have any degree of probability less than .5; whatever the probability of G, it cannot exceed, or even equal, that of not-G on the same basis. Hence we may say that G's obtaining is evidentially insufficient or theoretically unjustified for S. If S hopes for G, S cannot be in a position to know, or even justifiably to believe, that G will obtain (more probably than not), on the basis of the evidence available to S. S's epistemic status with respect to believing that G

139. There are analogous, or even identical, problems for utilitarians in gaining interpersonal absolute measures of utility (e.g., "hedons"), as opposed to intrapersonal relative measures (e.g., S's preferences).

will obtain is therefore less than ideal, although it may be the best that S can do under the circumstances.

Lack of theoretical justification means that there is an ineradicable element of risk in faith according to the hope model. The risk is not only the theoretical possibility of being mistaken in one's beliefs; more important are the practical stakes. In hoping for G, one is committing oneself to acting and living in a certain way, a way that is appropriate if G does (eventually) obtain but a waste of time and energy—or worse—if G does not obtain. In the extreme, one may stake an entire life on awaiting, anticipating, and expecting this good.

Finally, it is important to note that S may be aware or unaware of faith's improbability. Many persons of hope are no doubt unaware of the theoretical and practical risks involved in their faith because they are self-deceived, lax, dull, or just plain ignorant (excusably or not). But there is an additional risk in such unaware faith: It is unstable. Unstable faith is faith that can be undermined, often easily, by confrontation with evidence or by honest self-scrutiny. It is of course quite possible to live a life of self-deception (Who does not, in some way or other, deceive oneself with regard to some aspects of one's life?); but a life of self-deceptive faith carries the burden of maintaining a large and central self-deception, a task that requires substantial investments of energy in averting one's gaze from the facts of the matter (the facts as one would see them if one honestly looked). Still, not all faith as hope need be unstable; it is also possible for S to become and remain aware of the improbabilities involved in her faith but nevertheless to continue to have this faith. Such faith is stable, capable of withstanding honest self-scrutiny in light of present and future available evidence.[140]

4. The faithful person confidently awaits, anticipates, and expects the desired good in the face of its improbability. Despite all the theoretical and practical risks, S remains confident in awaiting, anticipating and expecting G (that is, G's obtaining), just because S so strongly desires G.[141]

140. Such stability would play an important role in any defense of the rationality of faith on the hope model, but I do not venture such a defense here.
141. My treatment in this section differs importantly from Muyskens, 1979, and

S is *confident* about G in the face of G's improbability. Such confidence displays many of the same qualities depicted in the confidence
model of faith. S is in a conscious state characterized by a persistent,
enduring, deep feeling of serenity, tranquility, calm, peace, and the
like. But hope is a relational state, not a nonrelational one, since the
confidence of hope is directed toward an object (an apparent supreme
good). Moreover, the elements of self-confidence and imperturbability may be muted or possibly absent, and hope occurs in the face
of (theoretical and practical) improbability, whether or not this improbability is acknowledged.

Confidence about G may also be characterized as being strongly
convinced, even to the point of feeling certain, that G will obtain.
Once again, "feeling certain" should not be confused with "being
certain." Being certain is a normative epistemic concept, a matter
of S being in the best possible epistemic condition in a certain situation (for example, where S's belief that p has the highest degree
of evidence possible for S). Feeling certain, on the other hand, is a
descriptive psychological concept, a matter of S being strongly and/
or thoroughly convinced (for example, where S tenaciously clings
to the belief that p). Faith as hope requires being confident but
precludes being certain.

Finally, there is a definite source for S's confidence on this model
of faith: S's strong desire for G. S confidently expects G just because
S so greatly desires G—even while (recognizing that) G is improbable. This makes S's confidence seem like wishful (irrational) thinking, and so it may be, but not necessarily. Although the matter is
too complicated to pursue here,[142] it seems at least possible for S to
be justifiably confident though not evidentially warranted in expecting G under some such conditions as the following: Neither G
nor non-G is certain; S's evidence for and against G is absent or
nearly equally balanced; S is correctly aware of S's evidential situation (S is not epistemically self-deceived); S is justified in believing
that G is at least possible; S's confidence about G does not sacrifice
any greater good; S's desire is stable; and so on.

S *awaits* G. Awaiting a good is a matter of being ready for the

---

Pojman, 1986b, especially in not precluding belief that G will obtain while retaining
the disposition to act appropriately to such a belief.

142. Moral arguments for theism may be viewed as attempts to justify confident
theistic beliefs on nonevidential grounds. See Sessions, 1982, 1985.

good by being disposed to welcome the good whenever (if ever) it should obtain. In faith as hope, such a disposition is not a superficial trait or habit but something deeply rooted and persistent in S's character. S confidently awaits G by keeping this disposition fresh and vivid, so that it can blossom into joy when and if the good arrives. S is therefore patient, "standing by" until G obtains without losing S's strong desire for G—awaiting is a matter of not losing heart.

S *anticipates* G. Anticipation means taking whatever present steps or actions one can, in order to (help) bring it about that a future good will obtain.[143] There is a present behavioral component to hope. In being confident about G, S is more than a patient person waiting to respond; S is also an active agent whose desires are shown in dispositions to act as well as to react. S seeks to obtain as well as to await G, so far as (S believes) that lies within S's power. There may be little or nothing that S can do to bring about G, and what S can do may remain unknown or unclear to S. Yet insofar as S sees that an action or line of action lying within S's power would help to obtain G, S will be strongly disposed to undertake such action, and S will also be disposed to search out and learn about such actions.

S *expects* G. To expect a future good minimally implies confidence that it is possible for this good to obtain in the future, that this good can obtain. But does this confidence extend also to the proposition that this good will obtain? Does S's confidence amount to a belief that G will obtain?[144] For those philosophers who think that S's beliefs are only involuntary products of how S assesses the available evidence, there can be no honest (non-self-deceived) belief that G will obtain, since by hypothesis the evidence goes against G's obtaining. Their view does not even seem to permit S to be confident

143. As Jim Keller reminds me, there is another behavioral sense of "anticipates": S acts now in a way appropriate to G's obtaining—"as if " G had already obtained—even though G does not now obtain and acting so does (and perhaps can do and is intended to do) little if anything to bring G about. Apocalyptic movements occasionally urge this kind of anticipatory behavior as a way of experiencing the eschaton in the present. But such behavior is not clearly a matter of hope; it is more living "in the light of " G as a (subjunctive) present reality rather than looking forward to G as a (potential) future reality.

144. Muyskens, 1979, and Pojman, 1986b, bend over backwards in attempting to have belief that G is possible without belief that G will obtain; to have, as they express it, hope without belief. Their views are considered in Chap. 4, sec. D.

that G will obtain: Confidence implies belief, beliefs are tied to evidence assessment, and evidence is insufficient for belief. But the hope model of faith partially disconnects belief from (available, assessed) evidence and so is able to view S's expectation of G as S's confident belief that G will obtain, a belief which is produced and maintained not by evidence but by S's desire for G and which can withstand scrutiny and knowledge of its desirous roots.

Still, there may be other reasons for thinking that faith on the hope model should not require expectation as confident belief. Could S strongly desire G without expecting G (to obtain) at all, much less confidently believing G will obtain? And could (belief in) G's nonoccurence fuel S's desire for G: Absence (or improbable appearance) makes the heart grow fonder? But these reasons fail to dislodge the proposed condition. Strongly desiring G without expecting G at all is mere idle wishing, and hence not faith; desiring G without confidently expecting G is not strongly desiring G, and hence not faith; and desiring G because G is not expected is a form of despair, not a kind of faith.

On the first point, if S strongly desires G but does not expect G at all, then not only must S believe, however weakly, that G is not likely (or is unlikely) to obtain but also S must either not believe that G will obtain or else believe that G will not obtain. But to desire G while either not believing G will obtain or believing G will not obtain is to have an idle wish for G. Faith is not idle wishing.

On the second point, if S desires G but does not confidently expect G, then either S does not expect G at all, which is once again only idle wishing, or else S expects G but not confidently, that is, S expects G with a lack or defect of confidence. Lack or defect of confidence in expecting a good can be due to either of two factors: lack or defect of evidence supporting the likelihood of the good, or lack or low degree of strength of desire for the good expected. In faith on the hope model, evidence is necessarily lacking or defective (S cannot be certain of G), so if S does not confidently expect G it can only be because S does not strongly desire G. But, as we have seen, S must strongly desire G in order to have faith. In order to have faith, S must confidently expect G because S strongly desires G.

On the third point, no doubt some people do desire goods (solely? in large part?) because these goods are unobtainable, or believed to be so—where S not only does not expect G to obtain but in fact expects G not to obtain. But why should such desires be considered hope or faith? They seem rather a subtle form of despair. Wanting what you believe (or know) you cannot have is not "hoping against hope" but rather not hoping at all. It is as if what S really wants is not G itself (which S believes will not or cannot obtain) but rather being in a state of wanting G; the hope, if any, is not for the good itself but for one's own desire for the good. Such desires provide no reason to remove the condition of expectation (as confident belief) from the hope model of faith.

It should be noted, however, that S's confident expectation of G's obtaining does not necessarily include any very definite expectation of when, where, how, or by what means G will obtain. Of course one may also expect these things, but this is, as it were, surplus expectation. In order to expect a future good, no one need be in a position to know the time and place of its coming, or even its means, cause, or purpose. Confident expectation is compatible with confident awaiting. S believes G will obtain, and awaits and anticipates its obtaining.

5. The opposites of faith are despair, evidential assurance, hesitancy, and dread. All four conditions oppose faith by canceling out, in different ways, the strong desire for a supreme future good that is at the heart of faith according to the hope model.

To *despair* of a good is not, or no longer, to desire it strongly enough: Despair is hopelessness or hope-lost-ness. The desire may be absent or lost altogether, or may be weakened or diffuse, or, as we have just seen, its loss or diminution may be concealed under apparent desire. In all these cases, S lacks faith's requisite strong desire. Causes of this lack or loss of strong desire vary greatly, but there are three prominent sources for many people: coming to think that G is not (or is no longer) possible, coming to think that G will not obtain, and acquiring new desires contrary to G (that is, desires for goods one believes to be incompatible with G or with desire for G). The completely lukewarm temperament discussed earlier is therefore a form of despair, and so are idle wishing and desire based on improbability and impossibility.

Strangely enough, *evidential assurance* is also opposed to hope, insofar as evidence is the sole or fundamental basis for one's confidence in the desired good's obtaining. By "evidential assurance" I mean being confident on the basis of the weight of one's evidence (subjective probability). Such assurance displays a lack or loss of hope to the extent that one would not be confident on any nonevidential basis, such as desire. One simply does not desire the good strongly enough to have faith, according to this model. S cannot have faith in G where S's confident expectation of G's obtaining is due solely or fundamentally to the probability of G on S's evidence, for then not only would S not expect G were the evidence otherwise but also so long as G is probable S runs little epistemic risk in expecting G.[145] In faith as hope, S should be confident of G (solely or fundamentally) on the basis of strongly desiring G, not on the basis of G's evidential probability.[146]

*Hesitancy* where decisive and confident action is called for likewise represents a lack of faith because desire for a good is not strong enough. To hesitate when action needs to be taken with respect to G (for example, in awaiting, anticipating, and expecting G) is to act as if G were not secure. It is not so much a lack of faith as a betrayal of faith, a betrayal of the supreme good by desiring it so weakly that its supremacy is lost or compromised.

To *dread* something good is to fear it because of its (perceived) connections—as cause, effect, concomitant, or condition—with something as bad as G is good, or perhaps even worse. It is not so much that one does not desire G (or ceases to desire it) as that one's desire for G is overcome by a stronger, or qualified by an equal, aversion to something bad connected with G. Desire for G once again proves to be insufficiently strong to constitute hope.

---

145. Could S be confident of G, have adequate evidence for G's obtaining, yet not base this confidence on the evidence available? Since having adequate evidence is a normative epistemic condition and being confident is a descriptive psychological state, it does seem possible for the two to be present independently of one another. But it would be a strangely bifurcated self in which this occurred: Either S would not be aware of his own evidential condition and/or confidence about G, or else if S were aware of both he would find it odd that his confidence is not based on his evidence when it both could and should be so based.

146. Of course it is only being confident on the basis of evidence and not being confident per se, that is incompatible with faith on the hope model. Being confident per se is in fact required by this model, but only as otherwise based—on desire, not on evidence.

To recapitulate: According to the hope model, faith is strongly future-oriented. It is a matter of deep yearning for some supreme, future, apparent good—fervently awaiting, anticipating, and expecting it—where the occurrence of that good is not subjectively probable. Its opposites are lack of a sufficiently strong desire for the future good (despair, hesitancy, dread) or denial of its improbability (evidential assurance).

# [ 3 ]

# The Models Compared

We have now explored the structures of six different models of faith deeply enough to enable us to examine some further issues about the models together. These issues first arise concerning the various relations among the models, one to another, next extend to the models' relations to particular conceptions of faith, and then concern the models' relations to the overall concept of faith. In addition, there are implications for the relations of conceptions of faith to the concept of faith and to the quest for a category of faith.

## A. Relations of Models to Models

There are many different kinds of relations among the models. This account considers five such relations, all of them fundamental: difference, commonality, consistency, completeness, and structure.

1. Difference. Some differences among the models are merely apparent, more a matter of emphasis and exposition than of substance. Such apparent differences occur because no model of faith is as rich as a fully developed conception; each model highlights a few interrelated features of faith, but in doing so it inevitably obscures or omits other features that are prominent or at least present

in other models.[1] Features that are not mentioned or not prominent in a model are not necessarily features that are excluded or precluded from that model. For example, propositional belief is at the forefront of the belief model, while it is subordinate in the personal relationship model and absent from the attitude model. However, neither of the latter treatments precludes propositional belief from accompanying, being compatible with, or even being somewhat useful to faith that exemplifies either model.

A closer look at this example is instructive. Clearly a certain sort of propositional belief (with conviction, inadequate evidence, and a nonevidential basis) is essentially required by faith on the belief model; that is what the belief model is all about. In the personal relationship model, propositional belief is also present, but subordinately. S must believe certain propositions about A ("articles of faith") in order to be in a trusting personal relationship with A, but these propositional beliefs are grounded in S's trust of A. If S did not trust A, S would not believe those propositions, or would not believe them in the same way, with the same kind of intensity and persistency. In the attitude model, however, propositional belief is not even mentioned; instead, a prepropositional attitude that is radically constitutive, fundamental, totalizing, and significant takes center stage. Nevertheless, propositional belief is not ruled out by being left out; it is at least an open question whether propositional beliefs are necessary or useful in expressing, carrying through, and living with such an attitude. At the very minimum, propositional belief is permitted in faith according to the attitude model. Apparent differences among the models may be less significant—or significant in more complicated ways—than meets the eye.

Still, there are differences among the models that are real, not merely apparent, and some of these are fundamental and important. Such deep differences occur especially when one model requires, and another proscribes, a certain feature. It also occurs when one model says a certain feature is essential to faith while another holds it to be optional. In the following section I look at six apparent differences among the models, and attempt to determine which of them are real and deep.

What looks to be the most fundamental kind of difference concerns

---

1. This is what I earlier called "conceptual chiaroscuro."

the logical structure of a concept of faith: Does faith have an object or not? Recall that "object" is used here in a purely logical or formal sense; it does not imply materiality, being a thing (as opposed to a person), or even objectification. It simply is a way of indicating whether faith is *relational*—requiring a relation between a subject of faith and something distinguishable, though not necessarily separable, from that subject. Of the six models, five require such logical objects; only the confidence model prohibits there being an object of faith.[2]

This difference is not only apparent but real, and it is deep, marking a watershed in conceptions of faith. Lacking an object (being a nonrelational conception) is as essential to the confidence model as having an object (being a relational conception) is to the other five models. Any attempt to find or create an object for faith on the confidence model is not an optional addition or supplement but rather a rejection of that model as a proper conception of faith. Likewise, any attempt to remove or ignore the logically proper kind of object of faith according to the other five models is to reject that model, for according to it faith requires an object of that kind.

Among the five relational models there are five different *kinds of objects*,[3] as summarized in the following list.

| Model | Type of Object of Faith | | |
|---|---|---|---|
| Personal Relationship | A | = | Person |
| Belief | p | = | Proposition |
| Attitude | X | = | Horizoned world |
| Devotion | W | = | Way of life |
| Hope | G | = | Apparent good |

Clearly these objects appear very different; but how deep are the differences? Are some objects less fundamental than others? Can some be reduced to others? Are any two of them identical, in extension if not in intension? Are any of them incompatible? These are interesting and important, but very complicated, questions. An-

2. The standard locutions for the models express this point; the five relational models all use prepositions to speak of faith in or that or toward or for something, whereas the confidence model uses "faith" without any preposition.

3. Once again, I have tried to convey these differences in the standard locutions by using different symbols, even different kinds of symbols.

swers to them will partially depend upon one's preferred ontology and axiology.

In my view, propositions and ways of life are both abstract entities; conceivably one could regard a way of life as a (very, perhaps infinitely, complicated) proposition, though of course not every proposition is or implies a way of life. But persons, horizoned worlds, and apparent goods are not (completely) abstract entities; all three are more or less concrete. Persons are very complex particular entities; horizoned worlds are environing contexts that include both concrete particulars and such abstract features as propositions; apparent goods as such are future potentials—not present actualities but also not complete abstractions. None of these concrete entities is reducible to propositions or some other kind of abstract entity, and only an extreme commitment to ontological monism (whether of concrete particulars or abstract universals) could motivate attempting such a reduction. Persons, worlds, and apparent goods are not concrete entities of the same kind; they do not seem reducible to one another. There is, however, a certain ontological priority to persons; a horizoned world is necessarily an environing context for some person, and an apparent good is necessarily good to some person.

The differences among objects of faith are more than apparent and superficial. They represent fundamental and irreducibly different orientations in faith. But they do not necessarily represent incompatible kinds of faith; a single person can combine two or more kinds of objects in one life of faith. For example, taking the personal relationship model as our focus:[4] S might simultaneously have faith$_P$ in A (trusting in A's authority); have faith$_B$ that p (where p expresses essential propositions or articles of faith about A or S's relationship to A); have faith$_A$ toward X (the horizoned world or environing context of significance within which S trustingly relates to A and believes the appropriate articles of faith); have faith$_D$ in W (a way of life leading to communion with A, involving and expressing trust in A); and also have faith$_H$ in G (an apparent, future, supreme good—perhaps S's own ultimate happiness—to be realized through, and perhaps only through, the way of life expressing trust in A).[5]

4. Different but parallel accounts of coincidence could be constructed by focusing on any of the other four relational models.

5. It is also possible that this complex concurrence of different kinds of faith might produce or lead to S having faith$_C$, faith as a state of pure awareness char-

Not only do the five relational models have different kinds of objects; they also express different ways in which the subject is *related to those objects*. Alternatively, we might say that the different models involve different kinds of faculties or capacities on the part of the subject of faith, the expression of which involves different kinds of relations to appropriately different kinds of objects.

| Model | Type of Relation or Faculty |
|---|---|
| Personal Relationship | Trusting personal relationship |
| Belief | Propositional attitude |
| Attitude | Radically constitutive attitude |
| Devotion | Voluntary choice |
| Hope | Great desire and confident expectation |

Once again these differences are more than superficial. Attitudes differ according to how their kinds of objects differ, so that the kind of attitude a person may take toward another person is not the same as the kind of attitude the person may take toward a proposition, an environing context, a way of life, or an apparent good. Likewise, and correlatively, different faculties are exercised with respect to these different objects. Believing something (a proposition) to be true is quite distinct from voluntarily choosing something (a way of life); and both are distinct from desiring or expecting something (a future apparent good) or constituting something (a horizon of significance). Not only are these attitudes distinct, they can also occur independently of one another. The types of relations that a subject may have to an object of faith (and the correlative types of faculties that are exercised) are irreducibly different and independent.

The different types of relations and faculties are not necessarily mutually exclusive. On the contrary, just as a human person may exercise several different capacities in performing a single action (in that sense doing more than one thing at a time) and likewise may exemplify several different relations (in that sense standing in more than one kind of relation at once), so a single act of faith may combine, in many different ways, the five relational models. For

---

acterized by a deep and persistent feeling of confidence, which might then be regarded either as a desirable side effect of the fivefold relational faith or perhaps even as its consummation. But such confidence could not coexist with the other five kinds of faith, for relational and nonrelational faith are essentially different states or conditions, not merely distinct but separate experiences.

example, taking the belief model as our focus,[6] S may simultaneously believe that p (where p expresses an article of faith about, say, a way of life W); believe p on the authority of A (thereby trusting A, at least on this score); constitute a horizon of significance (embracing A and W and giving sense both to p and to the believing of p); voluntarily choose to follow W (which p partially expresses); and also greatly desire some future good (which S confidently expects to flow from, or at least to require, belief that p).[7]

There are two questions regarding the role of *propositional belief.* First, is propositional belief required by, optional for, or excluded from faith? Second, if optional, is it desirable or useful for faith? There are important differences among the six models on both questions.[8]

On the first question, three models require certain appropriate propositional beliefs as essential for faith. On the belief model, in fact, propositional belief is more than required: It is central to faith. Faith is a certain way of believing propositions (with conviction and without inadequate evidence, that is, on a nonevidential basis). Any attitude or state or activity that does not centrally involve propositional beliefs is not faith. The personal relationship model also holds that faith requires propositional belief, but here belief is subordinated to and grounded in trust. Trust in another person comes first, and even though that trust essentially involves believing certain propositions about the object of trust ("articles of faith"), these beliefs are not necessarily prominent in the trusting personal relationship. Finally, the hope model requires of faith at least the (confident) beliefs that the strongly desired, apparent, future, supreme

---

6. Once again, parallel treatments could be developed from the standpoint of any of the other four relational models.

7. To reiterate, it is possible that having this complex of relations (or jointly exercising these various faculties) may produce or lead to S having a confident state of pure awareness. But confidence exercises a capacity for feeling that not only is prepropositional but nonrelational—any presence of relational capacities or attitudes is inimical to pure awareness as such—and therefore it cannot coexist with belief and the other kinds of relational states (though it may follow or precede them). Once again the confidence model stands alone.

8. Hence the inadequacy of any account of faith that holds that propositional belief is essential or inessential to all forms of faith. This is yet one more reason why a univocal account of faith—positing a single model or universal category of faith—just will not do.

good can and will obtain, for this is part of the requisite expectation of that good. Such expectation is not entirely a matter of propositional belief, of course, for feeling and disposition to action are also involved; and expectation is not all that is involved in hoping, for desiring a good is not itself a propositional attitude. While hope requires propositional belief, it also does not make it central.

Propositional belief is not mentioned in the other three models. Reading between the lines, however, we can see that two of them permit and one prohibits such belief. Propositional belief seems to be optional in the attitude and devotion models. Although the attitude model views faith as prepropositional, there is no reason to think that its fundamental, totalizing, significance–bestowing/embracing attitude cannot also be expressed, however partially and inadequately, in propositional beliefs.[9] Likewise the devotion model at least permits the holding of beliefs that are relevant to the voluntary choice of, and perseverance in, a way of life; certainly beliefs about the nature and value of the chosen way, and about alternatives not chosen, would seem to be permitted by this model, if not quite required.[10]

The remaining model, the confidence model, excludes propositional belief from faith. Since propositional belief is or implies a relation between a subject and a (propositional) object, and since confidence is a nonrelational conscious state, such belief can play no part in faith as confidence. Indeed, it seems, no propositional attitude at all is permitted in faith on this model, for all such attitudes are or imply a relation between a subject and a proposition. Of course, propositional beliefs may be useful in engineering faith as a state of confidence in oneself or others, but they must eventually be eliminated or transcended in order actually to achieve (or in achieving) such a state.

We turn now to the second question: Is propositional belief useful to faith (and if so, useful in what ways)? Our focus must be on the two models for which propositional belief is optional, as there can

---

9. Whether it should be so expressed is another matter.

10. S's voluntary choice of and devotion to a way of life W does not entail or require propositional beliefs by S about W because S could follow W through some other means, for example, S could know how to follow W, where such "know-how" is neither reducible to nor entailed by any set of propositional beliefs.

be no question of the utility of something required or prohibited.[11] Initially it may seem that such beliefs are more useful for faith on the devotion model than for faith on the attitude model.

On the devotion model, faith is lasting, persevering, wholehearted, voluntary commitment to a way of life. Propositional beliefs are useful, though not essential, both in coming to faith and in having faith. It is conceivable that someone could learn about a way of life (and its alternatives) and how to live it from simply observing the behavior of a trusted guru (faith on the personal relationship model as a means to faith on the devotion model), without ever formulating, much less believing, propositions describing that way, its methods, aims, and pitfalls. But clearly such beliefs could often be useful, especially for a beginner, by serving both as signposts marking the way and as red flags signaling deviations from the way. Once one learns how to follow the way, propositional beliefs may seem dispensable altogether, but such is not the case. What happens is that the formerly explicit beliefs, which were useful in learning to follow the way, now become mostly implicit. Though there is no longer any need to express or reflect on those beliefs, that does not mean they are no longer present; it is just that one holds them in a different way.[12]

The utility of propositional beliefs for faith on the attitude model seems less clear. It appears that one could have, and come to have, a radically constitutive, prepropositional, fundamental, totalizing, significance–bestowing/embracing attitude toward one's environing context without expressing (or being able to express) this attitude in propositional form, and also without believing such propositions. Beliefs about the constitutive attitude, the self, and its horizon might seem not only subsequent and superfluous but also harmful to the perpetuation of the attitude, by directing attention and energy away from the horizoned world and toward the isolated proposition, thereby inverting the true priority of fundamental attitude to propositional belief. However, faith on this model does permit and indeed

11. Though in the former case one may ask various questions about how much, how many, what kinds, or in what ways, the propositional beliefs are useful.

12. Perhaps an analogy will convey these points. An expert cyclist's lack of explicit, conscious concern for propositions about the art of cycling does not mean either that he (now) has no propositional beliefs about cycling nor that these beliefs were not useful (earlier) in learning how to ride so well.

may find quite useful such propositional attitudes as beliefs toward certain propositions describing crucial features of self and context. These propositional beliefs need not be very definite or explicit (they need not form an explicit creed); but they are useful for having, maintaining, and expressing faith, according to this model. The real question of utility for this model arises not about having faith but about coming to have faith. In logical priority, propositional beliefs do not precede the constitutive attitudes they express. Still, it is possible that, for some people, propositional beliefs can be helpful in inducing a new radically constitutive attitude—perhaps by making alternative attitudes dubious or unpalatable, or by partially preparing one's mind for the completely new orientation involved in a constitutive attitude. Not all persons will be helped to glimpse a new horizon of significance by believing propositions describing that horizon, but some might be.

The six models appear to involve different *time orientations*. The hope model uniquely emphasizes futurity. According to it, the supreme apparent good that is greatly desired in faith is the obtaining of a future state of affairs that the faithful one confidently awaits, anticipates, and expects. Similarly, though less emphatically, the personal relationship and the devotion models are tied to the past. On the former, faith self-consciously views itself as having been brought about and being currently sustained by its object, the trusted authority; on the latter, S has faith only through some previous (and currently reaffirmed) voluntary choice. The other models are much more present-oriented. Believing, having confidence, and having a constitutive attitude focus on a present state or act of consciousness.

These differences are merely apparent. All models consider faith to be lasting, enduring through time, and all imply—if they do not explicitly state—some orientation toward past, present and future. The expected future good (on the hope model) is the present object of desire, often stimulated by previous foretastes. A trusting personal relationship is past-regarding but also involves present reliance and future loyalty. Devotion to a way of life is not a single past or present voluntary choice but an ongoing series of decisions persevering on into the future. Finally, concentration on the present by the other three models does not preclude elements of pastness and futurity. Nonevidentially based beliefs have a history, and firm convictions have consequences; a constitutive attitude brings into being a new world of significance, but not ex nihilo and not without results; even a nonrelational conscious state grew out of, or at least was preceded by, some other kind of consciousness, and it will or will not be perturbed in the future. Differences in time orientation are more superficial than deep, more matters of emphasis than of opposition.

The six models initially appear to occupy quite different points along a scale of *activity to passivity*, that is, the extent to which the subject of faith is active or passive both in bringing about faith and in having faith. Once again, these differences are only apparent, and perhaps not very important, for there are elements of activity and passivity in all models.

At the active extreme appears the devotion model, for which faith comes about through a subject's voluntary choice of a way of life and continues as the person's wholehearted commitment to that way. None of this precludes external causes and conditions from exercising considerable influence, for example, in determining which possible ways of life are options open to S, in making W an attractive option to S, in helping or hindering S's successful (or unsuccessful) commitment to and perseverance in W, and so forth. Similarly, at the passive extreme, the confidence model seems to picture faith as a completely inert feeling-state, not an active choice or deed at all. Again the appearance is deceptive. Confidence is basically self-confidence, and both its achievement and its persistence are due to the self's agency. The self somehow engineers its own nonrelational state of mind. The imperturbability of (self-)confidence is both the subject's fundamental activity of self-recognition and self-acceptance, and also that subject's fundamental passivity in being self-recognized and self-accepted.

Likewise, the other four models embrace various kinds and degrees of activity and passivity. On the personal relationship model, S is active in coming to trust A and in formulating and believing articles of faith about A, but passive insofar as these acts are also caused (so S believes) by A. Such beliefs share with all beliefs a certain passivity in the face of evidence: Given that there is adequate evidence for p available to S, S generally just believes that p. On the belief model, there is inadequate evidence for belief, so that S can actively determine belief by other means; but at the same time

S is passive in believing. On the attitude model, S may be active insofar as the radically constitutive attitude S takes toward self and world is chosen, prepared for, maintained, and defended, and also in how S bestows significance through this attitude; but S is also passive in embracing antecedent significance and in having the meaning of self as well as of world constituted by this attitude. Finally, on the hope model, S is active in recognizing G's uncertainty and apparent desirability, and in confidently awaiting, anticipating, and expecting G; but S is passive in finding G supremely desirable yet improbable, and in being confident of G's obtaining.

Differences of activity and passivity, therefore, like those of time relations, are matters more of degree or emphasis than of radical kind or depth.

2. Commonality. The six models not only differ importantly in several respects but there are also some important common elements. At least there appear to be important common elements. In this section, I examine six candidates for commonality, in order to see if they are really common to all models, as well as to determine their importance.

In each conception of faith there is a logical and a *personal subject* of faith. Even if faith (as according to the confidence model) has no object, nonetheless it is inconceivable save as the faith of someone, some subject, some person, some self. Faith must have a personal "locus." We must be careful here, however. Having a personal locus does not imply that faith is (completely) causally produced, much less owned, by that person, or that faith is individualistic (having no reality beyond individual persons), or that the subject of faith is the only or best judge as to whether faith is present and in what this faith might consist. A person is "where" faith occurs or resides, not necessarily an authority on why or how or whether faith occurs or what faith is.

There is, however, considerably less to this point than initially meets the eye. No doubt each model requires a person as the subject or locus of faith; but it does not follow that it must be the same individual or kind of person for different models, that is, a person or self in the same sense in each model. Rather, different models might have different conceptions of the self, and in ascribing faith to the self they may be referring to different (kinds of) entities. As we take note of a second apparent common element, this point can be comprehended more fully.

Faith realizes or *fulfills the self* whose faith it is. This feature is explicit only in the confidence model (where faith is said to realize S's "deeper" self or Self), but it is implicit to some extent in all the others as well.[13] For example, faith according to the hope model is based on S's great desire for the obtaining of a supreme, apparent good that includes at least the apparent good of S's self; were this desire not satisfied through having faith, S would not be self-fulfilled. According to the personal relationship model, faith is trust; since trust is involved in nearly any personal relationship insofar as it is personal, and since one can fulfill oneself as a person only in relationship to other persons, it follows that trust is required to fulfill oneself. Similar points are true of other models. Nevertheless, though faith always aims at self-fulfillment, it is not necessarily the same (kind of) self that is fulfilled. Once again, the self may be quite differently conceived in different models of faith.

One way to express this point is as follows. If we view self-fulfillment as the development or actualization of certain fundamental capacities or faculties of the self, we notice that different models of faith ascribe different faculties to the subject of faith: the capacities for trust, (propositional) belief, constitutive attitude, feeling, volition, and desire. These capacities are not mutually exclusive, and so they do not necessarily represent capacities of different selves or kinds of selves. Ordinarily, in fact, we think that all of them are thoroughly compatible with one another and indeed that all (and many more) are essential to being a human person, or at any rate to being a normal or mature human person. Nevertheless, incompatibilities do arise when these capacities are taken to the extremes portrayed in the models of faith.

For example, on the attitude model, faith (partially) constitutes not only the environing world but also the perceptive self. In a horizon of significance, a self is correlative to a world and is realized only in relation to it. But the confidence model also claims to realize the self (or Self)—not, however, in relation to anything else but

13. See Connolly, 1980, on the "search for self-identity" in relation to "belief and unbelief" about the transcendent.

only in a persistent, enduring, deep, nonrelational feeling of self-confidence. It is difficult to see how the same self, or even the same kind of self, could be realized only in relation to a horizoned world and also fully in a nonrelational feeling.[14]

While the models agree in ascribing faith to a self (the personal locus of faith) that finds self-fulfillment therein, we must beware of assuming that it is the same self in every case that is the fulfilled locus of faith—in fact, there is good reason for doubting that this is the case.

In each model of faith, *propositions are secondary*; that is, some nonpropositional attitude, state, or relation (or more than one of them) is prior to and more important than anything propositional, although the obviousness as well as the nature of this priority varies considerably.

The confidence model obviously excludes relation to anything, including propositions, and so the priority of feeling to propositional attitudes is by default. The attitude model posits a radically constitutive attitude as prepropositional, not in the sense of excluding all propositional attitudes but in the sense of preceding and grounding them. Likewise in the personal relationship model, personal trust is temporally prior to and grounds propositional beliefs gained through the trusting relationship. Perhaps less obviously, but equally firmly, the devotion model makes choice of and commitment to a way of life logically (and usually also temporally) prior to any attitudes toward propositions descriptive of that way. On the hope model also, desire for a supreme, apparent good precedes and grounds propositional attitudes (such as those embedded in expectation of the good) toward that good.

Even the belief model ascribes a kind of secondary status to belief, the paradigm attitude toward propositions. Although on this model propositional belief is essential and central to faith, the evidence for such belief must be inadequate so that the belief can be noneviden-

14. Similar points could be made in comparing the confidence model with any of the other four relational models. For instance, the self that realizes itself in an imperturbable feeling of self-confidence is not the same as the self that realizes itself in a trusting relationship with another person. The two models are compatible if one or the other does not truly involve self-realization (but only something preliminary to it), or if either or both involve only partial realization (realization of different levels or aspects of the same self). The point is that they cannot both truly be realizations at the same level of the same (kind of) self.

tially based. This nonevidential basis conceivably might be some other beliefs that do not count as evidence (though it is hard to see how beliefs could serve as a basis for other beliefs without also serving as evidence for them); but more plausibly the nonevidential basis is something independent of, prior to, and more important than propositional beliefs, for example, wishes, desires, global attitudes, commitments, and hopes to which S fervently clings.

Even though the features of *confidence and evidential risk* are in tension, every model maintains both of them, with varying emphases. Faith on all accounts requires a high level of psychological comfort or confidence (feeling certain; being confident, convinced, or committed; confidently expecting); all models also agree that faith requires a lack of evidential security (being certain; having adequate evidence; possessing theoretical justification). Moreover, all recognize that it is at least possible, perhaps even desirable, for the faithful person to recognize the tension between these two requirements (for confidence and for evidential insecurity). Faith is therefore confidence in the face of risk, although the exact form this takes varies from model to model.

On the belief model, for example, S must be firmly convinced that p even while recognizing that there is (or that S has) inadequate evidence for p (that is, either S lacks evidence for p altogether or else S's evidence is insufficient to justify S believing p with such a high level of confidence or conviction); hence, S's strong belief that p must be nonevidentially based. Similarly, on the hope model, S must confidently await, anticipate, and expect G, a supreme, future, apparent good, despite G's obtaining being theoretically and practically improbable for S; S's high level of confidence with respect to G's obtaining is based not on S's evidence but on S's strong desire for G. Likewise, to take one more example, on the attitude model S's attitude toward X is implicitly confident because it is totalizing (involving the whole person and the whole environing context), yet at the same time it is not evidentially based (in fact it is not based on anything at all). This is what it means for an attitude to be radically constitutive both extensively (constituting both subject and object in relation to each other) and intensively (conditioning other constitutive features of subject and object).

Some tension between evidential insecurity and psychological comfort is therefore an important feature common to all six models—indeed, one is tempted to say that it is an essential feature of faith.

All models state or at least imply that faith is not transient or fleeting but something that endures, persists, or perseveres. In short, faith is *lasting*. Clearly personal relationships, constitutive attitudes, and hopeful stances are more than momentary, and it is explicitly part of the confidence and devotion models that faith is lasting. But what about faith on the belief model? It seems possible (just barely) that S's belief that p could be only a momentary act or fleeting state, but it is hard to see how S could be firmly convinced that p except as an ongoing condition or disposition. We may take lastingness as a feature common to all six models.

Once again, we must be careful not to push this point too far. Faith is lasting, all models agree; but what is it that lasts, and what is it to last? These are questions about which there is considerable disagreement. Does faith last as an activity that continues through time? Does it last as a sequence of such activities that has a history through time? Is it a static quality that remains the same over time? A dynamic relation that continuously changes while remaining stable through time? An enduring disposition discontinuously expressed at different times? For example, a personal relationship is a complex whole consisting of mutual acts, states, and dispositions on the part of (at least) two persons; it is dynamic, varying in strength and content over time according as the persons alter. On this model, faith lasts insofar as the relationship continues, however altered in strength and content. A belief, however, in the sense relevant to faith, is a disposition (to occurrent acts of believing) that lasts over time and that may vary in its strength and mode of expression, but not in its content. Similarly, a radically constitutive attitude is an all-embracing, enduring disposition, whereas a feeling of (self-) confidence is a profound, continuing occurrence. Finally, although devotion and hope are both lasting dispositions, they are nonetheless different sorts of dispositions: Persevering commitment (faith on the devotion model) continues a prior loyalty, while confident anticipation (faith on the hope model) actively looks forward to a future realization.

Lastingness, therefore, is only formally a common feature; materially, what it is that lasts and how it lasts vary significantly among the six models of faith.

A final feature often thought to be common, important, and even central to all conceptions of faith is its *totalizing* or holistic character. Faith, says Paul Tillich, "claims ultimacy" because of its "demand of total surrender to the subject of ultimate concern."[15] This claim requires considerable qualification if it is to apply to all six models of faith. Totalization is indeed present in all the models, but not to the same extent or in the same way. In language both more cautious and less committed to elements of the personal relationship model of faith than Tillich's, we may say that faith either wholly involves the whole person or else tends to do so—drawing more or less fully on all or most capacities of the person and manifesting itself in all or most dimensions of that person's life.

A radically constitutive attitude explicitly requires totalization, for it constitutes a whole self in relation to an environing context. Not every feature of that self and world is engaged, for faith on the attitude model is only partially constitutive, determining some but not all essential aspects. Likewise, devotion to a way of life explicitly requires wholehearted commitment, a kind of totalization. But the other models do not require totalization, even though they do possess what we might call totalizing tendencies. Trusting another can sometimes be partial and tentative, but it tends toward totality as the relationship grows more important to the subject of faith; similarly, belief acquires greater firmness of conviction as its nonevidential basis matters more to the believer; and hope's underlying desire consumes more or less of the hopeful person depending on the degree of supremacy of the apparent good. Confidence, however, seems totalizing in a different way—not so much by including all capacities and aspects of S but by excluding everything except what is essential for achieving the supremely prized nonrelational state of confident consciousness (although this state is said to realize all of S's "deeper" self or Self). In short, totalization cannot be considered a common feature of faith without important qualifications. There are great differences between inclusive and exclusive forms of totalization and between the requirement of totalization and the mere tendency toward totalization.

15. Tillich, 1957, 3. Another facet of faith's ultimacy, according to Tillich, is its promise of "total fulfillment" and threat of exclusion from such fulfillment "if the unconditional demand is not obeyed" (2). We have noted the feature of self-fulfillment just above, but without the requirement of totality.

Overall, then, the features common to the six models turn out to be less clear-cut and important than initially appears. Confidence in the face of evidential insecurity takes pride of place, but none of the features, individually or collectively, suffice to constitute much of a univocal concept or category of faith, especially in light of the deep differences mentioned previously, as well as issues surrounding consistency to which we now turn.

3. Consistency. Each model, I assume, is internally consistent; at least there seems to be no reason to suppose that any of the models includes self-contradictory features. But what about mutual consistency in the relation of the models to one another? As we have portrayed the models, there are no narrowly logical inconsistencies; there are no substitution instances of logical contradictions, where, for example, one model explicitly affirms p while another explicitly affirms not-p (or denies p), or where one affirms that A is Φ while another affirms that A is not Φ (or denies that A is Φ). Moreover, a number of differences (concerning the kinds of objects of faith, time-modalities, and the active/passive contrast) that appear to generate inconsistencies do not really do so.

Still, there are two intractable disagreements among the models that amount, I contend, to broadly logical incompatibilities.[16] First, there is the opposition between the nonrelational confidence model and the other five relational models: Faith must have an object for the latter, but faith cannot have an object for the former. Second, there is the tripartite disagreement as to whether propositional beliefs are required by faith (the belief, hope, and personal relationship models), prohibited by faith (the confidence model), or merely optional for faith (the attitude and devotion models). These inconsistencies do not mean that all pairs of models are inconsistent; at least the belief and personal relationship models, and the attitude and devotion models, respectively, seem to be mutually consistent. Nevertheless, a major implication of the two incompatibilities is that one cannot consistently conjoin all six models (in their entirety) to form a single concept—or category—of faith.

There is a secondary kind of inconsistency. Quite often, even when there are features common to all models of faith, the common

16. See A. Plantinga, 1974, 2, on the idea of "broadly logical" modality.

features tend to be expressed quite differently in different models. For example, having a personal locus and being self-fulfilled are common to all models, but each model involves different persons or selves (or different conceptions of person and self); propositional beliefs are always secondary in faith, but they are subordinated to different sorts of things and in different ways; confidence is in tension with evidential insecurity, but this tension takes quite different forms; faith lasts, but in different modes; and totalization may be inclusive or exclusive, required or merely a tendency. The common features seem common to all models only at a certain high level of generality; when further specified, they tend to vary—and to vary in incompatible ways—among the models. This incompatible variation is a kind of inconsistency, and it is one further obstacle in the way of forging a single category of faith out of the six models.

In sum, each of the models is internally consistent; at least two pairs of the models seem mutually consistent, although there are also various general features shared by many or all of the models; and, most importantly, there is no consistent way of combining all of the features of all six models so as to form a single category of faith.

4. Completeness. Are these six models all the models there are? Unfortunately, there is no way to be sure. On the one hand, there is no a priori (logical or conceptual) assurance of completeness, for there seems to be no principled way of exhaustively specifying all the possibilities.[17] On the other hand, there is no empirical assurance either, and this for two reasons. First, with respect to the past, there is no guarantee that every previous conception of faith (held by anyone at any time up to the present) is covered by one or the other of the six models or by some combination of them. My extensive research has failed to uncover any others, but this is scant guarantee that there are no more than six models. It is altogether possible that there exist or have existed other conceptions of faith that require another model or two to illumine their essential features. Second, with respect to the future, there is no guarantee that there will be no new developments such as the creation of new models and/or conceptions of faith that go beyond the six presented here.

17. In Kantian language, there is no "metaphysical deduction" of the models.

Both kinds of limitation (past and future) must be taken seriously, even while we show how many extant conceptions of faith can be viewed as specifications of, and as illuminated by, the six models. While no ironclad guarantee of completeness can be given, it is plausible to contend that little, if anything, is left out.

5. Structure. Concerns about structure are twofold: first, how conceptual features are organized within each model, and second, how models may be combined to form more complex structures.

The first kind of structure is internal to each model. Each model emphasizes or *highlights* some features not prominent in (or even absent from) other models, and each downplays or *shadows* other features prominent or present in other models. As we have seen, a highlighted feature of one model may, but need not, be found in other models. Indeed, it may even be common to all the models. A feature so shadowed as to be unmentioned may, but need not be, excluded from the model. For example, propositional belief is prominent and required in the belief model, prominently excluded by the confidence model, and shadowed but permitted by the attitude model; evidential insecurity coupled with psychological confidence is highlighted in some models, shadowed in others, but common to all.

But what is this notion of "highlight" and "shadow"? In part, and most deeply, it is the "conceptual chiaroscuro" noted earlier, which is ingredient to models themselves. Here, however, I focus on another aspect: the highlight and shadow due to the exposition of a model—how the model is portrayed or presented by someone to someone. Expository shading is by no means trivial or merely subjective.

Suppose that a model is or essentially contains a coherent (consistent, nonarbitrary, relevant) set of features or feature-schemata. An exposition of a model, then, is someone's attempt to list (name, describe, characterize) those features, as many as desirable, as perspicuously as possible, and as accurately as necessary, in order to make that model clear (or clearer) to someone. No exposition should claim definitive clarification of a model, for several reasons. For one, an exposition may misapprehend or fail to notice some features, especially relevant permissive or exclusive features (ones where a model permits or excludes certain features perhaps contained in other models). Second, any finite exposition must choose to focus on certain features as deserving lengthier treatment, because they are deemed more centrally or structurally important than others, and such choices may prove injudicious or unilluminating. Third, any exposition not merely displays the understanding of its author but also invites the understanding of some audience, so that limitations and interests of audience as well as author inevitably infect any exposition.

For all these reasons, therefore, there are both highlights (features clearly and centrally presented) and shadows (features omitted or unclearly presented) in any exposition of a model. As a result, there is considerable margin for error (errors of commission, omission, and emphasis) as well as occasion for manipulation (via techniques of rhetoric and force of personality). But there is no alternative save silence.

The second kind of structure concerns the ways in which models may be *combined*. First, one may combine features from two or more models to form a new model of faith. But in order to create a new model, as opposed to cleaving or cloning old models, or merely conjoining features at random, this combination must be a synthesis introducing novelty, not sheer addition or division. The borrowed features must be organized or structured by some novel feature or way of highlighting the old features.[18] As we have seen, there is no guarantee that this cannot be done, so we must admit it as a possibility, though in the absence of viable candidates for the role of a seventh model of faith, this must remain an empty possibility.

Second, one may combine two or more models, or features from different models, in a particular conception of faith. A conception may exemplify not just one but several models, so that each model illuminates a different facet of the complex conception. But, unlike models, a conception's combination of features need not be a consistent one—a conception may be confused, paradoxical, or just plain inconsistent. I consider some of the resulting possibilities later.

Third, one may combine two or more models via a temporal succession of conceptions, where first one conception (exemplifying one model or set of models) and then another (exemplifying another model or set of models) is adopted or considered by someone. Such

18. Of course, the features must also be mutually consistent, relevant to the phenomenon of faith, and so forth.

combination of models is not via abstraction (in another model or in an exemplifying conception) but via concretion (in a life). For example, S might first live a life exemplifying the personal relationship model of faith, trusting another person as to the best or only means of achieving a nonrelational state of self-confidence, which when achieved becomes independent of its guiding guru, so that S then lives by (a conception of) faith exemplifying the confidence model. Or S might trust an authority as to which is the best way of life to follow, and when this life is followed long and diligently enough it becomes self-guiding and self-inspiring, so that S then lives by (a conception of) faith exemplifying the devotion model.[19]

It might be thought that the models possess yet a third kind of structure: Although no model can be reduced to another (they are conceptually or logically independent), some are more important than others, are somehow closer to the center of the concept of faith, while others are merely peripheral. This I deny. Granted, from the standpoint of some particular conception of faith, one or more models of faith will be more important for illuminating that conception, and as the conception is valued, so will the model be valued. But this importance is entirely because one is wedded to some particular conception that exemplifies one or another model(s). From a different standpoint (that of another conception), other models will assume greater importance. The relative importance of the models is not intrinsic to the models themselves but is a function of one's standpoint, which in turn is a function of the conception of faith one has or values.[20]

## B. Relations of Models to Conceptions

So far I have considered only relations among models. I turn now to relations between models on the one hand and conceptions on

---

19. One may also imagine, and live, a way of life that includes abiding by different conceptions of faith as stages of life. One example is the Hindu notion of four *āśramas*: student (*brahmacārin*), householder (*grhasthin*), forest dweller (*vānaprasthin*), and renunciant (*samnyāsin*). See also the aesthetic, moral, and religious "stages on life's way" in Kierkegaard, 1988.

20. Of course, one or another model might be more important than the others for various particular purposes, perhaps for teaching about some conception or tradition of faith, but again this is not an intrinsic variation in importance.

the other.[21] Recall that a model is an idealized, reflective, moderately abstract, explicit, univocal concept, somewhat like a Platonic Form or Idea; a conception is an actual, reflective or primary, moderately concrete, usually implicit, often analogous concept, rather like a complicated and indefinitely fringed set of rules. The uses of models are primarily theoretical, secondarily practical; the uses of conceptions are the reverse.

The principal relations between models and conceptions are reciprocals: exemplification and illumination. A conception exemplifies a model when it contains the conceptual features delineated in the model, usually in a more elaborated, further specified, or even somewhat altered form.[22] A model illuminates a conception when it clarifies the distinctive and important features of a conception and enables the latter to be understood in relation to other conceptions. Since they are reciprocals, models should illuminate conceptions that exemplify them, and conceptions should exemplify models that illuminate them. Of course, a conception may exemplify and be illuminated by more than one model, and a model may illuminate and be exemplified by more than one conception. But no conception can consistently exemplify all features of all the models since the models contain mutually incompatible features. However, a single conception could consistently exemplify compatible parts or aspects of all of the models, as well as inconsistently exemplify incompatible models. Conversely, no model can illuminate all features of all conceptions, though it may illuminate a few common (but very general) features of all conceptions.

Two types of question arise concerning these primary relations of models to conceptions: questions of adequacy and questions of utility.

1. Adequacy. Do conceptions adequately exemplify models, and do models adequately illuminate conceptions? Since adequacy is a

21. My comments are rather general, dealing mostly with the relations of any or all models to any or all conceptions, not with the relations of particular models to particular conceptions. Specific questions about these latter relations are addressed in Chap. 4.

22. Exemplification is not instantiation. Concepts (conceptions, models) exemplify other concepts (etc.). Persons (or their lives) instantiate conceptions (also models and concepts) they employ to live their lives. Conceptions are not concrete individuals like persons, and so their relations to models are different.

matter of degree and is relative to standards and ends, these are very expansive questions. However, since exemplification and illumination are reciprocals, and since conceptions are generally prior to models in being, value, and inquiry, we may somewhat narrow our concern to the following: To what extent are the models—individually and collectively—adequate to actual conceptions of faith? Clearly no model or set of models can capture all of the indefinitely large number of conceptual features of any particular conception; rather, the worry is whether enough central features are captured to make the model a true model of faith (as opposed to something else). Few would dispute the devotion and attitude models, and fewer still the personal relationship model, as genuinely illuminating of many conceptions of faith. But questions may be lodged against the other three models:

The belief model has been roundly, even venomously criticized during the past century or so, especially in Neoorthodox Protestant Christian circles.[23] In part this criticism registers a vehement protest against secular tendencies to constrict faith merely to propositional belief; but such protest need not imply any criticism of the belief model, which qualifies propositional belief with a variety of other essential features. In part, the criticism also expresses a preference for a conception of faith that differs from the belief model either by making propositional belief completely optional (as in the attitude and devotion models) or by excluding it altogether (as in the confidence model);[24] but it is no defect of the belief model that it is not some other model.

The crux of the matter is whether the belief model is a model of faith at all. Here two points need to be stressed. First, many people do in fact use conceptions of faith that reflect this model, as we see in Chap. 4. To call their usage incorrect or mistaken seems disingenuous, or at any rate it is to turn a value judgment as to the best or highest form of faith (true or saving faith) into an exclusive claim

23. See, e.g., Karl Barth, 1936, 1959; Brunner, 1946, 1956; Buber, 1951; Ebeling, 1961; Gogarten, 1959; Kierkegaard, 1941, 1970, 1985; Kroner, 1943; Lindbeck, 1984; and Phillips, 1966, 1970, 1976.

24. Others—e.g., Buber, 1958—have tried to fashion a conception or model of faith as personal relationship ("I-Thou relationship") without propositional belief, but I do not think their efforts are successful. See Hepburn, 1958, chaps. 2–4, for a trenchant critique.

about the concept of faith (truly faith). Second, though propositional belief is central to the belief model, so also are firm conviction, inadequacy of evidence, and nonevidential basing of the belief. These latter features are ones that most neoorthodox critics of propositional belief would recognize as belonging to faith, and so even they would have to recognize some affinities of the belief model to faith as they view it.

Hope, some have urged, is not faith but a more rationally defensible substitute for faith.[25] They hold that, whereas faith requires that one believe that G (the supreme, future, apparent good) does exist or will obtain, hope merely requires belief that G is possible and that one should act as if G does or will exist. Whether this notion of hope is an alternative to faith or just a variant of it is open to question.[26] Moreover, this notion of hope differs crucially from the hope model, which requires belief that G does or will exist in addition to belief that this is possible. The hope model requires confident awaiting, anticipation, and expectation, not instead of belief but in addition to it. The case for thinking that the hope model is not a model of faith is very weak.

The confidence model, since it differs so profoundly from the other models of faith (especially in having no object, but also in prohibiting propositional belief), constitutes the most difficult case. Surely, one might suppose, faith must have an object—it must be in or that or toward something or other—and one must be at least able to believe some propositions about both the subject and object of faith. But the matter is not so clear-cut; there are reasons for thinking that the confidence model does indeed give a picture of (one kind of) faith. For one, some writers use the English word "faith" to name a conception that exemplifies the confidence model.[27] For a second, everyone accepts the phrase "faith in oneself," where the subject and object of faith are the same person; and this confident relation to oneself is not far from the feeling of (self-) confidence. For a third, the kind of feeling the confidence model

25. See Muyskens, 1979.
26. Pojman, 1986b, diverges from Muyskens on precisely this point; see Chap. 4, sec. D below.
27. Park, 1983; admittedly the word is applied in translation of a Korean term, but there are good reasons for the translation. Similar remarks apply to translating the Japanese Shin Buddhist term *shinjin* as "faith." See Chap. 4, sec. F below.

highlights (a feeling of profound and imperturbable confidence, serenity, or peace) is a frequent and intimate adjunct—if not quite an
essential feature—of faith according to most conceptions. So, at the
very minimum, the confidence model portrays something very like
faith (or something ingredient in profound faith) if not quite faith
itself. Beyond this, the model may prove useful in East-West comparisons in religious studies.[28]

2. Utility. There are many uses one might make of models with
respect to conceptions of faith, but the primary ones are theoretical.
Since models are fairly well structured sets of fairly clearly delineated
conceptual features, they may be used as patterns, of a sort, to place
alongside somewhat amorphous and opaque reflective conceptions
of faith, in order to highlight the latter's distinctive fundamental
features and to clarify their fundamental differences and similarities.
These are all useful steps on the road to understanding.

Achieving theoretical understanding of distinct conceptions of
faith need not be the only use for models. Understanding similarities
and differences in various conceptions may stimulate further reflection about concepts that might serve to bridge conceptual chasms,
reconcile conflicting claims, and harmonize divergent points of view.
In short, understanding at one level may be a spur to further inquiry
at another level, by clarifying the essential issues and showing what
remains to be done.

Moreover, for persons of goodwill it is even possible that, to
bend a French proverb, *tout comprendre, c'est tout tolérer* (to understand all is to tolerate all). That is, understanding another's different
conceptuality is at least a first step toward tolerating not only the
other's different conceptions but also her divergent way of life.
Of course toleration is not necessarily agreement (with the other's
views) nor acceptance (of the other's conceptions for her or even
for one's own uses), much less adoption (of the way of life that
those conceptions condition and express). But tolerance is an important step away from outright rejection, not to mention per-
secution.

---

28. In Chap. 4, we see how the confidence model illumines some (aspects of)
conceptions of faith that exemplify it.

3. Secondary relations. In addition to the primary relations of exemplification and illumination, there are several secondary relations between models and conceptions that are worth mentioning.

Priority in *inquiry* may work either way. Our six models were found through reflection on, or rational reconstruction of, a variety of conceptions. But it is also possible to learn of models before conceptions—for example, by reading about them, or simply imagining them for oneself—and only then to conduct an empirical exploration into the extant conceptions. The priorities of inquiry are only partially set by the priorities of a subject matter; they are also determined in part by the inquirer's starting points, methods, aims, and uses for the inquiry.

Models are more *abstract* than conceptions. By this I do not mean that models necessarily have been abstracted from conceptions but rather that conceptions are more fully featured or richly detailed than models, and in this sense models are less concrete; and the features in models are often more general versions of fairly specific ones found in particular conceptions, so that the latter are specifications of the former, and the former generalizations of the latter. In these ways models are more abstract than conceptions. Now the ontology of this work is more Aristotelian than Platonic: The concrete is ontologically prior to the abstract. Hence, actual entities and their specific features, including persons with their particular conceptions of faith, are ontologically prior to more abstract entities, such as models of faith and their conceptual features. The undoubted advantages of models over conceptions for inquiry (their relative clarity, precision, structure) does not confer ontological priority on models over conceptions.

Most of the *value* of the theoretical uses of models depends on the value of the practical uses of conceptions; here is one form of the vaunted "primacy of the practical." Models can be contemplated as mere forms or structures, and I do not want to underestimate the intrinsic enjoyment such contemplation may bring. But the primary value of contemplating conceptions lies in fulfilling the primary purpose of illuminating conceptions or understanding them, which is practical. Illumination is to be sought not (just or primarily) for its own sake but for the sake of living life with and through the illuminated conceptions. As an end in itself, theoretical understanding via model building has some value; but as a means to greater practical facility with conceptions, as well as to their more beneficial employment, it can be worth much more.

## C. Relations of Models and Conceptions to Concept

A *concept*, in the special sense intended here, expresses the over-arching or underlying unity of a set of conceptions. If this concept is a univocal one, expressing a coherent group of essential features found (only) in every member of a set of more concrete conceptions, then it is a *category*; if the concept is not univocal but also not completely equivocal, expressing overlapping likenesses but not commonalities in features among the various members of a set of conceptions, then it is an *analogy*. It is my contention that the concept of faith is an analogy, not a category. That is, the manifold conceptions of faith are related to one another not by possessing some common essential features but rather by resembling one another, in sundry conceptual ways. Models, then, may be seen as useful aids to the exploration of an analogical concept such as the concept of faith. Models of faith epitomize the varying, but resembling, conceptions of faith by bundling their prominent conceptual features into distinct and highlighted clusters, thereby clarifying the important commonalities and likenesses among the conceptions, as well as their deepest differences. The number, complexity, and articulation of the models is only a partial representation of the rich variegation of an analogical concept, but if the models receive a perspicuous exposition their highlights and shadows may greatly illumine the concept above as well as the conceptions below. The very selectivity of models of faith is key to a greater understanding of the concept of faith.

Still, a worry remains: How may we be sure that differing models all belong to one analogous concept and not to two or more different (analogical?) concepts?[29] The answer is that we have no such assurance. In the case of a category, of course, one has the assured unity of a distinct set of essential features; any divergence from this set

29. Alternatively: What constitutes the unity of an analogical concept? When do we have one family of conceptions, united by various strands of resemblance, or more than one, differentiated by various kinds of dissimilarity? How much likeness do we need for unity, or how much unity?

marks a different concept. But in the case of an analogy, resemblance—or recognition of resemblance—is bedrock. Resemblance, however, is a matter of degree, so that there is always latitude for making different choices in differentiating and grouping conceptions under different concepts. What constitutes "sufficient" resemblance or dissimilarity among conceptions and features must rest on judgment, perhaps finally on decision. Moreover, no matter where cuts and connections are made, there will always be difficult borderline cases (as well as clear-cut central ones).

None of this, however, means that all choices are equally good, that no decision to separate or to group together distinct models or conceptions is any better than any other. On the contrary, even though there are no ironclad assurances, there may still be very good reasons for preferring one choice over another. Even if there are equally good, though contrary, reasons for making two or more different choices—especially if these are made by different persons, from different standpoints, with different purposes and interests—this does not render the choices arbitrary. A diverse group of conceptions may be seen as one family by one person (from some standpoint, for some purposes) and with equal cogency as two or more families by another person (from another standpoint, for other purposes). Each person can see all the commonalities, differences, and likenesses the other sees; and each can see that the other's choice makes sense from the other's standpoint. Neither choice is necessarily mistaken. Still, one choice might be preferable to the other.

Our question about the unity of analogous concepts now takes the form: Do the six models of faith we have sketched sufficiently resemble one another so as to be usefully combined under a single concept of faith (for the purpose of theoretical understanding, if not also for the purposes of practical toleration and harmony)? We have seen that the resemblances are many and the degrees of resemblance are generally strong, certainly among five of the six models. The confidence model initially seems the odd one out, but, as we have argued, even here there are a number of important resemblances that warrant its inclusion along with the other models in a single (analogous) concept of faith. By highlighting different major features that are variously prominent in different but similar conceptions of faith, therefore, the six models may fairly be regarded as models of the same (analogous) concept. The models together constitute a single analogy of faith.

# [ 4 ]

# Seven Conceptions of Faith

Before we turn to an examination of some conceptions of faith in light of the proposed six models, two questions need to be addressed: By what criteria are these and not other conceptions selected for consideration? And, what is the point of considering these conceptions?

Concerning the first question, it is of course impossible to consider all extant conceptions of faith, much less all possible ones; they are too multitudinous and multifarious. Choices must be made, not just of sample conceptions but also of criteria by which to select these samples. I have employed five criteria in selecting the conceptions:

They are all fairly *definite* conceptions. A conception is definite to the extent to which it is complex (combining a number of distinct features), precise (containing few indeterminate features, and these only peripherally), articulated (its features are in more or less identifiable relation to one another), unified (the features form a coherent whole), and explicit (the features have actually been set forth by someone). I say "fairly definite" because of course it will be impossible to achieve completion—there is no way fully to make explicit everything contained in any actual conception—and so there will always be unanswered questions. Nonetheless, definiteness is desirable if obtainable. It is easier to apply models to relatively definite conceptions than to relatively indefinite ones, since fewer guesses need be made about content and structure.

They are all quite *diverse* conceptions, exemplifying different models of faith in different ways. Since there are an indefinitely large number of particular conceptions of faith, differing from one another in many ways, we cannot inspect or display them all.[1] It will be enough to explore conceptions exemplifying the entire spectrum of the models we have presented, for essential differences among these models constitute some of the more important conceptual differences among conceptions. Conversely, exploring a diverse group of conceptions will display the powers of illumination possessed by each of the six models individually and all six collectively.

They are all *representative* conceptions, sampling a number of historically important traditions of faith—traditions, that is, not only of conceiving faith but also of practicing or living faith in conformity to some conception of faith. Once again we must be very selective; there is no way to capture the full extent of any tradition, so we must be content to sample it at carefully chosen points, in the form of some individual's presentation of a conception that is broadly shared. The conceptions we examine are particular and personal in that they are specified by individuals respected for their powers of clear representation, but they are also general and communal in that they have been widely shared, at least in broad outline, by a large number of people, even by many who would not acknowledge this particular individual's account as authoritative.

We may perhaps view these individually expressed conceptions as especially clear distillations of some particular tradition of conceiving faith. Some of these distillations have in fact played, and been recognized as having played, a foundational role for some tradition; they are the conceptions articulated by some acknowledged founder, leader, or central thinker of a tradition. Others are less important historically, the product of some relatively minor figure in a tradition or some clearheaded commentator on a major or minor figure. But all are representative, whether or not they are historically foundational.[2]

---

1. I am tempted to say that the exploration of other conceptions in light of these models is left as an exercise for the reader—as usual, such exercise is not only strenuous but also decidedly nontrivial.

2. It is no part of this book to show how these different conceptions have arisen and functioned in actual traditions, much less how differences in conceptions of

Presentations of these conceptions are selected from *committed* authors—persons who do not merely use the conceptions but who also accept the legitimacy of using them and even advocate their use. Some may question this choice, claiming that advocates are likely to be blind to the defects and damages of their heartfelt conception and that an outsider (one who had no stake in the continuance of the tradition of faith) would be more likely to give a fairer, more neutral, presentation. I admit that there are dangers in advocacy, and I agree that in order to give an accurate depiction of a conception it is not necessary to use or accept, much less to advocate, a conception. One could very well describe a conception without employing or enjoying that conception in one's own life. Still, there are contrary dangers: Antagonists of a conception of faith cannot be counted on to present it fairly or fully, and indifferent outsiders may be unaware of the subtler aspects of a conception simply because they are unfamiliar with it at an existential level. Insiders who feel something important is at stake in the use of a particular conception are generally more appreciative of its nuances as well as more tenacious in grasping its essentials. Insiders may tend to overestimate the resources of a conception, but they will seldom omit any features; outsiders will seldom make excessive claims, but they may tend to underestimate the conception's resources. In my judgment, for purposes of understanding the distinctive features of a particular conception of faith it is safer to trust insiders than outsiders. One can more readily discard excess than supply deficiency.

The presentations of the conceptions are all relatively *accessible* to nonspecialists outside the traditions they represent. At the very least, in order to gain some (incomplete) level of understanding and appreciation of these conceptions one need not imbibe a whole tradition. This is one reason why I have relied on conceptions presented in English, many of them (secondhand) commentaries on conceptions initially expressed in other languages. There are obvious dangers to this approach. A commentator may fail to appreciate, or be unable to articulate, the subtleties of an original thinker; supple thoughts and subtle nuances may ossify into rigid rules; and many linguistic, conceptual, historical, and experiential resonances can

---

faith have contributed to the distinctiveness of each tradition; these are jobs for theologians, historians, and sociologists.

scarcely be conveyed in a different cultural context. But there are also advantages. The main outlines of a conception may be made clearer at some cultural remove; decades, often centuries of reflection on the conception may lead to greater clarity, or at least to greater explicitness; and only in this way are comparative questions accessible to readers (and authors) who are not polymaths.[3]

Concerning our second question (the point of our examination of conceptions), this account has four major aims. First, it seeks to display, as clearly as possible, the major features and central structures of some actual conceptions of faith that are fairly definite, diverse, representative, committed, and accessible.[4] Second, it seeks to display the connections between these conceptions and the six models. This involves showing how each conception exemplifies one or more models, how one and the same model may be variously exemplified, and how relations and tensions among the models are reflected in the conceptions. Third, since exemplification (of a model by a conception) is the flip side of illumination (of a conception by a model), we should also be able to gain a deeper understanding of each conception, both in itself and in relation to other conceptions, and thereby a more complete understanding of the full (analogical) concept of faith. Fourth, by applying models to conceptions—seeing how conceptions exemplify, specify, and develop models—we may gain a better understanding of the models themselves: an understanding of what might be called models-in-use.

## A. A Thomistic Conception

### Pieper's Version

There are almost as many Thomistic views as there are Thomists; there is even considerable discussion as to what, exactly, is the view

---

3. In fact, the weight of studying any single concept in its full personal, cultural, and historical context is so great that few specialists could hope to shoulder even one such burden, much less to heft more than one comparatively.

4. All these conceptions are labeled "faith" by their authors. Whether they are, in fact, conceptions of faith is a question on which our approach can perhaps shed some light. The extent to which a conception exemplifies one or several models of faith provides some confirmation that it is indeed a conception of faith (on the assumption, of course, that the six models are all models of faith).

that Saint Thomas Aquinas himself might have held.[5] Rather than enmesh ourselves in the delicate details of Thomas-exegesis, we sample the Thomistic tradition considerably later in its development, in order to benefit by centuries of reflective clarification of Thomas's conception, as well as by the subsequent light shed by other conceptions. Such a version is set forth in particularly lucid form by Josef Pieper in his short book *Belief and Faith*.[6] I note eleven features of this Thomistic conception.

1. Faith is a propositional attitude; it involves holding a proposition (or "statement") to be true in an unreserved or unconditional way.[7]

2. Faith resembles knowing in excluding doubt, but it differs from knowing in lacking "insight" into a subject matter; that is, faith is "firm assent" without full, adequate, or sufficient evidence, but not necessarily without any evidence at all. The certainty or assurance of faith is not founded or based on whatever evidence is available or obtainable.

3. Faith requires believing someone as well as believing something; it requires not only believing that some proposition is true but also believing in the truthfulness of some person as well. Indeed, believing the other person is the sole, or at any rate the fundamental, "reason" for believing the proposition. The prop-

---

5. See, e.g., Anscombe, 1979; Bars, 1961; Baum, 1969; Burrell, 1986; Chénu, 1968; D'Arcy, 1976; Fries, 1969a; Gilson, 1938; Grisez, 1975; Joly, 1958; Mouroux, 1959; Penelhum, 1971, 1977; Persson, 1970; Rahner, 1967, 1978b; Rahner and Vorgrimler, 1981; J. F. Ross, 1969, 1982; Stump, 1989; Weigel, 1961.

6. Pieper, 1963; page references in this section are to this text. Pieper takes himself merely to be explicating Aquinas, but this is questionable. For example, Pieper does not develop the distinction between "faith" and "formed faith" (faith formed by love of the divine good) precisely as Thomas does. See *Summa theologiae* 2.2 Q 4, especially articles 3–5. I do not explore the extent to which Pieper is in fact completely faithful to Aquinas's own conception; though no slavish imitator of Thomas, Pieper clearly gives us a "Thomistic" conception of faith.

A further complication is this: Aquinas's Latin term for the conception in question is "*fides*," Pieper's original German term is "*Glaube*," and the Winstons' English translation of both is "belief." Since it seems clear that all of these terms are intended to name a single conception, and that this is a conception of faith, I feel justified in using "faith" interchangeably with the translators' "belief."

7. According to Pieper, "belief [=faith] in the proper sense really means *unqualified* assent and *unconditional* acceptance of the truth of something" (14). This initial feature undoubtedly is what tempts the translator to read "belief" for "*fides*" and "*Glaube*."

osition is believed not on evidence but precisely on the other person's testimony.[8]

4. Faith requires "unreservedly" believing a proposition solely on the authority of another, so that a "wholehearted believer must logically accept as true *everything else* that his authority has said or ever will say in the future" (21).

5. Faith requires an uncoerced act of will. Since the believer does not "see" (know, deduce, have adequate evidence) that the proposition is true, something other than a cognitive capacity must produce assent; that cause is a desire for some good, and "it is the will, not cognition, which acknowledges the good" (27). The primary "object" of the act of will—the good that is sought—is neither the proposition believed nor the act of believing but rather the person believed.[9] Willing here is a matter of commitment to a person and to the good of "communion" with her. Hence, faith is ultimately a matter of love (30).[10]

6. The cognitive status of faith is grounded in the knowledge that the authority antecedently possesses; the authority's secure hold on truth is contracted by the believer's faith, giving the believer a kind of "knowledge" or "certainty" that she could not obtain in any other way. In order to gain knowledge by accepting another's testimony, one needs to have evidence that the other is indeed an authority.[11] So if faith is to yield "knowledge," there must be *præambula fidei* (preambles of or to faith); according to Saint Thomas, "*cognitio fidei præsupponit cognitionem naturalem*" (faith's knowledge presupposes natural knowledge).[12] This evidence for credibility is

8. "Belief itself is not yet 'purely' achieved when someone accepts as truth the statement of one whom he trusts, but only when he accepts it *for the simple reason* that the trusted person states." (21).

9. "The will of the believer is directed towards the person of the witness, toward the warrantor" (29).

10. The good toward which the will aims is "communion with the eyewitness or knower who says 'it is so' " (31). Here Pieper conflates faith with formed faith.

11. "Before we, as believers, accept the testimony of another, we must be sure that he has authentic knowledge of those things which we accept on faith," and this reliance "must be founded upon some knowledge on the part of the believer if it is to be valid" (38). The two musts may be construed as requirements either for faith or for rationally acceptable faith (in the latter case they could be replaced by "rationally should").

12. Pieper (41), quoting Saint Thomas Aquinas *Quaestiones disputatae de veritate* 14. 9 ad 8; 1. 2. 2 ad 1.

not coercive; trusting another person must always remain a fundamentally free act.

These six conditions, according to Pieper, are satisfied in what might be called "secular" or "human" faith, that is, ordinary faith in other human persons. But they obtain pre-eminently in (theistic) religious faith, where the authority is God and the content of the testimony concerns God. God is a logically unique authority—omniscient, unswervingly veracious,[13] and therefore inerrant. If God tells you or otherwise causes you to believe that something is true, then you rationally may and should be certain that it is true; your belief will then indeed approach "cognition" or "knowledge."[14] (Of course, you need not be certain that the proposition is true even if God tells you that it is, because you might not believe that it is God speaking, or because you might not trust in God.[15]) Pieper then goes on to note five further features of distinctively religious faith.

7. God, the object and author of religious faith, must be understood as "a personal Being capable of speech" (59). Religious faith cannot be in or from an impersonal principle, abstract ideal, or inscrutable transcendent principle.

8. Human receptivity to "divine speech" or supernatural revelation is a natural, not a supernatural, capacity.[16] Hence, "Unbelief contradicts what man is by nature" (62). Not every case of not believing a revealed proposition, or even every case of disbelieving such a proposition, is a case of unbelief. "Unbelief in the precise sense of the term is only that mental act in which someone *deliberately*

13. Why cannot God lie? Pieper provides no argument for this debatable assumption.

14. "[Religious] belief is more certain than any imaginable human insight—not insofar as it is belief, but insofar as it properly rests upon *divine speech*" (50).

15. Adapting or interpreting a tripartite distinction found in Aquinas *Summa theologiae*, 2a2ae. 2.2 Responsio, Pieper holds that truly religious (theistic) faith involves not only believing that what God says is true (*Deo credere*), but also believing that the speaker is God (*Deum credere*), as well as believingly to love or trust in God (*in Deum credere*) (54).

16. Of course, Pieper holds, all capacities are divinely created. But faith does not require the special creation of a faculty not present at birth in all; human beings are "by nature open to the divine speech, capable of being reached by it" (60). Pieper calls this innate capacity "an ontological openness to the original Source of all things" (101, n. 16). It does not follow from its natural or essential possession, however, that it is easy to actualize this capacity. On the contrary.

*refuses* assent to a truth which he has *recognized with sufficient plainness* to be God's speech."[17]

9. Though there is a natural human capacity to hear divine speech, no argument or evidence, nor any human act of will, can by itself bring about the actualization of this capacity; instead, a "spiritual inner light," divine "in-spiration," is required to recognize that *God* is speaking, that something is indeed *divine* speech (78).

10. In religious faith, what is believed, who is believed, and the inspiration to believe, are one and the same: God (90).

11. Faith is a kind of union with God that is a very great good, indeed the highest good possible for humans, fulfilling the very deepest human needs.[18]

Human faith as Thomistically conceived by Pieper is unreserved assent to a proposition on the authority of someone trusted (for good reason, if one is rational), even though evidence or insight into the truth of that proposition is lacking. Human faith is a cognitive condition, approaching certainty or knowledge if the authority is supremely reliable, but it is produced not through actualizing a cognitive or intellectual capacity on its own but rather though a collaborative (and foundational) act of the will—the free choice of a desired good, especially the good of relationship to or with one's authority. Religious faith embodies all the conditions of human faith and exercises a natural human receptivity to the supernatural, but it involves a unique set of propositions believed (divine truths), a unique authority ("divine speech"), a unique generating cause (divine inspiration), achieves the highest kind of certainty or knowledge, and realizes the greatest good for human beings, meeting our deepest needs. In brief, religious faith is communion with God via propositions believed on divine authority.[19]

17. Pieper (72; emphasis added). The conditions specified by the italicized words likely entail that, in Pieper's mind at least, genuine "unbelief" is a rather rare phenomenon.

18. "Man can scarcely find anything better and more meaningful to do than 'believingly to unite with the knowledge of God' " (Pieper [87], in part quoting Aquinas *De veritate* 14.8). "If God has really spoken, then it is not only good to believe Him; rather, the act of believing generates those things which in fact are goodness and perfection for man" (91).

19. This account, as one might expect, corresponds closely to the formulation of the first Vatican Council: "The Catholic Church teaches that this faith, which is the beginning of human salvation, is the supernatural virtue whereby, inspired and assisted by the grace of God, we believe the things which he has revealed as true,

## The Models Exemplified

Pieper's Thomistic conception of faith exemplifies both the belief and the personal relationship models—with some minor but interesting deviations. Both duality of exemplification and deviation from each model contributes to the complexity of his conception. One might characterize Pieper's conception as an ambiguous and somewhat aberrant exemplification of the two models of faith.[20]

The centrality of propositional belief in Pieper's Thomistic conception of faith is evident. Moreover, all of the features of the belief model are clearly present: propositional belief, "certainty" (firm conviction), lack of adequate evidence, and nonevidential basing. It may therefore seem as though this conception is nothing more than a straightforward illustration of the belief model. There are, however, several problems with this way of viewing things.

1. Pieper goes beyond the belief model in several ways. For one, he holds that faith's certainty must entirely exclude all doubt and must involve the willingness to accept anything the authority says. But on the belief model, there can be qualified, partially reserved, and wavering faith, at least in human cases, as well as faith that encompasses certain kinds and degrees of doubt and also faith that is committed to accepting only part of what the authority says.[21] Of course, absolute certainty of belief and willingness to believe are

---

not because of their intrinsic truth as perceived by the natural light of reason, but because of the authority of God himself who reveals them, and who can neither be deceived nor deceive" (quoted in Dulles, 1985, 4).

20. There are also residual features of the hope and devotion models in Pieper's conception, for example, the great desire for a future self-fulfilling good of the former and the wholehearted and lasting commitment of the latter. Pieper, like Aquinas, presumably could treat these not as parts of faith, much less as alternative conceptions of faith, but rather as partial explications of the other two great theological virtues, hope and love.

21. This is true even where S unreservedly believes that p on the authority of A. In such cases it may be that S is, and should be, committed only to accepting whatever A says insofar as A is (or S believes that A is) an authority for S. An authority for someone on some topic or in some area need not be an authority on everything for that person. Furthermore, if Pieper is right in holding that S's acceptance of p on A's authority entails that S is willing to believe anything A says, then it is doubtful whether any case of so-called "human" faith—where A is a human person—could be rationally warranted or even acceptable. What human person is or could be so great an authority that whatever he says ought to be believed by someone else? Finally, is it even possible for someone to believe anything and everything another human says?

consistent with the belief model; it is just that they are not required by this model.

2. Pieper apparently conflates, and confuses, certainty as an epistemic concept (related to knowledge) and certitude as a psychological concept (related to assurance and confidence); only the latter is required by faith according to the belief model (where it is labeled "conviction"), though one may readily comprehend why the former is sought as well.

3. Pieper seems to incorporate criteria of evidential rationality into his conception of faith. According to him, faith requires evidence of A's authority or credibility. But it is unclear how to interpret Pieper here. Does he mean that S must have conclusive or preponderant evidence of A's authority, or only some evidence (which might be outweighed by contrary evidence)? Does Pieper propose such evidence as a condition of faith or as a condition of rational faith? The former claim would be that in order for S to believe that p on A's authority, S must have (some? conclusive?) evidence that A is an authority with regard to p, and the latter claim would be that in order for S's faith in A to be rationally justified S must have (some? conclusive?) evidence of A's credibility. Perhaps the best construal of Pieper's intentions consistent with the belief model of faith is this: Belief on another's authority requires some evidence of A's credibility, and rational belief on another's authority requires conclusive evidence of A's credibility.

All in all, perhaps it is best to attribute Pieper's stringency about certainty and willingness to believe to his desire to promulgate a religious—specifically Roman Catholic—view and evaluation of faith. His conception of specifically Catholic Christian faith bears affinities to other, more ordinary or widespread notions of faith insofar as all are (differing) exemplifications of the belief model.[22]

Still, it is misleading to view Pieper's conception of faith solely in terms of the belief model. There can be no doubt that propositional belief takes the lead in his presentation, but features of the personal relationship model turn out to be just as important, and these must not be ignored in appreciating his conception of faith.

22. Pieper's conception is more specific or stringent than ordinary conceptions in the two conditions mentioned—excluding all doubt and believing whatever the authority says. Other conceptions that relax or avoid these conditions may still exemplify the belief model, perhaps regarding as optional what Pieper makes mandatory.

Pieper clearly holds that faith is a personal relationship involving trust as well as believing propositions, and that believing propositions about God on God's authority must be firmly rooted in the love of God, which is perhaps the deepest aspect of trust.[23]

Furthermore, for Pieper the major, if not the only, propositions that must be believed in faith are the very "articles of faith" on which the personal relationship model lays stress, and the fact of, if not also the belief in, divine causal efficacy in originating faith is contained in Pieper's emphasis on "inspiration." Two problems arise in connection with his treatment of the latter point. First, Pieper insists that faith is at once a human act of free (evidentially "uncoerced") assent to another's authority as well as a matter of having evidence for the other's authoritativeness, and it is not clear how it can be both. One construal might require evidence for A's authoritativeness, but not base assent to A's authority on this evidence. Another attempt might retain only free assent as part of a conception of faith and regard the question of evidence as a matter not of faith per se but of the rationality of faith. Pieper gives no indication of which, if either, approach he would take. Second, Pieper claims that in religion the free act of faith involves both a natural receptivity to supernatural revelation and also a special work of divine grace and "illumination" or "light." This view of the relative causal roles in faith of natural subject and supernatural object seems unnecessarily restrictive; the personal relationship model no doubt permits Pieper's view, but it also allows other, more radically theocentric conceptions in which God specially (and not innately or "naturally") gives humans not only illumination but also the capacity to be illumined.

### Recapitulation

Pieper's Thomistic conception of faith exemplifies both the belief and the personal relationship models, though with additional or deviating features in both instances; both exemplification and deviation are illuminating. In terms of Pieper's actual exposition, the

23. Indeed, the tradition out of which (and for which) Pieper speaks has since Vatican II brought such features of faith to the fore. Baum, 1969, notes that in Roman Catholic thought since Vatican II greater emphasis has been laid on divine self-disclosure to the entire human person (not just communication of propositions) and on the universal dimension of faith (outside the church). The net effect, he adds, is to move the Thomistic conception toward the views of the Protestant Reformers. But even so there are differences, as we shall see.

belief model clearly predominates, but in terms of logical structure both models are equally co-present. In fact, the two models' consistency at a general level is shown by their consistent mutual exemplification in Pieper's conception. At the same time, however, we see that there are more ways than one to exemplify each model (and to exemplify them both together), as Pieper introduces several optional specifications of features drawn from both models. One conception may exemplify more than one model, and one model may be exemplified in more than one conception, and both may be variously accomplished. Grasping these points further helps us to see the analogical nature of the concept of faith: There are different conceptions belonging to the same concept, and models may illumine both difference and sameness.

## B. A Calvinist Conception

### Shepherd's Version

In considering a Reformed or Calvinist conception of faith, we once again rely on the work of a recent commentator on Calvin, rather than looking to John Calvin himself. Centuries of scholarship may not have settled what Calvin meant, or might have meant, or should have meant, but they have at least clarified many issues. Victor Shepherd's book, *The Nature and Function of Faith in the Theology of John Calvin*, admirably analyzes various texts of Calvin and presents a clear portrait of a Calvinist conception of faith. Our concern is with the conception, and not with its (more or less plausible) ascription to Calvin.[24] I note seven distinctive features of the conception he portrays.

   1. Faith is necessarily saving faith, and, since in Shepherd's view

---

24. Shepherd, 1983; page references in this section are to this text. Although the extent to which the conception Shepherd presents is precisely *Calvin's* conception is not an issue here, it would be well to keep in mind Calvin's own famous Trinitarian definition of faith as "a firm and certain knowledge of God's benevolence toward us, founded upon the truth of the freely given promise in Christ, both revealed to our minds and sealed upon our hearts through the Holy Spirit" (*Institutes of the Christian Religion* 3.2.7, tr. Battles, ed. McNeill, 551). Other interpretations of Calvin on faith are found in Berkhof, 1949; Berkouwer, 1954, 1958; Brunner, 1946, 1949, 1956, 1964; Bulman, 1953; Dowey, 1952; Gogarten, 1959; Parker, 1969; Thielicke, 1977; and Warfield, 1931.

only Jesus Christ saves and can save, saving faith is uniquely faith in Jesus Christ. There is no such thing as generic human faith; faith is and can be nothing more, but also nothing less, than distinctively Christian faith. Faith is conceptually restricted to having only Christian instances.[25]

One important line of argument Shepherd uses to reach this rather startling uniqueness claim is as follows. Faith is not some common human attitude that can be attached to almost any object, religious or not, as if Christian faith were but an instance—an extension or heightening perhaps—of ordinary human faith. Rather, the attitude and entire nature of faith are determined by the nature of its "object"—what or who the faith is in—and by the nature of its "author"—what or who produces the faith. Where object and author are unique, so are the attitude and nature. Jesus Christ is unique, because Christ is the unique Word of God, "the Father's eternal decree to save" (2), and God Himself is unique because God is sui generis. Christ, then, is the sole object and author of faith, since faith in God just is faith in Jesus Christ.[26] The character of faith is likewise unique, having nothing in common with anything else called "faith."

2. Faith is a pure gift, God's free bestowal of life on sinners who are "dead" and "hence utterly incapable of responding were life offered to them" (1). Only God can guarantee the continuance of faith once granted. At every moment, and in every respect, faith's existence is completely dependent on God's mercy; it is "entirely the gratuitous gift of God" (2). Faith is not a human action going

25. This is a crucial point. On this view there is only one, or at any rate only one "true" conception of faith, the Calvinist Christian conception; all other conceptions do not truly speak of faith but of something else. Shepherd recognizes that there are other uses of the term "faith"—"religious alternatives," he sometimes calls them (99)—and he even admits that there may be a "phenomenological similarity" between the phenomena they denote and what "faith" in its true Christian use denotes (104). Nevertheless, he insists that these other phenomena are not properly called "faith" at all; rather, they should be labeled "religion" or "piety." Religion lacks saving force; it is "a monument to human concupiscence. . . . One can be both pious and condemned" (102). A distinction implicit in Shepherd's presentation is that between religion with a determinate object that is other than Jesus Christ and religion with no determinate object at all. Concerning the latter, Shepherd states: " 'Faith' of [sic] an indeterminate object is no faith at all; exhortations to 'have faith' are of themselves mere incentives to God-defiant idolatry" (30).

26. "God *is* he whose Son is Jesus Christ. Not to have the Son is not to have God incomplete or even distorted; it is simply not to have God" (103).

out to meet a divine action that recognizes and completes it. The act of faith is not something humans naturally do, nor is the capacity for having faith something humans innately possess. Humans even lack the desire or capacity for wanting to receive a capacity for having faith. Everything, absolutely everything, about faith must be given by God in Christ. There are no *præambula fidei*.[27]

In fact, in a sense, faith is not even something a human being "has." Faith is neither a human creation nor a human possession; faith is not possessing Christ but being possessed of Christ (30). Moreover, faith's (soteriological) effects are also gifts. For example, faith does not, by itself, justify or sanctify. Faith is only the contingent instrument of justification used by Christ (30), an empty vessel into which Christ's righteousness is poured (36). Salvation is wholly God's merciful gift, his "election."[28] Indeed, on Shepherd's interpretation of Calvin's notorious doctrine of double predestination, God eternally ordains not only election but also reprobation; humans do not even have the power to frustrate God by rejecting his offer of mercy; rejection as well as acceptance is foreordained.[29]

3. Despite the heavy emphasis on the sheer gratuity of faith, Shepherd nonetheless affirms that, according to Calvin, faith involves a genuine human affirmation, an act of will. This is not to say that humans have the power to create the renewed will that alone can produce faith's affirmation; the capacity to will faithfully must be created anew by the Holy Spirit (36). Nevertheless, Shepherd insists, faith is a human affirmation; in this much at least, he maintains, humans are not mere automatons (82–83).[30]

27. This is one of the (surprisingly few) points on which Shepherd's Calvinist conception of faith differs significantly from Pieper's (1963) Thomist one.

28. Calvin says that "whatever excellence there is in men is not implanted by nature, so that it can be attributed to nature or heredity, nor is it procured by our own free will so as to put God under our control, but it flows from his mercy which is pure and free" (Calvin, *Commentary* on 1 Cor. 4:7, quoted in Shepherd, 40). Shepherd adds: "Election forces upon faith" (i.e., upon those who have faith) the recognition that the engendering of faith is sheer miracle: "Dead men do not resurrect themselves" (44). "Thus the doctrine of election upholds the truth that God's faith-engendering activity is utterly gratuitous" (45).

29. According to Calvin, the doctrine of predestination—eternal election—has the threefold function of extolling God's mercy (election is a free and benevolent gift), upholding his glory (if we did anything, God's glory would be diminished), and preserving believers' humility (faith is not due to oneself) (46–48).

30. There is a certain tension here. On the one hand faith is solely a divine gift—both the act of faith and the capacity for faith are God's new and special creation. On the other hand, faith is a responsible human act of affirmation. To reduce this

4. Christian faith as a relationship with Jesus Christ—not "union," "absorption," or "identity," but "fellowship," "participation," "society," "sonship," "incorporation," and "engrafting"— is the realization of "authentic humanity," but it is not the fulfillment of our native endowment, our inborn human nature. Rather, faith involves a conversion that is more than just a matter of changing one's will; proper relationship with Jesus Christ requires the transformation of the entire human person. This transformed being may be considered a new creation. Revelation, therefore, is not "the dissemination of information" but "the act of God wherein he effects a new reality" (21).[31]

5. Even though the true object of faith is the person Jesus Christ, and although faith is definitely not identical with "ideology" or assent to any set of doctrines about him, apprehension of Jesus Christ as the living Word of God does involve apprehension of doctrines, which are propositions believed to be true.[32] The central set of doctrines concerns God's will toward us. It is not so much a structured set of propositions—"articles of faith"—as it is a single doctrine, the entire or at least the fundamental propositional content of the Christian gospel: God is for us; God is benevolent and beneficent toward us; God loves us; God is merciful to us. Even such a fundamental doctrine, however, is still secondary in faith. Apprehension of God's mercy goes far beyond assent to the proposition that God is merciful; such apprehension is an intimately personal realization and appreciation of the reality of God's mercy. Only in this latter sense is God's mercy a necessary condition of faith, something that is "logically prior" to faith (11).[33]

---

tension, if not to remove it, Shepherd and Calvin seem to go in different directions. Calvin clings to divine omnipotence, as manifested in the doctrine of election, thereby casting a "shadow of unreality over virtually everything he [Calvin] says about human affirmation. . . . Semi-Pelagianism of any hue must be avoided" (89). Shepherd, however, thinks that Calvin's fixation on omnipotence is a refusal to let God's will really be mercy—a mercy that could grant the room for human affirmation that sheer omnipotence cannot allow (95–96).

31. This act is the work of the Holy Spirit. "The Holy Spirit is the power in which the exalted Christ acts on men so as to draw them to himself, incorporate them into himself, and give them what is his" (22).

32. "Hence faith is neither engendered nor sustained without doctrinal teaching" (5). Still, it must be constantly born in mind that faith is not merely human assent to propositions; anyone who thinks faith is propositional belief lacks Christian experience.

33. "Only God's act of mercy wherein he reconciles the world to himself can establish faith" (12); "it must be *understood* that mercy *is* God's will towards us"

6. Faith is certain knowledge. Faith lies between ignorant believing and clear comprehension; it is neither the affirming of something not understood on the authority of another (so-called "implicit faith"[34]), nor a kind of totally lucid understanding. Still, faith is knowledge.[35] Faith is knowledge of God, which is knowledge of God's will as effectual mercy, which is knowledge of Jesus Christ. Faith's knowledge is knowledge of Christ. In knowing Christ, humans cannot employ any natural capacity like sense-experience or reasoning, for no human capacity can reach to God. Still, faith is not opinion or wishful thinking; faith is certain, indeed more certain than sense-experience, metaphysical speculation, or rational demonstration. Faith is not strong or highly probable opinion, for opinion is always open to revision, at least in principle, while faith is final (99). Faith is not wishful thinking, for it is authorized not by human wants but by divine inspiration. In short, faith's certainty needs no authentication from any other capacity in order to yield knowledge (19).[36] At the same time, however, faith is never pure

---

(16). In the *Institutes of the Christian Religion* 3.2.2, Calvin holds that saving faith is not affirming what some authority such as the church prescribes, but only a person's (transpropositional) "knowledge" or "explicit recognition" of God's mercy toward us.

34. Calvin often attacked "implicit faith," which he viewed as a major error in the Roman Catholic conception of faith. For Calvin, faith rests on, and is, knowledge, not the "pious ignorance" of believing what one does not understand (105). Not the church but Jesus Christ alone authenticates faith; the church only bears witness. In terms of distinctions introduced in Chap. 2, sec. A., Calvin seems to be chiefly concerned to rule out secondhand faith of any kind (faith in Christ on another's authority); his remarks have less force against firsthand implicit faith (S would believe p if p were proposed for S's belief by A). In addition, Shepherd fails to distinguish between two issues: whether S's faith in A can be solely or completely based on S's faith in B (exclusively secondhand faith); and, whether S's faith in A can be at all based on S's faith in B (exclusively firsthand faith). Shepherd seems to urge that since faith (in Jesus Christ) cannot be exclusively secondhand it must therefore be entirely firsthand. The personal relationship model agrees in ruling out exclusively secondhand faith, but it does not require, though it would permit, faith to be exclusively firsthand. It would also allow faith to be a mixture of firsthand and secondhand faith. Shepherd's conception requires one to vest authority exclusively in God, while the personal relationship model permits both this exclusivistic notion as well as other more tolerant conceptions.

35. "Unless there is knowledge present it is not God that we worship but a specter or a ghost" (Calvin, *Commentary* on John 4:22; quoted by Shepherd, 97).

36. In addition to being certain, faith is also a "constant assurance and perfect confidence" (Calvin, *Institutes of the Christian Religion* 3.13.3). This assurance does

or perfect knowledge; Jesus Christ is never fully understood before the eschaton (119).

7. The presence of faith is not "empirically discernible" (95). On the one hand, there is no external or public test of someone's faith (as opposed to a test of her confession of faith). Faith's authentic affirmation has no reliable behavioral criterion. On the other hand, ascertaining one's "standing-in-faith" cannot be a matter of passing some inner or subjective test—a matter of "psychospiritual introspection"—for that would imply, Shepherd thinks, that faith's assurance rests finally in humanity, not in God. "From a human standpoint faith will always be defective" (91). In fact, someone who worries about her own spiritual health would be well advised to turn away from herself toward Jesus Christ instead. As humility may be destroyed by constant self-assessment and comparison with others, so faith may be undermined by an excessive self-scrutiny that seeks evidence of rebirth, calling, or virtue.[37]

In sum, then, according to Shepherd's Calvinist conception, faith is fundamentally a unique personal relationship with Jesus Christ, and only with Jesus Christ, which necessarily derives from Jesus Christ; Jesus Christ is the sole author as well as the sole object of faith; and this faith cannot be understood at all in purely human, secular, or psychological terms. Faith is a pure gift, not just as an

---

not absolutely preclude anxiety, doubt, and the sin of unbelief, "yet Christ dwelling in believers does not allow such sin to overturn faith" (27).

37. Shepherd, 95. Shepherd here departs from Calvin, as well as many later Calvinists who sought fervently, even desperately, for assurance that they were among the elect—even while condemning Anabaptists for introspection. According to Shepherd, Calvin himself ironically ends up as a kind of Anabaptist: "The pledge (*pignus*) of our salvation becomes not Christ (the Word *extra nos*) but the 'inner call'. . . . Calvin is left urging believers to introspect. Calling becomes *evidence* of election to faith. Believers are turned back in on themselves; *they* are the arbiters of the veridicality of their calling" (92). What appears to bother Shepherd is not that there is or is not evidence of election or even that people are or are not able to ascertain what that evidence is or how much evidence there is, but rather that people should be—or put themselves—in the position of determining what counts as the right kind of evidence and the sufficient amount of evidence that confirms election. Presumably Shepherd would allow that God could set up evidential standards and endow humans with the capacities to detect evidence and apply those standards, but not that humans could do this on their own. Even so, there would be the inevitable temptation for those so endowed to consider—consciously or not—this special endowment as their own. Could God endow a creature with a self-humbling capacity for discernment?

actual relationship but also as an exercise of capacities and tendencies specially created by Christ. Christ gives not only himself but also the capacity and desire to receive him (as well as the capacity to want to receive him). Still, faith requires a genuine human act of affirmation: an act not simply of assent to propositions, of willing the good, or of feeling wholeheartedly, but an act of the whole human person relying on Christ without qualification. Faith is a cognitive condition and may be called "certain knowledge" (to distinguish it from merely probable opinion and wishful thinking), but it cannot be confirmed or disconfirmed by ordinary human means since the presence of faith is not "empirically discernible," either via observation of behavior or via introspection.

### The Question of Uniqueness

In examining Shepherd's conception of faith in the light of our models of faith, we must immediately address his contention that faith in Jesus Christ is unique, conceptually unique, such that alleged "faith" in anything but Jesus Christ does not count as faith at all. If this contention is sustainable, then there is no use for models such as I have sketched (which not only differ among themselves but which can also be instanced in a number of different cases, both religious and nonreligious alike), much less for an examination of an analogical concept of faith like that I propose. Shepherd's claim of conceptual uniqueness, however, cannot be sustained in crucial respects.[38]

Shepherd's major reason for holding that faith is conceptually unique is this: Faith in Jesus Christ is unique because Jesus Christ is unique, and Jesus Christ is unique because God is unique.[39] But the

38. Other versions of the uniqueness claim are found in K. Barth, 1936, 1959; Brunner, 1946; Ebeling, 1961; Ellul, 1983; Forde, 1982; Kraemer, 1957, 1969; Thielicke, 1977; and Van Noort, 1961. See also Penelhum, 1983, for a sustained critique of "fideism," which sometimes embodies similar uniqueness claims.

39. Another reason is less prominent in Shepherd's presentation. Right relationship with Jesus Christ is uniquely important: Only through such relationship can salvation be obtained, and nothing can be more important than salvation. Nothing else, therefore, is nearly as important as Christian faith. Hence, such faith is conceptually unique. This argument also fails. The most important instance of a concept is not thereby the only instance. Unsuccessful faith, failed or flawed faith, even trivial faith—all are still faith.

conclusion about the uniqueness of the conception of faith does not follow from the points about the uniqueness of relationship to God. Let us grant that God is unique not merely as every individual person is unique (necessarily, nothing else can be this individual person) but also as a kind of person may be unique (necessarily, nothing else can be this kind of person). Even if it follows that relationship to God is unique in some respects (necessarily, one could not be in quite this particular relationship or this kind of relationship to anything else), it does not follow that the conception of faith that this relationship instances is unique to this instance or this kind of instance. On the contrary, faith in God may still have a number of structural features in common with other relationships, and insofar as those common features are the very ones essential to what we have called a model of faith, we may see this case as exemplifying the model. To be more specific: Relationship with Jesus Christ exemplifies the personal relationship model of faith even though it is distinctive or unique in various respects.

There can be little doubt that faith as Shepherd portrays it exemplifies the personal relationship model of faith. Granted, personal relationship with a unique person has features no other personal relationship can have, and the more distinctive the person the more distinctive the relationship. But such faith is still a personal relationship,[40] which instantiates trust, contains some propositional beliefs, and is caused (more or less) by its object—the major essential features of the personal relationship model of faith. Clearly, Shepherd's Calvinist conception is not the only (actual or possible) exemplification of the personal relationship model of faith. While it offers certain important qualifications and extensions of the model, it must resemble other exemplifications of the model. Hence, the claims to conceptual uniqueness on behalf of Christian faith are confused or vastly overstated.[41] Insofar as his conception exemplifies

40. Shepherd is insistent that God is a personal being, indeed the very person who is the divine Father of Jesus Christ.

41. I do not dispute the possibility of certain kinds of uniqueness. Faith in Jesus Christ may be uniquely salvific (or salvific in a uniquely maximal way), and the agency of God in and through Jesus Christ may differ from other forms of divine and human agency (though this need not preclude the possibility of similar divine agency); and so forth. But none of these possibilities is a matter of conceptual requirement on the concept of faith; the uniqueness of faith in Jesus Christ, if any,

the model, it is not conceptually unique, for other conceptions also exemplify it; and insofar as it qualifies and extends (but does not contradict) the model, it specifies the model in ways that may resemble or even be the same as extensions in other conceptions.

On the one hand, consider how multiple exemplification of the personal relationship model ensures that Shepherd's conception of faith will resemble other conceptions. Faith for Shepherd is fundamentally a trusting personal relationship, a relationship between a human person and a divine person. This is so even though relationship with Jesus Christ takes on the unique quality and flavor of its distinctive object and author; the relationship still involves trust, propositional belief, and object-authorship, which are the bedrock features of the personal relationship model. This minimal structural coincidence ensures that faith in Jesus Christ cannot be completely different from a faithful relationship with a human being; there will be at least a formal resemblance with respect to these features, however different in kind the persons involved may be.

On the other hand, there are a number of qualifications and extensions of the model in Shepherd's conception, but none of them implies that Christian faith is conceptually unique.

1. Propositional belief, while present and essential, is severely downplayed in Shepherd's conception. Faith requires believing that God is merciful to us, but this is only the tip of a massive existential dependence on the one who is believed to be merciful. Propositional belief is de-emphasized almost, but not quite, to the vanishing point. This is why Shepherd's Calvinist conception seems so utterly opposed to the belief model of faith. But seeming is not being. In reality, the two have no quarrel over the presence of propositional belief; both hold it to be an essential feature of faith. The only question concerns the relative prominence of such essential beliefs in one's conceptual portrait. Nor does Shepherd's conception specify a unique degree of prominence (or rather lack of prominence) of propositional belief in faith; other exemplifications of the personal relationship model could do as much (or as little).

2. The personal relationship model stresses trust (acceptance, loyalty, and love) as the predominating quality of faith, whereas Shep-

---

is not due to its exemplifying a unique conception of faith, one that contains all of the meaning of the full concept of faith.

herd's conception stresses obedience (to the merciful lawgiver) and thankfulness (for the absolute gift) in response to the divine initiative. Again, these are not conflicting views, for obedience and thankfulness are not opposed to trust. They may even be viewed as varieties of trust: For S to obey A in the right way (with a grateful heart) is largely for S to trust in A's authority; and for S to be thankful toward A is largely for S to recognize and trust in A's goodness and goodwill toward S. Trust need not be specified in terms of obedience and thankfulness; one could imagine more egalitarian and less grateful forms of trusting personal relationship. But these are differences within the boundaries of trust; they mark degrees of conceptual resemblance and dissimilarity, not absolute otherness.

3. Shepherd's conception approaches (or even reaches) an extreme position with respect to the divine authorship of faith. At times it appears he holds that every aspect of faith is due to some special divine gratuitous act. Not only the human response but the capacity and desire to respond, and the desire to have the capacity to respond, are freely given by a merciful God. Clearly this position goes considerably beyond what the personal relationship model requires, which is only that the object of faith at least partially cause the relationship. But since "at least" states only a minimal requirement, more is permitted—even the near-maximum claimed by Shepherd. The model permits various degrees and extents (not to mention kinds) of causality by the object of faith. This Calvinist conception of faith is one permissible specification of the personal relationship model of faith. Because it is not the only possible one, it is not uniquely faith.

4. Shepherd's conception takes as the central "doctrine" of faith (the most important article of faith) the nature of God's will toward us, how God is disposed toward us. This is no more than a specification of the personal relationship model, which does not indicate which propositions are articles of faith but only delineates what an article of faith is. This is not a contradiction of the model but an optional specification of it; other conceptions (exemplifying the personal relationship model) could adopt different articles of belief while still remaining conceptions of faith.

5. Faith, according to Shepherd's conception, necessarily involves conversion—the radical transformation of one's entire self—and not merely a partial or limited alteration of, for example, some prop-

ositional beliefs. One cannot be naturally born with faith; one must be spiritually "reborn." Shepherd's conception specifies as a necessary feature of faith what the personal relationship model of faith regards as optional; but this specification does not entail that Shepherd's conception is totally unlike all other conceptions of faith, including those that consider faith to be only a partial or limited self-transformation. Such specification is a permissible option of the model, not a rejection of the model or a badge of conceptual uniqueness.

6. Finally, Shepherd (and Calvin) strongly insist that faith is knowledge, indeed certain knowledge, albeit knowledge that cannot be confirmed or disconfirmed by any ordinary human means but that must be divinely inspired and authenticated. Shepherd's account fails to distinguish certainty (as rational justification) from certitude or conviction (as personal commitment or involvement).[42] Faith, Shepherd claims, is unrevisable, divinely confirmed, fervent, and lasting. These claims, it seems, might better be expressed in terms of psychological conviction than in terms of epistemic certainty. Indeed, to insist on epistemic certainty in these matters may entail losing something vital for faith according to the belief model: its evidential riskiness. If faith is simply an appeal to some transhuman evidential source (where not only the evidence but also the capacity for recognizing it as evidence is given to some but not all humans), then faith achieves epistemic certainty at the expense of those kinds of fidelity, trust, venture, and zest that can exist only where the evidence is inadequate.

Some light may be shed on this latter point by the belief model of faith (despite the vigorous rejection of this model by the Calvinist conception). The belief model sharply distinguishes evidential certainty from firm conviction. Faith requires propositional beliefs, but excludes basing such beliefs on evidence (both available and forthcoming). Faith must take a risk with respect to the evidence. Still, such risk does not prevent faith from achieving a high degree of confidence that is tenaciously retained or maintained in the face of various obstacles. Faith simply has a nonevidential basis, and that

---

42. Compare a similar confusion in Pieper's (1963) Thomistic conception. It would be an intriguing study as to why this confusion has been so prevalent in accounts of religious faith.

basis might be a trusting personal relationship with another. For this reason, Shepherd's Calvinist notion would do well to eschew evidential certainty, and if it does there is no conflict with the personal relationship model of faith.

We see, therefore, that even Shepherd's extensions and qualifications of the personal relationship model of faith do not support his claims to conceptual uniqueness. In a number of cases Shepherd's conception treats as mandatory what the personal relationship model considers to be optional, while in others it sets up conditions that (presumably) only one kind of instance—the Christian one—can meet, but does not thereby remove the other, resembling features. The main thrust of these extensions and qualifications, it appears, is to ensure that faith can be found nowhere but in the lives of Christians (if indeed it can be found even there), by making faith conceptually unique.[43] Such an attempt necessarily fails. But even were it to succeed, its triumph would be a hollow one, for the following reasons.

1. As Shepherd admits, there are, in addition to great differences, also great formal and phenomenological similarities between specifically Christian faith and faith according to other conceptions of faith; the uniqueness conditions tend to overemphasize the differences and to overlook the resemblances. Considering both difference and resemblance together leads us to see that Shepherd's conception of faith, with its alleged uniqueness, is but one kind of exemplification of one model of faith (the personal relationship model); other exemplifications of the same model, as well as exemplifications of other models, might be less concerned to stake out differences and more inclined to observe and tolerate resemblances. Seeing this should undermine any desire to pursue the quest for conceptual uniqueness.

2. Even if faith could successfully be made into a parochial concept—one with necessary applicability to at most one religious tradition—there might be certain practical side effects. Interreligious dialogue might be blocked; some persons (both insiders and outsiders) might be encouraged to remain in willful ignorance of the

---

43. Ironically enough, such a drive toward conceptual uniqueness is not unique to Shepherd's conception of faith, or to Calvinist conceptions, or to Christian ones, or even to theistic ones. The problems raised by Shepherd's conception have considerably wider significance.

religious lives and traditions of others; and encouragement might be given to religious intolerance. Such potential side effects of insisting on conceptual uniqueness will seem acceptable to some, but they will give pause to others with an eye on historical excesses.

3. There are also theological resources within Shepherd's own tradition that caution against excessive claims to conceptual uniqueness. Such claims are often vehicles of piety draped with scriptural citation, but it is at least a formal possibility that they convey not humble obedience to divine will but rather prideful human self-assertion—the self-assertion of an individual, a group, or even an entire cultural tradition of thinking about God. Whether this is so in a particular case perhaps only humble, honest, strenuous self-examination will show—or perhaps God alone can know. At any rate the call to relentless honesty about the depths of human sinfulness is as much a part of traditions of faith such as Shepherd's as is exclusivism, and appreciation of both elements may temper one's evangelical zeal for conceptual uniqueness.

### Recapitulation

While there may be unique features to Shepherd's Calvinist conception of faith as faith in Jesus Christ alone, they are not sufficient to prevent other conceptions, which permit faith to be a different (kind of) relation to a different (kind of) object, from being or being regarded as conceptions of faith. Instead, Shepherd's conception is illuminated by viewing it as exemplifying the personal relationship model of faith while also qualifying this model in several respects (mostly a matter of taking features to an extreme or making mandatory in the conception features that are merely optional in the model). Shepherd's conception of faith, therefore, is not conceptually unique but rather fairly close kin to other exemplifications of the same model, as well as a more distant relative of exemplifications of other models.

## C. A Lutheran Conception

### Aulén's Version

In considering a distinctively Lutheran conception of faith, we turn to a twentieth-century scholar, Gustaf Aulén, rather than to

Martin Luther himself. Instead of getting bogged down in interpreting an effusive and unsystematic thinker like Luther, we will benefit from the relatively clear and organized presentation found in Aulén's book, *The Faith of the Christian Church*. While admitting that different meanings have been given to the term "faith" at different times, Aulén nonetheless specifies a broadly Lutheran version of this "principal concept of Christianity" (23).[44]

According to Aulén, faith is fundamentally a comprehensive, immediate, and personal relationship between a human being and God, a relationship that is not symmetrical or egalitarian but rather "theocentric"—a relationship where "God is the center and in which life is dominated by God alone" (23–24). Of course, since Aulén believes Jesus Christ is God's sole and authentic revelation, theocentric relationship turns out to be Christocentric faith (60). At any rate, Aulén begins his exposition with relationship to God, not to Christ.

1. This theocentric relationship is comprehensive in the sense that it engages all major human capacities: intellect (believing certain propositions that God reveals to humans), feeling (wholehearted trust in God), and will ("audacious" personal decision to be committed to God), and much more. However, there are several qualifications on faith's comprehensiveness. Most obviously, the engagement of human capacities is not the whole of a relationship, for there is also the other's capacities and activities, as well as the roles and interactions between the persons. More importantly, involving all major human capacities does not entail determining everything in a life or engaging these capacities to their fullest or most harmonious or most excellent actualization. Moreover, engaging all of one's capacities in theocentric relationship does not entail that this is the only or the best way of engaging them. Finally, although he insists that all human capacities are indeed engaged in faith, in the main Aulén tends to think of theocentric relationship primarily in terms of action or volition, relegating feeling and cognition to sec-

44. Aulén, 1948; page references in this section are to this text. At the risk of taxing the reader with redundancy, I insist once more that our concern is not with Aulén's fidelity to Luther, but with the distinctive elements in Aulén's own conception. Whether or not it is precisely Luther's view, it is at least a Lutheran conception. For other discussions of Luther's conception of faith, see Alles, 1985; Blanshard, 1975; Buri, 1976; Ebeling, 1961, 1963; Higgins, 1988; Holmer, 1978; Ingram, 1971; Ishihara, 1987; Kerr, 1943; Kolp, 1976; Laube, 1983; Thielicke, 1977.

ondary status.[45] In characteristically vivid language, Aulén describes faith as an "affirmation" or "decision"—even "an audacious personal decision and a bold *yes*" (107).[46]

2. The relationship with God is immediate in several senses.[47] It is a relationship that does not depend on any other relationship. In particular, trusting God does not rest on trust in any human witness or in the teaching authority of the church. Furthermore, the evidence for the authenticity of the relationship—how one can tell whether a putative case truly is relationship with God—somehow lies within the relationship and is not supposed to depend on any other fact, experience, or capacity; the faith-relationship is "self-authenticating." In a third sense, the relationship involves the direct disclosure—indeed the divine self-disclosure—not only of the existence but also of the character, attitudes, and intentions of the divine person. God's existence and being-for-us do not have to be inferred from clues God cleverly plants in nature, history, or personal experience; rather, God's being and character are directly given. Granted, revelation does take place through historical means—through events and actions in human history that are discernible by more than one person—but the revelatory content and power of these means is available only to someone who has faith. Finally, faith's immediacy does not remove but rather heightens consciousness of the immense gulf that separates divine from human life; this is precisely the "distance" of sin (25).

3. Theocentric relationship is personal, not simply in the sense that it is a relation that holds between two persons, but also in the sense that it involves their use of distinctively personal capacities—their apprehension, discernment, and appreciation of the other's personality, character, attitudes, values, and intentions. It follows,

45. This is a divergence from Pieper (1963) and Shepherd (1983), who tend to insist that faith is preeminently a matter of knowing (in some sense), not of feeling or acting. But this divergence is not deep.

46. One reason why Aulén prefers volition to cognition or affection may be that willing seems to encompass, or at least to engage, all of the other capacities in ways that none of them can match. Thinking about God, even correct thinking about God, need not involve appropriate kinds and levels of feeling, much less responsible commitment and action, just as appropriate feeling need not involve much if any correct thought. But willing an entire way of life brings with it appropriate kinds of feeling, thought, and action.

47. It is also mediated in several other senses, but we follow Aulén's stress upon immediacy over mediacy.

according to Aulén, that knowledge or conviction of the truth of propositions, even the truth of propositions about the persons involved, can at best be a secondary or subsidiary aspect of the relationship.

4. Further, according to Aulén, faith and revelation are correlative or reciprocal concepts. There are several ways of expressing what might be meant by correlativity, and Aulén probably accepts them all: "Faith" and "revelation" are different names for the same relationship; the terms name distinguishable though inseparable ways of looking at the same relationship; understanding either one requires understanding the other. But Aulén goes even further to urge that in order to understand revelation one must have faith, and in order to have faith one must possess revelation. So receiving revelation is necessary to understanding revelation.[48]

5. Still, even though he affirms this latter, very strong sense of the reciprocity of faith and revelation, Aulén nonetheless maintains that "in principle revelation is primary in relation to faith," because the divine standpoint is more "profound" (30). Minimally, this primacy of revelation to faith means that the revealer is not only more important but also more efficacious than the faithful one. The entire theocentric relationship, while genuinely involving two persons, is—entirely, or overwhelmingly, or at least fundamentally—produced by the divine partner; the relationship as a whole is initiated and preserved by God; it is God's gift, an act of "divine self-impartation." Such "self-impartation" is more than the transmission of information about God to humans; it is the very giving of God's own self to us.

6. In a vein reminiscent of Shepherd, Aulén holds that the faith/revelation relationship is unique because of the *sui generis* nature of the divine partner. Aulén goes beyond Shepherd in insisting that this relationship is unique precisely because even to the eye of faith God is absent (*Deus absconditus*). Aulén holds that faith may be present even when one does not "see" or "know" God, so long as one is committed to a way of life of devotion to God. In Lutherans such as Aulén, there is a much greater appreciation of—at times, almost

48. "On the one hand, faith has its origin and nourishment in revelation, and on the other, revelation is discerned and recognized only by the eye of faith" (29). Aulén means that faith is required not only to recognize that revelation occurs and what its content is, but also to comprehend what revelation as such is.

a glorying in—the evidential precariousness of faith, as compared with Thomists such as Pieper or Calvinists such as Shepherd, who wish to stress the presence of God in faith and hence the security of faith in God.

7. It is both possible and necessary to speak of faith or revelation and its "content," according to Aulén. As a result of theocentric faith's uniqueness, however, all such depictions must inevitably be couched in the language of paradox. Paradox results when one tries to preserve in statement form both sides of an essential religious tension, as when someone holds that though revelation "makes use of historical means, persons, words, acts, and the like. . . . [it is] also God's immediate fellowship with the soul" (45), or when one contends that God's essence as revealed is an "impenetrable mystery" (47). It follows that articles of faith—those beliefs about the object of faith that are essential to having faith—will also be paradoxes; indeed, articles of faith seem to be paradigms of paradox.

At any rate, Aulén clearly holds that the paradoxical character of faith's "affirmations" shows that religious "statements" are neither ordinary hypotheses based on empirical evidence nor extraordinary metaphysical claims resting on argument or proof; rather they are "symbolic" vehicles using finite expressions to speak of an infinite God. No words are adequate to the subject matter, even though the symbols may be "filled with the richest content" (97). This is yet another reason why Aulén declines to assimilate faith to knowledge, since knowledge on his view rests on some nonparadoxical apprehension of meaning and evidence (or argument). Instead of being a cognitive achievement, faith, according to Aulén, involves "an audacious and daring decision" (96). This decision is incomprehensible; it transcends all human rational understanding or comprehension. "Faith cannot be transformed into a rational world view. . . . Every pregnant affirmation of faith bears the mark of incomprehensibility" (99–100).[49]

49. Aulén is insistent on faith's incomprehensibility. "The more faith penetrates into the realm of divine revelation, the more it is confronted with the unsearchable" (100). In this insistence, of course, Aulén is only following Luther, although Luther's language is bolder and more vivid: "But faith killeth reason. . . . So all the godly entering with Abraham into the darkness of faith, do kill reason, saying: reason, thou art foolish; thou dost not savour those things which belong unto God: therefore speak not against me, but hold thy peace: judge not, but hear the word of God and believe it. . . . God setteth forth himself otherwise than reason is able either to judge

Without removing the inevitable incomprehension, however, Aulén believes it is nonetheless possible to see that the paradoxical tensions in faith are due to the need to take two quite different points of view on faith, even while conceding that for those who have faith there is a certain priority to the first point of view. For example, concerning whether faith is a divine or a human activity, on the one hand it seems that faith is entirely God's activity, a matter of humans "being subdued and dominated by God."[50] On the other hand, it seems that faith necessarily involves human choice and decision—"a turning and a commitment to God" (27). In short, "Faith is altogether a work of God, but it is at the same time man's choice and decision" (102). Neither side of this paradox should be suppressed or explained away; both must be firmly held, although from different points of view. Paradox is therefore essential in speaking of faith.

8. Faith is indeed certain, according to Aulén, but only in relation to divine revelation. This restriction has two aspects. First, faith's certainty does not extend to ordinary empirical claims; faith is not an alternative source of scientific or commonsense information. Second, and conversely, there can be no ordinary verification (or falsification) of revelation.[51] Further, faith's certainty is not "pragmatic," in the sense that it can be tested via its cultural products such as ethics. Faith lives in a kingdom not of this world; faith is communion with God, not human morality. Nor is the certainty of faith based on the evidence of religious experiences.[52] In the end,

---

or conceive. . . . Kill reason and believe in Christ" (Luther, *Commentary* on Gal. 3:6; quoted in Blanshard, 1975, 132–33, 137, 138).

50. Aulén claims that, "nothing is more essential to the peculiar outlook of faith than its awareness of the fact that the basis of faith is the divine revelation which dominates and subdues. . . . The real reason for our *yes* is, from the viewpoint of faith, nothing but that the hand of God has overwhelmed us" (29).

51. Once again, faith is "an audacious personal decision and a bold *yes*. This may be expressed by saying that for faith revelation is always an unveiling of Reality in secret" (107). The "Reality" thus seen can be glimpsed *only* "in secret."

52. Aulén quotes Luther: "*haec est ratio, cur nostra theologia certa sit: quia rapit nos a nobis et ponit nos extra nos, ut non nitamur viribus, conscientia, senseu, persona, operibus nostris*" (This is the reason why our theology is certain: because it snatches us away from ourselves and places us outside of ourselves, lest we rest upon men, conscience, feelings, character, our own work) (111). Aulén adds, "Because faith is not a faith in experiences, but altogether a faith in God alone, it can live even under those circumstances when God seems most remote, and can carry on to new experiences and a new vision of 'the glory of God' " (112).

faith's only certainty is "an inner conviction of being overwhelmed by God, or . . . an encounter with something which validates itself as a 'revelation' of God"; this inner conviction is identified as the testimony of the Holy Spirit.[53] No other evidence or support of faith's certainty is either possible or necessary.

In sum, on Aulén's conception faith is a comprehensive, immediate, personal, and theocentric divine-human relationship that can only be spoken about in a paradoxical way because it lies beyond rational comprehension, just as God lies hidden in "impenetrable mystery" (47). One such paradox concerns the causality of faith. From the standpoint of one who has faith, faith is entirely due to divine activity—a matter of revelation or grace, a gift from God to humans. From an ordinary human standpoint, however, faith essentially involves an active human response to the divine initiative, an act of acceptance of the gift. This response involves the entire self—intellect, feeling, and will—but it is perhaps least misleading to say that faith is a comprehensive act of will, an "audacious" personal decision. Further complicating the paradox, however, is the conviction that the certainty of the human response is nothing more or less than "an inner conviction of being overwhelmed by God."[54] We have, then, according to Aulén, just one more inevitable paradox in thinking and speaking about faith: Faith is a relationship that is authored completely by God and also partially by a human.

### Exemplifications and Distinctiveness

1. It is clear that Aulén's Lutheran conception of faith primarily exemplifies the personal relationship model of faith, although in a different way than either Pieper's Thomistic conception or Shepherd's Calvinist conception. On Aulén's view, faith is fundamentally a distinctive personal relationship, involving trust, propositional belief, and divine causality, even though each of these latter features receives a distinctive twist. That faith according to Aulén's concep-

---

53. "In this inner, inescapable compulsion the certainty of faith is hidden. This is *testimonium spiritus sancti internum*" (114). See Abraham, 1990, for a discussion of the relations between certainty and the work of the Holy Spirit.

54. Aulén, 113. Like Shepherd's (1983) Calvin, Aulén's Luther wants to make God, not human feeling, the final authority or criterion of faith, and hence the ultimate source of faith's certainty.

tion also exemplifies certain features of two other models of faith, the attitude and the devotion models, further complicates the conceptual situation.

Turning to the latter point first, Aulén's stress on the comprehensiveness of faith exemplifies some features of the attitude model of faith that are not contained, or at any rate are optional, in the personal relationship model. For Aulén, faith is comprehensive when it decisively engages all human capacities, although this does not entail that only faith engages all human capacities nor that all capacities are fully engaged in faith, to the highest possible degree and extent. Comprehensiveness exemplifies three features of a radically constitutive attitude: It is prepropositional, fundamental, and totalizing. An attitude is radically constitutive when it contributes essentially to both subject and object (in relation to each other) as self and horizoned world; it is prepropositional in preceding propositional specification; it is fundamental in not being based on any other attitude or experience; and it is totalizing in being both an attitude of the whole person as well as an orientation toward one's context as a whole. Aulén does not touch on the second element of totalization, but it is clear that the other features of a radically constitutive attitude are present in his account.[55]

In addition, Aulén's voluntarism—his stress on faith as affirmation or decision as opposed to seeing or knowing—has strong affinities with the devotion model, for which faith is a voluntary, wholehearted, lasting, and persevering choice. Although Aulén is always concerned more with the process of constant recommitment to God than he is with the pattern to and by which one is thereby committed, it is clear that he thinks that faith's commitment embraces an entire way of life: the life of loving God and neighbor (16). Although his overwhelming sense of the priority of divine agency in setting up the conditions for faith tends to overshadow or preempt any account of human agency aside from a stress on comprehensiveness, it is clear that Aulén requires human agency to be wholehearted, lasting, and persevering.[56]

---

55. Aulén does not discuss anything resembling the attitude model's notion of faith as significance-bestowing and significance-embracing, but one might find it implicit in his affirmation of the overwhelming importance of faith in God.

56. It is tempting to view lastingness as an implication of wholehearted, perse-

Aulén's Lutheran conception of faith therefore exemplifies not one but three models of faith, although one model (personal relationship) seems more fundamental, and more fully exemplified, than the other two. There are two important implications of this point. First, these three models of faith are consistent, at least in major respects, insofar as they may be conjointly exemplified, as in Aulén's conception. Second, some differences among conceptions of faith, all of which exemplify the same model of faith, are due to the fact that one conception exemplifies portions of other models not (explicitly) exemplified by the others.

2. Aulén's conception of faith differs from the conceptions of Pieper and Shepherd. The most obvious differences are Aulén's stress on volition (faith as decision) and incomprehensibility (faith as paradox), as opposed to Pieper and Shepherd's insistence on cognition (faith as knowledge) and doctrine (articles of faith). But these are differences more of emphasis than of substance.[57] On the one hand, Aulén agrees with Pieper and Shepherd that faith is "certain," and his paradoxes contain a kind of comprehensibility as well as a kind of mystery (they are resolvable to a certain extent when different points of view are taken into account, and they are capable of being expressed in "symbols"). On the other hand, Pieper and Shepherd agree with Aulén that faith's assurance has nothing to do with evidence (at least with anything ordinarily called "evidence"), that faith is somehow self-authenticating (or "immediate"), and that faith's propositional beliefs about God are very far from being clear or intelligible even to believers, much less to nonbelievers. The differences do not mark opposing doctrines so much as distinct emphases.

Still, emphasis matters. The three conceptions of faith look like different conceptions because they do differ in emphasis. It is possible for these different emphases to play importantly different roles in expressing and guiding piety and practice in different communities of faith. These roles may be even more important than the ones that

---

vering commitment to God. A merciful, steadfast God would not withdraw assistance once granted, and such assistance could not fail to produce its intended result.

57. One might also mention the relative propensity of our three writers to speak of God or of Jesus Christ as the "object" of faith, but this seems only a minor difference in emphasis, since all affirm that saving faith in God comes only via Jesus Christ.

are played by substantively differing features that are not emphasized, or even not mentioned. From a sociological perspective, a
community struggling to maintain its identity will often find it useful
to emphasize its differences with competing communities—even
when those differences are only degrees of emphasis. Communities
may remain distinct or even opposed when there is no substantive
disagreement between them, so long as there is some reason to insist
on their characteristically different emphases.[58]

3. There are certain twists in Aulén's conception of faith that seem
to distance it from the personal relationship model. Aulén does not
speak of trust but rather of decision and affirmation; faith for him
is necessarily correlative with divine revelation; the uniqueness of
Christian faith seems built into his conception of faith; and faith on
his view is certain without being unverifiable. None of these twists
negates the personal relationship model; they are optional extensions
and specifications of the model, not contradictions of it.

First, not only is decisive commitment arguably not opposed to
the trust required by the personal relationship model of faith, but
overemphasis on the role of volition in faith may work directly
contrary to Aulén's major concerns. While Aulén does hold that
faith is "an audacious personal decision and a bold *yes*" (107), one
needs to place this contention alongside another one: Faith is a personal relationship where "God is the center and in which life is
dominated by God alone" (23–24). Aulén wants to maintain decision
and domination together in paradoxical tension, and to increase the
tension so far as possible. But there are ways of reducing or understanding such tensions that do not involve much if any paradox.
One way is to take account of point of view. For example, from
the standpoint of someone who has faith, life may be dominated by
God alone, while from the standpoint of someone who lacks faith,
an audacious personal decision may be required.

There is another way of reducing the tension between volition
and trust, and that is by recognizing that faith itself may knit them
together. For example, S may be decisively committed to a personal
relationship in which S completely trusts or relies on A, such that

---

58. I do not mean that differences in conceptions of faith are the only, or even
necessarily the basic or the major, differences between communities of faith; there
are many other forms of distinction, not to mention opposition and antagonism.

this commitment is a part or aspect of the reliance. The faithful person's decision to be committed (comprehensively) to the "object" of faith is not a defiant act of self-assertion but only an aspect of her wholehearted trust in the other. Decision and trust need not be antagonists in faith. But further, all trust involves an element of continual decision in the following sense. Even when trust is not produced through choice (S does not decide or choose to trust A, but simply responds with trust to A's evident trustworthiness), still one is always faced with the possibility, which on awareness may become a live option, of ceasing to trust, or of refusing to trust any longer or to the same extent or degree. This element of (potential) negative volition is part of what distinguishes trust from other forms of dependence.

Second, revelation is not a requirement of the personal relationship model of faith, but Aulén maintains that faith and revelation are correlative: S has faith in A if and only if A reveals something to S. Aulén hangs three qualifications on this basic contention. (a) He holds that what is primarily revealed in faith is (some part or aspect of) the revealer, A, and only secondarily some proposition about A; what is revealed of A is more fundamental than what is revealed about A. (b) Aulén does not mean merely that something of or about A is revealed to S, for this could be done by someone or something other than A. Rather, he wants to claim that what is revealed to S of A must be revealed to S by A and only by A; S can have faith in A if and only if A alone does the revealing of A to S. (c) It is clear that Aulén thinks of revelation as a divine prerogative; in the proper sense of revelation only a divine being A can reveal A to S.[59]

Even with these qualifications, however, Aulén's conception of faith as correlative with revelation seems unduly restrictive. There may be cases where faith occurs, or even is possible, only when revelation occurs; and perhaps the kind of Christian faith Aulén is so concerned to present and promote is such a case. But surely there

59. Aulén is not clear on why this must be so. Presumably he would hold that with nondivine persons there is always some way of learning anything, or nearly anything, about the person without having to rely on the person's self-disclosure, whereas with God nothing (or very little) could be known without God disclosing it. God is a privileged source of awareness of God in a way that, say, Aulén is not a privileged source of awareness of Aulén.

are many other cases of religious and ordinary faith that lack revelation in Aulén's sense. S may have faith in A not because of what A has done or does to inspire S's trust and confidence in A, but rather because of S's inherent credulity (not brought about by A), or because S has, independently of A, obtained sufficient evidence to warrant trust or has had certain experiences that create general trust, and so forth. This feature of Aulén's conception of faith (that faith and revelation are correlative) is therefore a specification permitted but not required by the personal relationship model of faith. Other conceptions lacking this specification, or making it in a different way (for example, by denying that revelation is exclusively a divine prerogative), may nonetheless exemplify the personal relationship model of faith; they may be perfectly proper conceptions of faith. Aulén's belief that revelation is a necessary condition and correlative of faith as such is likely the result of his unduly narrow focus on a certain version of specifically Christian faith.

Third, like Shepherd but unlike Pieper, Aulén thinks no account of ordinary or everyday "faith" is necessary; only one putative kind of religious faith, Christian faith in God, measures up to the conceptual requirements of faith as such.[60] It appears that Aulén, again like Shepherd, thinks that this narrow focus is justified on something like the following grounds: The human–divine relationship in Christ is unique because God is unique,[61] and only such a unique relationship truly counts as faith. Aulén draws the wrong conclusions from the alleged uniqueness of personal relationship with God. The uniqueness of a (kind of) relationship does not entail the uniqueness of a conception of that relationship. Human–divine personal relationship is still personal relationship. Moreover, even if some uniqueness implying features are essential to Aulén's conception of faith, they need not be found in other conceptions of faith that also exemplify the personal relationship model. Only if the personal relationship model required these features instead of merely permitting them would their absence entail that one was not dealing

60. Whereas Shepherd's conception of faith is explicitly Christocentric, Aulén's conception is explicitly theocentric; but this is a distinction without a difference, as both writers affirm that relation to God must be, or be mediated by, a personal relationship with Jesus Christ.

61. Aulén also, and curiously, alleges uniqueness on the grounds that God is deus absconditus—as if absence could make the thought profounder.

with a conception of faith; even then, it might exemplify some other model of faith. Aulén's conception is so unduly restrictive because it improperly imports uniqueness into the very concept of faith from the special features of one particular "object" of faith.

Fourth, although he is distressingly vague on the precise sense of "certainty" he wishes to assert, Aulén wants to claim that faith's certainty has two important features. Negatively, faith's claims are disconnected from empirical verification and falsification, as well as from testing via moral behavior or religious experience. Positively, faith's certainty is an "inner" conviction due to the testimony of the Holy Spirit. These claims may suggest—they are at least consistent with—reading Aulén's "certainty" as "certitude" or "conviction." If we do so, there is no contradiction between Aulén's conception and the personal relationship model of faith: Conviction is required but not certainty. However, even if Aulén's "certainty" contains a surplus of meaning beyond conviction, his conception of faith may still be compatible with the personal relationship model so long as this surplus is optional, and does not entail truth (faith is still epistemically risky).

### Recapitulation

According to Aulén, faith is a comprehensive, immediate, and personal relationship with God—an "audacious and daring decision" uniquely founded on divine self-disclosure. Such faith is alleged to be unique and incomprehensible, generating only paradoxical symbolic expression. However, it is clear that this conception of faith does not stand alone; rather, it is a characteristically Lutheran conception that primarily exemplifies the personal relationship model of faith but also, and secondarily, the attitude and devotion models. Such hybrid exemplification is far from unusual and constitutes one way of individuating conceptions of faith. Each model is also exemplified in a distinctive way, via optional qualifications and specifications, thereby providing a second mode of individuation.

## D. A Contemporary Reconstructive Conception

The previous three conceptions of faith were all intended by their authors to be faithful representations of traditional Christian positions—Catholic, Calvinist, and Lutheran. Our next conception of faith differs from them in several important respects. It is not a clarification of someone else's conception but a conception newly minted—or rather reconstructed out of traditional and modern materials—for which its author assumes full responsibility. Its author's purpose is primarily to promote a view of faith that is more rationally responsible in and to the modern world, not to remain faithful to ancient ideas that seem to be outmoded and deleterious. Finally, it is not religiously exclusive; while aimed to accommodate religious impulses, it also seeks to establish continuities between religious and nonreligious varieties of faith, and between different varieties of religious faith, in terms that all can understand and embrace. Such a reconstructive conception of faith has been put forth by the contemporary American philosopher James Muyskens, in his book *The Sufficiency of Hope*.[62]

### Muyskens's Version

Muyskens wants to reconceive religious faith in terms of hope, not belief; in fact, he calls his reconstructive project a "*retreat* from belief to hope" (xii, emphasis added). He thinks this "retreat" is necessary in order to understand ordinary religious commitment as it actually exists in the modern world and, especially, to justify such faith according to contemporary standards of rational justification. Faith construed as hope may be rationally justifiable even though faith construed as belief is not, because of the way in which belief but not hope is "evidence-sensitive." Muyskens holds that where evidence for a proposition is lacking or inconclusive, then believing that proposition is rationally unjustified; it is not just lacking in rational justification but contrary to such justification. The modern epistemic situation, according to Muyskens, is such that central religious propositions, such as "God exists," are evidentially deficient (for anyone, apparently). If religious faith is then construed to require believing such propositions, religious faith must neces-

---

62. Muyskens, 1979; see also his 1985; page references in this section are from the first source. Louis Pojman, 1986b, has presented a very similar proposal. For other discussions of faith in relation to hope see Bars, 1961; Brunner, 1956; Day, 1969, 1970; Desroche, 1979; Macquarrie, 1978; Marcel, 1951a, 1951b; Moltmann, 1967, 1971, 1978, 1979; Radford, 1970a, 1970b; and Wheatley, 1958.

sarily be unjustified, a matter of "bad faith" for a rationally sensitive person. A "theology of belief" therefore lapses into absurdity.[63] But even when belief that a proposition is true is not justified or is unjustified, hope that the proposition is true may still be justified. This is because hope entails believing only that the proposition is possible, not that it is true. Such hope is not only rationally justifiable but also (and most importantly) religiously adequate, sufficient for "providing contemporary man with the ultimate guidance for his life" (146).

Muyskens formulates what he takes to be the necessary and sufficient conditions for hope and for justified hope as follows:

> S hopes that p[64] if and only if:
> (5a) S desires that p.
> (5b) It is not the case that p is not preferred by S on balance, or that S believes that q, which S prefers on balance, is incompatible with p.
> (5c) Neither p nor not-p is certain for S.
> (5d) S is disposed to act as if p. (18)[65]

63. "To my mind, Kierkegaard has very honestly and effectively demonstrated that a distinctly Christian theology of belief obliges one to reject every effort to reconcile religious-belief with ordinary criteria of reasonably justified belief " (143). Muyskens adds that in his view any "theology of belief" is a "bold but utterly irresponsible epistemological position" (143). Whether this is actually Kierkegaard's view and whether it is a correct view, may be questioned; in any case, our concern is with Muyskens's view.

64. Muyskens is aware of the distinction between believing in and believing that (42), but he does not make a parallel distinction between hoping in and hoping that. The way he formulates his conception of hope, however, indicates that he is primarily thinking of "hope that." Some parallels between belief and hope are sketched in Marcel, 1951b, 32.

65. Pojman's analysis of hope essentially relies on Muyskens, although its four conditions are somewhat different: (a) Hope "involves belief in the possibilities of a state of affairs obtaining. We cannot hope for what we believe to be impossible" (Pojman, 1986b, 161). (b) Hope "precludes certainty. . . . Hope entails uncertainty, a subjective probability index greater than 0 but less than 1" (162). (These first two conditions roughly amount to Muyskens's condition [5c].) (c) Hope "entails desire for the state of affairs in question to obtain or the proposition to be true," but it does not entail belief that it does obtain or is true (162). (This is the analogue of Muyskens's [5a].) (d) "If one hopes for *p*, one will be disposed to do what one can to bring *p* about, if there is anything that one can do to bring it about" (162). (This parallels Muyskens's [5d] but is doubly distinctive: Pojman adds a rider about S's ability to bring about p, whereas Muyskens says nothing of this; and, one may act as if p [Muyskens] without being able or disposed to do anything at all to bring about p [Pojman]. The only real disagreement between Muyskens and Pojman

S's hope that p is justified if and only if:

1. S's hope that p withstands provisional objections against it, especially those regarding S's right to want or desire that p (the "moral" or "evidential" requirement);
2. S's hope that p is not foolish, silly, or contrary to S's best interests (the "pragmatic" test);
3. S believes, and has adequate evidence for believing, that p is at least possible (the "real possibility" test);
4. "Any belief that [hope] presupposes must meet the conditions for [evidentially] justified belief" (the "background beliefs" test). (47)[66]

If and when hope passes these four tests, the strength of S's desire that p and the strength of S's evidence for p "combine to determine the [rationally] appropriate *strength* of S's hope that p" (47).[67]

Muyskens holds that religious faith-as-hope is continuous with nonreligious hope. Religious hope differs only in being a more "profound" hope, where the desire that p is considerably deeper and stronger than in ordinary hope, because S "sees p as constructively connected with his own well-being and/or concept of himself as a person" (36).[68]

---

centers on Muyskens's condition (5b). According to Muyskens there can be no incompatible hopes (though there can be conflicting wishes), while according to Pojman there can be incompatible hopes, even though they would be irrational or unjustified. On the "desiderative" side, Pojman holds that a hope is irrational if it is not preferred on balance or is incompatible with what is preferred on balance.

66. Muyskens thinks that for the specifically Christian hope to be vindicated, or at least not to be in vain, at the minimum an omnipotent God must exist. "Functionally, the question of God's existence is the question of the possibility of an open future. To deny that there is a God is to deny the framework within which alone men hope that the suffering, tragedy, and injustice that penultimately obtains is ultimately defeated" (129).

67. "The appropriate strength of a hope that satisfies that [fourfold] test is, in effect, the sum of the strengths of the desire and of the supporting evidence" (48). Muyskens does not explain why he thinks strengths should be summed—as opposed to multiplied, divided, subtracted, exponentiated, or otherwise combined—nor why each kind of strength should count equally—as opposed to giving a greater weight to desire over evidence, or conversely, on some occasions.

68. Pojman also speaks of "profound" hope, where one is deeply disposed to risk something significant, but adds that this profound hope is not rationally justified if it is "desperate" hope, where one hopes against the evidence. "Profound hope is distinguished from ordinary hope by the intensity of the desire and willingness to take great risk towards obtaining one's goal, and desperate hope is a type of profound hope where the estimative aspect is low" (1986b, 168).

Moreover, according to Muyskens, faith (as hope) in God does not entail believing, much less being confident or certain, that God exists; one who hopes need only believe that it is possible that God exists. To be sure, one may believe that God exists, but only in a tentative or hypothetical way that is open to new evidence, whether confirming or disconfirming. Only a theology of hope that abandons "cosmic security and acceptance" in order to be epistemically responsible can still provide contemporary people with "ultimate guidance" for life (146). Justified religious hope can coexist with doubt and dispense with dogmatism (144).[69]

In sum, Muyskens conceives (or reconceives) of faith as hope, not belief. Faith-as-hope is not fundamentally a cognitive condition—though it has its epistemic responsibilities—but rather a matter of desire and disposition to action. Still, such faith is, or can be, rationally justified for thoroughly modern epistemologists (indeed, this seems to be the primary motivation for Muyskens's proposal). Faith necessarily has an (intentional) "object," and possibly even an (actual) "author," but it necessarily lacks knowledge, or even unreserved affirmation, of that intentional object and putative author; moreover, reference to object or author is not included in the definition of faith-as-hope. Religious faith is differentiated from ordinary faith only by certain empirical features on the side of the subject of faith—chiefly depth of desire and strength of commitment to action—and not by essential reference to a certain kind of object (transcendent entities) or a particular object (God) or by any kind of supernatural causality. A single conception of faith, faith-as-hope, is univocally applicable to different religious traditions, as well as to nonreligious views.

### Exemplification

The first thing to note about Muyskens's conception of faith-as-hope is that it is not always clear what role he thinks this conception

---

69. Faith-as-hope is therefore what Pojman calls "experimental faith" (1986b, 171), the kind of faith that he supposes to be the only kind adequate for sophisticated modern religious persons. Decisive assent, or total and unconditional commitment independent of the evidence, is "morally repugnant" because it prematurely closes the door to inquiry and is incompatible with the ethics of belief. In Pojman's view, "honest doubt" may be as much "a state of reverence for God" as "fearful prohibition of doubt" (1986b, 174–75).

plays and should play. More particularly, it is not clear whether Muyskens is seeking an alternative (re)conception of faith (one that is more rationally defensible and perhaps more suited to "ordinary, contemporary commitment" than other conceptions) or a reconstructed substitute for the concept of faith (for the same reasons).[70] Nevertheless, since one of our models of faith does illuminate the conception he presents, we shall continue to speak as though he has indeed produced a conception of faith.

At the minimum, it is abundantly clear that Muyskens's conception exemplifies most of the features of the hope model; indeed, it is almost a paradigmatic instance of this model. On the hope model, faith is great desire and confident waiting for (anticipating, expecting) a supreme, future, apparent, uncertain good. Muyskens's conception deviates only slightly from this model. For one, he succumbs to the philosopher's temptation to overemphasize the role of propositional beliefs in hope, particularly the belief that the object of faith is at least possible; but overemphasis is after all only a matter of emphasis, not necessarily of substance. More significant is that the hope model requires "great" desire, while Muyskens's conception merely asks for desire.[71] This difference may be only a matter of degree. Presumably Muyskens would agree that a very weak desire (coupled with the other conditions) would not amount to hope, but would be only an idle or ineffectual wish. There is a threshold of strength of desire beneath which hope is not present. Whether this threshold is called "strong" desire or just plain "desire" is immaterial, so long as the desire is strong enough.

A final divergence from the hope model is harder to reconcile. According to the hope model, S has faith in G only if S confidently awaits, anticipates, and expects G, despite G's uncertainty. Muys-

---

70. Muyskens at one point suggests a third possibility. Faith cannot be adequately analyzed either in terms of belief or in terms of hope, but still hope is a "closer analogue" to faith than is belief (53). In effect, this proposal would tend to invalidate both the belief and the hope models of faith. Rather than examine this unelaborated suggestion, I explore the conception that Muyskens actually presents, a conception of faith as hope.

71. I suspect that Muyskens's (and Pojman's) avoidance of qualifiers like "great" in defining hope has irenic motives. Two plausible ways in which religious hope differs from ordinary hope are the intensity of the desire and the extent to which the whole person's being is involved, so that removing any reference to these features allows the conception to apply equally to religious and ordinary cases.

kens accepts the first two conditions—awaiting is being disposed to welcome G should it obtain, which is a part of desiring G; and anticipation is taking whatever present steps one can to (help) bring about G, which is a part of acting as if G obtains. But expectation is a different story. If S expects G, S believes not only that G is possible but also that G will obtain or occur. Muyskens is adamant that faith-as-hope lacks this latter belief; according to him, someone desiring G (strongly enough) must be disposed to act as if G will obtain without actually believing that G will obtain. In Chapter 2, section F, I argued that desiring G without expecting G (and hence without believing that G will obtain) is not hope but only an idle wish; here I wish to add two more arguments for believing that Muyskens is mistaken on this point in his conception of faith.

The first argument concerns hope's compatibility with conviction or confidence. According to Muyskens, faith-as-hope implies that S believes that p is possible (where p is some proposition about G's obtaining), but disallows the possibility that S (also) believes that p is true. However, it is possible for S to be convinced or confident that p only if S believes that p. For Muyskens, hope is incompatible with conviction or confidence. But it is not clear why this should be so; in fact, intuitively it seems that someone could both be convinced that p and also hope that p. It is important to remember that we are speaking of conviction or confidence, not (evidentially-backed) certainty. Presumably if S were certain that p or that not-p then S could not also hope that p; there is no sense hoping for (what one has the best of evidence to regard as) the inevitable or the impossible. But conviction is, or can be, independent of evidence, so presumably it could be present to any degree or strength even where the evidence is far from adequate to produce or warrant certainty. It seems that Muyskens's conception would permit only a weak and tepid form of faith-as-hope, and it is hard to agree with his restriction of the concept of hope in this way.[72]

The second argument connects up with one important possible

___

72. Perhaps Muyskens would seek to connect rational confidence as well as certainty to evidence, in such a way that S could be rationally confident that p (to a high degree) only if S has good evidence to support that confidence. At the very least, he provides no argument for this claim, which I believe to be false and implausible anyway.

ground for hope: trust. It is quite possible, indeed it may be quite normal, for S to hope that p because S trusts A, where A is an authority with respect to the possibility, certainty, or desirability of p. If Muyskens were right in thinking that when S hopes that p S can believe only that p is possible, not that p is true, then S's trust in A (or in A's authority) would remain limited or qualified in important ways. This does not bother Muyskens, for whom apparently all authorities are, or even must be, limited. Muyskens appears to distrust trust, either because there is not enough evidence to warrant great (total or "absolute") trust—the kind of trust most prominent in religious cases—or because great trust is not sufficiently evidence-sensitive. In Muyskens's eyes, one of the great merits of his conception of faith-as-hope is that it is a more evidence-sensitive conception and hence (he believes) a more rationally responsible conception than faith-as-belief. But Muyskens, it seems to me, is too distrustful of trust. It is not necessarily irrational (or rationally irresponsible) to trust to a greater or lesser degree than the evidence warrants. In fact, making trust *too* evidence-sensitive is a way of adopting an unjustified trust in evidence and in nothing else. There may be good reason to trust in advance of evidence or beyond evidence: Bargaining in "good faith" is not always, or usually, foolish. The hope model of faith does not require that trust be total or that it go beyond the evidence, much less that it go against the evidence, but at least it allows for the possibility of such non-evidential "absolute" trust, contrary to Muyskens's conception.

Muyskens's conception of faith-as-hope—precisely in order to remain a recognizable notion of hope—requires the following emendation: It must admit at least the possibility that there are propositions ("articles of faith about G,"[73] one might label them) that S must believe to be true (and not merely believe to be possible) in order to have faith-as-hope in G. So emended, Muyskens's conception is thoroughly compatible with the hope model of faith. Whether such a conception (or model) of faith is the only kind that is rationally justifiable in the contemporary world, as Muyskens believes, is another question, as is whether such a (re)conception could become a useful or acceptable part of any extant or proposed tradition of faith.

73. These must include at least one proposition to the effect that G will obtain.

Our descriptive account of the concept of faith does not adjudicate competing normative claims.[74]

## Recapitulation

Contemporary reconstructions of the concept of faith can be illuminated by the models of faith they exemplify. Muyskens's analysis of hope (if indeed it is intended to be a conception or reconception of faith and not a replacement for it) clearly exemplifies the hope model, with only a few deviations. The most important deviation concerns whether the hopeful person must believe that the hoped-for good will obtain or only that it is possible. But believing in a mere possibility is arguably insufficient for hope. Emending Muyskens's conception at this point would bring it more nearly into line with the hope model of faith, though perhaps it would no longer meet contemporary standards of evidential justification for beliefs, at least as Muyskens construes them.

## E. A Tripartite Hindu Conception

Having glimpsed four distinct Western conceptions of faith, all of them with strong Christian roots, it is clear that even within the bounds of a single tradition of faith there are different conceptions of faith—although there are also distinct family resemblances. As we move outside Christian tradition to examine other traditions of faith, we should expect to encounter even greater diversity. The first step we shall take—to India—may seem a rather large one, for it takes us outside Western theism altogether. Although the geographical distance is enormous, the conceptual distance turns out to be considerably smaller, because the Hindu conception we consider is the reflective product of a twentieth-century scholar who has been greatly influenced by Western currents of thought and who draws on Indian devotional traditions that considerably resemble Western

74. There is plenty of room for disagreement on all of the following questions: Is there a single coherent set of contemporary standards of rational justification? If so, has Muyskens correctly and adequately characterized these standards? How do these standards apply to religious beliefs, or to the beliefs ingredient in hope? Are these standards the only ones applicable to such beliefs?

theism. K. Satchidananda Murty, in his *Revelation and Reason in Advaita Vedanta*, presents a contemporary reflection on ancient Hindu thinking about faith that yields a tripartite Hindu conception—or perhaps one should speak of three distinct Hindu conceptions of faith rolled into one.[75]

## Murty's Version

Murty affirms many views with which Christian writers such as Pieper, Shepherd, and Aulén could agree, including, that "our awareness of God is his self-revelation" (283), that faith involves "reliance on a self-authenticated source of evidence" (301), or that faith is "a total response of our personality" (313). Nevertheless, there are important differences. What is fundamental for Murty are the following three claims: Faith is "preeminently an act of affirmation" of truth (280); revelation is preeminently the disclosing of knowable truth; and both essentially involve the apprehension of propositions and assent to them. In short, there is "an intellectual core" to revelation, which faith affirms and which theology may formulate into "dogma."[76] Moreover, this "genuine intellectual content" is "for ever final" for a person in the sense of revealing "absolute truth" to that person (297), even though "the credible formulae in which it is embodied tend to become obsolete" (281).

Furthermore, Murty acknowledges not just one but three distinct kinds or conceptions of "revelation." Since revelation both makes and mirrors faith, he in effect proposes three distinguishable con-

75. Murty, 1959; page references in this section are to this text. Murty's title is misleading, for Murty's own position departs considerably from Śamkara's orthodox school of Advaita Vedanta: "In general, my views on Revelation in this book are in agreement with those of the Nyaya writer Jayanata, while my conception of God differs very little from that of Ramanuja" (ix). Moreover, with regard to Vedic scripture, Murty declares he is not a "Hindu fundamentalist." Once again our concern is with Murty's own conception, not with its historical antecedents or accuracy of attribution. Other treatments of early Hindu conceptions of faith (in particular, discussions of *viśvāsa, āstikya, śraddhā,* and *bhakti*) may be found in Carman, 1968, 1974; Das Gupta, 1930; De Smet, 1973; Gokhale, 1980; Halbfass, 1991; Lala, 1986; Otto, 1930; Plott, 1974; Rao, 1971; and Sawai, 1987.

76. "Revelation through a person involves belief in him as a revealer of God, and this is impossible without that person revealing something about himself and our believing it to be true; and this 'something about him' must involve an intellectual core, which, however little, can be expressed, at least inadequately, in a proposition" (280).

ceptions of faith.[77] The first two kinds are or involve personal relationships, while the third is more "impersonal."

1. A person (divine or otherwise) can disclose information to
someone about herself and be believed on the credit of her word.
For example, James believes what Joan tells him about her intentions
because James trusts Joan to speak the truth (at least about herself
or, yet more narrowly, about her intentions). Here Murty apparently means that James has reasons to trust Joan that go beyond
Joan's present content and manner of discourse (for example, Joan's
testimony has proved reliable in the past, others praise her credibility, one can independently ascertain the truth of what she says,
and so forth). Still, the person believed (trusted) is an authority for
the person who believes, an authority at least concerning propositions about herself. All of this is quite familiar to us from the personal
relationship model (faith is propositional belief on another person's
authority), together with the notion of *præambulae fidei*.

2. Murty also holds that a person can disclose herself to another
person, and be believed in a "self-authenticating" way, without
appeal to any further authority than this very disclosing.[78] For example, James accepts what Joan shows him of the (kind of) person
she is precisely because it is Joan who shows him this concerning
herself and because of the way in which Joan does this. Here the
person believed (trusted) is both object and final authority of belief;
faith is basically self-generating trust of another. Such faith may lead
to propositional beliefs (accepted on the other's authority), as in the
first conception of faith, but it need not do so; all that is required
is a kind of implicit belief, where S is willing to believe that p if A
so proposes.

Both kinds of personal revelation, Murty holds, occur only
through and for the "devotee" who has faith. This is not just because
only a person can affirm a proposition or apprehend another person
as such, but also, and more importantly in religious contexts, because the revelation of A to S must be by A and therefore under

---

77. Or so it seems. Murty does not explicitly distinguish these three conceptions,
nor does he explicitly connect or correlate revelation with faith, nor does he specify
precisely how these different conceptions interrelate. Nevertheless, I believe his usage
in the text implies the points I make.

78. Murty calls this type of revelation "direct disclosure and immediate contact"
(282).

A's control. Personal religious revelation is always self-revelation (that is, either revelation of A or of truths about A), and the self-revealer must be able to set her own conditions for being apprehended by another.[79] These conditions typically include wholehearted commitment, allegiance, and devotion on the part of the receiver of revelation.[80] Still, Murty does not think that divine personal revelation (and its correlative faith) is sui generis. Instead, general revelation is present in "a kind of direct awareness, which is essentially similar to our awareness of ourselves and our neighbours" (283).[81] This kind of "direct awareness" exists in all humans, though to different degrees of self-consciousness. "Unless there is such a general revelation, the claim of many world-religions to be in possession of special revelations is unintelligible" (283).

3. The third kind of revelation Murty discusses differs considerably from the first two kinds. Stemming from the age-old practice of meditation, this kind of revelation is insight into "absolute truth," an insight that is neither given by another person nor experienced as given by another person. This is revelation without a revealer, an "impersonal" kind of revelation. In this sense, revelation is fundamentally the unveiling and apprehension of a nonordinary, unapparent kind of truth. This is absolute truth and not the communication of a particular private personality or the conveyance

79. It is not clear why Murty thinks that this must be so, and even less clear that it is so. Can A *not* set such conditions and instead allow S to find out about A by using S's own cognitive devices? Furthermore, why should it necessarily be in A's power to control A's own self-revelation? Perhaps A has an unavoidable "body language" or "expressive signature" from which others can discern (something of) A, no matter what A does to conceal himself? Finally, can S learn about A from some other person B without thereby becoming a devotee of A or of B? Murty assumes that these questions have received different answers in religious as opposed to nonreligious contexts; but one would appreciate arguments instead of assumptions.

80. Murty quotes the *Bhagavad Gita* at this point: "By devotion alone can I be perceived, known and seen in essence, and entered into" (*Bhagavad Gita*, 11.54; quoted by Murty, 283; see also 18.55; 8.22). Murty's use of the *Gita* here seems more than just a scholarly passing reference; one suspects that it is the kind of reflexively obvious reference that carries a subconscious aura of appeal to revelation.

81. Murty is not clear about the exact sense of "direct." He does not mean "unmediated," for awareness of others occurs through sense-experience of them, and self-awareness occurs through feelings, volitions, and cognitions. Rather, he has in mind something like "basic." Direct awareness is not inference from awareness of something else, and trust in or belief about the "object" of direct awareness is not based on any other attitude (trust, belief, etc.) about anything.

to another of ordinary kinds of truth about that personality. According to Murty's third conception, both the manner of revelation
(how revelation occurs) and its content (what is revealed) differ, in
connected ways, from the first two conceptions of revelation/faith.

Concerning the content of revelation, Murty distinguishes between two kinds of truth: universal and absolute truth. Universal
truth can be revealed in either of the first two ways (and may or
may not be accessible independently of revelation), but absolute
truth can only be revealed in the third way. "Absolute truth is that
by which a man lives, and for which he dies, and from which he
derives a sense of supreme 'repose in being' (i.e., integration in
himself and harmony with reality). On the other hand, universal
truth is relative, particular,[82] and obtained by all when they start
from finite premises and follow a definite method, and it is expressible in propositions, which are recognised as cogent by all who
understand them" (284). It is not that absolute truth is completely
nonpropositional, although it is more than propositional. Absolute
truth, like universal truth, can be expressed in propositions, but
these will usually not be commonly acknowledged to be true; persons need the special experience produced by meditation—or the
very experience of meditation itself—in order to understand, accept,
and "relive" absolute truth (285).[83] Though disclosed in particular
ways, absolute truth is "absolute" in being ultimate, final, and tran-
scendently important.

Murty holds that "religion" of all three kinds is fundamentally
cognitive, not affective or conative, and definitely not irrational or
even arational.[84] Feeling is important in religious experience, but
only as a vehicle for cognition: "In religious experience, man is

82. It is jarring to see "universal" truth called "particular." Perhaps what Murty
has in mind could be better expressed by "finite" or "limited" or "conditioned."
Universal truth is valid for all, but only under certain conditions that include various
acts and orientations on the part of the subject—conditions that need not obtain—
and is of only limited value and utility.

83. Actually, the difference here may be considerably less than Murty thinks.
Meditative experience is a condition for understanding absolute truth in the same
way as ordinary experience is a condition for understanding universal truth; the real
difference is that not everyone meditates.

84. Murty's usage here is illuminating. He tends to speak indifferently of "faith,"
"religious faith," and "religion." That Murty does not mark important distinctions
with these terms is itself an important difference between his conception of faith
and those of Shepherd (1983) and Aulén (1948).

aware of a presence that compels recognition, though it can only be imperfectly expressed in words" (317). Likewise, neither volition, choice, nor action is the essence of the religious life: "All the great religions are pre-eminently (not entirely) *theoria*, and not *praxia* [sic], and . . . the ultimate goal of all religion is the Vision of God" (319). Finally, religious faith is not irrational, in various respects. For one, its propositional content is not absurd or contradictory (322). For another, religious belief is not a voluntary action producing assent despite one's recognition of sufficient evidence to the contrary.[85] Again, although religious truth may be "above" reason, in the sense of outstripping reason's capacity to discover, express, prove, and understand it, still reason can play certain important roles. Negatively, objections to religious truth can be rebutted; positively, reason can to some extent clarify the content of revelation and elaborate doctrine (325).[86]

### Revelation without a Revealer

Much of Murty's account—especially his first two "personal" kinds of revelation—dovetails with the conceptions of Pieper, Shepherd, and Aulén. Like these Christian conceptions, Murty's first two Hindu conceptions primarily exemplify the personal relationship model of faith, although aspects of the belief model are also prominent. Both conceptions make revelation and faith correlative in a personal relationship: A gives p to S, and S believes p on A's authority.[87] The major divergence from the Christian conceptions is

85. "Any truth can be believed only when one knows that it is not opposed to reason; and not when he knows that it is opposed" (323). This seems too strong if "can" means "possible" or "able." We believe many things we do not know are not opposed to reason, and it may be that some believe—and even think they should believe—things they know are opposed to reason. But perhaps Murty is not describing doxastic fact but issuing epistemic injunction, laying down the following rules: "S should believe p only if S knows p is not opposed to reason," or at least, "S should not believe p if S knows p is opposed to reason."

86. Murty also holds that there is a *pramāna* (way of knowing) distinct from inference and perception that can show that "the existence of God is a necessary postulate, an implicit belief, involved in all experience" (332). This *pramāna*, he claims, is not an inference but "a meditation on existence" (332), though the nature of this meditation remains obscure.

87. The two conceptions differ from each other primarily on how A's authority is grounded for S: in other-evidence or in self-evidence.

that Murty tends to emphasize more strongly the cognitive side of faith, which in turn gives a more central role to propositional belief. Faith as knowledge may differ from other forms of cognition in its special experiential source of truth ("revelation"), as well as in the special kind of truth it obtains ("absolute" truth), but it does not differ in being expressible, more or less, in propositions that are believed to be true.[88]

Murty's third kind of "impersonal" revelation, however, is a different matter altogether. According to this conception it is possible to have revelation without a revealer, without personal relationship to another person; indeed, the truth disclosed or discovered here is available to individuals independently of any kind of relation to any other person.[89] "Absolute truth" may be "revealed" to S without S being aware that anyone has revealed this truth to S, and indeed without it being the case that anyone has revealed it to S.[90] Murty does speak of the "vision of God" as "the ultimate goal of all religion" (319), but he does not believe that this "vision" needs to be given to a person by God. Meditation that culminates in personal insight into absolute truth is, he believes, at least as capable of yielding such a "vision of God" as is devotion to another.

Indeed, one wonders whether the vision of God even requires the existence of God, on Murty's view. In fact, his use of "vision of God" seems to have several senses: (a) "seeing God" (where God is the actual "object" of the vision); (b) "appearing to see God" (where God is the apparent "object" of the vision); (c) "seeing what God sees" (where the subject sees the same content or truth that

88. Given the great similarity of conceptions of faith and revelation among Murty, Shepherd (1983), and Aulén (1948) here, it is interesting to note the considerable difference in the (allegedly) revealed contents of faith according to each. Their agreement is only formal or conceptual, not material or substantive.

89. Murty probably overemphasizes this point. Clearly the guidance of others (gurus) can be very useful to seekers of absolute truth—not just in providing helpful techniques, warnings of pitfalls, and encouragement to persevere, but also in calling to consciousness the very existence of such a goal and making it seem at once possible, vivid, and enticing. (Such roles are played as much by example as by precept.) Still, Murty would hold, an individual *could* discover the absolute truth without the help of any guru, however difficult this might be.

90. It does not follow, I think, that there is no one who could so reveal absolute truth to S, only that no one actually does so. In addition, what one person learns of absolute truth may be revealed by someone (perhaps a divine person), while what another person learns of the same truth may be "revealed" but by no revealer.

God sees); (d) "seeing as God sees" (where the subject sees in the way God sees); or (e) "seeing as God would see" (where God is the personification and objectification of a way of seeing). Senses (b) and (e) neither imply nor deny the existence of God; instead, the concept of God may be used in these senses merely to depict a kind of experience. Murty does not distinguish among these senses, but his "impersonal" view of revelation without a revealer seems to slide from (a) toward (e).

We can question whether Murty is equivocating on the meaning of "revelation" and "faith," since two quite different processes produce two quite different products. In all three conceptions, revelation is insight into previously unknown truth; but the resemblance stops there. In the first two conceptions, revelation's product is propositional belief based on personal trust, which is conveyed or produced by the process of another's self-disclosure; faith's object is a gift from another. In the third conception, revelation's product is an insight into absolute truth that (supposedly) is neither given nor produced by another. It necessarily results from one's own activity of meditation; faith's object is not a gift but a discovery (or even an invention) of one's own.

In fact, Murty's third conception of faith is a rather unstable hybrid, if not an outright contradiction. In the first place, it clearly exemplifies the belief model in its stress on firm conviction that certain propositions are true in the absence of ordinary evidence. But there are anomalies. Murty's appeal to meditation seems to seek a nonordinary source of evidence for faith's belief, whereas the belief model requires a nonevidential basis for such belief. More important, Murty's third conception exemplifies yet another model of faith, the confidence model, insofar as meditation produces (or just is) an imperturbable conscious state of deep (self-)confidence, the "sense of supreme 'repose in being' " (284). The problem here is that joint exemplification of the full belief and confidence models seems impossible, for the confidence model excludes (or at any rate is independent of) propositional belief, while the belief model requires such (or is essentially dependent on) beliefs. What might we say on Murty's behalf? Does he have a consistent conception?

A possible answer emerges from an awareness of what Murty is trying to preserve in his third conception of faith. Aside from his (not insignificant) historical allegiances, Murty deeply desires to maintain the cognitivity of faith. In doing so, he affirms two points: Faith is a kind of affirmation of truth (faith has an "intellectual content"); and, this affirmation involves the apprehension of something that can be expressed, however inadequately, in propositional form. But apprehension of propositional truth is a relational form of awareness, at odds with the nonrelational consciousness portrayed in the confidence model. A conception containing both features seems inconsistent.

Murty seems to have two lines of escape from this conflict.[91] One way is to soften his insistence on "an intellectual core" to revelation and instead to maintain that the meditation-produced experience of faith is not an intellectual matter at all, much less knowledge of truths expressible even to some extent in propositional form. This would involve giving up the cognitivity of faith that Murty so highly prizes. Alternatively, Murty might surrender the second point, holding instead that faith does have an "intellectual core" but that this core cannot be expressed in propositional form—not because doing so is inadequate but because it is fundamentally misleading. It is not that propositions that humans can apprehend convey some (but by no means all) of the truth disclosed in faith; rather, propositional expression is necessarily a distortion and disruption of religion's "absolute" truth. Religion's truth would therefore be quite different from the truth of daily life and science, which can be expressed, at least partially, in propositional form. In fact, the meaning of "truth" would alter dramatically, perhaps beyond recognition. Whether Murty would pursue either escape route is unclear. What is clear is that his conception is problematic; it contains a conceptual knot that can be unraveled only partially by use of (features of) our models of faith.

Some may think that Murty's third conception is too extreme to be taken seriously. After all, Murty tries to combine revelation without a revealer (or even without a revealed object), conviction with a quasi-evidential (but nonordinary) basis, absolute "truth"

91. There is another route, one which Aulén (1948) might well commend, yet it hardly avoids the problem and is not available to Murty: Since faith affirms propositional truth and yet faith's truth cannot be expressed in propositions, the relation between faith and (propositional) truth is paradoxical. Faith delights in this paradox; unfaith does not. But Murty is too much of a rationalist or intellectualist to pursue the path of paradox.

without (adequate) propositional expression, and nonrelational su-preme "repose in being." The central questions are: Does Murty's conception exemplify a consistent set of features so that it can qualify as a conception? Does it exemplify enough features of faith (whether from one or from several different models of faith) so that it can qualify as a conception of faith? We have already suggested an answer to the first question: Murty's third conception borders on inconsis-tency and needs some alteration, or at least clarification.

The second question places us in the realm of degrees of resem-blance. Murty's conception certainly resembles in various respects other conceptions that no one wants to deny are conceptions of faith; equally certainly, his conception differs from them in other respects. Murty apparently has no qualms about calling his third conception "faith," and my inclination is to agree with him. My agreement is based in part on the following similarities-in-difference between Murty's third conception and the personal relationship model. In-sight into absolute truth is not ordinary propositional belief but rather a kind of existential commitment involving deep transfor-mation of the self not unlike the "new life" of a deeply trusting relationship; the feeling of self-confidence gained by basking in the glow of self-illumined *satcitananda* (being-consciousness-bliss) re-sembles peaceful repose in an authority's arms; and the way in which one's higher self engineers, in some unfathomable way, one's escape from the unsatisfactory realm of *māya* (illusion) resembles the au-thority's (partial) authorship of the act of faith according to the personal relationship model.

The divergences of Murty's third conception even from the per-sonal relationship model are not as great as might be supposed. Moreover, these very differences can be matched with features drawn from other models of faith, for example, commitment with the attitude model, and self-confidence with the confidence model, so that even in cases of disanalogy to the personal relationship model there are similarities to other models. To be sure, the analogies are not overwhelmingly strong, but I do think they are strong enough to count Murty's third conception as a conception of faith.[92]

92. Some evidence to the contrary: When speaking of impersonal revelation, Murty tends to use the term "religion" and not the term "faith." It is quite possible that this usage reflects an awareness that "faith" is problematic, perhaps even in-appropriate, in this context.

Two additional points deserve mention, by way of contrasting Murty's view of faith with those of Shepherd and Aulén; both points show that the overall concept of faith—as opposed to some particular conceptions of faith—is less restrictive than many suppose.

First, whereas Shepherd and Aulén seek to reduce the scope of faith by particularizing the concept of faith, Murty holds that faith is widely distributed, perhaps even universally present. Murty's universalism is rooted in his view that faith is insight into truth, a kind of clarity or self-consciousness naturally open to anyone, with or without the aid of another person, whereas Shepherd and Aulén's particularism is rooted in the conviction that faith can only be relationship to a unique individual, a relationship that crucially depends on the elective causal agency of that particular person. For Murty, devotion (*bhakti*) and meditation (*dhyāna*) are optional means to the same end (possession of truth), not different means to different ends (personal relationship versus possession of absolute truth). Also, since all humans have some degree or level of insight into truth, faith for Murty is a matter of degree, not an all-or-nothing affair.

Although Murty's universalism conflicts with Shepherd and Aulén's particularism, it is important to see that both are permitted, and neither is required, by our models of faith. The universalism/particularism dispute concerning the scope and presence of faith cannot be settled by appeal to the concept of faith, and any normative appeal to a particular conception of faith must beg the question. Only careful empirical investigation can settle the question of how widely faith (according to some conception) is found, and only lengthy argument could hope to address the question of whether faith (according to some conception) should or should not be more or less widely present than it is.

Second, Murty's conception of faith has a distinctive view of reason's relation to faith. Murty agrees with Aulén that faith goes beyond reason, but disagrees that reason is therefore to be discarded, subverted, or "killed." On the contrary, since in Murty's view faith cannot conflict with reason and is never paradoxical, reason is not the enemy but the friend and ally of faith. Once again we have two conflicting views of faith (in relation to reason), and once again both of them are permitted, and neither is required, by our models of faith, particularly the personal relationship model.[93] Since the overall

93. Even if one or another model did require, or prohibit, a certain view of the

concept of faith does not contain any special view of the relations of reason to faith, different conceptions of faith are free to adopt a wide range of positions on this issue.

### Recapitulation

Two of Murty's conceptions of faith and revelation are distinctive but relatively unproblematic exemplifications of both the personal relationship and the belief models of faith: believing a proposition on someone's authority, where that authority is accepted extrinsically (on other-evidence) or intrinsically (on self-evidence). His third conception raises some important questions. If, as we have argued, this conception exemplifies features of two models (belief and confidence) that are mutually inconsistent, how are we to deal with this inconsistency? Should we simply "embrace" or accept the inconsistency (whatever that might mean)? Should features from one or the other model be subordinated, downplayed, or even discarded? Could a consistent subset of features be selected from both models (according to what criteria), and if so how rich a conception of faith would result?

Murty's insistence on the cognitivity of faith (insight into truth that can be expressed in propositions) suggests that he might want to qualify the confidence model in order to safeguard propositional belief; but his construal of "absolute" truth as existential and supreme "repose in being" is evidence for desiring the opposite qualification. Since Murty, unlike Aulén, does not delight in paradox as a sign of superiority to reason, he is faced with the task of altering, or at least clarifying, his third conception of faith. Once again our models of faith may be useful in this task—not as a template, or as a guru, but as a lamp and a guide.

## F. A Shin Buddhist Conception

Next we travel from Hindu India to Buddhist Japan, to consider a conception of faith developed in the Jōdo Shinshū, the "true Pure Land school," known in the West as Shin Buddhism. We take up

---

relations of faith to reason, not all models would agree, and so the overall concept of faith would neither require nor prohibit such a view.

a contemporary account, by Yoshifumi Ueda and Dennis Hirota, of the distinctive conception of *shinjin* elaborated by Shinran (1173–1263), the dominant figure in the Japanese Shin tradition.[94] As we shall see, the conception presented by Ueda and Hirota bears remarkable affinities to some of the Christian conceptions of faith we have considered, particularly to Aulén's Lutheran one;[95] but at the same time there are also major differences—differences so great as to raise considerable doubt as to whether "shinjin" should even be translated as "faith."[96] Both likenesses and differences, however, can be clarified by application of our models of faith, enabling us to see how shinjin embodies a unique kind of faith and not something altogether different.[97]

### Ueda and Hirota's Version

Ueda and Hirota set forth what they take to be the major positions of Shinran's thought within the context of Pure Land Buddhist

94. Ueda and Hirota, 1989; page references in this section are to this text. Our concern is not with the historical accuracy of Ueda and Hirota's account of Shinran, or with the adequacy of their or Shinran's conception for the rest of the Shin tradition, much less with this conception's relations to conceptions of faith found in other Pure Land schools, and least of all with how these conceptions developed within the wider contexts of Mahayana Buddhism and "original" or "primitive" Buddhism. It is quite enough for our purposes to consider their conception on its own merits. For other works on Shinran, Pure Land, and Shin Buddhist notion(s) of faith, see Bando, 1977; Bloom, 1959, 1965, 1968, 1984, 1989; Carter, 1986, 1987a, 1988; Cobb, 1982; Dobbins, 1989a, 1989b; Fox, 1986; Futaba, 1988; Gómez, 1983; Hirota, 1986, 1987, 1991; Johnston, 1976; Kaneko, 1965; Kasulis, 1981; Keenan, 1989a; Kikumura, 1972; Masutani, 1959; Nishitani, 1975; Pye, 1984; Sasaki, 1988; Shigefuji, 1980; Takahatake, 1987; Takeda, 1989; Tokunaga, 1985; and Ueda, 1981, 1984. (I am grateful to Minor Rogers for most of these references.) For works on early Buddhism that deal with the question of faith, though often only in passing, see la Vallée Poussin, 1908; Dutt, 1940; Ergardt, 1977; Gokhale, 1980; Hoffman, 1987a; Jayatilleke, 1963; Joshi, 1987; Ludowyk-Gyomroi, 1947; Nagao, 1989; Palihawadana, 1978; Thittila, 1956.

95. A good deal has been written about both the apparent and the profound resemblances between Shinran and Luther; see, e.g., Bloom, 1965; Buri, 1976; Doi, 1980; Higgins, 1988; Ingram, 1971; Ishihara, 1987; Kolp, 1976; Laube, 1983.

96. See, e.g., Carter, 1986; Gómez 1983; Kasulis, 1981; Nanamoli Thera, 1971; Ueda, 1981, and as gen. ed. 1981, 1983. Ueda and Hirota tend to translate shinjin—when they translate it at all—as "entrusting"; we see later how this translation may mislead.

97. Because of the controversial nature of translating "shinjin" as "faith," the former term is used for most of the following discussion, even though our analysis supports this translation.

thought, which in turn is set within the wider context of Mahayana Buddhist thinking and even, to some extent, in relation to Theravada and/or early Buddhism. We put aside these wider contexts, which are necessary for historical and "theological" understanding but which unnecessarily complicate the philosophical account we seek. In particular, a great deal of Ueda and Hirota's exposition deals with the historical development of *Shinshūgaku*, or Shinshū studies, the Buddhist analogue of Christian theology, which in the Pure Land tradition treats mostly of the transempirical nature, activity, career, and effects of Amida Buddha. But just as we were able earlier, for the most part, to prescind from Christian theology's account of God's nature and modus operandi in discussing Christian conceptions of faith, so here also we should be able—again for the most part—to prescind from *Shinshūgaku*'s account of Amida Buddha's nature and activity in discussing a Shin conception of shinjin.[98]

For expository purposes, I treat shinjin as the fundamental human quality of an extraordinary, paradoxical relationship between a human self and Amida Buddha, a relationship that transforms both difference and identity into difference-in-identity or identity-in-difference.[99]

Central to understanding this relationship is the Pure Land Buddhist practice of *Nembutsu*, which is simply (but profoundly) the act of "calling or thinking on" (*nem*) "the Buddha" (*butsu*). The practice of Nembutsu consists in saying and thinking over and over again the formula "*namu-Amida-butsu*," "the Name of Amida Buddha," and in doing so placing one's sole reliance on Amida for the gift of rebirth into the Pure Land. According to Ueda and Hirota,[100] Pure

98. The qualifier "for the most part" is vital, since we must to some extent come to grips with the unique "nature" of Amida Buddha as the unique "object" of shinjin, even though our focus is on shinjin itself.

99. I realize how problematic and unpromising it is to start off in this vein, since we shall have to qualify this "relationship" to make it much more intimate than any ordinary human interpersonal relation could be, and we shall have to qualify both the self and Amida Buddha to make them much less distinct from each other (and from other selves as well) than any ordinary empirical persons can be. Yet beginning here is illuminating.

100. See also Keenan, 1989b, for the historical development of "the remembrance of Buddha" from an Indian "meditative" aid to a Shin "invocational" practice, where the Nembutsu becomes "a calling to mind of the primal sacrament" (Amida's Vows) and where remembrance changes from recollection of the linear past to experiencing "the existential instant of *shinjin*" (40).

Land thinkers prior to Shinran thought of the Nembutsu as a kind of spiritual "practice" or activity of invoking and calling on Amida, who possesses both the power and the will to confer enlightenment—the enabling conditions for enlightenment—on anyone who sincerely and wholeheartedly engaged in the practice of Nembutsu.[101]

Shinran, however, held that on this traditional view Nembutsu amounted to nothing more than a magical exercise of "self-power" (*jiriki*), a way of securing one's own salvation or enlightenment by performing an act within one's power that triggers or calls forth Amida's complementary activity. Instead, according to Shinran, one must rely entirely on Amida's "other-power" (*tariki*). The very "practice" of Nembutsu itself (insofar as it enables enlightenment) must be entirely given by Amida. Hence, there are no rules to follow, no method to master, no guide as to how to call/think on Amida; there simply is no operating manual for the practice of Nembutsu. It is therefore a practice that is not a practice, a practice of "no-practice."

Shinjin is the central element, from the human side, in true Nembutsu.[102] It follows at once that there is nothing one can do to bring

101. The metaphysical—or mythical—mechanics of this process need not detain us, but in general the Pure Land view was that Amida, in fulfilling his bodhisattva vows over enormous stretches of time and against immeasurable obstacles and hardships, has accumulated a vast store of merit that can be transferred somehow to all other spiritual beings so as to enable them to attain enlightenment. Since Amida, out of compassion, deeply desires the enlightenment of all beings—it is the essence of his vows that he shall not rest in his own final enlightenment until he is joined by all others—he uses the best "skillful means" available to him. The Nembutsu is his primary vehicle of merit-transfer, an optimally "easy" way of translating everyone into Amida's Pure Land of bliss, wherein every occupant's enlightenment is assured.

102. Shinran's thought develops by way of commentary on his tradition; in particular, the notion of shinjin/entrusting springs centrally from the famous eighteenth vow of Amida Buddha (recorded in the Larger *Sukhāvati-vyūha, Adornments of the Land of Bliss*, a first-century C.E. sutra from Northwest India) never to rest until birth in the Pure Land is attained for all those who "with sincere mind entrust themselves, aspire for birth [in the Pure Land], and say my Name even ten times" (in F. Max Müller, tr., 1969, *Buddist Mahāyāna Texts*, pt. 2 [New York: Dover], 15). In Shinran's view, entrusting is the key to these "three minds" (sincerity, entrusting, and aspiring; see Ueda and Hirota, 143). Later Shin thought confirmed this view in deciding the *Sangō wakuran* controversy in favor of *shingyō* (trust and reliance) over *ganshō* (aspiration to be born in the Pure Land) as the essence of *shinjin* (see Dobbins, 1989a, 61).

about shinjin in oneself. "Both the entrusting of oneself to the Vow and the saying of the Name are given—unfolded in beings—through and as the activity of the Buddha" (144). Shinjin is the attitude or quality of the person who truly performs the Nembutsu; it is the distinctive character of the self in proper relation to Amida. But this attitude, quality, or character is not at all to be viewed as the self's own doing; it must be seen as entirely Amida's gift. This gift may be described in terms of the following nine features, all of them tightly bound together, however inadequate the depiction and however incompatible the features may at first appear.

1. First, shinjin is not worship or adoration of Amida, in the way that a human might be devoted to a divinity. Worship or devotion implies an abyssal and unbridgeable gulf between self and the divine other, whereas Amida Buddha's nature is not other than one's own. Every being is not only the expression (or "creation") of Buddha nature but is also capable of becoming a Buddha, of fully realizing one's Buddha-potential, of achieving enlightenment. Indeed, from a Buddha's-eye point of view, every being who will be enlightened (and on Ueda and Hirota's view this means every being) has already been enlightened and is therefore on a par with Amida. Shinjin is the realization (not an accomplishment or achievement but a state or condition) of one's own Buddha-nature.

2. Moreover, shinjin is not a mediated relation, where one achieves relationship to Amida through the Nembutsu, as if the Nembutsu were Amida's external and contingent means of relating to a human being. Rather, the Nembutsu just is Amida's self-manifestation to the self, "the natural manifestation of the Buddha's mind" in one (149). More forcefully, one may say that Amida and the Nembutsu are one, that the Nembutsu is the mind of the Buddha (at any rate the Buddha's mind in, or in relation to, human selves).

3. Further, shinjin and Nembutsu are inseparable. The one is present when and only when the other exists; one cannot truly call/ think on the Nembutsu without having shinjin, and conversely. Hence, by linking the first three points, we arrive at the view that shinjin marks a truly extraordinary and intimate relationship: Amida is not other than Nembutsu, which is not other than shinjin, which is not other than oneself. In short, Amida is not other than oneself!

However, shinjin is not (the experience of) sheer, blank identity. It is at once the recognition of the empirical duality of ordinary

experience, the transcendence of this condition, and then the transforming return to or dwelling within it. Aspects of these fundamental features are explored in the next few points.

4. Shinran is famous for insisting that shinjin is due to other-
power (*tariki*), the vow-power of Amida, and not the result of self-
power (*jiriki*). This means not merely that the conditions that
control, determine, or enable shinjin to occur are not within the
power of the (empirical) human self,[103] but also that, in some sense,
shinjin is a "self-less" act that does not even belong to this self.
Since it is not due to the (empirical) self's agency, it is not this self's
own activity. It follows that shinjin cannot be any kind of decision,
voluntary choice, or act of resolution or commitment, much less a
matter of calculation or instrumental activity. Shinjin is not something one does, or anything one could do; it is an act of a human
person without an (empirical) human agent. Any agency in (producing or enabling) shinjin must be ascribed to Amida. "It is the
Buddha's mind opened forth in the minds of beings, and the awakening of beings to a transformed and liberated existence in the complete givenness of genuine practice that results in enlightenment"
(148).

5. Even though shinjin is due to other-power, it is also *jinen*
(naturalness), "being made to become so of itself" (177). Naturalness
has two aspects. In one, shinjin is what is spontaneous, occurring
of and by itself without artificiality, internal directedness, or external
constraint.[104] In the other, shinjin is self-realization, the graceful
achievement of one's deeper self, one's own Buddha-nature, which
is not different from Amida's Buddha-nature. Putting these points
together with the previous one, we may say that although shinjin
cannot be viewed as the empirical human agent's act, it nonetheless
occurs naturally, gracefully, without flaw or error, in and through
that agent, and furthermore that shinjin is somehow a realization of
that person's deeper capacities, a realization that cannot be achieved
by the person's shallower self.

---

103. The qualification "empirical" is required to leave open the possibility of
identifying oneself with Amida Buddha. Since no Buddha as such is an empirical
agent (if indeed an agent in any ordinary sense at all), one's realization of Buddha-
nature and identification with Amida can only be at a nonempirical level.

104. Compare with the Protean Taoist notion of *wu-wei*, in at least some of its
many meanings.

6. It is not just that the shallow, empirical self cannot achieve shinjin. One who has (or is) shinjin perceives one's very (empirical) self as "evil"—not necessarily in the sense that one always does or wants to do deeds conventionally denominated "evil" (as opposed to "good"), but rather in the more fundamental sense of self-attachment. Shinran most often speaks of evil as a matter of "blind passions," but the notion expands to cover all empirically self-interested mental events. All ordinary thoughts, volitions, and attitudes, as well as all passionate feelings, are at root the expressions of self-attachment and incitements to further self-attachment. Whether what one desires for the self is (in conventional terms) "good" or "bad," and whether one succeeds in getting what one wants, the fact remains that one desires. One's desires ceaselessly, insatiably proliferate; there seems to be no end to desiring.

The heart of the matter is that a desiring being desires not only to have its own desires satisfied but also to have more desires, to go on desiring. This is self-attachment, attachment to the self that desires and desires to desire. But self-attachment is, on a Buddhist view, self-confinement, confinement to living as a self that feeds on its own needs, breeding ever more self-attachment—a process that extends throughout and beyond the duration of an individual life. This unending self-confinement truly is "hell" for a Buddhist. Finally, such an evil self is unable on its own to break free from its self-induced self-confinement. No matter what it does or wants to do—or even could do or want to do—it is doomed to remain in the clutches of desire, falling short of enlightenment, and condemned to an everlasting inferno of clinging, fearful, self-attached rebirths.

7. That is the bad news. The good news is that there is a way out of self-confinement, and it is through the door of shinjin. While we can do nothing to extract ourselves from self-confinement, Amida nonetheless makes available to us an exit, the complete "entrusting" of our entire self (sincerely, without a doubt) unto Amida. Ordinary trust is no way out of self-confinement, for three reasons: Ordinarily, S trusts A at least in part for the sake of S's own real or apparent good, in order to fulfill S's own needs or to satisfy S's desires; ordinarily, trusting A is thought to benefit S (only?) because A is able to satisfy S's desires; and ordinarily, S's act of trusting A belongs to S, is initiated by S, or is (at least partially) under S's control.

But trusting[105] Amida is radically different from ordinary trusting. Even though one can do nothing to escape self-confinement, even though one's best efforts at gaining control only make things worse, and even though one is fundamentally "evil" (self-attached), Amida is altogether beyond all that—beyond the calculating, discriminating pursuit of desired good and avoidance of unwanted evil. It is Amida, and Amida alone, who can save one from the evil one wants, the evil one does, and the evil one is. Shinjin is a condition where one does not "own" any actions that attempt to control or lay claim on Amida; in fact, one surrenders all efforts of self-attachment. Though passions and desires may arise, they are not connected to caring about one's self in such a way that one is pained when frustrated or fearful when successful. "Entrusting" oneself to Amida—or simply "trusting Amida"—means completely "forgetting" oneself and re-lying absolutely, unreservedly, fundamentally on Amida.

8. Shinjin therefore expresses, or indeed essentially is, heartfelt gratitude spilling over into repentance and joy. Since shinjin comes as an unexpected and overwhelming gift from Amida, a present from "outside" the ordinary grasping self (beyond its control and even beyond its ken), its phenomenology is that of an other-directed, grateful mind, a mind that thankfully accepts the gift that is given, and becomes available, only through shinjin—in fact, the gift is shinjin. This gift is in effect a completely new life, or a totally new way of living, or at any rate a radically new way of looking at life. Sincere acceptance of such a magnificent and all-encompassing gift entails that one repent of one's prior attachment to an "evil" exis-tence.[106] It also entails that one's transformed existence is filled with

105. Perhaps surprisingly, here "trusting" seems a better translation for shinjin than "entrusting." "Entrusting" connotes agency and action; it is something one does or brings about ("I entrust myself to your care"). "Trusting," however, is a condition that need carry no implication of agency; it is something one has, or a condition one is in, independently of who or what has brought it about ("To my surprise, I trust you" or "I find myself trusting him"). Clearly shinjin, as the cancellation of all self-effort and self-attainment, is more like trusting than entrusting in this respect.

106. Interestingly enough, Ueda and Hirota interpret repentance not in terms of guilt but in terms of shame. Repentance is having "a radical and pervasive sense of shame that transcends the moral and ethical dimensions of human life and goes to the core of one's personal existence" (164). Is shame, as opposed to guilt, a necessary feature of shinjin? Is guilt (versus shame) a necessary feature of a Lutheran (or even

joy, a positive tone of delight permeating one's entire being. Gratitude without repentance is insincere, and repentant gratitude without joy is hollow.

9. Finally, shinjin is "nonretrogressive." Achievement of its goal of enlightenment is assured and cannot be blocked or taken away. Ueda and Hirota construe this feature as the "immediate attainment of birth" in the Pure Land—now, at present, in daily life, and not just after death (169–70). The "place" for attaining enlightenment is not some otherworldly heaven or afterworldly spirit realm but the reality of here and now transformed through being viewed with a non–self-attached gaze and lived with the mind of Amida Buddha. In traditional Buddhist categories, "nirvana fills samsara" (171), i.e., the "place" of enlightenment is no longer distinct from but pervades and transforms the "place" of karmic *dukkha*, the damning cycle of self-confinement.[107]

Putting all of the nine features together we have an inherently paradoxical or apparently contradictory portrait of shinjin. It is a relationship between a completely "evil," self-confined being and an enlightened being transcending good and evil, a relationship that both heightens and overcomes their radical differences. It is the wholehearted trusting of another by a being who is completely unable on its own to take the least step toward escaping self-confinement. It is a gift that one cannot give or accept, and yet a gift that is compassionately given and gratefully accepted. It is the cancellation of one's evil self but not of one's evil passions, thoughts, and inclinations; at the same time, it is the spontaneous expression

a Christian?) conception of faith? There is no space to explore these tantalizing questions here.

107. It seems that Ueda and Hirota, in their interpretation of Shinran, wish to obliterate all distinction between being born into the Pure Land (as an optimal and effectual set of conditions for achieving enlightenment) and achieving enlightenment itself (actualizing the Pure Land conditions). First, they collapse any distinction between reaching the Pure Land after death and realizing nonretrogression in this life. Then they insist that the Pure Land is not some intermediary ideal world for continued practice but the very realization of enlightenment. Hence, there is no distinction among nonretrogression (in this life), reaching the Pure Land, and achieving enlightenment (172). Later, however, Ueda and Hirota bring back a functional equivalent of the distinction between the Pure Land and enlightenment by insisting that shinjin is "not yet supreme enlightenment" (176) and by asserting that there is room for growth in wisdom-compassion after death. They do not, however, elaborate how one might distinguish among kinds or degrees of enlightenment.

of one's own transcendent Buddha-nature which is the very same as Amida's Buddha-nature. It is attaining compassion for all other beings even while achieving the wisdom that they are not other than oneself. It is the recognition of an unbridgeable chasm between oneself and Amida, and then it is the bridging of that chasm. It is the passage from samsara to its utter opposite nirvana and thence to their identification. It is realizing "nonretrogressive" nirvana while remaining fully immersed in cyclic samsara.

### The Models Paradoxically Deployed

What are we to make of such a tangled, complicated, and apparently contradictory set of features? Do they even form a single conception at all, much less a conception of faith? Brashly to dismiss any of these features would be a mistake, I believe, even if we cannot give a completely satisfactory account of how they fit together, because it is the witness of the Shin Buddhist tradition, as interpreted by Ueda and Hirota, that all of these features are required to even begin to do justice to their experience. But merely to repeat the Shin thinkers' paradoxical accounts that simply preserve all of these features can be quite unhelpful to the outsider and otiose to the enlightened. What we can try to do, instead, is to see what light our models of faith can shed on shinjin.

My proposal is this: The concept of shinjin is paradoxical precisely because it exemplifies features of different models of faith that are strictly incompatible, in their full extension, but nonetheless somehow are conjoined as different aspects or "moments" of one unitary experience.[108] In particular, the coincident exemplification of three models of faith illumines most of the complicated features of shinjin. The elements of difference in shinjin chiefly exemplify the personal relationship model, the elements of sameness mostly exemplify the confidence model, and the elements of transformation (difference

108. Frank Hoffman rightly queries how incompatible features could possibly be conjoined in one experience: How could something impossible be actual? I readily confess that I do not know. Nevertheless, it seems to me that such a paradoxical depiction is the best characterization of shinjin as portrayed by Ueda and Hirota. Whether this means that I have misunderstood them, or that they have improperly depicted shinjin (as paradoxical), or that persons fundamentally committed to logic are on the wrong track, I do not know. (Perhaps explorations in "paraconsistency" would help; see, e.g., Da Costa and French, 1990.)

becoming sameness) largely exemplify the attitude model. We should glance first at the other three models, however, for each of them contains some features that shinjin exemplifies, or at least permits, even though each also contains other features that shinjin excludes.

1. The belief model essentially involves propositional believing, whereas shinjin appears to be an experience transcending all such propositional attitudes; indeed, believing propositions would seem to be a paradigm of "self-power." But these appearances are deceptive. The propositional beliefs required by the belief model lack adequate evidence and are nonevidentially based, and it is quite possible that the person who holds such beliefs is not the agent of their formation or of their being held in such a confident way. It may be that a person just finds herself firmly believing these things. So it is at least possible that shinjin permits having propositional beliefs, for example, about Buddha-nature or about Amida Buddha's "other-power" role in bringing about shinjin (in general or in one's own case).

All that shinjin requires is that the person having these beliefs not choose or otherwise cause these beliefs, not use them as a basis for choice or action, not take credit for having them, and indeed not even think of oneself as having them, for all of these would be forms of self-attachment. This explains how having propositional beliefs may be compatible with having (or being) shinjin. Still, shinjin is much more than propositional believing, however firmly convinced it may be, and so the belief model sheds very little light on shinjin.

2. The devotion model essentially involves voluntary choice (of a way of life open to the chooser). This may appear to be excluded by shinjin as reliance on "self-power," yet the devotion model highlights several features that are also to be found in shinjin. For example, faith involves an entire way of life, not just a limited set of beliefs or attitudes or actions (similarly, shinjin cuts at the very root of self-attachment and self); faith involves a person's wholehearted engagement in a way of life, not just the participation of some parts of a personality (shinjin transforms the entire self); and faith involves lasting perseverance, not episodic experiences (shinjin is "nonretrogressive").

3. The hope model appears to contravene the temporal and axiological structure of shinjin by its commitment to a future good,

as opposed to a transtemporal condition beyond all good and evil; moreover, it relies on desire, anticipation, and expectation, all apparently facets of the self-confined empirical self that is transcended in shinjin. Nevertheless, hope is not entirely foreign to shinjin—not merely in hope's confidence amid (evidential) uncertainty but even in its future-orientation. Although from an Amida Buddha-eye's point of view all beings are (transempirically) enlightened, and even though from the standpoint of shinjin "one becomes aware that one already is, and always has been, within the working of great compassion, just as one is" (158), still there is room for hope just because there *is* a difference (even for one with shinjin) between having shinjin and not having it.[109] Expectant futurity may therefore be seen as the measure of the unfulfillment of Amida's vows, just as nondiscriminating, enlightened presentness is the sign of the vows' fulfillment; both lack and fulfillment are to be found in shinjin. Even so, futurity is not a prominent aspect of shinjin, and so the hope model does not greatly illuminate this conception.

We turn now to the other three models of faith, for they do indeed illumine the three major elements, aspects, or moments in shinjin—difference, sameness, and transformation (difference becoming sameness)—even as they prove to be incompatible with one another, thereby also illuminating shinjin's paradoxicality.

4. The personal relationship model expresses what initially appears to many Westerners as the most striking feature of shinjin. It is a trusting relationship between two quite different persons or personal selves: an empirical self-attached self and a transcendent compassionate other. The differences between the two persons or selves—their "degree of otherness," so to speak—could scarcely be made more complete. Even while they are in intimate, trusting relationship, the empirical self acknowledges itself to be totally unable to break out of its self-confinement; this self cannot in any way even begin to trust the other; the relationship is in every respect a gift from the other. Shinjin is wholly due to "other-power," not at all due to "self-power," and recognition of this fact (just as in the personal relationship model) must be an article of faith for the be-

---

109. The need for hope is of course even more exigent for those who have not (yet?) reached shinjin, or for those who believe that they have not, or will not, or even might not, reach shinjin.

lieving self, as well as a reality acknowledged by feelings of gratitude and joy.[110] The personal relationship model goes far to illuminate the major elements of difference between self and Amida Buddha in shinjin.

5. But of course difference is not all there is to shinjin. There is also a deepening sense of sameness, unity, or identity between the initially distinct "subject" and "object" of the relationship. Amida's Buddha-nature must be seen as not other than the deeper self's own Buddha-nature, and it is therefore natural for Ueda and Hirota to speak of the Buddha "becoming one with" the self (157). This unity, or identity, is illuminated by the confidence model, for which faith is a nonrelational conscious state, realizing one's deeper self, characterized by a deep and imperturbable feeling of peace, tranquility, or confidence. On the confidence model, there is no difference between self and other, because there is no other—or perhaps one should say the only "other" is one's own (deeper) self, with which one becomes thoroughly unified through the intimacy of identity.

There are, of course, some difficulties in applying the confidence model to shinjin. For one, confidence is said to persist or endure through time; for another, the confidence model insists on a self—a "deeper," nonempirical self to be sure, but still a self. However, these obstacles are only apparent. First, the persistence of confidence need not connote the kind of substantial continuance rejected by all Buddhists; it is equally compatible with wholly fresh arising in every moment, so long as the novelty of the now preserves or constantly exemplifies the feature of tranquility, serenity, and peace. The confidence model merely requires that confidence not cease, not come to an end, not fail to occur in any future moment, and this requirement may be met equally well by an antisubstantial view as by a substantial one.

Second, the "self" that is realized according to the confidence model is not the grasping empirical self that is to be lost in shinjin, a self consumed with, by, and for desire. Rather, this requirement of a deeper self is thoroughly compatible with the Shin realization of a transcendent Buddha-self whose wisdom and compassion ex-

110. The personal relationship model's element of propositional belief—"articles of faith"—is certainly dormant in shinjin, but there seems to be no good reason why it needs to be completely absent.

tend to all beings alike, neither discriminating among them nor attaching itself to any one of them in particular. It is in these ways that the confidence model illumines the elements of identity in the conception of shinjin.

6. Finally, in shinjin difference and unity are transformed into unity amid difference, or difference infused by unity: "Samsara and nirvana are brought to stand simultaneously in mutual opposition and in identity" (152); or "nirvana fills samsara" (171). Here the attitude model sheds some light. According to this model, faith is a partial, radically constitutive attitude toward an environing context, an attitude that is prepropositional, fundamental, totalizing, and significant. Such an attitude constitutes both the self that is "in" the world and the world that environs it. Self and world are thus opposites—different and "other"—yet they are also necessary correlates and therefore states or conditions of a deeper "self" that "has" this and not some other attitude toward this and not some other world.

Of course, in the attitude model this radical self-world constitution is only partial, and one might suppose that shinjin requires something greater—a complete or total constitution. This is not necessarily so. In shinjin, all or most of the elements of samsaric existence remain (for example, desires, feelings, passions, as well as perceptions, conceptions, and ordinary mentation), save only for the self-attachment that glues them together. But without the glue of self-attachment, the way in which the samsaric elements are fashioned into a "world" is radically (= "at root") different than before; the world is radically reconstituted. Hence, shinjin requires only partial radical constitution.

We are now in a better position to appreciate the utility of our models of faith. On the one hand, they can shed light on even such a complex and paradoxical conception as shinjin by highlighting its distinct structural aspects, dimensions, or moments. On the other hand, they help to settle the question of whether shinjin is a conception of faith, and not something altogether different. Still, two problems remain.

First, Ueda-Hirota's Shin conception of shinjin posits a unique "object" of faith, Amida Buddha, and the entire quality of shinjin is thereby affected. The Nembutsu seems to be a "strait and narrow gate" for shinjin. Shinjin is necessarily that state or condition that is brought about by the "other-power" of Amida and by no other. It seems, for example, that Christian faith in "God the Father of Our Lord and Savior Jesus Christ" could not qualify as shinjin even if it were entirely due to the other-power of God, just because the other-power is God's, not Amida's. Shinjin can be considered faith, it appears, only if faith is conceptually matched with Amida Buddha; but doing so would rule out faith in any other (kind of) object, and, hence, would exclude faith in God, or even faith in another human being. Since this is absurd, one might argue, shinjin cannot be faith.

However, there are a number of ways around this extreme conclusion. For one, there are some structural similarities between Buddhist transformation and Christian conversion. In both, one's current empirical self (evil, grasping, sinful) is lost or left behind, and one receives—it is not an achievement—a new "self" (state of being, new life). For another, though Amida is expressly said not to be a god, he is also said to possess a number of godlike qualities (transtemporality, boundless compassion, irresistible power, and intimacy to self). Further, the Nembutsu and Christian prayer are phenomenologically similar in many respects, particularly in their other-mindedness, as expressed in dependence, gratitude, and joy. Finally, although shinjin paradoxically unites radical difference and unity (or transforms them into unity-in-difference), whereas Christian faith preserves the gulf between creature and creator, there are hints in Christianity of a kind of "unitive" or (better) "communitive" mystical state wherein the intimacy of God and human passes quite beyond ordinary limits and understanding. It is not entirely clear that shinjin in Amida necessarily precludes intimate faith in God, or conversely. The uniqueness clause in Ueda and Hirota's Shin conception of shinjin need no more exclude other conceptions of faith than the structurally similar (but contrary) uniqueness clause in Aulén's or Shepherd's Christian conceptions of faith.

Second, Ueda and Hirota's conception of *shinjin* is paradoxical; that is, it contains features that are inconsistent, or that lead to contradictions in their depiction. In the eyes of Ueda and Hirota, this is no defect; the experienced reality of shinjin requires all these features, however contradictory they may seem or be. Therefore, the contradictions that arise from applying all three of the models of faith we have used (personal relationship, confidence, and attitude models) are not an artifact of our account; the conflicts among the models mirror the tensions within the conception of shinjin. Further, one might say that joint application of the three models helps to pinpoint exactly what the essential tensions within shinjin are: the contradiction between a nonrelational view (such as the confidence model) and a relational view (especially the personal relationship model, but also the attitude model); and within relational views, the contradiction between relation with another person and relation to a (nonpersonal) "world" constituted by an attitude. From these two fundamental contradictions spring most, if not all, of the paradoxical aspects of shinjin. The tension between the otherness of Amida and his identity with one's own Buddha-nature, for example, reflects the former contradiction; and the tension between the personality of Amida and Amida's transempirical transcendence of all differences, including those of personality, reflects the latter contradiction. Use of the models, therefore, does not conceal or explain away the paradoxical character of shinjin; its paradox may even be heightened by being more clearly illumined.[111]

We may conclude with a surprising observation. The features of uniqueness and paradoxicality, far from differentiating shinjin from other conceptions of faith like those of Aulén, Shepherd, and the rest, have the diametrically opposite effect. Paradoxically, neither uniqueness nor paradoxicality is unique to shinjin, but both are common to and equally intelligible in the context of many other conceptions of faith. These features can only further secure shinjin's place in the family of conceptions of faith.

### Recapitulation

The conception of shinjin presented by Ueda and Hirota is many-faceted and paradoxical. Three of our models of faith help to illumine the major facets of shinjin: the personal relationship model highlights the elements of difference dividing an empirical, self-attached self from a transcendent, compassionate other; the confidence model

---

111. Paradox may be present but unwelcome, as we saw with Murty's (1959) Hindu conception of faith, in which case the models' illumination of the essential tensions enables clarification for the sake of altering or patching the conception. Here paradox is present and welcome, and so the models' illumination of the incompatibilities enables clarification without any desire to alter the conception.

illumines the elements of identity uniting their Buddha-natures; and the attitude model casts considerable light on the transformations of both difference and identity into difference-in-identity or identity-in-difference through its notion of partial radical constitution. The mutual inconsistencies among these three models crisply mirror, and therefore help one to discern, the paradoxical tensions within the conception of shinjin, just as they help one to see how shinjin both resembles and differs from other conceptions of faith. This shows, finally, that use of our models of faith need not be limited to consistent conceptions.

## G. A Sŏn Buddhist Conception

The last conception of faith we consider departs even further than Ueda and Hirota's Shin Buddhist conception of shinjin from the Christian conceptions with which we began. Yet it too can be seen as a viable conception of faith in its own right, insofar as it clearly exemplifies one of our models of faith, the confidence model. The conception is one that has emerged out of the Mahayana Buddhist tradition known as the *Dhyāna* (meditation) School, which has a long and complicated development in China and throughout East Asia. Its Japanese variant, Zen, is perhaps most familiar to Westerners, but there are similar versions in China (Ch'an) and Korea (Sŏn) as well. We consider the lucid presentation of a Sŏn Buddhist conception of faith that is found in *Buddhist Faith and Sudden Enlightenment*, written by Sung Bae Park, a monk of the Chogye order in Haeinsa, Korea.[112]

### Park's Version

According to Park, Sŏn Buddhism is a religion of faith as well as of meditation and enlightenment: "Without right faith, no practice

112. Park, 1983; page references in this section are to this text. Park is particularly reliant on the writings of Chinul, but, once again, neither the historical accuracy nor the doctrinal orthodoxy of Park's account is here in question. Works on the Sŏn Buddhist tradition include Buswell, 1983, 1986, 1989; Chang, 1969; Hakeda, 1967; Keel, 1986; and D. W. Mitchell, 1980. Buswell, 1983 and 1989 contain extensive bibliographies of ancient and modern works in both Asian and European languages.

can be initiated and no enlightenment attained in Buddhism" (1). Faith is not merely the origin and means but also the culmination of the Buddhist Way; faith is both necessary and sufficient for enlightenment (13). This faith is not the Westerner's customary "dualistic" or "subject-object" faith; it is not someone's faith that something is, has been or will be the case, nor is it someone's faith in a person, principle, or institution. Faith simply has no such "object," or, indeed, any object at all. Instead, "nondual" faith is "a natural function (*yung*) of one's own (originally enlightened) Mind" (1). It is a kind of self-confidence or "self-power," "a state of conviction or resoluteness that keeps one firmly rooted in practice" (2). More fully, it is "abiding firmly with resolute conviction in a state of clearness, tranquility, and freedom" (16). To have such faith is "to realize directly the nature of our own True Mind," not to hear or see or otherwise be related to the mind of some other person such as God (18).[113]

Following the Sŏn monk Chinul (1158–1210), Park calls nondual faith "patriarchal" faith (Korean *choshin*, Chinese *tsu-hsin*); it is a faith of and from the patriarchs but not a faith in the patriarchs (35–6). Patriarchal faith is to be carefully distinguished from "doctrinal" faith (Korean *kyoshin*, Chinese *chiao-hsin*). Whereas doctrinal faith is preparatory to practice and enlightenment, patriarchal faith is practice and enlightenment; whereas doctrinal faith is belief in a Buddha, patriarchal faith is the faith of a Buddha; whereas doctrinal faith is the belief that I can become Buddha, patriarchal faith is the affirmation that I already am Buddha—"a much more potent idea," Park dryly notes (4). "To arouse patriarchal faith is to become instantly enlightened" (19).[114] To be enlightened, to realize one's true Buddha-nature, is to realize in a most intimate way the dependent origination and true emptiness of all things. Hence, "Buddhist faith is quite

---

113. Park, unlike Murty (1959) in a similar situation, does not speak of "revelation," nor does he view faith as correlative to revelation. Park's view seems to be that nondual faith has no need of revelation because there is no personal relationship with a personal revealer. "Faith" and "revelation" are not correlative concepts for Park, precisely because he thinks there cannot be revelation without a personal revealer. Murty, of course, retains the correlativity of faith and revelation by holding that there can be (and is) revelation without a revealer.

114. Park translates the title of the basic Hua-yen text, the *Ta-ch'eng ch'i-hsin lun*, as "Treatise on Awakening Mahāyāna Faith" instead of the standard "Treatise on the Awakening of Faith in Mahāyāna" (37).

different from the faith of theistic religions, for it is not a belief in the truth of scriptures, in the divinity of a Savior, or in the existence of a transcendent God; rather it is the direct experience of dependent origination, in which all dharmas are empty" (26).[115]

Patriarchal faith is "nonbacksliding faith" (*pu-t'ui hsin*), an irreversible condition that cannot be lost, a state of enlightenment that always remains firm and steady. As such, faith's origin and continuance cannot be due to any fallible human capacity such as will or intellect; hence, Park infers, nondual faith cannot be reduced to a combination of human *fiducia* (trust) and *assensus* (assent).[116] Moreover, nondual faith is neither a gift from God nor the product of any human activity. In fact, nondual faith is said to have no cause or authorship at all, to be completely outside the causal nexus altogether—patriarchal faith just is Suchness, dependent origination, and emptiness all rolled into one. Nondual faith is a condition of "One Mind" or nondiscriminating consciousness, a condition that has no external source. This is why "backsliding is not possible in a mind free of discriminating thoughts. Since no distinctions are made, there is nowhere to backslide to and no one to backslide" (45).

In this Sŏn Buddhist conception, patriarchal faith is a condition of mind—or perhaps one should say it is a state of conscious being or a conscious state of being—that lacks an "object" and an "author." There is nothing such faith is in or about, and there is nothing by which it is caused or produced. It is not an attitude directed toward a proposition or another person. It does not involve believing or trusting anyone (except, in a peculiar sense, one's own true self), nor does it permit recognizing or submitting to the authority of anyone (that is, the authority of anyone else). It is not a relationship between a human person and a (or the) divine person or any other person. In fact, nondual faith is not a relationship at all but a quality; the term "faith" here names a one-place predicate: "abiding firmly with resolute conviction in a state of clearness, tranquility, and free-

---

115. Park compares this Buddhist conception of faith to Friedrich Schleiermacher's (1768–1834) conception of faith as "the feeling of absolute dependence," but notes that dependent origination is mutual interdependence, not one-sided dependence (27).

116. Here Buddhist "nonbacksliding faith" strongly resembles Christian "persevering faith." On the latter, see Berkouwer, 1958.

dom." Such abiding is also called "enlightenment." It is not directed toward or focused on anything at all—but it is nonetheless the realization of one's deepest, most real, true self.[117]

### Exemplification and Annexation

Unlike Ueda and Hirota's notion of shinjin, which paradoxically exemplifies three models of faith at once (personal relationship, confidence, and attitude models), Park's conception of patriarchal faith seems a clear and relatively straightforward instance of one and only one model of faith, the confidence model.[118] On the one hand, patriarchal faith ( = enlightenment) exemplifies the following essential features of the confidence model: It is a nonrelational, prepropositional, conscious state that is characterized by a deep, enduring, and imperturbable feeling of self-confidence and that realizes one's deeper (true) self. On the other hand, since it admits of no relational features whatsoever, patriarchal faith cannot consistently exemplify any of the other five models, all of which are relational concepts.

There are, however, two complications. For one, Park's conception does not quite confine itself to only one model of faith. It annexes, though it does not exemplify, the devotion model of faith. For another, even though it fully exemplifies the confidence model, Park's Sŏn Buddhist conception of faith is neither a reduplication nor the only possible exemplification of this model, just because of its rather extreme specification of some optional features in the confidence model of faith.

On the first point, although Park's conception of patriarchal faith exemplifies only the confidence model, Park still leaves open the possibility, as well as the desirability, of other kinds of faith (ex-

---

117. Is such faith a relation toward oneself, that is, toward one's true self? Yes and no. Insofar as identity is a relation, faith is a relation, for faith is being one's true self. But insofar as relation implies otherness, faith is not a relation, for faith essentially involves no one but one's own true self. Still, what about the relation between one's current, imperfect, empirical self and one's true self? This may be another kind of faith, but it is not the nondual faith that Park discusses as "patriarchal" faith.

118. By saying it is a "clear and relatively straightforward" exemplification, I do not mean to imply that the confidence model depicts all of the essential or important features of patriarchal faith, much less that patriarchal faith is easy (or difficult) to attain.

emplifications of other models) as useful adjuncts, helps, or means. In particular, doctrinal faith may be a helpful means to patriarchal faith. Having faith in the enlightened authority of a patriarch may inspire emulation of her life; believing true propositions about the possibility and importance of patriarchal faith may open options for one's life; desiring the great good of enlightenment may be better than hating or ignoring it; and so forth.

It is worth contrasting Park with Ueda and Hirota on this score.[119] As with Ueda and Hirota's Shin Buddhist conception of shinjin, Park's Sŏn Buddhist conception of patriarchal faith goes beyond the confidence model to make use of other models, but in a less essential way. Whereas shinjin paradoxically requires and exemplifies three incompatible models while excluding any kind or aspect of faith that resembles "self-power," patriarchal faith nonparadoxically requires and exemplifies only the confidence model, while at the same time permitting the use of other kinds and conceptions of faith (exemplifying other models) insofar as they are helpful means, whether or not they involve self-power.

Further, the other model that Park's conception chiefly employs is the devotion model; that contrasts with Ueda and Hirota's use of the personal relationship and attitude models.[120] Devotion involves voluntary choice of a wholehearted and lasting commitment to a way of life open to one. According to Ueda and Hirota's conception, devotion is excluded from shinjin because volition involves a "self-power" that is diametrically opposed to the total reliance on Amida's "other-power" required to produce (re-)birth in the Pure Land and achieve enlightenment. Shinjin is a personal relationship with Amida Buddha (a total reliance on another) as well as a radical reconstitution of one's fundamental attitude toward the world, and

119. Here models help to illuminate the differences between two Buddhist conceptions of faith. This illumination implies two important points: First, there are distinct conceptions of faith within traditions of faith other than the Christian tradition, as well as between the Christian tradition and other traditions. And second, our models of faith have the potential to clarify a variety of traditions both internally and in relation to one another; they are not parochial models useful only in Western theistic contexts.

120. I focus on the devotion model, but similar remarks might be made about the belief and attitude models in relation to Park's conception of patriarchal faith. For example, confidently believing certain propositions or adopting certain radically constitutive attitudes may assist one in attaining a confident state of mind; but they are strictly unnecessary.

both reliance and attitude are inextricably connected with enlightenment. Reliance on Amida, reconstituting experience, and (self-)
confidence go together, and to achieve any one of them is to achieve
the others.

For Park, however, self-power devotion to another is not totally
rejected. Of course, one should not be devoted to some superhuman,
semidivine Buddha, much less to a god; rather, one should be devoted to the way of life taught (and lived) by some human guru,
teacher, or helper, insofar as such devotion will help one to achieve
patriarchal faith and thus enlightenment. At the minimum, such
devotion may be less obstructive or harmful to attaining enlightenment than floundering about in its absence. Still, devotion is only
contingently connected with enlightenment; a useful means for some
or many, it is necessary for no one. Devotion is a matter of doctrinal
faith, faith in someone, and doctrinal faith is only a means to the
practice of patriarchal faith, not itself the practice of such faith. It
is at least possible that some gifted individuals will not need the
assistance of doctrinal faith in patriarchs in order to attain patriarchal
faith—after all, the first patriarch (if there was a first) presumably
did not require such assistance. Still, devotion may be useful for
some or many in achieving patriarchal faith, and making use of this
means—by one's own choice or act of "self-power"—is not merely
not excluded but also recommended by Park. Relying on oneself to
choose to be devoted to a teacher, rather than completely relying
on Amida's merit and power from the outset, can be an aid instead
of an obstacle to the achievement of patriarchal faith.

On the second point, Park's conception specifies the confidence
model in various nonobligatory ways, of which three may be mentioned.

1. The confidence model is neutral with respect to the accoutrement and independence versions of pure awareness, that is, a nonrelational conscious state (see Chap. 2, sec. D). On the accoutrement
version, pure awareness accompanies separable states of consciousness but is not itself a separable conscious state; on the independence
version, pure awareness is itself (also) a separable conscious state.
Park's conception of patriarchal faith adopts the independence version of pure awareness, since nondual faith, as "the direct experience
of dependent origination, in which all dharmas are empty," must

itself not be dependent on anything, including any (other) conscious state.[121]

2. The confidence model maintains only a minimal depiction of pure awareness as a psychological state, leaving considerable latitude for speculation about any further reality and value that this state might possess. Park's conception, however, goes far beyond this minimal depiction. Nondual faith is much more than a psychological condition; it is a state of being (or something beyond both being and nonbeing) that is of ultimate ontological and axiological significance. Such faith realizes (brings to consciousness and makes actual) ultimate reality, which is Suchness, emptiness, or dependent origination.[122]

3. The confidence model insists on imperturbability only in a conditional sense (an incapacity for S to be perturbed so long as S has a fundamental quality Q), not an absolute sense (S cannot lose Q and therefore cannot be perturbed, come what may). The model permits absolute imperturbability, but by no means requires it. Park's conception, on the other hand, does seem to require imperturbability in the absolute sense. Nondual faith or enlightenment is "nonbacksliding," which means that it is irreversible, lasting, and cannot be lost; its imperturbability cannot be brought to an end by any external or internal causes.

The point of these three brief examples is not just that conceptions are exemplifications of models and that what is obligatory in a conception may be optional in a model; it is also that conceptions all exemplifying the same model of faith may nonetheless differ greatly among themselves—they may even be incompatible exemplifications, where one conception forecloses what another leaves open. To focus on the differences without taking note of the underlying commonalities would be a major mistake.[123]

121. It seems that Ueda and Hirota want the notion of shinjin to work both ways; shinjin as the pure nirvanic awareness of samsara adopts both the accoutrement and the independence versions of pure awareness. Shinjin is a state of awareness that is not separable from ordinary samsaric consciousness, and yet it is also not in any way dependent on the latter.

122. Ueda and Hirota's conception of shinjin would seem to agree with Park's conception on this point and the next.

123. Note also that two conceptions of faith may share a specified feature while exemplifying two quite different models of faith, so long as the feature is common

*Is Choshin Faith?*

In moving from Pieper's Thomistic conception of faith to Park's Sŏn conception, we have traveled a very great conceptual distance. Some may even think that we have gone over the edge of the world, having arrived in Sŏn Buddhism at a conception that is not even a conception of faith at all. Clearly Park thinks "choshin" is a conception of faith, since "patriarchal faith" is how he unapologetically translates the term into English. Further, since Park's conception clearly exemplifies the confidence model, his conception of choshin is a conception of faith if the confidence model is a model of faith. Still, some may question whether the confidence model indeed models faith. If the confidence model, and its diverse exemplifications, is a member of the "family of faith," it surely belongs to a fairly remote and exotic lineage, differing in many fundamental respects from its (putative) kinfolk. Some, delighting in extending the bonds of kinship, may welcome this model and Park's conception into the household of faith; others, keeping closer track of the degrees of kinship, may make distinctions and discriminate accordingly. Let us hear what may be said on both sides.[124]

On the latter score, recall the enormous divergence of Park's conception from exemplifications of the personal relationship model such as the Christian conceptions of Pieper, Shepherd, or Aulén. Choshin is not a personal relationship or a relation between two distinct persons, or even a relation between two stages, aspects, or levels of the same person; in fact, choshin is not a relation at all but a quality—a state or condition of a single mind or person. Hence, there is no "object" of faith, no (external) authority whom the subject trusts, no author or (partial) external agent-cause of faith. Choshin is self-reliance, not dependence on or trust of another. Moreover, and not least, there are no articles of faith in or prior to

---

to, or at least optional in, the two models (occurring there in a relatively general form). Not every conceptual agreement stems from the same roots.

124. In the following pages, I use "choshin" untranslated, so as not to prejudge the question of whether it names a kind of faith. I also focus on Christian conceptions of faith, not because Christianity is imagined to have a monopoly on faith or conceptions of faith, but rather because the Christian conceptions are undeniably conceptions of faith and also apparently so opposed to Park's conception of choshin.

choshin, no propositions to be handed down, to be believed, or even to be considered.[125]

Given these fundamental and obvious points of difference, it may seem hopeless to view choshin as a conception of faith. Yet noting differences is by no means the end of the story. Quite apart from historical considerations (traditions of translation and piety whose linguistic usage is as open to question as anything else), there are good systematic reasons supporting Park's use of "faith" in translating choshin. Choshin resembles as well as differs from standard notions of faith such as Christian faith in God; the following are among the more salient likenesses.

1. Enlightenment plays roughly the same (absolutely central and controlling) role in Sŏn Buddhist thought as does salvation in Christian theistic thought. Choshin is said to be necessary and sufficient for the supreme goal of enlightenment, while faith in Christ is thought to be necessary and sufficient for the supreme goal of salvation. Moreover, both are essential constituents of their respective goals, although choshin comes closer to being identical with its goal than does Christian faith. Choshin is enlightenment, whereas Christian faith is an earthly approximation to and foretaste of the vision of God. Choshin resembles personalistic faith because both play similar roles with respect to the (different) supreme ends of their respective religious traditions.

2. Negatively, choshin is not dependent in any way on fallible human capacities, while faith in Christ is not producible (wholly or partially) by human activities as such. Neither can be attained or achieved by ordinary empirical effort, by one's "own power" or "works"; phenomenologically, both appear as "gifts," or at any rate as effortless occurrences that are neither chosen nor willed but rather come unbidden to the grateful subject of faith.

3. Of course, the giftedness of choshin is neither experienced as coming from an external agent nor ascribed to such an author (indeed, the state or condition of choshin is said to be uncaused) while the giftedness of faith in Christ is usually experienced as coming

125. Of course, kyoshin ("doctrinal faith") requires such dealings with propositions, but kyoshin is no more than a useful but still optional means to choshin, not an essential part or aspect of choshin.

from, and ascribed to, a divine person (God the Father or the Holy Spirit). However, one should not place too much weight on these apparent differences. The phenomenological feature, wherein the experience is or is not felt as coming from an external author, is only a preliminary guide to the ascription (or not) of authorship of the experience to a transcendent agent. From an ordinary empirical point of view, there is little to choose between an experience that is not produced by any node of the world-causal nexus and one that is produced by a cause entirely transcending nature. Both are essentially "supernatural" as regards their "causality," if indeed "causality" is the right category to use in this connection. Perhaps the point is precisely to block appeal to causal explanation or inquiry of the usual (empirical) sort altogether. Here choshin does resemble Christian faith.

4. The authoritativeness of choshin-experience resembles the authoritativeness of Christian faith-experience. The state or condition of choshin is one of "abiding firmly with resolute conviction in a state of clearness, tranquility, and freedom." Such a state possesses firm, deep, and lasting authority over the person's entire life, an authority that is fundamental or basic, not derived from any other state or condition. Of course, God is the ultimate authority for Christians, but still faith in Jesus Christ is often held to be certain, basic, and "self-authenticating," possessing fundamental epistemic authority,[126] as well as exercising basic practical guidance, for a Christian's whole life.

5. Choshin is both self-realization and self-transformation. It is the attaining of one's deepest self—one's original, enlightened, "true" mind—as well as the transforming (and transcending) of one's ordinary self—one's conditioned, ignorant, suffering soul. Moreover, the state or condition of having transcended one's ordinary self and realized one's deeper self is irreversible; it is a nonbacksliding condition. Coming to have faith in Christ also involves both self-realization and self-transformation. It is a new birth or a fundamental conversion (*metanoia*) of the same yet profoundly altered self. Of course, there are different Christian interpretations of this new birth.

---

126. Alvin Plantinga's defense of belief in God as properly basic (1981, 1983) is one version of this feature of Christian faith; it is by no means the only possible one.

Sometimes it is said to involve the donation and actualization of some new (infused) capacity, sometimes the fullest realization of one's fundamental native capacities, and sometimes both, but in any event the self is both profoundly transformed and fully realized. Likewise, the majority Christian view is that no one can fall from a state of grace (or prevent God from saving those whom He has chosen). In this way, both choshin and Christian faith agree on the paradoxical need to lose oneself in order to gain oneself—to leave behind one's ordinary, superficial, and merely apparent self in order to gain one's deeper self, one's true, real, or genuine self.

6. Many of the effects of choshin resemble those of faith in Christ: tranquility ("the peace of God, which passes all understanding" [Phil. 4:7; RSV]), freedom ("for freedom Christ has set us free" [Gal. 5:1; RSV]), calm assurance ("now faith is the assurance of things hoped for" [Heb. 11:1; RSV]), integration of personality ("the unity of the faith and of the knowledge of the Son of God, . . . mature manhood, . . . the measure of the stature of the fullness of Christ" [Eph. 4:13; RSV]), depth ("the Spirit searches everything, even the depths of God" [1 Cor. 2:10; RSV]), and so forth. Two things having similar consequences may be presumed similar; once more choshin and Christian faith are alike.

7. Choshin is a firm settling on and setting out upon the Way, "a state of conviction or resoluteness that keeps one firmly rooted in practice," the practice of meditation.[127] Similarly, faith in Christ requires lasting loyalty, a *fiducia* guiding one throughout life, an agapeistic way of life that must be "practiced" and not merely "preached." In both there is enduring commitment to a way of life that subsumes, transforms, and transcends the myriad details of ordinary existence.

The considerable similarities between choshin and faith in Christ are all the more impressive the closer and deeper one looks. I mention them not in order to claim that choshin is the same as or even very closely resembles Christian faith; on the contrary, the fundamental differences cannot be ignored. My point, rather, is this: There are profound similarities and deep differences, and both must be taken

127. Note that the practice of meditation is not practice in meditation, that is, it is not practicing meditation but rather actually meditating. Likewise, the practice of Christian faith (thinking, acting, living faithfully, with the mind of Christ) is not practice in or for faith (learning how one can be faithful).

into account in coming to a decision as to whether to welcome Park's Sŏn Buddhist conception of choshin (and also the confidence model) into the conceptual family of faith.

We may go even further, albeit rather tentatively. Even if, contrary to fact, there were relatively few similarities that were vastly outweighed by the differences, it might still be possible for two conceptions or models to belong to the same conceptual family, that is, to be specifications or versions of the same concept, provided they play essential complementary roles. The general argument to this conclusion is as follows.

Consider two concepts, $C_1$ and $C_2$. Suppose that $C_1$ and $C_2$ have various kinds and degrees of conceptual resemblance and difference, but that there is at least prima facie reason to regard $C_1$ and $C_2$ as kindred concepts, perhaps different conceptions of the same concept, $C^*$. Now despite their conceptual differences, which perhaps even outweigh their resemblances, $C_1$ and $C_2$ might still be regarded as members of the same conceptual family, provided that they play essential complementary roles. By this I mean, first, that their roles in the lives of different people (or perhaps the same person's life at different times) are essential to living those lives (that life); second, that these roles are incompatible in the sense that $C_1$ and $C_2$ could not perform their respective functions at the same time in the same person's life; and, third, that these functions fit together not merely as instancing different aspects or dimensions of the same concept $C^*$ but also as contributing different means to and parts of the same overarching end or ends.

On this view, then, conceptual family ties are formed not only from conceptual resemblances between two concepts (though there are indeed many similarities), nor just from similarity of function or role (though these also are similar), but also from the complementary and harmonious functioning of the concepts in the lives of different people (or the same person at different times) with regard to some common end.

To make this line of thought less abstract, consider the following (admittedly limited and controversial) analogy with human families.[128] Let us assume that sex differences are important, that no

128. This analogy works, if it works at all, only on a traditional, and strictly false, view of the biology of sex; in a brave new world of bisexuality, asexuality,

person can be of more than one sex at one time, and that each sex is conceptually distinct (so that the concepts of male and female are similar yet different). Still, persons of different sexes may belong not merely to the same species but also to the same tribe or even to the same family; indeed, a (traditional) family requires there to be persons of different sexes (at least one of each) in order to exist and persist over time—for marriage and procreation—and arguably also for (one kind of) self-definition and even self-fulfillment—for personal identity and happiness. The function of each sex in these ways is different yet essential and complementary toward the important ends of marriage, procreation, self-identity, and happiness.

Similarly, then, if two otherwise incompatible conceptions essentially function in complementary ways toward the same end, then both might be considered members of the same conceptual family—conceptions of the same concept, conceptual kin. Now choshin, I am inclined to believe, complements personalist notions of faith in just this way. It exhibits another essential facet of the wider concept of human faith, a facet that should not be ignored by anyone interested in "the unity or coherence of humankind's religious history."[129]

Nevertheless, it seems to beg the question to speak of "the wider concept of human faith" when we are exploring whether choshin is a kind (and conception) of faith lying beyond the borders of familiar Christian ones. We could remove this fallacy if we could somehow indicate more neutrally the larger end or ends to which choshin and Christian faith are essential and complementary. This I do not know how to clearly do. But it is clear why such ends—if indeed they exist—cannot be easily or clearly specified. Since faith is so profound and pervasive a feature of people's lives, such ends must be very general—as general, perhaps, as living a fully and distinctively human life as a whole.

Perhaps the case may be put this way. There are essentially different ways of living a fully, distinctively human life, but any such life must be (in essential part) a life of faith. Since every fully, distinctively human life of faith must be conceived and lived as a

---

XYY chromosomes, in vitro fertilization, extrauterine gestation, embryonic genetic selection, surrogacy, parthenogenesis, and cloning, the analogy breaks down.

129. W.C. Smith, 1981, 3.

life of faith, and since no single conception of faith could possibly fit or capture the variety of fully, distinctively human lives, it follows that we will need an array of variously differing conceptions of faith to conceive and live human life fully and distinctively. There will be a variety of irreducibly different conceptions of faith, but these will form a harmonious family: the conceptual family of faith. In fact, the only way adequately to conceive of fully, distinctively human life as a whole will be via a concept of faith that encompasses a variegated range of conceptions of faith. Anything less is a partial view of faith because it is a partial view of fully, distinctively human life as a whole.

Such a view is antipodal to sectarian conceptions of faith that make uniqueness claims for one particular (Christian or other) conception of faith.[130] On the contrary, instead of resting on the exclusive laurels of one or another particular conception of faith, this line of speculation leads to the view that faith itself, in order to function as it should, requires transcending any particular conception of faith. Admittedly, this line is both obscure and incomplete. Much more needs to be said about faith's role in living a fully, distinctively human life as a whole. Yet despite its deficiencies, I think this line of argument tends to support the inclusion of Park's Sŏn Buddhist notion of choshin in the family of faith.

Despite the difficulties, even dangers, therefore, I think it is both possible and desirable to extend the concept of faith to include Park's Sŏn Buddhist notion of choshin.

### Recapitulation

Park's Sŏn Buddhist conception of choshin, or nondual patriarchal faith, not only exemplifies and is illuminated by the confidence model more clearly and fully than any other conception we have considered (even though there are important optional specifications) but it also supports permitting at least some nonrelational conceptions to count as conceptions of faith. Choshin is indeed faith if the

---

130. Sometimes these uniqueness claims rest on views about the uniqueness of God or of Christ; sometimes they are an essential expression of the overriding authority of church, pope, or Bible; and sometimes they are grounded on the unique finality of salvation as Christianly conceived (there is no higher end and no other possible means). Clearly, this last position is most troubling for our argument here.

confidence model indeed models faith, and there are good reasons for accepting such modeling. As a bonus, the different ways in which choshin and shinjin exemplify the confidence model help to illuminate some central differences within the Mahayana Buddhist tradition between Korean Sŏn and Japanese Shin thinking. The house of faith has many rooms, and not all of them are in the Christian wing.

# [ 5 ]

# Conclusion

We have traveled far and wide in our exploration of faith, and it is time now to settle back, to reflect on some central features of our journey, and to ask where we might go from here. First, I offer some reflections on faith's conceptual diversity, the great variation in conceptions of faith. I follow with some thoughts on faith's conceptual unity, how amidst the welter of conceptions of faith one may still discern some kind of unity in the concept of faith. Finally, I touch on some of the many problems that remain for—and some that are created by—this inquiry.

## A. The Diversity of Conceptions of Faith

The seven conceptions of faith we have examined represent only a few of the many options to be found in and out of various traditions of faith, not to mention the even larger set of possible conceptions that have yet to be realized (recognized and made actual). These seven were selected because, among other reasons, they jointly exemplify every one of our six models of faith, in varying combinations, and thereby show how all of the models variously illuminate their exemplifications. Despite this sevenfold variety, however, one might wish for more. It would be nice, for example, to be able to list all actual conceptions of faith, or to classify all possible conceptions, or even to sketch the major kinds. This is well beyond what is possible; there are simply too many conceptions of faith, and they are too diverse in too many different ways.

Still, it may be worth scanning and naming a few additional variations in conceptions of faith (in outline, not in their full particularity). This exercise may seem unnecessary to some, who are already fully convinced of the diversity of conceptions of faith, but it may benefit others, who want to increase their awareness and appreciation of faith's enormous diversity. In addition, it provides an opportunity to clarify further uses for these models of faith, since models can illuminate conceptual deviations just as well as conceptual exemplifications.

When a conception exemplifies a model, it adopts some or all of the essential features of the model as its own.[1] Almost invariably, though, it will contain different conceptual content than is provided by the model's rather general features, in any or all of the following ways. It may specify the general features in various optional ways;[2] it may extend or alter general features without replacing them; it may add (general or specified) features to those in the model; it may reject one or a few of the essential features of the model, while retaining enough features to preserve some connection with the model; or it may replace one or more such features with other features, perhaps drawn from other models. Specification of models (singly and in various combinations) is illustrated in Chapter 4; this section illustrates some of these other ways in which conceptions of faith may deviate from models of faith. To simplify, I focus on deviations involving only the first two models, the belief model

1. More precisely, a conception is a complete exemplification of a model if it adopts all of the model's features, a partial exemplification if it adopts only some of them, and a pure exemplification of a model (or models) if it adopts features only from that model (those models). There are few pure exemplifications of any single model of faith. Moreover, as fewer and fewer features of a model are exemplified, it becomes increasingly problematic whether one has a (very) partial exemplification or no exemplification at all.

2. A conception may require what is merely optional in the model (specifying a different modality of some feature). This is not a rejection or contradiction of the model, so long as we recognize that there may be other exemplifications of the model that differ from the given conception precisely in not requiring this feature. A requirement in a model must be required in a conception that exemplifies that model, but a requirement in a conception need not be required in a model it exemplifies.

and the personal relationship model, since these have been most prominent—if not altogether too prominent—in English-language philosophical and theological discussions during the twentieth century.[3]

One group of variations concentrates on *propositional beliefs*. The major feature of the concept of faith, from this standpoint, is the role to be played by believing propositions about the "object" of faith. Some variations within this group may be cataloged as deviations from the belief model of faith. For some thinkers—not all of them critics of religion—faith is merely or centrally stubborn belief, nearly always irrational. More precisely, faith is a certain kind of propositional belief, unrestricted in content, where S's degree of conviction greatly outstrips S's evidence for p. Typically, S believes p with great conviction but with little evidence for p and/or considerable or even overwhelming evidence against p.[4] This view may seem identical to the belief model, but there are two crucial differences. This view does not require a nonevidential (possibly rational) basis or justification for faith's firm belief, and, it is not interested in important features other than propositional belief. On this view, indefensible belief exhausts faith, it is all there is to faith. This is, of course, an extremely reductionist view, and that it should have gained any credence at all is rather surprising.[5]

3. Many of the formulators of these conceptions have been driven by the aim not of describing, clarifying, or interpreting some tradition of faith, but rather of devising a conception that will meet some modern standards of rational acceptability; in doing so they have often sought more to justify than to analyze their conceptions. The diversity and tenacity of their efforts at justification testify to several important points: the persistent modern desire to be found acceptable at the bar of reason; the continuing rub of "faith and reason"; and the lack of a unique diagnosis or therapy for this irritation. Those who claim to speak for or against "faith" and "reason" *überhaupt* nearly always have in mind only some particular conceptions or reconceptions of faith and reason, and in assessing their claims it is vital to bear in mind the tremendous diversity of alternative conceptions.

4. See Mark Twain's quip that "Faith is believing what you know ain't so." A character in Martin Gardner's autobiographical novel maintains, "The secret of faith is that it doesn't have *any* cognitive support. God wants uncompelled love" (Gardner, 1973, 270; see also Gardner, 1983, chap. 13). Penelhum suggests that "the concept of faith has increasingly come to be used to refer to any state of mind which someone, for commendable or at least forgivable motives, hangs on to some belief that he has no evidential right to hang on to" (1971, 117). See also Ducasse, 1953; Freud, 1928; O'Hear, 1984.

5. Gabriel Marcel suggests that this reductionist view of faith typically originates in someone who does not share that faith; faith becomes an "opinion" and then a

Since for every extreme position there is an equal and opposite reaction, there are also views that hold that faith has nothing at all to do with propositional belief, and that this lack is crucial to faith.[6] On this view, S can have faith in someone or something without believing any propositions about that person or thing, or even perhaps without believing any propositions whatsoever. This view directly and centrally negates the belief model, which requires articles of faith (about the object of faith) that are propositional beliefs. This view may be developed in several different ways.

First, there are differences in the range of propositions that are excluded from faith (in the sense that believing them either is prohibited or at least not required). Some views require, or at least permit, the exclusion of all propositional beliefs.[7] Others exclude only explicit beliefs, or occurrent beliefs, or beliefs that involve the conscious apprehension of definite propositions, while permitting implicit, dispositional, or dormant beliefs. There may also be variations in whether the latter could be converted into the former, *salva fidei*. Others permit beliefs about many facets of faith but none directly about the object of faith, perhaps on the grounds that the object of faith is a paradox or mystery. Exception is usually granted for believing the proposition that the object of faith, or faith in this object, is indeed a paradox or mystery.[8] Others permit characterizing beliefs about A ("A has such-and-such properties") but not existential beliefs about A ("A exists"). Others allow incidental beliefs about the object of faith but permit no (mandatory) articles of faith. No doubt there are other variations.

Second, there are the various proposals as to what should replace

---

"claim," and this transformation may even be internalized by the faithful one (1964, 121–24). In addition, part of the (scant) plausibility of equating faith with propositional belief may be due to the diversity of conceptions of belief as well as to the diversity of conceptions of faith. Believing that a proposition is true is not the same as believing a person, or believing in a person, institution, or cause; and some nonpropositional senses of belief are more congenial to other aspects of faith.

6. "Faith has practically nothing to do with believing statements about anything, however much or little evidence there may be for those statements" (K. D. Smith, 1983, 3).

7. See Bouwsma, 1984; Brunner, 1946; Buber, 1958; W. C. Smith, 1964.

8. See Whittaker, 1981, who characterizes faith as commitment to value-principles without any accompanying metaphysical beliefs in objects as existing entities.

belief, if belief is disallowed,[9] as well as proposals as to what roles these nondoxastic elements play or should play in the lives of the faithful. Some hold that faith is essentially or exclusively a matter of passional fervor;[10] others think it merely a matter of holding and acting on intentions or policies;[11] others seek to compress faith into pure decisiveness;[12] and yet others focus on something like the trust that is central to the personal relationship model of faith.[13] Others may find a multifactorial analysis more attractive (faith is passion plus decisiveness, or some other combination).[14] Common to all these proposals is the view that faith is something quite distinct from and independent of propositional belief.

Third, the relations between faith and propositional belief may be variously construed. One extreme holds that faith is in every respect inimical to propositional belief. Not only is faith not the same as belief, but having or even attempting to gain true beliefs hinders, limits, damages, or even destroys faith. A more moderate view is that while faith is not at all a matter of believing propositions, such beliefs need not be destructive of faith; they are at best harmless curiosities, strictly irrelevant to faith.[15] A third view is that beliefs can be useful for faith, even though they are not centrally important. Holding these beliefs may be propaedeutic to obtaining faith, or prophylactic against weakening or losing faith.

An intermediate kind of position on the issue of propositional beliefs is that faith is, or essentially includes, firmly held propositional beliefs, but these are limited to only a certain subset of possible beliefs about the object of faith. These are the beliefs for which

9. More accurately, these are proposals about what faith does contain if it does not include propositional beliefs. I do not mean to endorse any view that faith can or should dispense with propositional belief; I merely note that many thinkers in attempting to conceive of faith without such belief have substituted quite different features.

10. See Kierkegaard, who speaks of "that happy passion which we call faith" (1985, 61). Burgess, 1975, develops this theme.

11. See Braithwaite, 1955, on faith as belief-less adherence to an "agapeistic way of life."

12. "Belief [Tro] is not a knowledge but an act of freedom, an expression of will" (Kierkegaard, 1985, 83). Ferreira, 1990, provides judicious commentary on Kierkegaard's notion of a "leap of faith." See also, F. R. Sullivan, 1978.

13. See Brunner, 1964; Buber, 1958; Cupitt, 1984; W. C. Smith, 1979a.

14. "Faith is venture dictated by human interest" (Tennant, 1956, 299).

15. "It is said that oil and water do not mix. And so it is with evidence and faith" (Bouwsma, 1984, 18).

ordinary evidence—as opposed to divine revelation—is inadequate or insufficient to support, in a rational way, their being held with such a high degree of conviction. In beliefs held on faith, according to this view, there must be no evidence at all in support of the belief, or else weak or inadequate evidence, or evidence that is evenly balanced pro and con.[16] However, there are disagreements over exactly which if any (kinds of) propositions are believable on faith in this sense. Some hold that all or only metaphysical beliefs fit into this category, and that such metaphysical beliefs are ingredient in all matters of faith. Others hold that only beliefs in transcendent entities are believable on faith; still others that only probable (non-certain) beliefs are matters of faith; and so on. In this type of view the belief model of faith is basically accepted but with severe qualifications: a strong condition is placed on how or why the evidence is, or must be, inadequate for S to believe that p with such a high degree of conviction.

Quite a different position identifies propositional belief with faith, or with a central portion of faith, but holds that evidence (at least probable if not conclusive evidence) is both proper and available for such beliefs.[17] Either all beliefs are held to be matters of faith, or else some way is found to distinguish those beliefs that are matters of faith from those that are not. Perhaps only probable beliefs qualify, or only probable beliefs acquired in a certain way, or only probable beliefs about matters of great importance or of "ultimate concern," and so forth. Conviction, on this view, varies directly with evidence, and with evidence alone—or at least it should vary in this manner if one is rational. Hence, contrary to the belief model, when the evidence is inadequate or balanced, faith does not require certitude or firm conviction. The central rational question about faith, on this view, is, Which beliefs about matters of greatest importance have the greatest evidential support? This view is certainly very latitudinarian, but its plausibility is often tainted by a failure

16. Often this evidential inadequacy is thought to be noncontingent—perhaps because the "object" of faith transcends all possible human evidence, or because human evidence gathering and evidence assessing mechanisms are ineradicably corrupted by sin, and so forth. On the former view, see Sessions, 1980a; on the latter, see A. Plantinga, 1983.

17. "Faith, then, is conviction based on convincing private evidence" (Davis, 1978, 86). See also, Ehrlich, 1975; Geisler, 1976; Habermas and Flew, 1987; Sire, 1976.

to distinguish certainty from certitude (the former having to do with evidence, the latter with psychological conviction).[18] The belief model, of course, carefully distinguishes between these concepts.

Another cluster of conceptions of faith has tended to predominate in twentieth-century Christian theology, especially but not exclusively in Protestant theology. Here the focus is on faith as an *extraordinary kind of personal relationship*, and the major options may be construed as deviations from the personal relationship model of faith.

Faith may be viewed as an interpersonal relationship characterized by trust, as in the personal relationship model, but such trust may be thought possible without the subject of faith holding any propositional beliefs about the object (or even about the subject) of the relationship. This is a frequent temptation in "existentialist" theologies, which sometimes seem unconsciously to embrace Ludwig Feuerbach's program of transforming theology into anthropology.[19]

There are many ways to specify this view. In one version, a trusting relationship may exclude all beliefs about one's partner and oneself, because entertaining and holding such beliefs "objectifies" an essentially "subjective" relation, turning self and other into "things" or "objects" and not treating them as persons ought to be treated. Or, the view may exclude from the faithful relationship merely all explicit (occurrent, consciously entertained) beliefs about oneself and the other, while permitting implicit (dispositional, unconscious) beliefs. Alternatively, the view may exclude all characterizing (as opposed to existential) beliefs about self and other; or it may exclude some narrower class of beliefs. Whether trust without belief is even possible, it is distinct from trust according to the personal relationship model, which requires believing at least the appropriate articles of faith.

Another variant makes trust a matter of voluntary choice or decision, a willful or arbitrary commitment that is neither entailed nor supported by beliefs or evidence.[20] Faith is entirely, largely, finally,

18. For examples of this confusion, see Dubay, 1985; Sire, 1976.
19. See Feuerbach, 1957; see also J. Baillie, 1956; K. Barth, 1936, 1956, 1964; Brunner, 1946, 1949, 1956; Buber, 1951, 1958; W. C. Smith, 1964, 1977, 1979a. By way of criticism, see Hepburn, 1958.
20. See K. Barth 1959, 18–20; Bartley, 1984; Ebeling, 1961, chap. 6; Emmet, 1966, chap. 6; Hutchinson, 1956; and Kierkegaard, 1970. Some variants would make

or essentially up to the subject of faith. This point should be carefully distinguished from faith's necessary asymmetry, wherein one person depends on, relies upon, or even clings to another person, but not conversely. Rather, the point has to do with the perceived and/or real "authorship" or causality of such asymmetrical dependence. On this view of faith, A, the one to whom S is committed, plays little or no essential, important, or helpful causal role in engendering or sustaining the dependent relationship between them. Rather, S and not A is the sole, central, most important, or essential author of S's faith in A. According to this view, then, faith is a leap, an act of the subject; it is not a gift, an act of the object. This view of faith is not consonant with the personal relationship model. According to the latter the relationship of faith is at least partially—but also essentially, importantly, and finally, perhaps even dominantly—causally produced by the object of faith. Willful decision, far from being the essence of faith, tends to destroy faith by intruding an attitude that is antagonistic to grateful acceptance of a gift.[21]

Several variants construe trust differently from the personal relationship model, that is, in terms other than acceptance, loyalty, and love. One considers trust to be unconditional, unquestioning, or "blind" obedience; "self-surrender, submission";[22] being prepared to do, say, feel, and believe whatever the authoritative object of faith says—even to do what one believes to be absolutely wrong, to affirm what one takes to be nonsense, and to expect what one cannot understand to be even so much as possible.[23] On another

---

evidence merely peripheral to the consciousness of the faithful person, others would require the presence and acute awareness of evidential insufficiency.

21. In Shinran's terminology, any human agency in faith is a matter of "self-power" (*jiriki*) as opposed to "other-power" (*tariki*). Of course there is wide variation in the amount or range or kinds of agency different views require or prohibit for the subject of faith. A minimalist position is that faith, as a response to grace, requires only the single act of sincerely accepting the gift, as in Paul Tillich's famous admonition: "Do not seek for anything; do not perform anything; do not intend anything. *Simply accept the fact that you are accepted!*" (1948, 162, emphasis in original). For discussions of the relations of divine and human agency, see Abraham, 1990; Farrer, 1961, 1974; Sessions, 1991a; Tanner, 1988; Tracy, 1984, 1990.

22. Brunner, 1946, 35.

23. See the disturbing interpretation of Genesis 22 that Søren Kierkegaard—under the pseudonym "Johannes de Silentio"—develops in *Fear and Trembling*. Unqualified divine command ethical theories often elaborate such extreme views of what it means to trust God, but not when they are "modified" by requiring obedience only to a

construal, faith is a kind of fear. This not so much distrust or the lack of trust but rather antitrust, which is a kind of negative trust in the capacities, desires, and intentions of the other to do one evil instead of good. On a third construal, trust is reduced (or perhaps subordinated) to expectation, a disposition based on predicting another's behavior via evidence gained of her intentions, desires, beliefs, character, and so forth. All such construals of trust deviate from the personal relationship model, although in interestingly different ways. For example, blind obedience is uninterested in the question of rational justification or acceptability, fear is the opposite of love, and expectation is not really trust but rather more or less evidentially justified belief.

In Shin and Sŏn Buddhism, trust in another seems to be displaced by the paradoxical notion of trust in oneself, where the subject and object of faith are one and the same person.[24] In part, self-trust may be viewed as a limiting case of the trust which is central to the personal relationship model. Of course, these are deep and murky waters, and it is always dangerous to construe relations to oneself on the analogy of relations to others. Nonetheless, there are resemblances, particularly if one makes some kind of distinction between surface self (apparent, phenomenal, empirical) and deeper self or Self (real, true, transcendent). Self-confidence is relying on one's own deeper capacities for apprehending truth or achieving salvation, even while truth is unapparent or salvation seems hopeless; it is a kind of loyalty, love, and acceptance of one's true self (or Self). There are also disanalogies: Ultimately, or in principle, both selves are one self, and their otherness can be overcome to a much deeper degree than in the case of two irreducibly different persons.

Various conceptions of faith may be characterized in terms of how they qualify, limit, replace, or even reject the central notion of personal relationship. One line of modification construes faith as relationship to another person that is not (specifically) personal, for example, radical dependence or reliance on another person, such as

---

God who is loving, just, wise, and so forth. See the seminal essays in Adams, 1987, pt. 3, "God and Ethics"; also Green, 1978, 1982, 1988; and Perkins, 1981.

24. See the interesting twist on this point in Kierkegaard, 1967, 9.A32 [1848]: "Faith is precisely this infinite self-concern which keeps one awake in risking everything, this self-concern about whether one really has faith—and precisely this self-concern is faith."

expecting necessary goods from a predictable donor. Second, one might have a distinctively personal relationship to something that is not a person at all, for example, trusting in an institution (the judiciary, the state), a tradition (the American way), a community (the Sangha, the party), a coming event or condition (the Last Judgment, the revolution), a machine or mechanical process (a computer, a functioning Turing program), or truth (*Dhamma*), or the universe as a whole (Spinoza's *"deus sive natura"* [God or nature]). Third, the object of one's putative "personal" relationship may not even exist; it may be a fictitious or imaginary object that would be a person if only it existed. Fourth, the subject of faith may be extended from an individual person—either "downwards" toward beings that are not persons (animals, computers) or else "upwards" toward beings that are collections of persons (groups, communities, traditions).[25]

Sometimes the nonpersonal object of faith is not a person but may be personified or "personalized" to the point that one seems to be in a distinctively personal relationship with it. This personification may be due to ignorance (S believes O is a person or a certain kind of person, when O is not that sort of being at all) or with full knowledge (S is aware that O is not a person but nonetheless believes that personalistic language is appropriate, or not inappropriate, or the least misleading sort of thing to say). Finally, differences among kinds of persons (human, extraterrestrial, immaterial, divine) will condition the kinds of personal and nonpersonal relations one may intelligibly have with them. It may even happen that, without quite being aware of it, one's radical qualifications of an object of faith transform it from a person in the full sense to something that is (somewhat) personal or even to something that is (thoroughly) nonpersonal, as when differences between divine and human beings are magnified to such an extent that it seems pointless to maintain that "the divine" is a person at all.

These variations in (types of) conceptions of faith by no means exhaust the possibilities; that we stop here does not mean that the concept of faith stops here. But we have seen enough diversity in

25. Some representative sociological extensions: "Human society is faith itself" (Lynch, 1973, 57). Faith is "the *way of being* of a community"; "*any* community, to be a community at all, is possessed of an unspoken mutual giving-over, a basic trust, the alternative being a kind of chaos below the level of the brutes. . . . Faith is the very *fact* of a community" (Giurlanda, 1987, 3, 7).

conceiving faith to make us more acutely aware of both the utility
of our models in understanding aspects of different conceptions of
faith and the difficulty, if not quite the impossibility, of issuing
blanket generalizations about the entire concept of faith. What we
say about and through some particular conception of faith need not
apply to all exemplifications of the same model, much less to the
overarching concept of faith. Models help us to comprehend some
commonalities among diverse conceptions, but also to understand
the many diversities both within and between communities of conceptions.

## B. The Unity of the Concept of Faith

A second concluding reflection concerns the kind of unity possessed by the concept of faith. Provocatively put, there is no such
thing as "the concept of faith" in its usual sense. The usual understanding is that faith is somehow an invariant universal phenomenon, with certain central or essential features shared across time and
space by all of its varying instances. On such a view, there is, or
may be (re)constructed, a universal concept or category of faith that
explicitly and univocally articulates these common features. As I
have repeatedly argued, no such category applies to faith, because
faith has no such common features. On the contrary, inquiry into
even a few of the many conceptions of faith actually held by different
people around the world—as well as speculation about other kinds
and types of conceptions of faith—discloses a great variety of conceptions that differ from one another, more or less, in many different
ways. Such a variety cannot be comprehended in the univocal embrace of a category: Faith as a categorical phenomenon simply does
not exist.

As I have also argued, however, the enormous diversity in conceptions of faith is no mere hodgepodge. The various conceptions
resemble one another in disparate and overlapping ways, so as to
give us reasonable hope of finding, or assembling, a single concept
of faith—not a category but an analogy of faith. An analogy, in this
usage, is an analogical concept that achieves its unity via resemblance, not via identity or commonality. Its various instances resemble one another and variously share partially overlapping

features, even though there is no essential or important set of features held in common.

Two features of analogical unity deserve special notice. First, analogical unity is a matter of degree, not of digital presence or absence. One analogical concept may be more or less unified than another, and neither need be very unified at all. The greater, more numerous, and more fundamental the resemblances among its instances, the greater the degree of unity the concept possesses; conversely, the greater, more numerous, and more fundamental the differences, the lesser degree of unity it has. Second, analogical concepts are fundamentally and irreducibly vague. Such concepts do not have intrinsically sharp and distinct boundaries; instead, a twilight region of indeterminate application surrounds more clear-cut paradigm cases. People may draw distinct boundaries around the concept for some purpose or other, but since different persons may draw such boundaries more or less tightly or sharply, it follows that they may disagree about whether a particular conception falls within the concept's range. However, differing boundary-drawing decisions need not be haphazard or arbitrary, even though they will undoubtedly be influenced by various kinds of purposes, commitments, and biases. Just because no single line can be drawn, it does not follow that all lines are equally well drawn, with equal justification.

Since faith is not a category but an analogy, the term "faith" is not univocal in all its applications; it bears no single core meaning or invariant type of referent—not throughout history, not worldwide today, not even within "single" traditions of faith such as Christianity or Buddhism. Faith is not one single thing but many different things that more or less resemble one another, in various ways. To return to an analogy we used earlier, faith is like a family of variously related but vastly differing individuals, not like an assembly of variously garbed genetic clones.[26]

Understanding an analogical concept like faith requires considerable experience with many of its widely varying instances; it will not do simply to focus on one particular conception, either in itself

26. The analogy naturally calls to mind Wittgenstein's remarks about "family resemblance" (1953, §§65–67). But Wittgenstein's families are related solely by resemblance and not also by heredity or history. My usage allows both synchronic and diachronic features.

or as yielding (by abstraction) a set of generic features. But how is one to make headway among the bewildering variety of conceptions? To shed some light on the family of faith, one could of course try to interview every single family member, or even to construct a genealogy (a history of conceptions of faith). But these are daunting tasks, given the vast diversity of conceptions, the linguistic inaccessibility of many of them (save to specialists), their intricate nuances (even to specialists), and especially the typical inexplicitness of such conceptions in the minds of those who use them. A more promising enterprise is to search out groups or clusters of conceptions of faith and to analyze each group's common features; combining such analyses will provide a limited account of the full (analogical) concept of faith. This, in effect, is what I have done in this book by proposing six models of faith. These models are tools for the investigation and understanding of the vast analogy that is the overall concept of faith.

Recall that a model is an idealized, reflective, moderately abstract, explicit concept. Constructing and applying models contributes toward two important theoretical aims. Models help to clarify the general concept of faith (by depicting some of its analogous strands in themselves and in relation to one another) and they help to illuminate various particular conceptions of faith (by displaying important features of the conceptions as exemplifications of and deviations from the models). The latter task is especially important. Consideration of our seven cases in Chapter 4 shows, I believe, the considerable theoretic power of our six models of faith. They can shed surprisingly strong light not only on the affinities of particular conceptions of faith so diverse as Christian, Hindu, and Buddhist ones but also on the differences among apparently very similar conceptions within each of these traditions of faith.

The result of our philosophical investigation of faith, then, is this: There is after all a single concept of faith, but its overall unity is not great. Certainly there is no categorical unity across all instances of all conceptions of faith. Rather, faith's unity is analogical, a matter of resemblance, similarity, likeness. Some models—the attitude, devotion, and hope models—considerably resemble one another, but other models are rather further apart conceptually—the personal relationship and the confidence models. Nevertheless, there are enough important overlapping resemblances among the models (and therefore conceptions) of faith to constitute a single overarching concept that may fittingly be titled "the" (analogical) concept of faith. Faith is whatever exemplifies in its conception one or more of our models of faith.

There is one further, rather speculative, consideration about the unity of the concept of faith. What happens, or might happen, to actual conceptions of faith as their possessors become aware of not only the differences and resemblances in others' conceptions of faith but also the kind of analogical unity one finds in the overarching concept of faith? One possibility is that differences would swamp likenesses, tending to produce not convergence or coalescence but further differentiation of conceptions. The development of ever more varied conceptions of faith would then resemble biological evolution: The process of faith would be anisotropic and divergent. A second possibility is that neither differences nor resemblances would prevail; neither diversity nor unity would increase, though there might be a marginal if salutary boost to toleration of conceptions other than one's own. There is also a third possibility. As faithful persons become increasingly aware of differences in conceptions of faith, they might be stimulated into taking substantive account of these differences, or even to incorporating them, in their own conceptions. Beyond simply noting differences and similarities, these pioneers of piety might be moved to alter their own conceptions in light of the conceptions of others, and by so doing they might introduce further degrees and kinds of unity into the concept of faith. In this way, they might promote not so much convergence of conceptions as their greater resemblance or harmony. To my mind this is the most entrancing possibility of them all.

## C. Some Remaining Problems

A third concluding reflection is more humbling, but perhaps also more inspiring. Whatever success I have achieved, I certainly have not provided a complete account of faith; indeed, it should be obvious to all that the surface is barely scratched. As a way of recognizing—without removing—this inevitable incompletion, it is worth noting a few of the many tasks that remain.

First, there are no doubt many questions that might be raised about the particulars of the model-theoretical account, for example, concerning the tripartite distinction among concept, model, and conception; the notion of an analogical concept; the characterization of the six models of faith individually and in relation to one another; and the application of the models to the seven particular conceptions of faith. This account constitutes only a beginning on these facets; critical scrutiny by others is most welcome.

Next, even supposing that this account is moderately successful as far as it goes, it is not easy to extend it to the rest of the vast array of human conceptions of faith. This task is daunting not simply because there are so many different conceptions of faith. In addition, many conceptions lie buried beneath the sands of time, along with the persons and cultures that once enlivened them; they appear only in ancient documents, artifacts, and traces that require considerable efforts of conceptual archaeology to uncover their meaning. Many other conceptions, though governing the lives of persons today, and so in principle more accessible, nonetheless remain hidden from philosophical view because they have not been made very explicit by their own users. It is no small feat for an insider, and nearly impossible for an outsider, to provide an accurate articulation of implicit conceptions. But only when conceptions are made (partially) explicit can they fruitfully be considered in light of our models of faith.

Further, individuals and communities not only have different conceptions of faith but they also change in their conceptions over their lifetimes. Are there any universals of development here, or only variously resembling and differing stories of growth?[27]

Finally, there are a number of important but seemingly intractable philosophical issues about faith that may profitably be addressed in

27. I have omitted discussion of the burgeoning literature on the individual psychological development of faith and faith-conceptions. Such developmental accounts of which I am aware (in particular Chirban, 1981; Droege, 1983; Fowler, 1974, 1976a, 1976b, 1981, 1982; Stokes, 1982; Wuthnow, 1982) presuppose that there is a single universal category of faith, and that conceptual development is from conceptions of faith that are less adequate to those that are more adequate to this universal category. This line of thinking ignores the central contention of this book: the diversity of conceptions of faith. A faith-developmental account more consonant with this work would chart a number of different styles of growth in faith by noting which models apply, and in what combination, at various times in different individuals' and communities' lives—without prejudging which, if any, style is normatively "mature."

terms of our models. Some of them may be briefly characterized as follows:

1. The authorship problem. In theistic faith, the central act(s) of faith seem both to be caused or "authored" essentially and completely by the divine "object" of faith and also to be authored essentially though partially by the human "subject" of faith. Do different models of faith generate, or at any rate shed light on, the two contending sides?[28]
2. The certainty problem. What kinds of certainty are compatible with or even required by faith? In particular, how can views of faith exemplifying the personal relationship and propositional belief models permit epistemic (evidence-sensitive) certainty?[29]
3. The ultimacy problem. Does faith truly require, or even always admire, complete commitment, absolute devotion, ultimate concern, and the like?[30]
4. The duality/unity problem. Faith typically is dual, a relation between two distinct individuals of entities. But faith also presses toward a more intimate union: putting on the mind of Christ, experiencing God's presence, Self-realization. Do different models of faith underlie the two parts of this problem?[31]
5. The value problem. What is faith's value or worth? There are two aspects to this problem, and perhaps different models of faith yield different answers in each case.
   a. The "worth" problem. Is faith intrinsically valuable? How valuable is it? What makes it valuable? Is faith also (or merely?) extrinsically valuable—a means, instrument, part, or cause?
   b. The "fruits" problem. How much of the value (and disvalue) of faith comes from its effects? What kind of effects? Is faith essential to producing these effects?
6. The rationality problem. Is faith rationally warranted, justified, grounded, supportable, or defensible?[32] Again there are two major

28. For quite different kinds of solution to this problem, traditionally called the "problem of freedom and grace," see Abraham, 1985, chap. 12, 1990; Alston, 1989; Aulén, 1948; Dalferth, 1988, pt. 2; D. D. Evans, 1980, chap. 6; Helm, 1979; McPherson, 1974, chap. 5; Morris, 1988; Sessions, 1991a; Tanner, 1988; Tracy, 1984, 1990.

29. See Audi, 1988; Davis, 1978; Dubay, 1985; Maitzen, 1992; Miller, 1978; Sessions, 1991b; Tennant, 1956.

30. See Adams, 1986; Banner, 1990, chap. 5.

31. See Cobb, 1982; Oakes, 1990; Park, 1983; Smart, 1968.

32. The rationality of faith is distinct from, though related to, the value of faith, the truth of faith, and the evidence for faith. It is an interesting question why rationality should even matter to faith. Do problems of "faith and reason" bulk so

areas of concern, and again differences in models may produce significantly different answers.

   a. Can use of or adherence to some particular conception of faith be rationally justified?

   b. Can living a life of faith according to some particular conception of faith be rationally justified?[33]

  7. The truth problem. Are different kinds of truth relevant to different models of faith? For example, propositions believed on faith are true, interpretations made on faith are correct, commitments chosen on faith are authentic, and so forth.

  8. The evidence problem. How is evidence related to faith? This question also divides in two and also receives different responses from different models.

   a. How are (propositional) beliefs related to faith?

   b. How is evidence related to (propositional) beliefs?

Doubtless there are further problems, but this list is long enough to drive home my final point: Although considerable progress has been made in understanding the concept of faith via models of faith, there is still more work to be done. Of inquiry into faith there is no end, and that is why we return with deepened comprehension to the words with which we began: "If it were all to be recorded in detail, I suppose the whole world could not hold the books that would be written" (John 21:25; NEB). To believe anything less about faith is to be unfaithful to faith, as well as to ourselves.

---

large in Western philosophy of religion simply because of pressures from outside faith? The uneasy relationship between religion and science may be largely responsible; see Austin, 1976; Banner, 1990; Clayton, 1989; Lyas, 1977; and Murphy, 1990.

  33. There are two prominent subproblems here. Can beliefs entrained by some particular faith (specific "articles of faith") be rationally justified? Can believers (living by some particular conception of faith) be justified on nonevidential grounds? There are also connections with the so-called "ethics of belief." See Blanshard, 1975, chap. 4; Davis, 1978; Dupré, 1972.

# Selected Bibliography

Abelson, Raziel. 1961. "The Logic of Faith and Belief." In Hook, ed., 1961, 116–29.

Abraham, William J. 1982. *Divine Revelation and the Limits of Historical Criticism.* Oxford: Oxford University Press.

———. 1985. *An Introduction to the Philosophy of Religion.* Englewood Cliffs, N.J.: Prentice-Hall.

———. 1990. "The Epistemological Significance of the Inner Witness of the Holy Spirit." *Faith and Philosophy* 7 (October), 434–50.

Abraham, William J., and Steven W. Holtzer, eds. 1987. *The Rationality of Religious Belief: Essays in Honor of Basil Mitchell.* New York: Oxford University Press.

Adams, Robert M. 1986. "The Problem of Total Devotion." In Audi and Wainwright, eds., 1986, 169–94.

———. 1987. *The Virtue of Faith and Other Essays in Philosophical Theology.* New York: Oxford University Press.

———. 1990. "The Knight of Faith." *Faith and Philosophy* 7 (October), 383–95.

Akishige, Yoshiharu. 1977. *Psychological Studies on Zen,* vol. 1. Tokyo: Komazawa University Zen Institute.

Allen, Diogenes. 1966. "Motives, Rationales, and Religious Beliefs." *American Philosophical Quarterly* 3, 111–27.

———. 1989. *Christian Belief in a Postmodern World: The Full Wealth of Conviction.* Philadelphia: Westminster/John Knox Press.

———. 1990. "The End of the Modern World: A New Openness for Faith." *Princeton Seminary Bulletin,* n.s. 11, 11–31.

Alles, Gregory. 1985. "When Men Revile You and Persecute You: Advice, Conflict, and Grace in Shinran and Luther." *History of Religions* 25 (November), 148–62.

Alston, William P. 1989. *Divine Nature and Human Language: Essays in Philosophical Theology.* Ithaca, N.Y.: Cornell University Press.

Ammerman, Robert Ray. 1964–1965. "Ethics and Belief." *Proceedings of the Aristotelian Society*, n.s. 65, 257–66.

Anscombe, G. E. M. 1979. "What Is It to Believe Someone?" In Delaney, ed., 1979, 141–51.

Armstrong, D. M. 1973. *Belief, Truth, and Knowledge.* Cambridge: Cambridge University Press.

Ashcroft, Richard. 1969. "Faith and Knowledge in Locke's Philosophy." In John W. Yolton, ed., *John Locke: Problems and Perspectives.* Cambridge: Cambridge University Press, 194–224.

Audi, Robert. 1988. *Belief, Justification, and Knowledge: An Introduction to Epistemology.* Belmont, Calif.: Wadsworth.

Audi, Robert, and William J. Wainwright, eds. 1986. *Rationality, Religious Belief, and Moral Commitment.* Ithaca, N.Y.: Cornell University Press.

Augustine, Morris J. 1986. "The Sociology of Knowledge and Buddhist-Christian Forms of Faith, Practice, and Knowledge." In Ingram and Streng, eds., 1986, 35–51.

Aulén, Gustaf. 1948. *The Faith of the Christian Church*, tr. Eric H. Wahlstrom and G. Everett Arden. Philadelphia: Muhlenberg Press.

Austin, W. H. 1976. *The Relevance of Natural Science to Theology.* London: Macmillan.

Azraf, Dewan M. 1987. "Faith and Reason in the Great Traditions." *Dialogue and Alliance* (Spring), 78–85.

Baillie, D. M. 1927. *Faith in God and Its Christian Consummation.* Edinburgh: T. and T. Clark.

Baillie, John. 1928. *The Interpretation of Religion.* New York: Charles Scribner's Sons.

———. 1956. *The Idea of Revelation in Recent Thought.* New York: Columbia University Press.

———. 1959. *Our Knowledge of God.* New York: Charles Scribner's Sons.

———. 1963. *A Reasoned Faith: Collected Addresses.* New York: Charles Scribner's Sons.

Bainbridge, William Sims, and Rodney Stark. 1986. *A Theory of Religion.* New York: Peter Lang.

Baker, Judith. 1987. "Trust and Rationality." *Pacific Philosophical Quarterly* 68 (March), 1–13.

Bando, Shojun. 1977. "The Dual Aspect of Faith." In Yusuf Ibish and Ileana Marculescu, eds., *Contemplation and Action in World Religions.* Houston, Tex.: Rothko Chapel Book, 16–27.

Banner, Michael C. 1990. *The Justification of Science and the Rationality of Religious Belief.* Oxford: Oxford University Press.

Barber, Bernard. 1983. *The Logic and Limits of Trust.* New Brunswick, N.J.: Rutgers University Press.

Barbour, Ian G. 1974. *Myths, Models, and Paradigms.* New York: Harper and Row.

Bars, Henry. 1961. *Faith, Hope, and Charity*. London: Burns and Oates.

Barth, Karl. 1936. *The Doctrine of the Word of God*. Vol. 1, pt. 1 of *Church Dogmatics*, tr. G. T. Thomson. Edinburgh: T. and T. Clark.

———. 1956. *The Doctrine of the Word of God*. Vol. 1, pt. 2 of *Church Dogmatics*, tr. G. T. Thomson and Harold Knight. Edinburgh: T. and T. Clark.

———. 1959. *Dogmatics in Outline*, tr. G. T. Thomson. New York: Harper and Row Torchbook.

———. 1964. *Evangelical Theology: An Introduction*, tr. Grover Foley. Garden City, N.Y.: Doubleday Anchor Books.

Barth, Markus. 1969. "The Faith of the Messiah." *Heythrop Journal* 10, 363–70.

Bartley, W. W., III. 1984. *The Retreat to Commitment*, 2d ed. rev. LaSalle, Ill.: Open Court.

Barua, B. M. 1927. "Faith as in Buddhism." In *Sir Asutosh Mookerjee Silver Jubilee Volumes*. Calcutta: Calcutta University Press, 3:3, 237–256.

———. 1931. "Faith in Buddhism." In Bimala Churn Law, ed., *Buddhist Studies*. Calcutta: Thacker, Spink and Co., 329–49.

Batchelor, Stephen. 1990. *The Faith to Doubt: Glimpses of Buddhist Uncertainty*. Berkeley, Calif.: Parallax Press.

Bauer, Joachim M. 1930. "The Modern Notion of Faith." Ph.D. diss., Catholic University of America.

Baum, Gregory. 1969. *Faith and Doctrine: A Contemporary View*. Paramus, N.J.: Paulist Press.

Bavinck, Herman. 1953. *The Philosophy of Revelation*. The Stone Lectures, 1908–1909. Grand Rapids, Mich.: William B. Eerdmans.

Bazan, Bernardo Carlos. 1980. "La Reconciliation de la foi et la raison." *Dialogue* (Canada) 19 (June), 235–54.

Bendall, Kent, and Frederick Ferré. 1962. *The Logic of Faith: A Dialogue on the Relations of Modern Philosophy to Christian Faith*. New York: Association Press.

Benson, John E. 1988. "Justification by Faith in a Wider Context [compared with Hinduism, Buddhism]." *Dialog* (Minnesota) 27 (Fall), 285–90.

Berkhof, Louis. 1949. *Systematic Theology*. Grand Rapids, Mich.: William B. Eerdmans.

Berkouwer, G. C. 1954. *Faith and Justification*, tr. Lewis B. Smedes. Grand Rapids, Mich.: William B. Eerdmans.

———. 1958. *Faith and Perseverance*, tr. Robert D. Knudsen. Grand Rapids, Mich.: William B. Eerdmans.

Bettenson, Henry, ed. 1963. *Documents of the Christian Church*, 2d ed. London: Oxford University Press.

Blanshard, Brand. 1975. *Reason and Belief*. New Haven, Conn.: Yale University Press.

Bligh, J. 1968. "Did Jesus Live by Faith?" *Heythrop Journal* 9, 414–19.

Bloch, Ernst. 1986. *The Principle of Hope*. 3 vols., tr. Neville Plaice, Stephen Plaice, and Paul Knight. Cambridge, Mass.: MIT Press.

Bloom, Alfred. 1959. "Is the Nembutsu Magic?" *Japanese Religions* 1:3, 31–35.

———. 1965. *Shinran's Gospel of Pure Grace*. Tucson: University of Arizona Press.

——. 1968. "The Life of Shinran Shōnin: The Journey to Self-Acceptance." *Numen* 15, 1–62.

——. 1984. "Shinran's Praises on the Nembutsu of True Faith: Reality of Faith in History." *Junshin Gakuhō* 3 (December), 1–30.

——. 1989. "Introduction to Jōdo Shinshū." *Pacific World: Journal of the Institute of Buddist Studies*, n.s. 5 (Fall), 33–39.

Bogdan, Radu J., ed. 1986. *Belief: Form, Content, and Function.* Oxford: Clarendon Press.

Borhek, James T., and Richard F. Curtis. 1975. *A Sociology of Belief.* New York: John Wiley and Sons.

Bouwsma, O. K. 1984. *Without Proof or Evidence: Essays of O. K. Bouwsma*, ed. J. L. Craft and Ronald E. Hustwit. Lincoln: University of Nebraska Press.

Braithwaite, R. B. 1955. *An Empiricist's View of the Nature of Religious Belief.* Cambridge: Cambridge University Press.

Brams, Steven J. 1983. *Superior Beings: If They Exist, How Would We Know? Game-Theoretic Implications of Omniscience, Omnipotence, Immortality, and Incomprehensibility.* New York: Springer-Verlag.

Brenneman, Walter, Stanley O. Yarian, and Alan M. Olson. 1982. *The Seeing Eye.* State College: Pennsylvania State University Press.

Brown, R. M. 1974. *Is Faith Obsolete?* Philadelphia: Westminster Press.

Brown, Stuart C., ed. 1977. *Reason and Revelation.* Ithaca, N.Y.: Cornell University Press.

Bruce, Steve. 1984. *Firm in the Faith.* Brookfield, Vt.: Gower Publishing.

Brunner, Heinrich Emil. 1946. *Revelation and Reason: The Christian Doctrine of Faith and Knowledge*, tr. Olive Wyon. Philadelphia: Westminster Press.

——. 1949. *Our Faith.* London: SCM Press.

——. 1956. *Faith, Hope, and Love.* Philadelphia: Westminster Press.

——. 1964. *Truth as Encounter.* London: SCM Press.

Buber, Martin. 1951. *Two Types of Faith*, tr. Norman P. Goldhawk. New York: Macmillan.

——. 1958. *I and Thou*, 2d ed., tr. Ronald Gregor Smith. New York: Charles Scribner's Sons.

Bulman, J. M. 1953. "The Place of Knowledge in Calvin's View of Faith." *Review and Expositor* 50, 323–29.

Bultmann, Rudolf. 1961. *Existence and Faith: Shorter Writings of Rudolf Bultmann*, tr. Schubert M. Ogden. London: Hodder and Stoughton.

Bultmann, Rudolf, and Artur Weiser. 1961. *Faith.* Vol. 3 of *Bible Key Words*, from Gerhard Kittel, *Theologisches Wörterbuch zum Neuen Testament*, tr. Dorothea M. Barton, P. R. Ackroyd, and A. E. Harvey. New York: Harper and Brothers.

Burgess, Andrew J. 1975. *Passion, "Knowing How," and Understanding: An Essay on the Concept of Faith.* AAR Dissertation Series, 9. Missoula, Mont.: Scholars Press.

Buri, Fritz. 1976. "The Concept of Grace in Paul, Shinran, and Luther." *Eastern Buddhist* 9 (October), 21–42.

Burrell, David. 1983. "Faith and Religious Convictions: Studies in Comparative

Epistemology." Review of W. C. Smith, 1977, 1979a, 1981, and Rodney Needham, 1972. *Journal of Religion* 63, 64–73.

——. 1986. *Knowing the Unknowable God: Ibn-Sina, Maimonides, Aquinas.* Notre Dame, Ind.: University of Notre Dame Press.

Buswell, Robert E., Jr. 1983. *The Korean Approach to Zen: The Collected Works of Chinul.* Honolulu: University of Hawaii Press.

——. 1986. "Chinul's Systemization of Chinese Meditative Techniques in Korean Sŏn Buddhism." In Peter N. Gregory, ed., *Traditions of Meditation in Chinese Buddhism.* Honolulu: University of Hawaii Press, 199–242.

——. 1989. *The Formation of Ch'an Ideology in China and Korea: The "Vajrasamādhi-Sūtra," a Buddhist Apocryphon.* Princeton, N.J.: Princeton University Press.

Caporale, Rocco, and Antonio Grumelli, eds. 1971. *The Culture of Unbelief: Studies and Proceedings from the First International Symposium on Belief Held at Rome, March 22–27, 1969.* Berkeley: University of California Press.

Carlton, Eric. 1973. *Patterns of Belief.* 2 vols. London: George Allen and Unwin.

Carman, John B. 1968. "Is Christian Faith a Form of Bhakti?" *Visva-Bharati Journal of Philosophy* 4, 24–37.

——. 1974. *The Theology of Ramanuja: An Essay in Interreligious Understanding.* New Haven, Conn.: Yale University Press.

Carr, Stephen. 1992. "F. H. Bradley and Religious Faith." *Religious Studies* 28, 371–86.

Carter, John Ross. 1986. "*Shinjin*: More Than Faith?" *Annual Memoirs of the Ōtani University Shin Buddhist Comprehensive Research Institute* 4, 1–40.

——. 1987a. "On Conferences and Faith [interreligious dialogue]." *Japanese Religions* 14 (July), 14–30.

——. 1987b. "Towards an Understanding of What Is Inconceivable." *Eastern Buddhist*, n.s. 20 (Autumn), 32–52.

——. 1988. "On Celebrating Our Faith." *Shinshugaku Journal of Studies in Shin Buddhism* 78 (March), 25–43.

Chang, Chung-yüan. 1969. *The Original Teachings of Ch'an Buddhism.* New York: Pantheon Books.

Chénu, M. D. 1968. *Faith and Theology*, tr. Denis Hickey. New York: Macmillan.

Chirban, John T. 1981. *Human Growth and Faith: Intrinsic and Extrinsic Motivation in Human Development.* Washington, D.C.: University Press of America.

Chisholm, Roderick M. 1968. "Lewis' Ethics of Belief." In P. A. Schilpp, ed., *The Philosophy of C. I. Lewis.* LaSalle, Ill.: Open Court.

——. 1977. *Theory of Knowledge*, 2d ed. Englewood Cliffs, N.J.: Prentice-Hall.

——. 1982. *The Foundations of Knowing.* Minneapolis: University of Minnesota Press.

Chittick, William C. 1989. *The Sufi Path of Knowledge: Ibn al-'Arabi's Metaphysics of Imagination.* Albany, N.Y.: SUNY Press.

Clark, Stephen R. L. 1986. *The Mysteries of Religion.* Oxford: Basil Blackwell.

Clayton, Philip. 1989. *Explanation from Physics to Theology: An Essay in Rationality and Religion.* New Haven, Conn.: Yale University Press.

Clegg, J. S. 1979. "Faith." *American Philosophical Quarterly* 16 (July), 225–32.

Coady, C. A. J. 1992. *Testimony.* New York: Oxford University Press.

Cobb, John B. 1982. *Beyond Dialogue: Toward a Mutual Transformation of Christianity and Buddhism.* Philadelphia: Fortress Press.

Coburn, Robert. 1988. "Metaphysical Theology and the Life of Faith." *Philosophical Investigations* 11 (July), 197–217.

Connolly, John R. 1980. *Dimensions of Belief and Unbelief.* Washington, D.C.: University Press of America.

Cook, J. Thomas. 1987. "Deciding to Believe without Self-Deception." *Journal of Philosophy* 84 (August), 441–46.

Coward, Harold G., ed. 1987. *Modern Indian Responses to Religious Pluralism.* Albany, N.Y.: SUNY Press.

Craft, J. L., and Ronald E. Hustwit, eds. 1984. *Without Proof or Evidence: Essays of O. K. Bouwsma.* Lincoln: University of Nebraska Press.

Craig, Charles H. 1952. "A Layman's Definition of Faith." *Review and Expositor* 49 (April), 150–60.

Creel, A. B. 1978. "The Concept of Revelation in Sarvepalli Radhakrishnan and H. Richard Niebuhr." *Journal of Dharma* 53 (July-September), 253–67.

Creel, Richard E. 1984. "Philosophy's Bowl of Pottage: Reflections on the Value of Faith." *Faith and Philosophy* 1 (April), 230–35.

——. 1991. *Religion and Doubt: Toward a Faith of Your Own,* 2d ed. Englewood Cliffs, N.J.: Prentice-Hall.

Crumbine, Nancy Jay. 1981. "On Faith." In Perkins, ed., 1981, 189–203.

Cupitt, Don. 1981. *Taking Leave of God.* New York: Crossroad.

——. 1982. *The World to Come.* London: SCM Press.

——. 1984. *The Sea of Faith.* London: BBC Publications.

——. 1985. *Only Human.* London: SCM Press.

——. 1986. *Life Lines.* London: SCM Press.

Da Costa, Newton C. A., and Steven French. 1990. "Belief, Contradiction, and the Logic of Self-Deception." *American Philosophical Quarterly* 27 (July), 179–97.

Dalferth, Ingolf U. 1988. *Theology and Philosophy.* Oxford: Basil Blackwell.

Danto, Arthur C. 1961. "Faith, Language, and Religious Experience: A Dialogue." In Hook, ed., 1961, 137–49.

D'Arcy, Martin Cyril. 1976. *The Nature of Belief.* Westport, Conn.: Greenwood Press.

Das Gupta, Mrinal. 1930. "Śraddhā and Bhakti in Vedic Literature." *Indian Historical Quarterly* 6, 315–33, 487–513.

Davies, Brian. 1982. *An Introduction to the Philosophy of Religion.* Oxford: Oxford University Press.

Davis, Stephen T. 1978. *Faith, Skepticism, and Evidence: An Essay in Religious Epistemology.* Lewisburg, Penn.: Bucknell University Press.

——. 1983. *Logic and the Nature of God.* Grand Rapids, Mich.: William B. Eerdmans.

Dawe, Donald G., and John B. Carman, eds. 1978. *Christian Faith in a Religiously Plural World.* Maryknoll, N.Y.: Orbis Books.

Day, J. P. 1969. "Hope." *American Philosophical Quarterly* 6 (April), 89–102.

——. 1970. "The Anatomy of Hope and Fear." *MIND* 79 (July), 369–84.

Decourt, Alexis. 1947. *L'Acte de foi. Ses éléments logiques. Ses éléments psychologiques.* Paris: Beauchesne.

Delaney, C. F., ed. 1979. *Rationality and Religious Belief.* Notre Dame, Ind.: University of Notre Dame Press.

Demos, Raphael. 1961. "Religious Faith and Scientific Faith." In Hook, ed., 1961, 130–36.

De Smet, Richard. 1973. "Highlights of the Life of Faith (Śraddha) in India." In Gispert-Sauch, ed., 1973, 39–58.

Desroche, Henri. 1979. *The Sociology of Hope,* tr. Carol Martin-Sperry. London: Routledge and Kegan Paul.

Dewey, John. 1934. *A Common Faith.* New Haven, Conn.: Yale University Press.

Dillenberger, John. 1958. "Faith." In Marvin Halverson and Arthur A. Cohen, eds., *A Handbook of Christian Theology.* New York: Meridian Books.

Dilman, Ilham. 1975. "Wisdom's Philosophy of Religion—Part I: Religion and Reason." *Canadian Journal of Philosophy* 5 (December), 473–95.

Dobbins, James C. 1989a. *Jodo Shinshu: Shin Buddhism in Medieval Japan.* Bloomington: Indiana University Press.

——. 1989b. "Shin Buddhism, the *Nembutsu* Experience, and Faith." *Pacific World: Journal of the Institute of Buddhist Studies,* n.s. 5 (Fall), 53–62.

Doi, Masatoshi. 1980. "Dynamics of Faith: A Dialogical Study of Pure Land Buddhism and Evangelical Christianity." *Japanese Religions* 11 (September), 56–73.

Dornisch, Loretta. 1990. *Faith and Philosophy in the Writings of Paul Ricoeur.* Lewiston, N.Y.: Edwin Mellen.

Dowey, E. A., Jr. 1952. *The Knowledge of God in Calvin's Theology.* New York: Columbia University Press.

Downing, F. G. 1964. *Has Christianity a Revelation?* London: SCM Press.

Dreyfus, Hubert L. 1991. *Being-in-the-World: A Commentary on Heidegger's "Being and Time," Division I.* Cambridge, Mass.: MIT Press.

Droege, Thomas A. 1983. *Faith Passages and Patterns,* ed. Allan Hart Jahsmann. Philadelphia: Fortress Press.

Dubay, Thomas. 1985. *Faith and Certitude.* San Francisco: Ignatius Press.

Ducasse, C. J. 1953. *A Philosophical Scrutiny of Religion.* New York: Rand Press.

Duff-Forbes, Donald R. 1969. "Faith, Evidence and Coercion." *Australian Journal of Philosophy* 47 (August), 209–15.

Dulles, Avery. 1969. *Revelation Theology.* New York: Herder and Herder.

——. 1977. "The Meaning of Faith Considered in Relationship to Justice." In John C. Haughey, ed., *The Faith That Does Justice.* New York: Paulist Press.

——. 1985. *Models of Revelation.* Garden City, N.Y.: Doubleday Image Books.

Duméry, Henry. 1968. *Faith and Reflection,* tr. S. McNierney and M. B. Murphy. New York: Herder and Herder.

Dupré, Louis. 1972. *The Other Dimension: A Search for the Meaning of Religious Attitudes.* Garden City, N.Y.: Doubleday.

Durka, Gloria, and Joanmarie Smith, eds. 1976. *Emerging Issues in Religious Education*. New York: Paulist Press.

Dutt, N. 1940. "The Place of Faith in Buddhism." *Indian Historical Quarterly* 16 (September), 639–41.

Ebeling, Gerhard. 1961. *The Nature of Faith*, tr. Ronald Gregor Smith. Philadelphia: Fortress Press.

——. 1963. *Word and Faith*, tr. James W. Leitch. Philadelphia: Fortress Press.

Edwards, Paul, ed. 1967. *The Encyclopedia of Philosophy*. 8 vols. New York: Macmillan and Free Press.

Ehrlich, Leonard H. 1975. *Karl Jaspers: Philosophy as Faith*. Amherst: University of Massachusetts Press.

Ellul, Jacques. 1983. *Living Faith: Belief and Doubt in a Perilous World*, tr. Peter Heinegg. San Francisco: Harper and Row.

Elster, Jon. 1979. *Ulysses and the Sirens: Studies in Rationality and Irrationality*. Cambridge: Cambridge University Press.

Emerson, Ralph Waldo. 1957. *Selections from Ralph Waldo Emerson*, ed. Stephen E. Whicher. Boston: Houghton Mifflin Riverside.

Emmet, Dorothy. 1966. *The Nature of Metaphysical Thinking*. New York: St. Martin's Press.

Ergardt, Jan T. 1977. *Faith and Knowledge in Early Buddhism: An Analysis of the Contextual Structures of an Arahant-Formula in the Majjhima-Nikāya*. Leiden: E. J. Brill.

Evans, C. Stephen. 1978. *Subjectivity and Religious Belief: An Historical, Critical Study*. Grand Rapids, Mich.: Christian University Press.

——. 1985. *Philosophy of Religion: Thinking about Faith*. Downers Grove, Ill.: InterVarsity Press.

——. 1990. "The Relevance of Historical Evidence for Christian Faith: A Critique of a Kierkegaardian View." *Faith and Philosophy* 7 (October), 470–85.

Evans, Donald D. 1963. *The Logic of Self-Involvement*. London: SCM Press.

——. 1974. "Faith and Belief." *Religious Studies* 10 (March and June), 1–19, 199–212.

——. 1979. *Struggle and Fulfilment: The Inner Dynamics of Religion and Morality*. London: Collins.

——. 1980. *Faith, Authenticity, and Morality*. Toronto: University of Toronto Press.

Farrer, Austin M. 1948. *The Glass of Vision*. London: Dacre Press.

——. 1961. *A Faith of Our Own*. Cleveland, Ohio: World Publishing Company.

——. 1964. *Saving Belief*. London: Hodder and Stoughton.

——. 1967. *Faith and Speculation*. The Deems Lectures, 1964. New York: New York University Press.

——. 1974. *Reflective Faith: Essays in Philosophical Theology*, ed. Charles C. Conti. Grand Rapids, Mich.: William B. Eerdmans.

——. 1976. *Interpretation and Belief*, ed. Charles C. Conti. London: SPCK.

Fenn, Richard. 1987. *The Dream of the Perfect Act: An Inquiry into the Fate of Religion in a Secular World*. New York: Tavistock Publications.

Ferré, Nels F. S. 1963. *The Finality of Faith and Christianity among the World Religions*. New York: Harper and Row.

Ferreira, M. Jamie. 1980. *Doubt and Religious Commitment: The Role of the Will in Newman's Thought.* Oxford: Clarendon Press.

———. 1987. "The Faith/History Problem, and Kierkegaard's *A Priori* 'Proof'." *Religious Studies* 23 (September), 337–46.

———. 1990. "Kierkegaardian Faith: 'The Condition' and the Response." *International Journal for Philosophy of Religion* 28, 63–79.

Feuerbach, Ludwig. 1957. *The Essence of Christianity*, tr. George Eliot. New York: Harper and Row Torchbook.

Fey, William R. 1976. *Faith and Doubt: The Unfolding of Newman's Thought on Certainty.* Shepherdstown, W.V.: Patmos Press.

Firth, Roderick. 1967. "The Anatomy of Certainty." *Philosphical Review* 76 (January), 3–27.

Flanagan, Philip. 1946. *Newman, Faith, and the Believer.* London: Sands.

Forde, Gerhard O. 1982. *Justification by Faith: A Matter of Death and Life.* Philadelphia: Fortress Press.

Forman, Robert K. C., ed. 1990. *The Problem of Pure Consciousness: Mysticism and Philosophy.* Oxford: Oxford University Press.

Forrest, Peter. 1986. *The Dynamics of Belief: A Normative Logic.* Oxford: Basil Blackwell.

Fosdick, Harry Emerson. 1951. *The Meaning of Faith*, rev. ed. New York: Association Press.

Fowler, James W. 1974. "Toward a Developmental Perspective on Faith." *Religious Education* 69 (March-April), 207–19.

———. 1976a. "Stages in Faith: The Structural Developmental Perspective." In Thomas Hennessey, ed., *Values and Moral Development.* New York: Paulist Press, 173–79.

———. 1976b. "Faith Development Theory and the Aims of Religious Socialization." In Durka and Smith, 1976, 187–208.

———. 1981. *Stages of Faith: The Psychology of Human Development and the Quest for Meaning.* San Francisco: Harper and Row.

———. 1982. "Stages of Faith and Adults' Life Cycles." In Stokes, 1982, 179–207.

———. 1984. *Becoming Adult, Becoming Christian: Adult Development and Christian Faith.* San Francisco: Harper and Row.

———. 1987. *Faith Development and Pastoral Care.* Philadelphia: Fortress Press.

Fowler, James W., Sam Keen, and Jerome Berryman. 1978. *Life-Maps: Conversation on the Journey of Faith.* Waco, Tex.: Word Books.

Fox, Douglas A. 1986. "Soteriology in Jodo Shin and Christianity." *Pure Land: Journal of Pure Land Buddhism,* n.s. 3, (December), 29–34.

Frankfurt, Harry G. 1962. "Philosophical Certainty." *Philosophical Review* 71 (July), 303–27.

Freud, Sigmund. 1928. *The Future of an Illusion.* London: Hogarth Press.

Fries, Heinrich. 1969a. *Faith under Challenge*, tr. William D. Seidensticker. New York: Herder and Herder.

———. 1969b. *Revelation.* New York: Herder and Herder.

Frye, Northrop. 1989. "The Dialectic of Belief and Vision." *Shenandoah* 39:3, 47–64.

Futaba, Kenkō. 1988. "Shinran and Human Dignity: Opening an Historic Horizon," tr. Kenryu T. Tsuji. *The Pacific World: Journal of the Institute of Buddhist Studies*, n.s. 4, 51–59.

Gambetta, Diego, ed. 1988. *Trust: Making and Breaking Cooperative Relations*. Oxford: Basil Blackwell.

Gardet, L. 1973. "ISLĀM, I. Definition and Theories of Meaning." In *Encyclopaedia of Islam* 4, fasc. 63–64, 171–74.

Gardner, Martin. 1973. *The Flight of Peter Fromm*. Los Altos, Calif.: William Kaufmann.

——. 1983. *The Whys of a Philosophical Scrivener*. New York: Quill.

Gaskin, J. C. A. 1984. *The Quest for Eternity: An Outline of the Philosophy of Religion*. Harmondsworth, Eng.: Penguin Books.

Geisler, Norman. 1976. *Christian Apologetics*. Grand Rapids, Mich.: Baker.

Geivett, R. Douglas, and Brendan Sweetman, eds. 1992. *Contemporary Perspectives on Religious Epistemology*. New York: Oxford University Press.

Gibson, Alexander Boyce. 1970. *Theism and Empiricism*. New York: Schocken Books.

Gilson, Étienne. 1938. *Reason and Revelation in the Middle Ages*. New York: Charles Scribner's Sons.

Gispert-Sauch, G., ed. 1973. *God's Word among Men*. Delhi: Vidyajyoti, Institute of Religious Studies.

Giurlanda, Paul. 1987. *Faith and Knowledge: A Critical Inquiry*. Lanham, Md.: University Press of America.

Godlove, Terry F., Jr. 1989. *Religion, Interpretation, and Diversity of Belief*. Cambridge: Cambridge University Press.

Gogarten, Friedrich. 1959. *The Reality of Faith: The Problem of Subjectivism in Theology*, tr. Carl Michalson et al. Philadelphia: Westminster Press.

Gokhale, Balkrishna Govind. 1980. "*Bhakti* in Early Buddhism." *Journal of Asian and African Studies* 15:1–2, 16–28.

Golding, Joshua L. 1990. "Toward a Pragmatic Conception of Religious Faith." *Faith and Philosophy* 7 (October), 486–503.

Gómez, Luiz O. 1983. "Shinran's Faith and the Sacred Name of Amida." Review of Ueda, ed., 1981. *Monumenta Nipponica* 38 (Spring), 73–84.

Gordh, G. 1954. "Calvin's Conception of Faith." *Review and Expositor* 51, 207–15.

Gordon, Jeffrey. 1993. "The Rational Imperative to Believe." *Religious Studies* 29, 1–19.

Govier, Trudy. 1976. "Belief, Values, and the Will." *Dialogue* 15 (December), 642–63.

Green, Ronald M. 1978. *Religious Reason: The Rational and Moral Basis of Religious Belief*. New York: Oxford University Press.

——. 1982. "Abraham, Isaac, and the Jewish Tradition." *Journal of Religious Ethics* 10, 1–21.

——. 1988. *Religion and Moral Reason: A New Method for Comparative Study*. New York: Oxford University Press.

Griffiths, A. Phillips. 1990. "Certain Hope." *Religious Studies* 26, 453–61.

Grigg, Richard. 1983. "Theism and Proper Basicality: A Response to Plantinga." *International Journal for Philosophy of Religion* 14, 123–27.

——. 1990. "The Crucial Disanalogies between Properly Basic Belief and Belief in God." *Religious Studies* 26, 389–401.

Grisez, Germain. 1975. *Beyond the New Theism: A Philosophy of Religion.* Notre Dame, Ind.: University of Notre Dame Press.

Gualtieri, Antonio Roberto. 1969. "Faith, Tradition, and Transcendence: A Study of Wilfred Cantwell Smith." *Canadian Journal of Theology* 15 (April), 102–11.

Gurrey, Charles S. 1990. "Faith and the Possibility of Private Meaning: A Sense of the Ineffable in Kierkegaard and Murdoch." *Religious Studies* 26, 199–205.

Gutting, Gary. 1982. *Religious Belief and Religious Skepticism.* Notre Dame, Ind.: University of Notre Dame Press.

Habermas, Gary R. 1990. *Dealing with Doubt.* Chicago: Moody Press.

Habermas, Gary R., and Antony G. N. Flew. 1987. *Did Jesus Rise from the Dead?*, ed. Terry L. Miethe. San Francisco: Harper and Row.

Hakeda, Yoshito S., tr. 1967. *Mahayanasraddotpadasastra: The Awakening of Faith, Attributed to Aśvaghosha.* New York: Columbia University Press.

Halbfass, Wilhelm. 1991. *Tradition and Reflection: Explorations in Indian Thought.* Albany, N.Y.: SUNY Press.

Hals, Ronald M. 1980. *Grace and Faith in the Old Testament.* Minneapolis, Minn.: Augsburg.

Hara, Minoru. 1963–1964. "Note on Two Sanskrit Religious Terms: *Bhakti* and *Śraddhā.*" *Indo-Iranian Journal* 7, 124–45.

Hardwig, John. 1991. "The Role of Trust in Knowledge." *Journal of Philosophy* 88 (December), 693–708.

Harrington, Walt. 1987. "Implacable Faith." *Washington Post Magazine,* July 26, 10–17, 38–39.

Harris, Errol E. 1982. "Hegel and Christianity." *Owl of Minerva* 13 (June), 1–7.

Harris, R. Baine. 1987. "Faith and Reason in the Early Neoplatonists." *Dialogue and Alliance* 1 (Spring), 6–17.

Harrison, Jonathan. 1987. "Some Reflections on the Ethics of Knowledge and Belief." *Religious Studies* 23 (September), 325–36.

Hartshorne, Marion Holmes. 1963. *The Faith to Doubt.* Englewood Cliffs, N.J.: Prentice-Hall.

Hatch, William Henry Paine. 1917. *The Pauline Idea of Faith in Its Relation to Jewish and Hellenistic Religion.* Cambridge, Mass.: Harvard University Press.

Haught, John F. 1980. *Religion and Self-Acceptance: A Study of the Relationship between Belief in God and the Desire to Know.* Lanham, Md.: University Press of America.

Hays, Richard B. 1983. *The Faith of Jesus Christ: An Investigation of the Narrative Substructure of Galatians 3:1–4:11.* Chico, Calif.: Scholars Press.

Heaney, James. 1980. "Faith and the Logic of Seeing-As." *Sophia* 18 (April), 33–41.

Hebert, A. G. 1955. " 'Faithfulness' and 'Faith'." *Reformed Theological Review* 58 (June), 33–40.

Hegel, G. W. F. 1977. *Faith and Knowledge,* tr. Walter Cerf and H. S. Harris. New York: SUNY Press.

Heidegger, Martin. 1962. *Being and Time,* tr. John Macquarrie and Edward Robinson. New York: Harper and Row.

Helm, Paul. 1969. "Faith, Scepticism, and Experiencing-As." *Faith and Thought* 97 (Summer) 51–64.

———. 1973a. *The Varieties of Belief.* New York: Humanities Press.

———. 1973b. "Locke on Faith and Knowledge." *Philosophical Quarterly* 23, 52–66.

———. 1979. "Grace and Causation." *Scottish Journal of Theology* 32, 101–12.

Henle, Paul. 1949. "Mysticism and Semantics." *Philosophy and Phenomenological Research* 3, 416–22.

Henze, Donald F. 1967. "Faith, Evidence, and Coercion." *Philosophy* 42 (January), 78–85.

Hepburn, Ronald W. 1958. *Christianity and Paradox: Critical Studies in Twentieth-Century Theology.* London: Watts.

Hermann, Ingo. 1966. *The Experience of Faith: A Contribution to the Biblico-Theological Dialogue,* tr. Daniel Coogan. New York: P. J. Kenedy.

Hick, John. 1957. *Faith and Knowledge: A Modern Introduction to the Problem of Religious Knowledge.* Ithaca, N.Y.: Cornell University Press.

———. 1967a. "Faith and Coercion." *Philosophy* 42 (July), 272–73.

———. 1967b. "Revelation." In Edwards, ed., 1967, 7:189–91.

———. 1969. "Religious Faith as Experiencing-As." in Vesey, 1969, 20–35.

———. 1971. "Faith, Evidence, Coercion Again." *Australian Journal of Philosophy* 49 (May), 78–81.

———. 1973a. *Philosophy of Religion,* 2d ed. Englewood Cliffs, N.J.: Prentice-Hall.

———. 1973b. *God and the Universe of Faiths: Essays in the Philosophy of Religion.* New York: St. Martin's Press.

———. 1978. *The Center of Christianity.* San Francisco: Harper and Row.

———. 1982. *God Has Many Names.* Philadelphia: Westminster Press.

———. 1985. *Problems of Religious Pluralism.* New York: St. Martin's Press.

———. 1989. *An Interpretation of Religion: Human Responses to the Transcendent.* New Haven, Conn.: Yale University Press.

———, ed. 1964. *Faith and the Philosophers.* New York: St. Martin's Press.

Higgins, Jean. 1988. "Luther and Shinran on *fides sola*: A Textual Study." *Pacific World: Journal of the Institute of Buddhist Studies,* n.s. 4, 23–41.

Hinchcliff, John C., ed. 1975. *Perspectives on Religion: New Zealand Viewpoints 1974.* Auckland: University of Auckland Press.

Hinton, J. M. 1970. "Hoping and Wishing." *Proceedings of the Aristotelian Society,* supp. vol. 44, 71–88.

Hirota, Dennis. 1987. "Religious Transformation in Shinran and Shōku." *Pure Land: Journal of Pure Land Buddhism,* n.s. 4, 57–69.

——. 1991. "Breaking the Darkness: Images of Reality in the Shin Buddhist Path." *Japanese Religions* 16, 17–45.

——, tr. 1986. *Tannishō: A Primer*. Kyoto: Ryūkoku University.

Hoffman, Frank J. 1987a. *Rationality and Mind in Early Buddhism*. Delhi: Motilal Banarsidass.

——. 1987b. "The Pragmatic Efficacy of *Saddhā*." *Journal of Indian Philosophy* 15 (December), 399–412.

——. 1991. "Towards a Philosophy of Buddhist Religion." *Asian Philosophy* 1:1, 21–28.

Holmer, Paul. 1978. *The Grammar of Faith*. San Francisco: Harper and Row.

Hook, Sidney, ed. 1961. *Religious Experience and Truth: A Symposium*. New York: New York University Press.

Howard, George. 1967. "On the 'Faith of Christ'." *Harvard Theological Review* 60, 459–65.

——. 1974. "The Faith of Christ." *Expository Times* 85, 212–15.

Husserl, Edmund. 1931. *Ideas: General Introduction to Pure Phenomenology*, tr. W. R. Boyce Gibson. London: George Allen and Unwin.

Hutchinson, John A. 1956. *Faith, Reason, and Existence: An Introduction to Contemporary Philosophy of Religion*. London: Oxford University Press.

Inge, William Ralph. 1910. *Faith and Its Psychology*. New York: Charles Scribner's Sons.

Ingram, Paul O. 1971. "Shinran Shonin and Martin Luther: A Soteriological Comparison." *Journal of the American Academy of Religion* 39 (December), 430–47.

Ingram, Paul O., and Frederick J. Streng, eds. 1986. *Buddhist-Christian Dialogue*. Honolulu: University of Hawaii Press.

Ishihara, John. 1987. "Luther and Shinran: *simul iustus et peccator* and *nishu jinshin*." *Japanese Religions* 14:4, 31–54.

Izutsu, Toshihiko. 1965. *The Concept of Belief in Islamic Theology: A Semantic Analysis of îmân and islâm*. Tokyo: Keio Institute of Cultural and Linguistic Studies; Yokohama: Yurindo.

Jacobs, Louis. 1968. *Faith*. London: Valentine, Mitchell.

James, William. 1979. *The Will to Believe*. Cambridge, Mass.: Harvard University Press.

Jaspers, Karl. 1949. *The Perennial Scope of Philosophy*, tr. Ralph Manheim. New York: Philosophical Library.

——. 1967. *Philosophical Faith and Revelation*, tr. E. B. Ashton. Chicago: University of Chicago Press.

Jayatilleke, Kulatissa Nanda. 1963. *Early Buddhist Theory of Knowledge*. London: Allen and Unwin.

Johnson, L. T. 1982. "Romans 3:21–26 and the Faith of Jesus." *Catholic Biblical Quarterly* 44, 77–90.

Johnson, Roger, ed. 1982. *The Anatomy of Faith*. Philadelphia: Fortress Press.

Johnston, William. 1976. "Pure Land Buddhism and Nembutzu, The Meditation of Faith." *Studia Missionalia* 25, 43–64.

Joly, Eugene. 1958. *What Is Faith?*, tr. Dom Illtyd Trethowan. London: Burns and Oates.

Joshi, Lal Mani. 1987. "Faith and Wisdom in the Buddhist Tradition." *Dialogue Alliance* 1 (Spring), 66–77.

Kaneko, Daiei. 1965. "The Meaning of Salvation in the Doctrine of Pure Land Buddhism." *Eastern Buddhist* 1 (September), 48–63.

Kasulis, Thomas. 1981. Review of Ueda, ed., 1978. *Philosophy East and West* 31 (April), 246–48.

Katz, Steven T., ed. 1978. *Mysticism and Philosophical Analysis*. New York: Oxford University Press.

———, ed. 1983. *Mysticism and Religious Traditions*. New York: Oxford University Press.

Kawashima, Keiko, and Yoshiharu Akishige. 1977. "Psychological Studies on Faith and Practice." In Akishige, ed., 1977, 77–90.

Kazi, Abdul Khaliq. 1966. "The Meaning of Īmān and Islām in the Qur'ān." *Islamic Studies* (Pakistan) 5, 227–37.

Keating, John, ed. 1968. *Faith in the Face of Doubt*. New York: Paulist Press.

Keel, Hee-Sung. 1986. *Chinul*. Berkeley, Calif.: Berkeley Buddhist Studies Series.

Keenan, John P. 1989a. *The Meaning of Christ: A Mahayana Theology*. Maryknoll, N.Y.: Orbis Books.

———. 1989b. "Nien-Fo (Buddha-Anusmrti): The Shifting Structure of Remembrance." *Pacific World: Journal of the Institute of Buddhist Studies*, n.s. 5 (Fall), 40–52.

Kellenberger, Bertram James. 1972. *Religious Discovery, Faith, and Knowledge*. Englewood Cliffs, N.J.: Prentice-Hall.

———. 1974. "God and Mystery." *American Philosophical Quarterly* 11 (April), 99–101.

———. 1976. "Problems of Faith." *Canadian Journal of Philosophy* 6 (September), 417–42.

———. 1981. "Three Models of Faith." *International Journal for Philosophy of Religion* 12, 217–33.

———. 1985. *The Cognitivity of Religion*. Berkeley, Calif.: University of California Press.

———. 1989. *God-Relationships with and without God*. New York: St. Martin's Press.

———, ed. 1993. *Interreligious Models and Criteria*. London: Macmillan.

Keller, James. 1985. "Reflections on the Value of Knowledge: A Reply to Creel." *Faith and Philosophy* 2 (April), 191–94.

Kennedy, Eugene C. 1977. *Believing*. Garden City, N.Y.: Doubleday.

Kennedy, Gail. 1961. "Some Meanings of 'Faith'." In Hook, ed., 1961, 109–15.

Kenny, Anthony. 1983. *Faith and Reason*. New York: Columbia University Press.

Kepnes, Steven, and David Tracy, eds. 1982. *The Challenge of Psychology to*

*Faith*. Vol. 156 of *Concilium: Religion in the Eighties*. Edinburgh: T. and T. Clark; New York: Seabury Press.

Kerr, Hugh T., ed. 1943. *A Compend of Luther's Theology*. Philadelphia: Westminster Press.

Kierkegaard, Søren Aabye. 1941. *Concluding Unscientific Postscript*, tr. David F. Swenson and Walter Lowrie. Princeton: Princeton University Press.

——. 1967. *Søren Kierkegaard's Journals and Papers* Vol. 1, A–E, ed. and tr. Howard V. Hong and Edna H. Hong. Bloomington: Indiana University Press.

——. 1970. *Søren Kierkegaard's Journals and Papers*. Vol. 2, F–K, ed. and tr. Howard V. Hong and Edna H. Hong. Bloomington: Indiana University Press.

——. 1985. *Philosophical Fragments*, tr. Howard V. Hong and Edna H. Hong. Princeton: Princeton University Press.

——. 1988. *Stages on Life's Way*, tr. Howard V. Hong and Edna H. Hong. Princeton: Princeton University Press.

Kikumura, Norihiko. 1972. *Shinran: His Life and Thought*. Los Angeles: Nembutsu Press.

King-Farlow, John, and William Niels Christensen. 1972. *Faith and the Life of Reason*. Dordrecht: D. Reidel.

Kinneavy, James L. 1987. *Greek Rhetorical Origins of Christian Faith: An Inquiry*. New York: Oxford University Press.

Kirk, Kenneth E. 1920. *Some Principles of Moral Theology and Their Application*. London: Longmans, Green.

Klein, Peter D. 1981. *Certainty: A Refutation of Scepticism*. Minneapolis: University of Minnesota Press.

Kolakowski, Leszek. 1982. *Religion: If There Is No God . . . On God, the Devil, Sin, and Other Worries of the So-Called Philosophy of Religion*. New York: Oxford University Press.

Kolp, Alan L. 1976. "Shinran and Martin Luther: Two Doctrines of Salvation by Faith Alone." *International Philosophical Quarterly* 16 (December), 341–58.

Kraemer, Hendrik. 1957. *Religion and the Christian Faith*. Philadelphia: Westminster Press.

——. 1969. *The Christian Message in a Non-Christian World*, 3d ed. Grand Rapids, Mich.: Kregel Publishing.

Kroner, Richard. 1943. *The Primacy of Faith*. New York: Macmillan.

——. 1951. *Culture and Faith*. Chicago: University of Chicago Press.

——. 1966. *Between Faith and Thought: Reflections and Suggestions*. Oxford: Oxford University Press.

Kuang, Stanislaus Lo. 1988. "Rapprochement between Modernized Confucian Thought and Christian Belief." *Ching Feng* 31 (August), 153–65.

Lai, Whalen. 1981. "Faith and Wisdom in the T'ien-t'ai Buddhist Tradition: A Letter by Ssu-ming Chih-li." *Journal of Dharma* 6 (July/September), 281–98.

Lala, Chhaganlal. 1986. *Bhakti in Religions of the World: With Special Reference to Dr. Sri Bankey Behariji*. Delhi: B. R. Publishing.

Lash, Nicholas. 1988. *Easter in Ordinary: Reflections on Human Experience and the Knowledge of God.* Charlottesville: University of Virginia Press.

Latourelle, René. 1966. *The Theology of Revelation.* Staten Island, N.Y.: Alba House.

Laube, Johannes. 1983. "Der Glaubensakt bei Luther und bei Shinran." *Zeitschrift für Missionswissenschaft und Religionswissenschaft* 67 (January), 31–49.

la Vallée Poussin, Louis de. 1908. "Faith and Reason in Buddhism." In *Transactions of the Third International Congress for the History of Religions.* Oxford: Clarendon Press, 2:32–43.

Lee, Shui Chuen. 1987. "The Confucian Conception of Reason and Faith." *Dialogue Alliance* 1 (Spring), 58–65.

Leibrecht, Walter, ed. 1959. *Religion and Culture: Essays in Honor of Paul Tillich.* New York: Harper.

Leith, John H., ed. 1982. *Creeds of the Churches: A Reader in Christian Doctrine from the Bible to the Present,* 3d ed. Atlanta: John Knox Press.

Léon-Dufour, Xavier, ed. 1973. *Dictionary of Biblical Theology,* 2d ed. New York: Seabury Press.

Lewis, C. S. 1960. "On Obstinacy in Belief." In his *The World's Last Night, and Other Essays.* New York: Harcourt Brace.

Lindbeck, George. 1984. *The Nature of Doctrine.* Philadelphia: Westminster Press.

Lipner, Julius. 1987. "A Modern Indian Christian Response." In Coward, 1987, 291–314.

Little, Donald P., ed. 1976. *Essays on Islamic Civilization presented to Niyazi Berkes.* Leiden: E. J. Brill.

Livingston, James C. 1974. *The Ethics of Belief: An Essay on the Victorian Religious Conscience.* Tallahassee, Fla.: American Academy of Religion.

Ljungman, Henrik. 1964. *Pistis: A Study of Its Presuppositions and Its Meaning in Pauline Use.* Lund: Gleerup.

Lossky, Vladimir. 1957. *The Mystical Theology of the Eastern Church.* London: James Clarke.

Lucas, J. R. 1971. "Pelagius and St. Augustine." *Journal of Theological Studies,* n.s. 22 (April), 73–85.

——. 1976. *Freedom and Grace.* London: SPCK.

Ludowyk-Gyomroi, Edith. 1947. "The Valuation of Saddhā in Early Buddhist Texts." *University of Ceylon Review* 5:2, 32–49.

Luhmann, Niklas. 1980. *Trust and Power.* New York: John Wiley.

Lührmann, Dieter. 1973. "Pistis im Judentum." *Zeitschrift für Neutestamentliche Wissenschaft* 64:1–2, 19–38.

——. 1976. *Glaube im frühen Christentum.* Gütersloh: Gerd Mohn.

Luijpen, William A. 1973. *Theology as Anthropology: Philosophical Reflections on Religion,* tr. Henry J. Koren. Pittsburgh, Penn.: Duquesne University Press.

Lyas, Colin. 1977. "The Groundlessness of Religious Belief." In Stuart C. Brown, 1977, 158–80.

Lynch, William F. 1973. *Images of Faith: An Exploration of the Ironic Imagination.* Notre Dame, Ind.: University of Notre Dame Press.

McBrien, Richard. 1974. "Faith, Theology, and Belief." *Commonweal* 101 (November 15), 134–37.

McCarthy, Gerald D., ed. 1986. *The Ethics of Belief Debate.* Missoula, Mont.: Scholars Press.

McClendon, James William, Jr., and James M. Smith. 1975. *Understanding Religious Convictions.* Notre Dame, Ind.: University of Notre Dame Press.

McCool, Gerald A., ed. 1975. *A Rahner Reader.* New York: Crossroads.

McDaniel, Jay B. 1985. "Faith without Foundations." *Q R (Methodist)* 5 (Spring), 9–26.

McDonald, H. D. 1959. *Ideas of Revelation.* London: Macmillan.

MacIntosh, J. J. 1970. "Belief-in." *MIND* 79 (July), 395–407.

Mackey, James P. 1972. *Problems in Religious Faith.* Dublin: Helicon.

——. 1975. "The Theology of Faith: A Bibliographical Survey (And More)." *Horizons* 2, 207–37.

MacKinnon, Donald M. 1990. "Does Faith Create Its Own Objects?" *Religious Studies* 26, 439–51.

Maclaren, Elizabeth. 1976. *The Nature of Belief.* New York: Seabury Press.

McPherson, Thomas. 1974. *Philosophy and Religious Belief.* London: Hutchinson University Library.

Macquarrie, John. 1978. *Christian Hope.* New York: Seabury Press.

McTaggart, John McTaggart Ellis. 1906. *Some Dogmas of Religion.* London: Edward Arnold.

Mahathera, Nyanaponika, ed. 1971. *Pathways of Buddhist Thought.* London: George Allen and Unwin.

Maitzen, Stephen. 1992. "Two Views of Religious Certitude." *Religious Studies* 28, 65–74.

Malcolm, Norman. 1963. *Knowledge and Certainty: Essays and Lectures.* Ithaca, N.Y.: Cornell University Press.

——. 1964. "Is It a Religious Belief that 'God Exists'?" In Hick, ed., 1964, 103–10.

——. 1977. *Thought and Knowledge.* Ithaca, N.Y.: Cornell University Press.

Malevez, Léopold. 1969. *Pour une théologie de la foi.* Paris: Bruges.

Marcel, Gabriel. 1951a. *Faith and Reality.* Vol. 2 of *The Mystery of Being,* tr. René Hague. Chicago: Henry Regnery.

——. 1951b. *Homo Viator: Introduction to a Metaphysic of Hope,* tr. Emma Craufurd. Chicago: Henry Regnery.

——. 1964. *Creative Fidelity,* tr. Robert Rosthal. New York: Farrar, Straus, and Giroux.

Martin, C. B. 1959. *Religious Belief.* Ithaca, N.Y.: Cornell University Press.

Masutani, Fumio. 1959. *A Comparative Study of Buddhism and Christianity,* 2d ed. Tokyo: CIIB Press.

Matthysse, Steven. 1969. "Faith and Evidence." *Religious Studies* 4 (April), 253–58.

Mavrodes, George. 1970. *Belief in God: A Study in the Epistemology of Religion.* New York: Random House.

——. 1988. *Revelation in Religious Belief.* Philadelphia: Temple University Press.

Meng, Heinrich, and Ernst L. Freud, eds. 1963. *Psychoanalysis and Faith: The Letters of Sigmund Freud and Oskar Pfister*, tr. Eric Mosbacher. London: Hogarth Press.

Michalson, Carl. 1963. *The Rationality of Faith: An Historical Critique of the Theological Reason*. New York: Charles Scribner's Sons.

Micklem, Nathaniel. 1963. *Faith and Reason*. London: Gerald Duckworth.

Miller, Richard W. 1978. "Absolute Certainty." *MIND* 87 (January), 46–65.

Mitchell, Basil. 1973. *The Justification of Religious Belief*. London: Macmillan.

——. 1980. "Faith and Reason: A False Antithesis?" *Religious Studies* 16, 131–44.

——. 1990. *How to Play Theological Ping-Pong and Other Essays on Faith and Reason*, ed. William J. Abraham and Robert W. Prevost. Grand Rapids, Mich.: William B. Eerdmans.

Mitchell, Donald W. 1980. "Faith in Zen Buddhism." *International Philosophical Quarterly* 20 (June), 183–98.

Mohler, James A. 1969. *Dimensions of Faith*. Chicago: Loyola University Press.

Moltmann, Jürgen. 1967. *Theology of Hope*. New York: Harper and Row.

——. 1971. *Hope and Planning*, tr. Margaret Clarkson. London: SCM Press.

——. 1975. *The Experiment Hope*, tr. M. Douglas Meeks. Philadelphia: Fortress Press.

——. 1979. *The Future of Creation*, tr. Margaret Kohl. Philadelphia: Fortress Press.

Moran, Gabriel. 1966. *Theology of Revelation*. New York: Herder and Herder.

——. 1972. *The Present Revelation*. New York: Herder and Herder.

Moravcsik, Julius. 1988. "Communal Ties." *Proceedings and Addresses of the American Philosophical Association* 62 (September), 211–25.

Morewedge, Parviz, ed. 1979. *Islamic Philosophical Theology*. Albany, N.Y.: SUNY Press.

Morgan, K. W., ed. 1956. *The Path of the Buddha*. New York: Ronald Press.

Morgan, W. 1928. "Faith, Christian." In James Hastings, ed., *Encyclopaedia of Religion and Ethics*, 5:689–94.

Morris, Thomas V., ed. 1988. *Divine and Human Action*. Ithaca, N.Y.: Cornell University Press.

Mortimer, R. C. 1972. *The Elements of Moral Theology*, rev. ed. London: A. and C. Black.

Morton, Adam. 1977. *A Guide Through the Theory of Knowledge*. Encino, Calif.: Dickenson.

Moule, C. F. D. 1962. "Revelation." In George A. Buttrick, ed. *Interpreters' Dictionary of the Bible*, 4:54–58.

Mouroux, Jean. 1959. *I Believe: The Personal Structure of Faith*. New York: Sheed and Ward.

Munson, Thomas N. 1968. *Reflective Theology: Philosophical Orientations in Religion*. New Haven, Conn.: Yale University Press.

Murphy, Nancey. 1990. *Theology in the Age of Scientific Reasoning*. Ithaca, N.Y.: Cornell University Press.

Murty, K. Satchidananda. 1959. *Revelation and Reason in Advaita Vedanta*. New York: Columbia University Press.

Muyskens, James. 1979. *The Sufficiency of Hope: The Conceptual Foundations of Religion*. Philadelphia: Temple University Press.

———. 1985. "What Is Virtuous about Faith?" *Faith and Philosophy* 2 (January), 43–52.

Nabe, Clyde M. 1980. "A Reflection on Faith and Reason." *Southwest Journal of Philosophy* 11 (Spring), 125–32.

Nagao, Gadjin. 1984. "Ascent and Descent: Two-Directional Activity In Buddhist Thought." *Journal of the International Association of Buddhist Studies* 7:1, 176–84.

———. 1989. *The Foundational Standpoint of Mādhyamika Philosophy*, tr. John P. Keenan. Albany, N.Y.: SUNY Press.

Nanamoli Thera, Ven. 1971. "Buddhism: A Religion or a Philosophy?; Does Saddhā Mean Faith?; Cessation of Becoming; Consciousness and Being." In Mahathera, ed., 1971, 13–48.

Nash, R. H. 1988. *Faith and Reason: Searching for a Rational Faith*. Grand Rapids, Mich.: Academic Books.

Needham, Rodney. 1972. *Belief, Language, and Experience*. Oxford: Blackwell.

Newman, J. H. 1955. *An Essay in Aid of a Grammar of Assent*. New York: Doubleday Image.

———. 1970. *Fifteen Sermons Preached before the University of Oxford, 1826–43*, 3d ed. London: SPCK.

———. 1976. *The Theological Papers of John Henry Newman on Faith and Certainty*, ed. J. Derek Holmes. Oxford: Clarendon Press.

Niebuhr, H. Richard. 1941. *The Meaning of Revelation*. New York: Macmillan.

———. 1961. "On the Nature of Faith." In Hook, ed., 1961, 93–102.

———. 1989. *Faith on Earth: An Inquiry into the Structure of Human Faith*, ed. Richard R. Niebuhr. New Haven, Conn.: Yale University Press.

Nielsen, Kai. 1981. "On the Rationality of Groundless Believing." *Idealistic Studies* 11 (Summer), 215–29.

———. 1982. *An Introduction to the Philosophy of Religion*. New York: St. Martin's Press.

Nikhilananda, Swami. 1946. *Essence of Hinduism*. New York: Rama-Vivek Center.

Nishitani, Keiji. 1975. "The Problem of Time in Shinran," tr. Dennis Hirota. *Eastern Buddhist*, n.s. 11:1, 13–26.

Northrop, Filmer S. C. 1944. "The Complementary Emphases of Eastern Intuitive and Western Scientific Philosophy." *Philosophy East and West*, 168–234.

Nozick, Robert. 1989. *The Examined Life: Philosophical Meditations*. New York: Simon and Schuster.

Oakes, Robert. 1990. "Union with God: A Theory." *Faith and Philosophy* 7 (April), 165–76.

O'Collins, Gerald. 1981. *Fundamental Theology*. Ramsey, N.J.: Paulist Press.

O'Connor, Edward D. 1961. *Faith in the Synoptic Gospels: A Problem in the Correlation of Scripture and Theology.* South Bend, Ind.: University of Notre Dame Press.

Ogden, Graham S. 1987. "Divine Revelation in the Old Testament and in Chinese Wisdom." *Ching Feng* 30 (May), 18–24.

Ogden, Shubert. 1979. *Faith and Freedom.* Nashville, Tenn.: Abingdon.

O'Hear, Anthony. 1984. *Experience, Explanation, and Faith: An Introduction to the Philosophy of Religion.* London: Routledge and Kegan Paul.

Oppenheim, Frank M. 1987. *Royce's Mature Philosophy of Religion.* Notre Dame, Ind.: University of Notre Dame Press.

O'Rourke, J. J. 1973. "*Pistis* in Romans." *Catholic Biblical Quarterly* 35, 188–94.

Otto, Rudolf. 1930. *India's Religion of Grace and Christianity, Compared and Contrasted,* tr. Frank Hugh Foster. New York: Macmillan.

———. 1932. *Mysticism East and West: A Comparative Analysis of the Nature of Mysticism,* tr. Bertha L. Bracey and Richenda C. Payne. New York: Macmillan.

Owen, H. P. 1960. *The Christian Knowledge of God.* London: Athlone Press.

Pagels, Heinz R. 1986. *Perfect Symmetry: The Search for the Beginning of Time.* New York: Bantam New Age Books.

Pailin, David A. 1969. *The Way to Faith.* London: Epworth Press.

———. 1989. *God and the Processes of Reality: Foundations of a Credible Theism.* London: Routledge.

Palihawadana, Mahinda. 1978. "Is There a Theravada Buddhist Idea of Grace?" In Dawe and Carman, 1978, 181–95.

Pannenberg, Wolfhart. 1969. *Revelation in History,* tr. David Granskou and Edward Quinn. London: Sheed and Ward.

———. 1971. "Faith and Reason." *Basic Questions in Theology,* vol. 2. Philadelphia: Fortress Press.

Pannikkar, Raimundo. 1971a. "Faith, A Constitutive Dimension of Man." *Journal of Ecumenical Studies* 8, 224–25.

———. 1971b. *Myth, Faith, and Hermeneutics.* New York: Paulist Press.

———. 1981. "Athens or Jerusalem: Philosophy or Religion." *Logos* 2, 21–39.

Park, Sung Bae. 1983. *Buddhist Faith and Sudden Enlightenment.* Albany, N.Y.: SUNY Press.

Parker, T. H. L. 1969. *The Doctrine of the Knowledge of God: A Study in Calvin's Theology,* 2d ed. Grand Rapids, Mich.: William B. Eerdmans.

Pascal, Blaise. 1966. *Pensées,* tr. A. J. Krailsheimer. Harmondsworth, Eng.: Penguin Books.

Patrick, John W. 1979. "Personal Faith and the Fear of Death among Divergent Religious Populations." *Journal of the Scientific Study of Religion* 18 (September), 298–305.

Patterson, David. 1982. *Faith and Philosophy.* Lanham, Md.: University Press of America.

Penelhum, Terence. 1971. *Problems of Religious Knowledge.* London: Macmillan.

——. 1977. "The Analysis of Faith in St. Thomas Aquinas." *Religious Studies* 13 (June), 133–54.

——. 1983. *God and Skepticism: A Study in Skepticism and Fideism*. Dordrecht: D. Reidel.

Perkins, Robert L., ed. 1981. *Kierkegaard's "Fear and Trembling": Critical Appraisals*. University: University of Alabama Press.

Perrett, Row W. 1984. "John Hick on Faith: A Critique." *International Journal for Philosophy of Religion* 15:1–2, 57–66.

Persson, Per Erik. 1970. *Sacra Doctrina: Reason and Revelation in Aquinas*, tr. Ross Mackenzie. Oxford: Basil Blackwell.

Pfurtner, Stephen. 1964. *Luther and Aquinas on Salvation*, tr. Edward Quinn. New York: Sheed and Ward.

Phillips, D. Z. 1966. *The Concept of Prayer*. New York: Schocken Books.

——. 1970. *Death and Immortality*. New York: St. Martin's Press.

——. 1971. *Faith and Philosophical Inquiry*. New York: Schocken Books.

——. 1976. *Religion without Explanation*. Oxford: Basil Blackwell.

——. 1986. *Belief, Change and Forms of Life*. London: Macmillan.

——. 1988. *Faith After Foundationalism*. London: Routledge.

Pieper, Josef. 1963. *Belief and Faith: A Philosophical Tract*, tr. Richard Winston and Clara Winston. New York: Pantheon Books.

Pierce, J. David. 1989. "Styles of Believing: Analytic and Imagistic." In J. Ashbrook, *Faith and Ministry in Light of the Double Brain*. Bristol, Ind.: Wyndham Hall Press, 243–61.

Plantinga, Alvin. 1974. *The Nature of Necessity*. Oxford: Clarendon Press.

——. 1979. "Is Belief in God Rational?" In Delaney, ed., 1979, 7–27.

——. 1981. "Is Belief in God Properly Basic?" *Noûs* 15 (March), 41–52.

——. 1983. "Reason and Belief in God." In Plantinga and Wolterstorff, eds., 1983, 16–93.

Plantinga, Alvin, and Nicholas Wolterstorff, eds. 1983. *Faith and Rationality: Reason and Belief in God*. Notre Dame, Ind.: University of Notre Dame Press.

Plantinga, Cornelius, Jr. 1979. *A Place to Stand: A Reformed Study of Creeds and Confessions*. Grand Rapids, Mich.: Christian Reformed Church Board of Publications.

Pletcher, Galen K. 1973. "Mysticism, Contradiction, and Ineffability." *American Philosophical Quarterly* 10, 201–11.

Plott, John C. 1974. *A Philosophy of Devotion*. Delhi: Motilal Banarsidass.

Pojman, Louis. 1979. "Rationality and Religious Belief." *Religious Studies* 15 (June), 159–72.

——. 1986a. *Religious Belief and the Will*. London: Routledge Kegan Paul.

——. 1986b. "Faith without Belief." *Faith and Philosophy* 3 (April), 157–76.

Presa, Kevin. 1968. "Assent, Belief, and Faith." *Sophia* 7 (October), 20–25.

Price, H. H. 1954. "Belief and Will." *Proceedings of the Aristotelian Society*, supp. vol. 28, 1–26.

——. 1964. "Faith and Belief." In Hick, ed., 1964, 3–15.

——. 1965. "Belief 'In' and Belief 'That'." *Religious Studies* 1 (October), 5–28.

Proudfoot, Wayne. 1985. *Religious Experience.* Berkeley: University of California Press.

Prozesky, Martin. 1984. *Religion and Ultimate Well-Being.* London: Macmillan.

Pruyser, Paul W. 1974. *Between Belief and Unbelief.* New York: Harper and Row.

Purtill, Richard L. 1974. *Reason to Believe.* Grand Rapids, Mich.: William B. Eerdmans.

Pye, Michael. 1984. "Other-Power and Skillful Means in Shin Buddhism." *Pure Land: Journal of Pure Land Buddhism,* n.s. 1, 70–78.

Quinn, Philip L. 1990. "Saving Faith from Kant's Remarkable Antinomy." *Faith and Philosophy* 7 (October), 419–33.

Radford, Colin. 1970a. "Hoping and Wishing." *Proceedings of the Aristotelian Society,* supp. vol. 44, 51–70.

——. 1970b. "Hoping, Wishing, and Dogs." *Inquiry* 13 (Summer), 100–103.

Radhakrishnan, Sarvepalli. 1955. *Recovery of Faith.* New York: Harper and Brothers.

Rahner, Karl. 1967. *Belief Today.* New York: Sheed and Ward.

——. 1978a. *Meditations on Freedom and the Spirit,* tr. Rosaleen Ockenden, David Smith, and Cecily Bennett. New York: Seabury Press.

——. 1978b. *Foundations of Christian Faith: An Introduction to the Idea of Christianity,* tr. William V. Dych. New York: Seabury Press.

Rahner, Karl, and Herbert Vorgrimler. 1981. *Dictionary of Theology,* 2d ed., tr. Richard Strachan, David Smith, Robert Nowell, and Sarah O'Brien Twohig. New York: Crossroads.

Rahner, Karl, and Karl-Heinz Weger. 1981. *Our Christian Faith: Answers for the Future.* New York: Crossroads.

Rahner, Karl, et al. 1968–. *Sacramentum Mundi: An Encyclopedia of Theology.* New York: Herder and Herder.

Randall, John Herman, Jr. 1958. *The Role of Knowledge in Western Religion.* Boston: Starr King Press.

——. 1968. *The Meaning of Religion for Man.* New York: Harper Torchbooks.

Rao, K. L. Seshagiri. 1971. *The Concept of Śraddha (in the Brahmanas, Upanisads, and the Gita).* Patiala: Roy.

Rao, O. M. 1984. "The Dynamics of Belief Compared between the Fourth Gospel and the Gita." *Independent Journal of Theology* 33 (October-December), 25–30.

Rauf, Muhammad Abdul. 1967. "Some Notes on the Qur'anic Use of the Terms Islām and Imān." *Muslim World* 57, 94–102.

Rawls, John. 1971. *A Theory of Justice.* Cambridge, Mass.: Belknap Press.

Redington, James D. 1983. "The Hindu-Christian Dialogue and the Interior Dialogue." *Theological Studies* 44 (December), 587–603.

Reid, Louis Arnaud. 1939. *Preface to Faith.* London: Allen and Unwin.

Rescher, Nicholas. 1980. *Scepticism: A Critical Reappraisal.* Totowa, N.J.: Rowman and Littlefield.

Richards, Glyn. 1987. "Faith and Praxis in Liberation Theology, Bonhoeffer and Gandhi." *Modern Theology* 3 (July), 359–73.

Richardson, Alan, ed. 1976. *A Dictionary of Christian Theology*. Philadelphia: Westminster Press.

Richman, Robert J. 1983. *God, Free Will, and Morality: Prolegomena to a Theory of Practical Reasoning*. Dordrecht: D. Reidel.

Ricoeur, Paul. 1977. "Toward a Hermeneutic of the Idea of Revelation." *Harvard Theological Review* 70, 1–37.

Rigaux, B., and P. Grelot. 1973. "Revelation." In Léon-Dufour, 1973, 499–505.

Roberts, Robert C. 1986. *Faith, Reason, and History: Rethinking Kierkegaard's "Philosophical Fragments."* Macon, Ga.: Mercer University Press.

Robinson, D. W. B. 1970. " 'Faith of Jesus Christ'—A New Testament Debate." *Reformed Theological Review* 29, 71–81.

Robinson, N. H. G. 1966. "Faith and Truth." *Scottish Journal of Theology* 19 (June), 144–59.

Rockefeller, Steven C. 1991. *John Dewey: Religious Faith and Democratic Humanism*. New York: Columbia University Press.

Rollins, C. D. 1967. "Certainty." In Edwards, ed., 1967, 2:67–71.

Ross, J. Robert. 1978. "Historical Knowledge as Basis for Faith." *Zygon* 13 (Summer), 209–24.

Ross, James F. 1969. *Introduction to the Philosophy of Religion*. New York and London: Macmillan.

———. 1972. "Religious Knowledge." *Proceedings of the Catholic Philosophical Association* 46, 29–42.

———. 1982. "Aquinas on Belief and Knowledge." Unpublished manuscript.

———. 1986. "Believing for Profit." In McCarthy, ed., 1986, 221–35.

Rousselot, Pierre. 1990. *The Eyes of Faith*. New York: Fordham University Press.

Rust, Eric C. 1981. *Religion, Revelation, and Reason*. Macon, Ga.: Mercer University Press.

Ryan, Cheyney. 1981. "Beyond Beliefs." *American Philosophical Quarterly* 18, 33–41.

Ryūkoku Translation Center, tr. 1966. *The Shōshin Ge: The Gatha on True Faith in the Nembutsu*, 4th ed. Kyoto: Ryūkoku University.

Samartha, Stanley J. 1979. "Can Mount Sinai and River Ganga Meet?" In Wegner and Harrelson, eds., 1979, 99–120.

Sasaki, Shōten. 1988. "Shinshū and Folk Religion: Toward a Post-Modern Shinshū Theology," tr. Jan Van Bragt. *Bulletin of the Nazan Institute for Religion and Culture* 12, 13–35.

Sawai, Yoshitsugu. 1987. "The Nature of Faith in the Śankaran Vedanta Tradition." *Numen* 34:1, 18–44.

Schaff, Philip, ed. 1983. *The Creeds of Christendom, with a History and Critical Notes*, 3 vols., rev. by David S. Schaff. Grand Rapids, Mich.: Baker Book House.

Schiffers, N. 1970. "Revelation." *Sacramentum Mundi* 5, 342–59.

Schillebeeckx, E. 1968. *Revelation and Theology*, vol. 2, tr. N. D. Smith. New York: Herder and Herder.

———. 1974. *The Understanding of Faith: Interpretation and Criticism*, tr. N. D. Smith. New York: Seabury Press.

———. 1987. *On Christian Faith: The Spiritual, Ethical, and Political Dimensions*, tr. John Bowden. New York: Crossroads/Continuum.

Schlatter, Adolf. 1963. *Der Glaube im Neuen Testament*. Stuttgart: Calwer.

Schlesinger, George N. 1988. *New Perspectives on Old-Time Religion*. Oxford: Clarendon Press.

Schuon, Frithjof. 1975. *The Transcendent Unity of Religions*, rev. ed., tr. Peter Townsend. New York: Harper and Row Torchbook.

Sessions, William Lad. 1980a. "Kant and Religious Belief." *Kant-Studien* 71:4, 455–68.

———. 1980b. "William James and the Right to Over-Believe." *Philosophy Research Archives* 6:1420, 48 pp.

———. 1982. "Religious Faith and Rational Justification." *International Journal for Philosophy of Religion* 13, 143–56.

———. 1985. "A New Look at Moral Arguments for Theism." *International Journal for Philosophy of Religion* 18, 51–67.

———. 1987. "Coherence, Proper Basicality, and Moral Arguments for Theism." *International Journal for Philosophy of Religion* 22, 119–37.

———. 1991a. "The Authorship of Faith." *Religious Studies* 27 (March), 81–98.

———. 1991b. "The Certainty of Faith." *Logos* 12, 57–68.

Sharma, Arvind. 1988. "A Third Way of Spirituality Beyond Faith and Reason in Buddhism." *Journal of Dharma* 13 (July–September), 282–90.

Shepherd, Victor A. 1983. *The Nature and Function of Faith in the Theology of John Calvin*. Macon, Ga.: Mercer University Press.

Shigefuji, Shinei. 1980. *Nembutsu—Nembutsu in Shinran and His Teachers: A Comparison*. Toronto: Toronto Buddhist Church.

Singh, Harbans. 1969. *Guru Nanak and Origins of the Sikh Faith*. Bombay: Asia Publishing House.

Sire, James W. 1976. *The Universe Next Door*. Downers Grove, Ill.: InterVarsity Press.

Sittler, Joseph. 1955. "The Necessity of Faith." *Christian Scholar* 38 (September), 198–205.

Smart, Ninian. 1968. *The Yogi and the Devotee*. London: George Allen and Unwin.

———. 1970. *The Philosophy of Religion*. New York: Random House.

———. 1988. Review of Proudfoot, 1985. *Journal of Philosophy* 85 (March), 151–54.

Smith, George Duncan. 1948. "Faith and Revealed Truth." In G. D. Smith, ed., *The Teachings of the Catholic Church: A Summary of Catholic Doctrine*, vol. 1. London: Burns, Oates, and Washbourne, 1–37.

Smith, Kent D. 1983. *Faith: Reflections on Experience, Theology, and Fiction*. Lanham, Md.: University Press of America.

Smith, Wilfred Cantwell. 1964. *The Meaning and End of Religion: A New Approach to the Religious Traditions of Mankind*. New York: Mentor Books.

———. 1971. "A Human View of Truth." *Studies in Religion/Sciences Religieuses*, 1:1, 6–24.

——. 1973. "Faith as a Universal Human Quality." Bea Lecture, Woodstock College, New York City, March 18, 1971. April typescript.

——. 1976. "*Arkān.*" In Little, ed., 1976, 303–16.

——. 1977. *Belief and History.* Charlottesville: University of Virginia Press.

——. 1979a. *Faith and Belief.* Princeton, N.J.: Princeton University Press.

——. 1979b. "Faith as *Tasdīq.*" In Morewedge, ed., 1979, 96–115.

——. 1981. *Towards a World Theology: Faith and the Comparative History of Religion.* Philadelphia: Westminster Press.

——. 1988. "Transcendence." *Harvard Divinity School Bulletin* 18 (Fall), 10–15.

Snellgrove, David. 1971. "Theological Reflections on the Buddhist Goal of Perfect Enlightenment." *Bulletin, Secretariatus pro non Christianis* (Vatican) 17, 76–98.

Söderblom, Nathan. 1966. *The Nature of Revelation.* Philadelphia: Fortress Press.

Solomon, Robert. 1976. *The Passions.* New York: Doubleday.

Sponheim, Paul R. 1985. *God—The Question and the Quest: Toward a Conversation Concerning Christian Faith.* Philadelphia: Fortress Press.

Stace, W. T. 1960. *The Teachings of the Mystics.* New York: New American Library.

——. 1961. *Mysticism and Philosophy.* London: Macmillan.

Stoeber, Michael. 1993. "Introvertive Mystical Experiences: Monistic, Theistic, and the Theo-Monistic." *Religious Studies* 29, 169–84.

Stokes, Kenneth, ed. 1982. *Faith Development in the Adult Life Cycle.* New York: W. H. Sadlier.

Stump, Eleonore. 1989. "Faith and Goodness." *Philosophy* 25 (Supplement), 167–91.

Sullivan, F. Russell, Jr. 1978. *Faith and Reason in Kierkegaard.* Washington, D.C.: University Press of America.

Sullivan, John Edward. 1979. *Ideas of Religion: A Prolegomenon to the Philosophy of Religion.* Washington, D.C.: University Press of America.

Surlis, Paul, ed. 1972. *Faith: Its Nature and Meaning.* Westminster, Md.: Christian Classics.

Sutherland, Stewart R. 1984. *God, Jesus, and Belief: The Legacy of Theism.* Oxford: Basil Blackwell.

Swinburne, Richard. 1981. *Faith and Reason.* Oxford: Clarendon Press.

——. 1992. *Revelation: From Metaphor to Analogy.* Oxford: Clarendon Press.

Takahatake, Takamichi. 1987. *Young Man Shinran: A Reappraisal of Shinran's Life.* Waterloo, Ontario: Wilfred Laurier University Press.

Takeda, Ryūsei. 1989. "Shinran's View of Faith: A Translation Issue of 'Shinjin' and 'Faith'." *Ryūkoku daigaku sanbyaku gojūshūnen: Kinen ronbunshū,* ed. Ryūkoku Gakkai, 2–30. Kyoto: Nagata Bunshōdō.

Taliaferro, Charles. 1985. "Divine Cognitive Power." *International Journal for Philosophy of Religion* 18, 133–40.

Tanner, Kathryn. 1988. *God and Creation in Christian Theology: Tyranny or Empowerment?* Oxford: Basil Blackwell.

Taylor, Michael. 1987. *The Possibility of Cooperation.* Cambridge: Cambridge University Press.

Taylor, Richard. 1961. "Faith." In Hook, ed., 1961, 165–69.

Temple, William. 1935. *Nature, Man, and God*. London: Macmillan.

Tennant, F. R. 1930. *Philosophical Theology*, vol. 1. Cambridge: Cambridge University Press.

———. 1956. *Philosophical Theology*, vol. 2. Cambridge: Cambridge University Press.

Thakur, Shivesh Chandra. 1981. *Religion and Rational Choice*. Totowa, N.J.: Barnes and Noble.

Thielicke, Helmut. 1977. *The Doctrine of God and of Christ*. Vol. 2 of *The Evangelical Faith*, tr. Geoffrey W. Bromiley. Grand Rapids, Mich.: William B. Eerdmans.

Thittila, Maha Thera U. 1956. "The Fundamental Principles of Theravada Buddhism." In K. W. Morgan, ed., 1956, 67–112.

Thornton, Jim. 1975. "Reason, Faith, and Freedom." In Hinchcliff, ed., 1975, 60–64.

Tillich, Paul. 1948. *The Shaking of the Foundations*. New York: Charles Scribner's Sons.

———. 1952. *The Courage to Be*. New Haven, Conn.: Yale University Press.

———. 1957. *The Protestant Era*, abridged, tr. James Luther Adams. Chicago: University of Chicago Press Phoenix Books.

———. 1958. *Dynamics of Faith*. New York: Harper and Row Colophon Books.

Tokunaga, Michio. 1985. "The 'Non-self' Aspect in Shinran's Concept of 'Faith'." *Pure Land: Journal of Pure Land Buddhism*, n.s. 2, 30–38.

Torrance, Thomas. 1957. "One Aspect of the Biblical Conception of Faith." *Expository Times* 68, 111–14.

Tracy, Thomas F. 1984. *God, Action, and Embodiment*. Grand Rapids, Mich.: William B. Eerdmans.

———. 1990. "Action: Created and Divine." Unpublished manuscript.

Trembath, Kern Robert. 1991. *Divine Revelation: Our Moral Relation with God*. New York: Oxford University Press.

Trigg, Roger. 1973. *Reason and Commitment*. Cambridge: Cambridge University Press.

Ueda, Yoshifumi. 1981. "Response to Thomas P. Kasulis' Review of *Letters of Shinran*." *Philosophy East and West* 31 (October), 507–12.

———. 1984. "The Mahayana Structure of Shinran's Thought," tr. Dennis Hirota. *Eastern Buddhist*, n.s. 17 (Spring), 57–78 and (Autumn), 30–54.

———, gen. ed. 1978. *Letters of Shinran: A Translation of "Mattōshō."* Kyoto: Hongwanji International Center.

———, gen. ed. 1979. *Notes on "Essentials of Faith Alone": A Translation of Shinran's "Yuishinshō-mon-i."* Kyoto: Hongwanji International Center.

———, gen. ed. 1980. *Notes on Once-Calling and Many-Calling: A Translation of Shinran's "Ichinen-tanen mon'i."* Kyoto: Hongwanji International Center.

———, gen. ed. 1981. *Notes on the Inscriptions on Sacred Scrolls: A Translation of Shinran's "Songō shinzō meimon."* Kyoto: Hongwanji International Center.

———, gen. ed. 1982. *Passages on the Pure Land Way: A Translation of Shinran's "Jōdo monruki jushō."* Kyoto: Hongwanji International Center.

———, gen. ed. 1983–1990. *The True Teaching, Practice, and Realization of the Pure*

*Land Way: A Translation of Shinran's "Kyōgyō shinshō,"* 4 vols. Kyoto: Hongwanji International Center.

Ueda, Yoshifumi, and Dennis Hirota. 1989. *Shinran: An Introduction to His Thought.* Kyoto: Hongwanji International Center.

Underhill, Evelyn. 1955. *Mysticism: A Study in the Nature and Development of Man's Spiritual Consciousness.* New York: Meridian Books.

Van Den Haag, Ernest. 1961. "On Faith." In Hook, ed., 1961, 150–55.

Van Der Leeuw, G. 1963. *Religion in Essence and Manifestation,* 2 vols., tr. J. E. Turner. New York: Harper and Row.

Van Fraassen, Bas C. 1984. "Belief and the Will." *Journal of Philosophy* 81 (May), 235–56.

Van Inwagen, Peter. 1987. Review of Craft and Hustwit, eds., 1984. *Faith and Philosophy* 4 (January), 103–8.

Van Noort, Gerardus. 1961. *The Sources of Revelation. Divine Faith.* Vol. 3 of *Dogmatic Theology,* tr. John J. Castelot and William R. Murphy. Westminster, Md.: Newman Press.

Veninga, Robert L. 1985. *A Gift of Hope: How We Survive Our Tragedies.* Boston: Little, Brown.

Vesey, G. N. A., ed. 1969. *Talk of God.* New York: St. Martin's Press.

Wainwright, William J. 1981. *Mysticism: A Study of its Nature, Cognitive Value, and Moral Implications.* Madison: University of Wisconsin Press.

Warfield, Benjamin Breckinridge. 1931. *Calvin and Calvinism.* New York: Oxford University Press.

Webb, Mark O. 1985. "Religious Experience as Doubt Resolution." *International Journal for Philosophy of Religion* 18:1–2, 81–86.

Wegner, Walter, and Walter Harrelson, eds. 1979. *Aspects of Interfaith Dialogue.* Jerusalem: Ecumenical Institute for Advanced Theological Studies.

Weigel, Gustave. 1959. *Faith and Understanding in America.* New York: Macmillan.

——. 1961. "Reflections on 'On the Nature of Faith'." In Hook, ed., 1961, 103–8.

Weigel, Gustave, and Arthur G. Madden. 1961. *Religion and the Knowledge of God.* Englewood Cliffs, N.J.: Prentice-Hall.

Wheatley, J. M. O. 1958. "Wishing and Hoping." *Analysis* 18 (June), 121–31.

Whittaker, John H. 1981. *Matters of Faith and Matters of Principle: Religious Truth Claims and their Logic.* San Antonio, Tex.: Trinity University Press.

Wiebe, Donald. 1981. *Religion and Truth: Towards an Alternative Paradigm for the Study of Religion.* The Hague: Mouton.

Wiles, Maurice F. 1982. *Faith and the Mystery of God.* Philadelphia: Fortress Press.

Williams, Bernard. 1973. "Deciding to Believe." In his *Problems of the Self,* chap. 9. Cambridge: Cambridge University Press.

——. 1985. *Ethics and the Limits of Philosophy.* Cambridge, Mass.: Harvard University Press.

Williams, C. J. F. 1974. "Believing in God and Knowing That God Exists." *Noûs* 8 (September), 273–82.

Williams, John N. 1982. "Believing the Self-Contradictory." *American Philosophical Quarterly* 19, 279–85.

———. 1992. "Belief-in and Belief in God." *Religious Studies* 28, 401–6.

Williamson, William B. 1985. *Decisions in Philosophy of Religion.* Buffalo, N.Y.: Prometheus Books.

Wisdo, David. 1987. "Kierkegaard on Belief, Faith, and Explanation." *International Journal for Philosophy of Religion* 21:2, 95–114.

Wittgenstein, Ludwig. 1953. *Philosophical Investigations,* tr. G. E. M. Anscombe. Oxford: Basil Blackwell.

———. 1961. *Tractatus Logico-Philosophicus,* tr. D. F. Pears and B. F. McGuinness. London: Routledge and Kegan Paul.

———. 1965. "Lecture on Ethics." *Philosophical Review* 74, 3–12.

———. 1972. *On Certainty,* ed. G. E. M. Anscombe and G. H. von Wright. New York: Harper Torchbooks.

Wolfson, Harry Austryn. 1942–1943. "The Double Faith Theory in Clement, Saadia, Averroes, and St. Thomas, and Its Origin in Aristotle and the Stoics." *Jewish Quarterly Review* 33, 213–64.

———. 1956. *Faith, Trinity, Incarnation.* Vol. 1 of *The Philosophy of the Church Fathers.* Cambridge, Mass.: Harvard University Press.

———. 1961. *Religious Philosophy: A Group of Essays.* Cambridge, Mass.: Harvard University Press.

Wolterstorff, Nicholas. 1990. "The Assurance of Faith." *Faith and Philosophy* 7 (October), 396–417.

Woods, Richard, ed. 1980. *Understanding Mysticism.* Garden City, N.Y.: Doubleday Image Books.

Wren, David J. 1981. "Abraham's Silence and the Logic of Faith." In Perkins, ed., 1981, 152–64.

Wuthnow, Robert. 1982. "A Sociological Perspective on Faith Development." In Stokes, ed., 1982, 208–23.

Yandell, Keith E. 1990. "The Nature of Faith: Religious, Monotheistic, and Christian." *Faith and Philosophy* 7 (October), 451–69.

Zaehner, R. C. 1957. *Mysticism: Sacred and Profane.* Oxford: Clarendon Press.

Zimmerman, Marvin. 1976. "Subjective Thinking." *Humanist* 36 (July-August), 32–33.

# Index

Abraham, William J., 186n53, 249n21, 257n28
Abstract, the:
  abstraction *in concreto*, 100n107
  accounts of faith, 17–18
  v. concrete, 17–18, 154
  models of faith, viii
  objects of faith, 132
  v. specific, 154
  way of life, 99
  *See also* Concept; Model
Alston, William P., 92n99, 257n28
Amida:
  Buddha-nature, 216, 220, 223, 226
  cause of shinjin, 216, 218
  and Christ, 213, 225
  and confidence, 223
  and hope, 221–22
  mind of, 215, 219, 222
  object of faith, 215, 224–25
  other-power v. self-power, 216, 218, 221–22, 231
  point of view of, 222
  and propositional beliefs, 221
  and Pure Land, 214, 219, 231
  trust in, 217–18, 222–23
  uniqueness of, 213
  unity with self, 213–16, 219–20, 223–24, 226–27
  vows of, 214nn101–2

*See also* Buddha
Analogy:
  of choshin and faith, 235–40
  degrees:
    of prominence, 176
    of resemblance, 156, 176, 209, 253
    of unity, 7, 156
  faith as analogical concept, 6–8, 155–56, 168, 252–55
  unity of, 6, 155–56, 252, 254–55
  vagueness, 7, 253
Aquinas, Saint Thomas, 8n4, 33n19, 36, 37n30, 161–65
Attitude:
  and basis, 80–81
  and belief, 79–80, 134, 137
  and confidence, 142
  constitutive, 70–71, 91
    partially v. completely, 70–72, 87–88
    radically, 71–73, 87, 187
  defined, 69–70
  as fundamental, 81
  and horizon of significance, 73–77, 84–85
  multiple subjects of, 70n75
  onlooks, 69
  pre-propositional, 77–80, 92, 141–42, 187

*Cornell Studies in the Philosophy of Religion*
Edited by William P. Alston

*(continued from front flap)*

superiority of any over all others, his models help us to discern the unity amid the diversity of these different conceptions.

"Perhaps a new way of viewing one's own conception of faith in concert with the conceptions of others," he writes, "may lead not to a weakening of personal faith—much less to heresy, apostasy, and infidelity—but rather to grateful acceptance of other faiths even as one is strengthened and confirmed in one's own."

WILLIAM LAD SESSIONS is Professor of Philosophy and Associate Dean of the College at Washington and Lee University. A graduate of the University of Colorado, he holds an M.A. from Columbia University and a Ph.D. from Yale University.

A VOLUME IN THE SERIES
Cornell Studies in the
Philosophy of Religion
EDITED BY
WILLIAM P. ALSTON